Some things for the children

2202.
2203.

Some Things for the Children

edited by Jane Waller

Duckworth

This book is dedicated to my mother and father who gave me such a perfect childhood J. W.

First published in 1974 by Gerald Duckworth & Co. Ltd.
The Old Piano Factory, 43 Gloucester Crescent, London N.W.1.

Designed by Alphabet and Image, Sherborne, Dorset

ISBN 0 7156 0742 1

Printed by Unwin Brothers
The Gresham Press
Woking

To give authentic representation, the articles in this book have been photographed direct from the original magazines. The publishers hope that the lay-out and designs will compensate for any imperfections in the reproduction.

Contents

Introduction

Ancient rules of thumb for bringing up children are rapidly being discredited. The old axioms – 'Spare the rod and spoil the child', 'Children should be seen and not heard' – and many others of the sort have been examined by modern science and found defective. It has been discovered that the child is a human being.

Freeing the children, 1919–29

Before the First World War, children had been strictly confined to the nursery or schoolroom under the care of the nurse, and were allowed to visit the 'parental precincts' only at stated times, and even then under the most 'stringent injunctions' as to behaviour and deportment. Now it was decided to let them out. Little children were permitted to be heard as well as occasionally seen. Parents were heard to say sadly: 'We have unintentionally neglected our children through ignorance; we have often failed to give them sufficient sunshine, provide a balanced diet or take the necessary precautions against disease.' They began to take an interest in their children's health, welfare and education. They learnt about child psychology and behaviour, and it was felt that every parent should have at his elbow 'the knowledge of the delicate, impressionable child's mind', as well as of his physical make-up. They read volumes on Household Management, Healthy Motherhood, and The Hygiene of Life; they devoured articles on child psychology; the Editor of *Woman's Weekly* persuaded the matron of a big welfare centre to give valuable advice to readers once a week. Armed with the two great weapons of the Twenties, Hygiene and Advice, parents set to work to put into practice all that they had learnt. Everything that was harmful to the child's physical and mental health was swept aside, and everything that stimulated his development was strongly encouraged.

The reform should start before the child was born. 'Remember that before baby comes it is your health that counts. Baby's whole future may depend upon it.' In a bid for healthier mothers, safer childbirth and better babies, advertising persuaded women to attend the new Ante-Natal Clinics and Infant Welfare Centres. As well as receiving help from Health Visitors, mothers learnt Home Nursing and First Aid: '. . . for hysterical fits, speak sharply to the patient, and avoid giving sympathy.'

When baby arrived, breast-feeding was encouraged for mothers 'of all classes' as being more nutritious, hygienic and natural. The baby was placed in his cot – a new, wickerwork cot, for 'gone are the hangings beloved of our grandmothers, harbouring the dust and keeping baby's stagnant breath hanging heavily above him'.

The voluminous robes of the infant's layette were also rapidly disposed of, and with them the frills, bows and lacy ruffles that were the pride of mothers of the previous generation, but which hampered and tormented the child. It was no longer the thing to dress one's child in a great weight of garments, one over the other. The health and comfort of the child were the first points to consider in the layette; the garments should be soft and comfortable: 'Baby cannot use his limbs and kick as nature would have him do if he is packed up like a parcel in a flannel wrapper.' His gowns were reduced to twenty-seven inches in length, and they were worn until the baby was 'shortened' at about the age of four months; by 1929 the modern baby was wearing gowns or night-gowns only twenty-four inches in length.

The nursery, instead of being shut away somewhere in the servants' quarters, became the most important room in the house after the drawing-room. It was advised that 'in a large house two rooms can be set aside for baby, and sometimes even a third as the nurse's bedroom. In a small house the difficulty is very much greater, but baby must have a room to himself. The nursery should face south, certainly never north. It should be well-ventilated, light and airy. The ideal is to have a balcony on which baby's cot can stand at all times, being brought in for necessary purposes. The furnishings should show simplicity of design, practicality and gay colouring.' It was now recognised

that 'children's surroundings should at all times express beauty and cleanliness'. Cork linoleum for the floor, cork carpets, washable wallpaper and a low dado of large coloured animals, or a dado of blackboard upon which a child could scribble, made excellent furnishings. Later a few good pictures could be introduced. Apart from the toy cupboard and a strong wooden table, 'the chief piece of furniture is a wardrobe, in which the children's outdoor clothes are kept', which saves 'scampering up and down the stairs to the night-nursery when they are going for a walk'.

Labour-saving devices of all kinds came as a boon to many mothers. A survey conducted in America in 1922 demonstrated that the proportion of American households able to boast domestic help was no more than eight per cent. In Britain, 'judging by present conditions in this country, where a shortage of household labour and higher wages paid to the domestics is forcing many mistresses to take on a larger share of the work of the house themselves, we are also gradually veering towards a situation where the average British housewife will find herself in a similar servant-less state. Already many women who formerly employed three or four servants now find themselves with only one.' In all the magazines, advice was given to women who found themselves learning how to wall-paper, clean carpets, and treat woodworm. Children were taught to help nurse by tidying away their toys and games in the right place; though care was to be taken not to go to extremes. 'We do not, after all, want to encourage in little ones such habits of extreme pernickertiness as shall render them later of that tiresome type that tidies up one's chair against the wall while one is still taking one's leave.' Nurse too had to be considered and appreciated more: 'It is of the utmost importance to give her a comfortable chair. Her duties are arduous and it is essential that when she has a chance to sit down she should be able to get a real rest.'

The physical condition of her children was of great concern to the mother, and she not only taught them the importance of cleanliness and hygiene, but also made sure that they had a well-balanced diet. She learnt the value of vitamins and nutritional foods, and how to present nourishing meals in an interesting way so that they would delight the eater and stimulate his appetite. She taught her children how to cook, and attended carefully to the cleanliness of her larder, so that there was little fear of 'either pets or obnoxious insects being allowed to play havoc among the stores'. She found that 'plain living' was best for health in the household, and that luxury was one of the worst forms of waste, being 'injurious, both morally, mentally and physically'. One should guard against rich cakes: 'Quite plain cakes may be made to look so attractive as to delight the small folk and yet can be eaten with impunity.'

To keep fit, children had to have plenty of exercise. The child was instructed to hold himself erect, to walk, run, leap and swim; and skipping, hoop-bowling and tennis were approved of. Whereas previously children's play had been controlled and genteel, and the child had been punished if he got his clothes dirty, now the minimum of constraint was the object to be aimed at. 'To laugh, to romp, make weird noises, and to get spotted with dirt are essential to health and to the normal growth of body and mind.'

In order to enjoy this unrestricted play, the

Twenties child wore the simplest frock or romper in the lightest of materials, and was able to run about easily. Skirts were cut well above the knee, and for infants were even shorter. If they got muddy, as it was now accepted that children should, the simple garments were easily washed. For the little girl the bloomer was especially recommended: 'When the small person takes playing seriously, bloomers are a necessity to wear with a linen frock.' The full bloomer could be worn instead of a skirt, and it protected the child from draughts and dirt. The most suitable garment of all for the small child, since this period of its life was so essentially the play period, was the romper or creeper, a one-piece garment fitting very loosely at the crutch.

When the little girl grew older, simplicity remained the keynote of her clothes; after 1925 her dress became less baggy, and fell in a straight line from the yoke to the hem, with the waist either missed out altogether or placed somewhere around the hips. Mother was told that 'the frills and ruffles that used to decorate the dress-up frock are never seen on the smart child of today. I do not approve of fussy dressing, overdressing or dressing a child too old.' The plainness was relieved by cleverly matching trimmings, embroidery, smocking, piping, faggotting, shirring or trimming with contrasting material. The long, carefully-curled hair secured with a large bow, that was worn by girls in the early Twenties, had changed by 1925 to the more convenient short 'bob' or 'shingle'. By the end of the Twenties, little boys had also adopted the straight line in clothing, and the watchwords for boys' clothes were 'Durability and Suitability'.

The emphasis on physical health, cleanliness, and practicality was matched by a new concern for the child's mental well-being. Parents found that they could 'get to know' their children by observing their behaviour. If the child misbehaved, the reasons behind it should be considered, and his point of view heard, before punishment was inflicted. Often the fault could be corrected through discussion; if not, the punishment must be seen by the child to be just – punishment that invoked fear was considered very harmful.

Many a nervous child is obliged to play a little tune on the piano.

The increasing interest in child psychology led the modern mother to realise that the foundations of character and temperament were laid in infancy. A good emotional environment was vital for the child's well-being. With the problematic only child, it was suggested that a young nurse, or governess, be appointed, so that there was a smaller age gap. Parents were encouraged to have larger families, to reverse the recent trend towards one-child families.

Parents found that they had to maintain a careful balance in their treatment of their children. It was observed that over-carefulness and sentimental love were as bad for the child as gross neglect; that it was a mistake for mothers to show off their children in public, because it made them either nervous or conceited; and that pocket money had to be carefully calculated, as 'the spendthrift has in his youth been the child with too much pocket money to spend; while the sponge was he to whom pocket money in reasonable proportion was denied.'

They had to be just as careful over choosing the child's clothes, since bizarre or ill-chosen clothes could cause psychological disturbances. 'Makeshifts should be avoided at all costs. The party dress that has seen its last party should not be pressed into service for school. Why should it be when skirts are so brief, and fabrics so inexpensive, and the laundress's little girl is just the same age? The ermine that grew yellow on Aunt Alice's black velvet must not be used to trim Amy's new coat. Much better let it go furless and use a woollen scarf, which would be warmer anyway. Almost all such makeshifts, that turn a child into a bad memory for herself in later years, do not spring from actual poverty, but from a mistaken reaching for the elaborate and unusual, which is a costly error psychologically even if not financially.'

The imagination of the child, having been stimulated at an early age by the attention of mother or nurse, could be further developed through play. 'A valuable accessory at bath time is the amusing sponge, floating soap or toy, that can be readily introduced as entertainment.' Later, children were encouraged to develop their imaginations through reading. 'Let them read the *Red*, *Blue* and *Green Fairy Books* of Andrew Lang, Andersen's *Fairy Tales* and Charles Kingsley's *Heroes*.' Children wrote and acted in their own plays, and disguised themselves in costume; fancy dress parties became more of a craze every year. The child was encouraged to see, hear and touch, and to appreciate objects. Even tiny babies were given soft toys and cuddly playthings to touch and hold; bells and rattles and soothing lullabies to listen to; and gay, colourful things to look at. 'If a nurse can blow soap bubbles through her hands, it is of course an added attraction at bath-time.'

Powers of observation were to be cultivated rather than suppressed. For little girls and boys and their friends, 'Pedestrian Excursions' were arranged, to enlarge their knowledge of the neighbourhood. For holidays an excellent suggestion was made: 'When packing the family trunk this summer, you will be well repaid for your forethought if you include in it at least one small text-book on sea-shells, another on minerals and possibly a third on the solar system.'

There had been a time when children were not allowed to ask questions, or speak unless first spoken to. Now it was recognised that the trait of insatiable curiosity in children was immensely valuable in their development. Their curiosity had to be satisfied, as through it they could acquire Wisdom and Knowledge, the two great foundations upon which a person's character and personality were built. The information needed was found in the abundance of Encyclopaedias, Boys' and Girls' Annuals, magazines and children's newspapers which began to appear. These volumes were written in simple, straightforward language and were often beautifully illustrated. They revealed to children the wonders of plant and animal life, adventures of travel and voyages of discovery; they told them about battles and heroes, and why aeroplanes flew. They taught the children games and how to solve puzzles and enter competitions, and created new hobbies for them. 'The young collector, naturalist, carpenter, or engineer should find that both mother and father are as keen as himself.' Talents shown for music, drawing, modelling, story-writing or verse should be encouraged. Games like chess and draughts, though of great educational value, 'should on no account be forced on children'.

In the schools, the child's education was continued along similar lines, but so many new methods were constantly being devised and advertised, and so much was written on education, that many parents were bewildered by what was going on. Conscientious parents tried to understand that 'it is an acknowledged fact among leaders in the educational world that there are three mighty forces upon which civilisation depends: they are first inherited ability, secondly the right kind of environment, and thirdly the developing will-power in man . . . it is called by various names . . . "self-activity", "self-making", "auto-education", "character-building", "ideal end", "freedom" etc.' This will-power or self-activity of the individual, they were told, began to show itself in the 'faintly conscious' mind of the infant and had to be developed early to give it the proper direction.

The two most important new methods of education were those designed by Montessori, the Italian educator, and Froebel, the German founder of Kindergartens. Dr Montessori taught that knowledge was gained through doing, testing, and experimenting. She thought that discipline cramped and denied the natural desires of normal children. The child's brain should no longer be moulded by the educator, who required only passive activity from the child. By lifting repression and inhibition, the teacher could free the child to express his individuality. This was to be done by giving him materials through which he would be able to correct his errors independent of his instructor. Montessori explains: 'A little girl is given the task of replacing cylinders of varying sizes into a wooden block in which there are holes of varying depths. If she errs, placing one of the objects in an opening that is too small for it, she takes it away and proceeds to make trial, seeking the proper opening for it . . . the didactic material controls every error and the child proceeds to correct herself.' Montessori toys could be given to children with great effect from the age of three – before they started kindergarten.

Froebel also believed in self-employment by the child, but looked at the spontaneous play of children for guidance. He thought that, given the freedom to express themselves in their own way and allowed to choose their own activities, children would automatically be interested in what they were doing and would therefore concentrate better. 'Learning through play' gave the child freedom to develop along his own lines. He suggested training the senses by letting the child judge for himself the different sensations of shape, colour and temperature. Little ones were taught to read – 'in play if possible' – and the idea of 'learning without tears' was developed. Like Montessori's pre-kindergarten toys, 'creative play' was encouraged in the nursery. It was suggested that a 'surprise box' of simple materials collected from time to time and kept secret from the child, such as paints, cardboard, clothes-pegs, pictures, and glue, should be brought out 'when the weather prevented the usual and necessary expenditure of energy out of doors, and even the best-loved toys lost their charm'. Both the Montessori and the Froebel teachings are combined in schools today.

For older children, conditions in school had also considerably improved. Classes were smaller, with more attention given to the individual child. Children were taught how to keep fit, and their changing-rooms and classrooms were made more hygienic. Out of school there were boys' clubs and the Scouts; and girls were allowed their own versions of these more masculine pursuits, such as the Girl Guides. In girls' education, 'concentrate on the boy' had been the prevalent attitude; but in 1918 the vote had been given to women over thirty, and by 1928 women had the vote on the same terms as men, at the age of twenty-one. It was now possible for a woman to have a career. Small girls no longer had to sit for hours over a sampler and study etiquette, but it was still felt that a woman's place was in the home, and instead she was given a thorough training in cookery, household management and the care of children. A magazine asks: 'Would you rather your daughter should know how to cook a meal for a man, or be the one he would want to share a dinner with? The alternative is false; she can easily be both.'

1930–1939

The children ruling the roost

The 'House' of the Twenties had, by the Thirties, come to be called 'the Home'. This home, purchased perhaps with the aid of a building society, was a bungalow, semi-detached or detached residence with a garden at the back and a garage at the side, and was lived in by the now small middle-class family, 'Hubby', 'Wifey' and the 'Kids', acting as a closely knit unit. The centre of the home was the living-room, a cheerful, comfortable room 'in which every member of the family can find relaxation, and which seems to extend a welcome to all who enter'. Around the cosy fireplace, Daddy would be reading the paper, his pipe in his mouth and his slippers on his feet; Mummy would be knitting or sewing garments for the children; and with the wireless on, the Kiddies would be playing with their toys, pursuing their hobbies or trying to do their homework.

The children had been transferred from the background to the very forefront of family life, and, apart

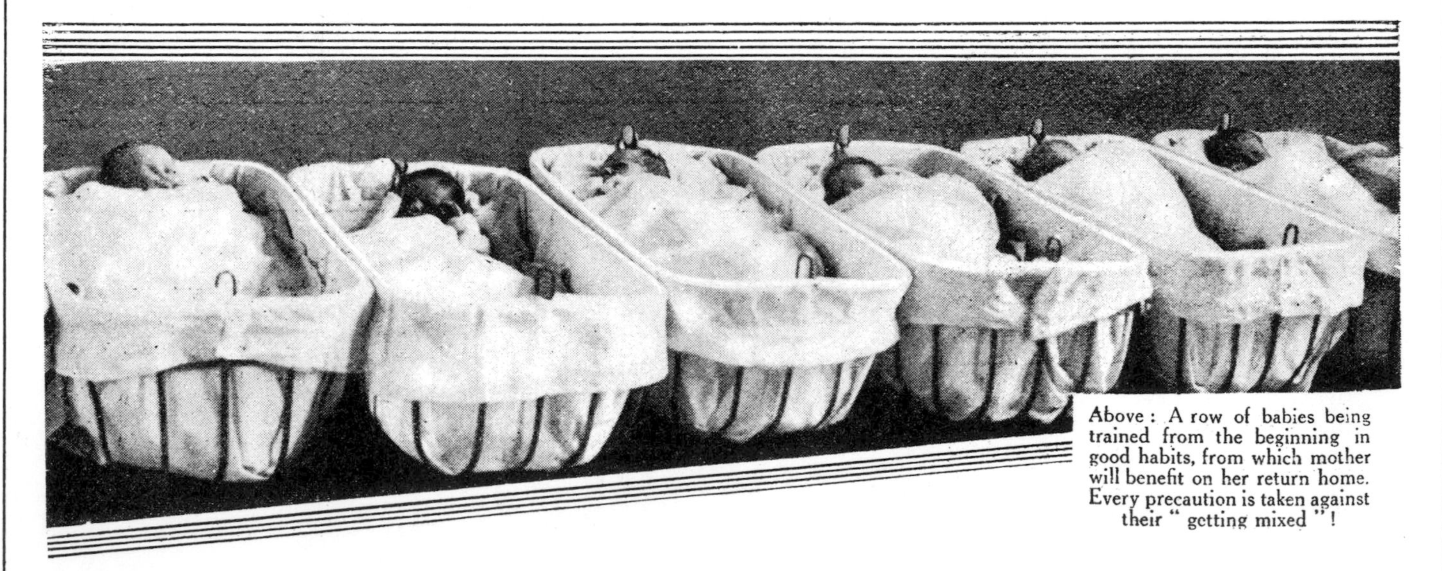

Above: A row of babies being trained from the beginning in good habits, from which mother will benefit on her return home. Every precaution is taken against their "getting mixed"!

from the great rituals of Spring-Cleaning and Jam-Making, life tended to revolve around the school terms and holidays. The celebrations of Christmas and Easter were arranged primarily for the enjoyment of the children, and in summer there was a trip to the seaside for them too, if the family could afford it. During term-time, Father took more and more interest in the progress of his little ones at school; he had realised that there was no reason why he should not take an active part in the bringing up of his children from the very beginning. He made them toys and nursery furniture, helped with their homework, tried to set a good example in front of them and tried to be fair in settling the disputes of the family. He realised that his character and manners had a great influence on his children's minds, for how can a small boy be expected 'to hand round his box of chocolates first, if he constantly sees his father helping himself to claret without passing it to his wife?'

The fashions and styles of children's clothes closely followed their seasonal activities. There were clothes for school, to wear after school and at weekends, clothes for visiting and parties, and sunsuits for the summer. Because of economic conditions, any or all of these clothes might be made by the mother, who had by force of circumstances become dressmaker for her children, as well as cook, housemaid and Hubby's comrade. Dressmaking was made more painless by the new Singer sewing machines, which made possible all kinds of professional-looking fancy sewing, and by the new ranges of Tootal and Tobralco anti-crease, anti-fade cottons and voiles: 'Never has it been easier to dress the child than this season, for materials are more plentiful than ever, and cheaper than we have ever known them.' She could also use cast-off adult clothing: 'If you follow my suggestion, I honestly don't think anyone would recognise your old left-over stockinette outfit in the smart little suit your son will wear this Christmas.'

The birth-rate of the middle classes was at this time declining rapidly, for a number of possible reasons. The economic climate made it necessary to keep the family small if it was to maintain its old standard of living, servants were scarcer and more expensive, and the modern middle-class house had too little space. More widely available birth control had its effect, but perhaps an important reason was that 'European women are giving birth to fewer children in a world so full of uncertainty, particularly the women of France and England, who are intelligent enough to hate war and refuse to produce children for furthering it. The contrary is true of Germany and Italy, the Fascist and activist states, and also of Japan, where mothers are encouraged to produce children as fast as they can.' Despite the threats of another war, there were many articles in the women's magazines encouraging women to have larger families: 'This disastrous idea of bringing down the population has got about, and if we don't watch out there won't be anyone left in a few hundred years to enjoy the new world which the biologists and physicists are ready to give us.'

The modern middle-class mother about to have a baby attended the clinic and joined the Women's Institute classes which taught Motherhood as a craft. She participated in National Baby Week, held during the first week in July, when mothers were shown new ways of managing babies. With mothers being persuaded to have their babies in a hospital or maternity home, far fewer babies died in their first year. In a public ward, mothers were charged according to their husbands' means; but for a private cubicle the charge was fixed at two guineas a week, and for a nursing home, four to twenty guineas a week. Magazines were continually giving advice on which to choose: 'Some types of women will make themselves almost ill going over and over in their minds the advantages and disadvantages incurred in staying at home with familiar objects around, or in going to a nursing home or hospital.' Mothers were also reassured over one of their biggest worries: 'There is really no need to fear, as many do, that the babies will get mixed up.'

So, having arrived home, hopefully with the right baby, she started to apply the new rules. 'Breast-fed is well-fed', she was told, and dummies were to be discarded as unhygienic. It was considered 'most desirable' for the mother to be the baby's nurse, but if a nurse or nanny were to be employed she should be of impeccable character and display the following qualities: 'She should have a real love of children, be strong and healthy, clean and tidy in her person and habits, good-tempered and patient. . . . The nurse must be capable of securing obedience; she should always be reasonable and never tyrannical. Nurse should speak well without any marked accent.' Her duties would be to take care of the children at home, of their clothes and rooms. She would also of course take baby out for airings in the pram, one of the modern 'baby carriages' that were considered so good. At this time English perambulators were renowned throughout the world for safety, comfort and style, the older high-built type having been superseded by a much lower-built body and smaller wheels. However, nurse was warned that it was often necessary to insert a thick mattress into these prams, 'or baby will be almost buried in the fashionable but unhygienic depths'.

Her charges had to be nicely turned out too. In the Twenties it had been enough for baby to be healthy and strong, but in the Thirties he had to be beautiful as well. Curly hair 'seems the natural frame for the curves of the chubby face, and it is worth any amount of care to keep it wavy'. A marvellous invention called

'Curly Top' came to the aid of mothers – a curling solution which in no way discoloured the hair, and which not only curled it in the most beautiful way, but even encouraged further curls to appear quite naturally! By the end of the Thirties many parents were dissatisfied with the plain simplicity of baby's layette, and wanted not just embroidery and smocking but frills and ruffles. However, the frills could be made of net or some other material easy to wash, and they were not expensive, as 'self-frill' could be bought at a shilling a yard. 'Besides their charm and daintiness, these layettes are thoroughly practical, as all the designs are on straight-down lines which are so comfy and healthy for baby.'

After the outing, baby would be placed in his cot or wicker-work Moses basket in the nursery. Frills were still kept out of the nursery, as they were likely to catch the dust. While it was felt that it was a mistake to have a nursery that looked too like a hospital ward, dust was 'an enemy to be fought tooth and nail'. The floor and walls should meet in a rounded curve, so as to be easy to clean, with the floor in linoleum of a plain colour, as it would in time 'have to represent the sea, the fields, the background of a railway line'. Inlaid rubber was also recommended as scrubbable, noiseless and warm, and since every child was now to be allowed to use the floor as his natural playground, it was an admirable idea to provide some floor cushions and a mattress, covered in a cheerful cretonne print, upon which he could play.

There was as little furniture as possible in the nursery, as it would only cause unnecessary knocks and falls. As far as possible, corners were rounded off on furniture, and it was made light and strong. A popular trend was to paint the furniture with a washable, gaily-coloured enamel paint, decorated with flowers in a contrasting colour. The three most useful pieces of furniture were the play-pen, easily made by Daddy, an ottoman for baby's clothes and a brick-box which, like the ottoman, could be padded and covered to act as a seat. Mothers were advised to be 'generous with the bricks as they are the best toy a child can have'. Safety first in the home required the use of a fire-guard, firmly attached, and bars at the window, which would look less menacing, it was suggested, if a wide cushioned window-seat were fitted snugly beneath, and for a town nursery at the top of the house, a low safety gate across the head of the stairs. Parents were advised to fill the spaces between the bannisters with three-ply wood 'to remove the temptation of investigation and perhaps getting stuck between them'. It was likely that a staircase would be involved, since very few houses boasted a third sitting-room, but most had a spare bedroom that could be turned into a nursery, and in town it was preferable to put the nursery at the top of the house where it would be away from the coming and goings of the home, and where the light and air were better. If it was impossible for each child to have his own room he had at least to have a space in which his own things were respected. Anyway, for the good both of his physical and of his mental health, the bare minimum air space recommended for each individual was one thousand cubic feet.

By 1935 a reaction had set in to the white enamelled nursery, as it was thought that the glaring white paint had a deleterious effect on children's eyes. Preferable were natural wood or varnished and distempered walls 'with a great deal of yellow in them'. Adhesive-backed cartoon cut-outs had arrived, which could be stuck on to almost any surface and frequently were, removing themselves from their traditional place on the dado and being stuck on to chairs, cupboard doors and even the corners of the table. The sight of Mother Goose flying across the ceiling with favourite characters attendant was too much for the more progressive magazines, who thought that these cut-outs provided too many cut-and-dried ideas, and did not allow full scope for the child's individuality and inventiveness. They thought the child should cut out and paste to a cloth dado his 'own weird choice' of pictures drawn by himself or taken from magazines.

By 1938 the ultimate in nursery design had arrived in the form of special furniture made entirely on 'small folk' scale: miniature wardrobes, toy-cupboards, chest-of-drawers, dressing-tables and book-shelves, all made with rounded corners and on the unit principle so that one piece could be added at a time, all built in and fitted. This furniture came in the prettiest of pastel shades.

The modern way to treat the tiny baby was not to 'coddle and fuss', but to follow a quiet, healthy programme all day long. The baby who was never talked to or played with was sure to become dull and unintelligent, but this did not mean that the mothers were advised constantly to amuse and stimulate their child.

One of the most influential theorists on how to bring up babies was a New Zealand farmer, Dr Truby King, whose wife, Mary Truby King, wrote a book describing their methods. He advised complete breast feeding until the ninth month, hourly feeds from birth and no night feeds. Babies were fed strictly by the clock, in order to establish good habits for the rest of their lives. He also advocated as much sun and air as possible – 'It is of little use opening a window one or two inches only; it should be flung right up from the bottom' – and banned refined sugar from both baby and adult diets. 'Natural sugar such as honey, dates, raisins and ripe bananas should take the place of white sugar, jams, chocolates, sweets and cakes.'

All toys given to the baby up to the age of eighteen months should be 'mouth toys', they were told, which could be chewed without harm and were too large to swallow. Toys that were sharp, too fluffy or covered with poisonous paint or material were to be discarded. A coloured ball on a string was thought a good toy as baby could reach out for it again and again, until he could touch it accurately whenever he wanted. At bed-time baby could be bathed in one of the new baths made of rubberised material slung between two wooden cross members, and his bath-time accessories could be kept in a row of gay pockets (made by Mummy) hanging on a wooden horse-rack (made by Daddy). If the mother was nursing baby, she should have a proper nursing chair.

There were two nursery rules: first, never to shut the window, and secondly that a fire in the baby's bedroom should be unheard-of except in illness. 'Baby's ideal day will end in dreamless sleep by windows open wide as they will go, summer or winter, in a cot with a firm mattress on good springs, and with as few blankets as is compatible with warmth.' Bed socks could be worn if necessary, or a sleeping suit with feet. Mothers were advised to keep their door and the nursery's open, to allow fresh air to circulate and so that she could hear her baby if it cried; if she could afford it, loud-speaker 'phones were just becoming

A-HUNTING We Will Go is our name for this gay nursery cretonne in blue, brown, green, orange and gold on cream.

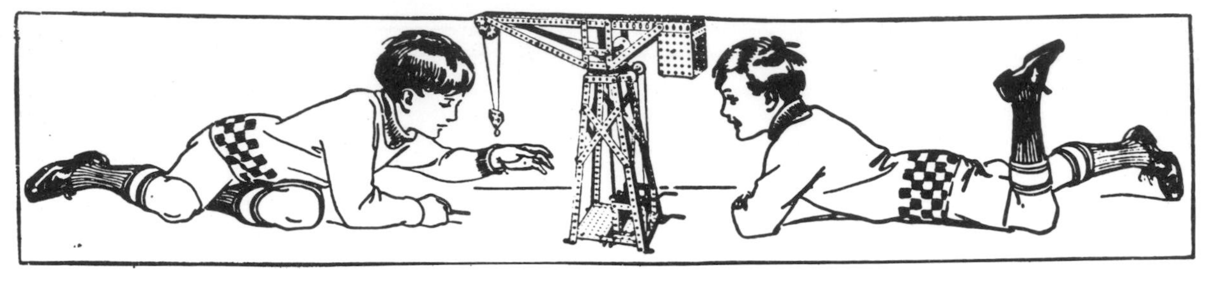

Meccano, the outstanding educational toy of the thirties, is still very much alive.

available which connected the nursery to any or every room in the house so that baby's cries could be heard immediately.

Following the lead of teachers such as Montessori, mothers tried to foster the child's independence. 'Goodbye to babyhood begins when the baby can scramble to his feet unaided, and stagger away from the shelter of his mother's arms on an ever-widening voyage of discovery.' When the child showed the first signs of wanting to dress himself he should be allowed to do so, even if it takes half an hour, for it was the greatest joy to the child to feel that he was 'helping Mummy'. Montessori taught that to work is a child's natural occupation. Give a child a duster or broom, she said, and he will help you as long as he is allowed, though to the child it was not the result but the occupation that mattered. For him play-time was really work-time, and parents were warned not to interrupt the child who was engrossed in what he was doing – concentration cannot begin too young.

'Let's pretend' games taught the child self-reliance and developed his imagination. He was given paints, potato printing equipment and clay, and encouraged to make presents for others. At Christmas he was given Meccano, bricks or other constructional toys. Parents were warned against elaborate or sophisticated toys such as freakish dolls in fancy dress, or 'complex mechanical toys which were a matter of passing fancy for the adult and child alike'. A rag doll, a hinged treasure box or some cotton reels on a piece of string for the child to pull around were home-made toys which would keep the kiddies amused hour after hour. Packing cases were as good a toy box as any, and Princess Elizabeth's favourite toy, it was pointed out, was a simple little rabbit called Peter.

It was considered essential that there should be perfect co-operation between husband and wife when dealing with the children. They had to take care not to quarrel in front of them, or deceive them by leaving promises unfulfilled; only by treating their children as rational and intelligent human beings would they win their respect. Parents discovered that by careful guidance, training and understanding, by praise seasoned with a good deal of prudence, and by intelligent reasoning, their children could be given almost complete freedom and independence without too much going wrong. They turned out to be ordinary, healthy children, with their fair share of naughtiness, and much more enjoyable company.

However, there were still some old-fashioned parents who did not believe in 'this freedom business'. They complained that children seemed to be everywhere, with no part of the house sacred to adults: 'Every room is more or less a play-room . . . one trips over an engine in the hall, and nearly comes to grief over a set of ninepins upon entering the drawing-room . . . one carries on conversations with one's hostess in rivalry with a musical-box.' They concluded that 'the child simply rules the roost', and that discipline was 'still important, as even the tiniest of children has a strong will of its own'. Once one started giving in to it one was well on the way to ruining the child's character.

Both sorts of parents were still largely agreed that the older child should be taught to go to bed at a given hour, after a 'proper' cold bath, and that he should be told cheerful, happy stories. It was thought better that this should be done before he was in bed, so that his mind would not be made too active just before sleep. Just William, Rupert Bear and Winnie-the-Pooh were among the best-loved heroes.

Some psychologists had come to the conclusion that many nursery tales had a bad effect on the thoughts and actions of youth. The popular cartoon films such as the new Walt Disney, 'Snow White and the Seven Dwarfs', though recognised as universally appealing and convincing, were thought to be frightening to a sensitive child, with their portrayal of a world where trees talked and grasshoppers played the fiddle.

Just as the adult world had its heroes, lone aviators

or film stars perhaps, so the children had figures they looked up to and whose tastes and manners they copied. Princess Elizabeth and Princess Margaret Rose were the most popular children in the land, and it was thought that they were 'more famous than any other children alive, and more photographed than any other children that ever lived'. If Princess Elizabeth preferred 'little tarts with lemon cheese fascinatingly concealed within', most other children would suddenly show a great liking for them; or if the nursery at No. 145 Piccadilly displayed a frieze of all the favourite fairy-story characters in a long procession round the wall, then that too was sure to become all the rage. If a Margaret Rose Dress was shown in a magazine, then everyone would knit it, or copy the style. Parents admired the 'simple homeliness' of the Royal Family, and were full of praise for the gracefulness and good behaviour of the two royal children.

Another popular star was Shirley Temple, who, dispensing 'light and sweetness' in the film 'Heidi', was almost idolised by children. 'This little girl, whose income is enormous, seems for some inscrutable reason, to arouse a great deal of scorn in adults, but her popularity with children is unbounded.' To get little girls interested in cooking, they could be encouraged to make Shirley Temple's face in pastry.

Little boys and girls were fitted into their masculine or feminine roles very early. Little girls, having tried cookery, were instructed in the arts of sewing and knitting by learning how to make their own dolls' clothes. Little boys were allowed to be messy, and get their clothes muddy and even torn, for 'boys will be boys'. While girls' hair had to be curly if possible, the small boy's hair was cut as soon as he ceased to be a baby: 'What a heart-break it will be to see sonny's curls lying on the hairdresser's floor. Goodbye to babyhood! He's to be a real man now, but the time has come, and like sensible mothers we must face it.' Boys were expected to look 'manly' directly they left the romper suit stage, and at the age of three wore a smart shirt and tie, while little girls wore clothes

which were 'frilly, not fussy, but pretty and feminine'. It was thought a good idea that a boy should have a dog as a pet to look after and feed regularly, to develop a sense of responsibility and instincts of protectiveness, qualities he would need as a good husband and father. A girl should have a rabbit, and so learn to develop the instincts of motherhood that lay deep down in every girl's heart. In spite of this sex distinction, however, the boy was often expected to help in the house, and do all the useful things his sister did, such as making a bed, tidying a room, mending and even cooking.

Children now ate with their parents, and had to be taught the right table manners. In fact meal times were considered a wonderful opportunity for character training, as 'the child who learns self-control and good manners in the face of the temptations of the table is likely to be strengthened in all ways'. Children were taught to wait until their elders had

One of Walt Disney's "Seven Dwarfs"
© Walt Disney Productions

Shirley Temple, an example of one of the many Pastry Faces you can bake with "Mr. McDougall's Pastry Faces Outfit"

finished at table, and never to break into their conversations. The right training would help the child avoid self-consciousness or faddiness.

Diet for the child was very important, and recommended were uncooked fruits and vegetables, wholemeal flour, fish and dairy products, and instead of sugar a few raisins or dates, or a little honey. A romp before breakfast, after a cold sponge down, would be an aid to a good appetite, and a good mother was careful to serve meals at regular times, unlike slapdash mothers who thought it made no difference whether the child preferred his slice of cake at three or four o'clock. 'The ideally-mannered child should be content with one piece of cake at tea, should give up his toys willingly to visitors, bear disappointments cheerfully without expecting a compensatory reward, and be quiet when he knew Mother was tired.'

The children of the Thirties were enthusiastic party-goers. Adults too played party games almost identical with those of the children, and would go to parties clad in the same fancy dress, gaily eat a fairy-tale or hedgehog cake, and express delight at those hard, bright jellies that came in individual waxed-paper cases and could easily keep a spoon upright. It was the age of jellies. January was the big party month, with the children's holidays packed with invitations. Parents were encouraged to let the children take their part in planning and entertaining, to choose which friends to invite and to write their own invitations. It was felt that if children were allowed to run their own parties and to feel that they were their very own, not only would they get more fun out of them, but they would not be spoiled by them. *Wife and Home* wrote in 1934: 'When Princess Elizabeth has the Queen's permission to invite a few of her friends to tea, her sea-blue eyes sparkle with delight. She writes the invitation cards herself and Princess Margaret Rose helps by carefully addressing the envelopes in her best handwriting, and then the stamps are jointly paid for out of the princesses' weekly pocket money. The Queen always insists that they meet such incidental expenses from their own allowances. It teaches them the financial values and encourages the use of thrift. Princess Elizabeth offers her guests slices of iced fruit cake which she has made herself.'

A party for younger children would start at three-thirty and be held in a brightly decorated room, cleared of everything except a gramophone or piano and chairs. The children would learn a great deal about the successful entertainment of friends by being taught how to receive their guests, hang up their coats and generally act as hosts and hostesses. Since most children were apt to be serious on arrival, a game of musical chairs was suggested as a good mixer. Some parents engaged a conjuror, a ventriloquist, a puppet show or even a cinema show, but this was not really considered necessary – it was thought much better to sing favourite songs round the piano. The children were allowed to choose the food for the party – within reason of course, for it had to be 'simple and wholesome'; a variety of fancy breads and buttered rolls, followed by iced sponge cake, fruit salad and jelly and crackers. A balloon and presents from a bran tub were given to the children when they left.

The most fashionable party dresses were fairy-like models in net, organdie or taffeta, with frills, ruchings, a wide sash and a cape. Pastel shades – pale tangerine, pink and turquoise – were thought most becoming for

girls; Princess Elizabeth chose primrose yellow and pink for her dresses, and another popular style based on a royal design was the Rosebud Dress, embroidered with posies on the collar, sleeves and pockets. Tiny tots would wear a smock made of Jap silk, Japsham or Shantung, since Prince Edward always wore smocks. A pretty party frock for a very small girl could be ankle length, with floppy bows, sashes and little net flowers, and the skirt entirely composed of short frills in rows one above the other.

The new middle class was all for doing things nicely. Parents had a great sense of occasion, and special celebrations such as the christening were properly observed with all decorum and etiquette. The guests should 'leave as soon as tea is over, and their farewells should include a tactful and congratulatory speech about the baby'. The desire to observe the proprieties often resulted in pathetic pleas for advice sent to the editors of the women's magazines: 'My hubby, although only a motor mechanic, is a clever, well-read man who could do almost anything and rise to almost any position. Without being a snob, I want to raise the standard of my small home to that of my neighbours' houses, but my hubby only laughs and gives no help. He doesn't realise the importance of doing things nicely.' The editor in this case tactfully replied: 'This is not so important as the true manliness and goodness which your husband without a doubt possesses. Try hard to put the polish on by all means, dear, but don't lose sight of the diamond underneath for a single moment, will you?'

One had to keep up with the Joneses not only in the purchase of the newest labour-saving devices, but in one's garden, which had to be as good as, if not better than, the neighbours. The kiddies were now, of course, freed from the nursery to romp all over the garden, and so there was rather a conflict of use, with the children clambering over their father's prize dahlias. The women's magazines, however, insisted that baby be given his full ration of sunshine and air, and for those families who could not afford to go away for a holiday, plans were suggested for turning the garden into a perfect holiday for the children. Daddy could make a swing, a slide, a house out of packing-cases, and even a see-saw out of a log and plank. A mock sea-side could be fashioned out of a sand-heap, bucket and spade, and a tin bath filled with water. Wearing his knitted sun-suit, baby could get his correct amount of ultra-violet, joining in the great craze for sun-bathing in the Thirties. It was suggested that a tent would be a fine acquisition for the older kids, or they could be given their own piece of garden and suitably child-size gardening tools. Perhaps they could plant their own initials in mustard and cress. The toddler's play-pen should be out in the garden in all but very bad weather. Later he should learn to acquire mastery over his own body by practice in 'balancing, carrying, fastening and unfastening, jumping and aiming'. Outdoor games, it was pointed out, requiring bats, hoops, skipping-ropes, balls, marbles and spillikins will develop different bodily skills. If it rained, Wellington boots were an exciting innovation, and suddenly every child was delighting in plodding through puddles and splashing water about.

Other ideas for those not able to go away for a long holiday in the summer were to have plenty of picnics or nature walks with Daddy, for not only could the children develop an interest in wild life, but they could satisfy their collecting instincts by picking wild flowers and pressing them in an album. If the child lived in the town, Daddy could take him on walks that taught him the different architectural styles, or the history of ancient buildings. Not only, it was thought, would this 'improve the natural taste of the child', but an opportunity could be taken to teach him the importance of road safety on the increasingly busy roads.

If one was lucky enough to go away, a cycling holiday was perhaps a good idea , or a trip to the sea-side. For this, the magazines pointed out, 'the wise

company of other children of his own age, and resolved to give their child the best schooling they could. They were told that choosing the right school is an individual matter, and 'instead of endeavouring to fit every child to a pre-conceived pattern, they should aim at furthering the child's latent possibilities'. The idea of a co-educational school was now becoming acceptable, and even those free schools where the children were allowed almost complete liberty. Parents were warned not to choose a school just because its fees were low; if they could not afford a good public school, they would do much better to send the child to a day school. The best situation for a boarding school was in the country, on a hill facing south, or on gravel, sand or chalk, or at the seaside. For girls there were some schools that made a great point of training in deportment and manners for London society, but this was of use, it was pointed out, for only a few girls!

This cosy home life, with its parties, jellies and social festivities, was brought suddenly to an end in September 1939, with the outbreak of war. Children and their schools were evacuated to the country, and their parents' energies were now diverted into the war effort.

The quotations in this introduction are taken mainly from the women's magazines mentioned in the credits, and also from *The Girl's Own Annual* 1920, 1922, 1923, *The Home Magazine, Woman at Home* 1923-24, *The Hygiene of Life* 1930, *The Motherhood Book* 1933 and *Mrs Beeton's Household Management*.

mother of a youthful family will choose any month but August, for then the children will have the sands more to themselves and are less likely to suffer from cricket balls and other exuberances of the older children; land-ladies smile cheerfully on them and the weather is very much better.'

Small boys and girls would wear a sunsuit at the seaside – the briefest possible garment, made of wool or cotton in bright colours: 'We do want little limbs to get as much sunshine as possible.' The most popular designs were backless costumes with the top striped and the bottom plain, and costumes in one colour with knitted-in designs of fish, seahorses or buckets and spades. With them went striped linen beach hats and pretty trimmed sun-bonnets.

Holiday time was fraught with danger for the nervous mother. She was warned to take care on the train journey lest the train should stop with a jerk and baby 'roll off the seat'. Nurse or mother was advised *not* to be too zealous in stopping her children from playing with 'those nasty rough boys' and taking them to a protected part of the beach, for 'protect them as we may while they are young, they must live in a world which presents danger when they are grown up'.

At the end of the summer holidays the same protective fears arose in the hearts of parents, for on the child's first day at school he 'definitely steps out of the house and into an alien and perhaps menacing world. This is the moment when a mother and father undertake the great surrender.' They realised the importance of school life, where the child would have the

Mickey's Circus

Come one! Come all! Step right inside!
The band's about to play!
And Mickey Mouse's Three-Ring Show
Is getting under way!

Presenting: Duke Donaldo and
His troop of juggling seals.
He's very gay! (He knows that they
Like fish—not duck—for meals!)

A thrilling, gripping tightrope act
By Mickey. Hold your breath!
He whizzes on his one-wheeled bike,
Defying sudden death.

See Donald Duck! He walks the wire
And stands upon his head
Without a parasol or pole.
(He has balloons instead!)

These things and many more besides—
Gigantic! Huge! Immense!
Wild Animals! A hundred acts!
Admission: Just three cents!

Paste the theatre on heavy cardboard or bristol board before cutting the slits. Then paste the strips of film together as indicated, or else cut off the "Paste here" sections and mount the films on one-inch adhesive tape, allowing eight inches of extra tape on either end. Double surplus tape over on itself, making two strong ends four inches in length with which to operate.

1920s

A rainy day will be welcomed by any child who owns such a mackintosh! It is made of rubber cashmere mackintosh, in brown and blue, and can be had for 25*s.* 6*d.* The sou' wester is 4*s.* 9*d.*

Trace these bland little Teddies by placing a piece of carbon paper under this page and outlining the bears with a sharp pencil.

Old Friends Are Best!

TEDDY bears embroidered on little garments are just the things to please the children most! Three of these Teddies are appliquéd and three are just outlined.

Marcus Adams.

Lady Cynthia Asquith's delightful book, "The Child at Home," was inspired by her own two children.

Make a Success of Your Daughter

By Lady Cynthia Asquith

SHALL she be charming or efficient, dependent or independent, manager or managed? If she is one thing cannot she be the other? Lady Cynthia Asquith says "Yes." As she beautifully suggests, a girl can be sturdy as a tree and yet have ivy moods.

THE other day I was asked whether I intended to bring up my daughter to be the kind of girl vaguely described as "independent." Did I mean to train her so that she should stand firmly on her own feet, or did I think competence unbecoming, and therefore wish her merely qualified, like her Victorian great-aunt, to lean gracefully on another's arm?

When I fondly pictured her future, was it to see her clinging like ivy or rather as a tree rooted in self-reliance? In short, did I wish her to become a woman capable of earning her own living, or one whose so-called "femininity" might inspire men to earn it for her?

Fortunately for our peace of mind, it is not given to us to decide on the details of our daughters' developments. Consider how one sister will differ from another, brought up in the same environment and subjected to identical influences, and you must admit that the selfsame sowing may yield entirely dissimilar harvests. You may decide on whether your daughter wears blue or red, but you can no more count on influencing the colour of her thoughts and emotions than you can determine her complexion.

I have no intention to belittle parental responsibility, and without doubt something may be effected by precept, much by example, and even more by *warning*. Remember your daughter will be more likely to react from the defects of your good qualities than to avoid such faults, however grave, as are without any symptoms inconvenient to herself.

For instance, how easy to make punctuality odious and indolence attractive!

I know a couple who, when faced with the responsibility of bringing up a child in the way it should go, early decided that the best way to keep his feet on the narrow path of duty was for one to act as an example and the other as a warning. Unfortunately both had settled on the less arduous if more effective *rôle* of the warning, and so the plan was abandoned, and both parents remained the usual piebald of good and bad habits.

But to return to the question.

Do I want my own daughter to be managing or managed? Shall I encourage her to be the type of woman who will be a mother to her own mother, or the type (it exists) who will be a daughter to her own daughter? My unhesitating answer is that I do not want her ever to be a woman to whom any ready-made label could be applied. She must not belong to any obtrusive type. Above all, let her be *adaptable*, responsive to the individual in people and the particular in circumstances. The most popular rhymester of our day divided Humanity into two kinds: "Those who lift and those who lean." This might be taken as an unsubtle way of summing up the difference between two opposing types of womanhood. Let us pray that our daughters may be able both to lift and to lean, that their nature fits them for both attitudes and that circumstances will give opportunities for each in succession. Both attitudes are admirable in season, both may be offensive out of season. Any woman who invariably leans must often be a burden too great for human endurance. On the other hand, she who will, so to speak, never accept the proffer of a strong and disengaged arm, on which temporarily to lean would be to economise her own force till the time for her to lift returns, shows no instinct for adaptability or for the becoming.

Efficiency is a glorious thing in any human being. No man but a fool will now consider it unfeminine, and even that fool will appreciate its results in the home. Competence should, however, never be claimed as a satisfactory substitute for charm; nor need any woman, so to speak, for ever wear her efficiency on her sleeve.

Concerning another question now out of date (surely no man still insists on illiteracy in the woman of his choice ?), it was once well said: "If the stockings are blue, the petticoat should be long." No doubt a certain degree of camouflage makes some of our best qualities more becoming. Perhaps if the muscles are big the sleeves should be long ?

Do We Confuse Womanliness and Subservience ?

Lord Chesterfield wrote: "Wear your learning like your watch in a private pocket, and do not pull it out and strike it merely to show that you have one. If you are asked what o'clock it is, tell it, but do not proclaim it hourly and unasked like the watchman." Similarly there is all the difference between the woman whose strength and resourcefulness always rises to an occasion and she who is for ever giving gratuitous displays of her physical or moral biceps in the drawing-room.

Just as the legs of dancers are spoilt by over-development, some women of strong character seem to become psychologically muscle-bound. It should be remembered that the Russians, so incomparably the best dancers, never suffer this self-disfigurement. They know how to counteract the outward and visible signs of their excessive activity. Is there not in some girls of to-day a tendency to flourish the banner of independence when not on parade, to confuse womanliness and subservience and therefore to despise it ? In reality there is no more connection between competence and unfemininity than there is between genius and long hair. It was the liking for a foil to their own qualities, I suppose, which made some men appreciate the old-fashioned type of girl who swooned on receipt of a letter or at sight of a mouse, and scarcely passed a day without having to have her "laces cut" and feathers burnt under her nose.

We cannot expect the healthy, well exercised girls of to-day to carry on in such a manner; as well expect them to sit all day at an embroidery frame. In spite of strong ankles and bobbed hair, there is however no reason why they should not occasionally display some flattering sense of obligation towards what is still called the sterner sex—perhaps suffer their luggage to be carried, sometimes even allow their minds to be made up.

Because ivy looks silly when there is no wall to support it, no reason why a woman should not, so to speak, have ivy moods.

You would not like your daughter to be dismissed as a butterfly, but would it be more bearable to hear her defined as a busybody ?

The New Year

By Helen Douglas Adam

(The twelve-year-old poet who has just published a book of poems, entitled "The Elfin Pedlar".)

TWIRL about and in and out,
A glimmer through the gray,
And a little lonely piper
On the edge of day.
Sweet the sound, oh! sweet the sound,
A broken pipe of reeds,
Yet, in it flowers and sunny hours
And long winds in meads.

Trembling down the valleys,
The lonely stars of night,
Sweet the music up the glens
Where the rain-mists light.
Just a broken pipe of reeds,
Yet calling sweet and clear
Through the half-shut gates of dawn
The little frightened Year.

Softly through the twilit sky,
When the hours were run,
'Fore the hesitating day
Came the Little One.
Perched upon the crescent moon
In a dream of spells
And all the listening air a-shake
With pealing of the bells.

Passed across the twilight
In a rush of song,
Leaving empty silence
So, the Year was gone.
Leaving wistful twirl about
A glimmer through the gray,
And a little lonely piper
On the edge of day.

It is so dreadful to be either at the wrong time, so sad not to be capable of being each in turn! A butterfly in a storm is certainly a pitiable sight, but is not a busybody in a "soothing solstice hushed and halcyon" almost as distressing ? In ceasing to be butterflies how many women with no instinct for compromise become squaws! The great mistake is to specialise as any type. In so doing you inevitably injure virtue by making it appear unattractive, and damage the harmony of your being. Surely life is long enough to dance as well as to housekeep ? Even though yours be the glory of earning your living, there is still time to do your hair becomingly. Have a care that in learning a profession you do not forget how to live, and lose the art of leisure, the capacity for lotus-eating.

Alas, in learning to earn, how many forget to spend !

Would you rather your daughter should know how to cook a good dinner for a man or be the one he would want to share a good dinner with ?

The alternative is false. She can easily be both. Instead of which how often are the means allowed to defeat the end, with the result that a house is made uninhabitable by the very housekeeping; the process of cleaning being more unendurable than the dirt, the economies worse than insolvency.

Again some women in themselves becoming performers, unnecessarily lose their charm as spectators.

Because you now drive your own golf ball, no reason why you should not applaud another's drive.

What Your Daughter Must Be ?

Which relationship would you wish your daughter to personify: mother, sweetheart, sister, aunt, mother-in-law, or what ? Surely the answer is *none* exclusively because *all* potentially.

She must be imaginable as excelling in every *rôle*. She who is now the ideal sweetheart will one day be the ideal aunt, and the best daughter of to-day should make the best mother of to-morrow. In short, one would like her to remind one of Wordsworth's unsurpassed poem :—

She was a Phantom of delight
When first she gleam'd upon my sight;
A lovely Apparition, sent
To be a moment's ornament;
Her eyes as stars of twilight fair,
Like Twilight's, too, her dusky hair;
But all things else about her drawn
From May-time and the cheerful dawn;
A dancing shape, an image gay
To haunt, to startle, and waylay.

I saw her upon nearer view,
A Spirit, yet a Woman, too!
Her household motions light and free,
And steps of Virgin-liberty;
A countenance in which did meet
Sweet records, promises as sweet;
A creature not too bright or good
For human nature's daily food.
For transient sorrows, simple wiles,
Praise, blame, love, kisses, tears or smiles.

And now I see with eye serene
The very pulse of the machine;
A being breathing thoughtful breath,
A traveller between life and death.
The reason firm, the temperate will,
Endurance, foresight, strength and skill;
A perfect Woman, nobly plann'd
To warn, to comfort and command;
And yet a Spirit still, and bright
With something of an angel-light.

A Child's Knitted Frock

THIS pretty little frock was worked in a pale amethyst shade of "Falcon" Linen Jumper Floss, with trimmings of white Angora.

Materials Required.

½ lb. of Knox's "Falcon" Linen Jumper Floss, ½ oz. of Angora wool, 1 pair of knitting-needles No. 8, and 1 pair No. 10.

Abbreviations used.

K = knit ; **p** = purl ; **s** = slip ; **o** = over (put the thread over to make a st) ; **n** = narrow (knit 2 st together) ; **st** = stitch or stitches.

The Skirt.

Cast on 97 st on the No. 8 needles, and knit in stocking-web stitch (a plain and a purl row alternately) for 30 rows. This forms skirt length.

The Frock measures 19 inches from neck to hem, and is designed for a child of from 2 to 3 years.

31st Row.—P 3, * drop 1 st off the needle, p 6 and repeat from * to the end of the row, finishing with p 3. Let the dropped st run right down to the hem, forming a ladder after the k 6. This should leave 84 st.

Now change to the finer needles and work 6 rows plain.

The Bodice.

Change back to the No. 8 needles and begin pattern, making sure you have the correct number of st on the needles (84).

1st Row.—S 1, k 1, n, * o and k 1 alternately 3 times, o, then n 4 times, repeat from * 6 times, finishing with k 1 in the front and back of next st to increase 1, k 2.

2nd Row.—P. *3rd Row.*—K plain. *4th Row.*—P.

Repeat these 4 rows until there are 13 patterns in the bodice. Work 6 rows of plain knitting, then cast off; this brings the work to the top of the shoulders. Work a second piece in exactly the same way.

The Sleeves.

Cast on 62 st and work the fancy pattern until there are 5 complete patterns, then change to the finer needles, and k 6 plain rows. Cast off.

To Make up the Dress.

Place the two pieces together and sew down from the plain knitting at the waist to the hem on each side seam. Sew along the top of the shoulders for about 2 in. on each side. Then fix the centre of the sleeve on the shoulder line, and over-sew on the wrong side, working from the top of the shoulder down each side to the full extent of the sleeve top, then sew up the sleeve seams and the remainder of the side seams of dress down to the plain knitting at the waist.

Finishings.

Take a No. 9 crochet-hook and work 1 row of d c round the neck, sleeves, and lower edge with Angora wool.

FASHIONS FOR SMALL PEOPLE.

"IT must be embroidered or it is not smart," says Fashion. "But I have not time to do embroidery on my clothes, nor on those of the children. I am a very busy person," you answer.

If you think that is the end of the matter, you are much mistaken. Dame Fashion, as we all know, comes from France, and from France she has brought us an embroidery which literally takes no time to do at all—it is the useful and always pretty *Broderie Rapide.*

True *Broderie Rapide* is nothing at all but straight stitches, which are long or short according to the needs of the design.

Broderie Rapide consists of straight, single stitches long or short, according to the design.

LET the stitches be much bigger on the right side of the stuff than on the wrong, and take great pains to keep them even and regular.

Rompers and Play Suits for Boys and Girls

CHILDREN'S FASHIONS

Some Suggestions for the Schoolgirl's Term Outfit

No. 10206.
Age 8–14.

On a dress of navy serge, a belt of scarlet leather strikes a cheerful note.

A narrow black sash and embroideries of black wool adorn baize green wool jersey.

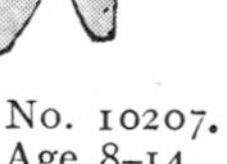

No. 10207.
Age 8–14.

No. 10210.
Age 8–14.

Black fur and braid trim an overcoat of cinnamon brown cloth.

A frock of rust red velveteen is embroidered in blue, red and black silk.

No. 10209
Age 8–14.

No. 10208.
Age 8–14.

Grey jacquard velour fashions a coat with buttons of bright blue.

JUDGING from appearances to-day, the "awkward age" does not exist. This is a wonderful testimonial for all mothers. It shows how successful they are in choosing attractive clothes for small daughters who have reached that most difficult stage of dressing.

Girls of eight to fourteen do not, as a rule, display any interest in the clothes problem. That these should be comfortable and not fussy is all that they ask. It is for their parents to add "attractive" to this list of qualifications. The girl who is naturally careful of her things presents no difficulties; it is the tomboy who is the cause of many an anxious moment where the school outfit is in question.

It will not be until after Easter that bright days will permit of light frocks; so the choice lies among warm, serviceable materials. There is a large range of delightful ones to choose from, corduroy velvet being one of the most hardwearing and becoming. No longer does it appear solely in the well known guise; there are numerous charming figured varieties obtainable printed in effective designs.

Plain wool corduroy is also nice for a morning frock, and should be made very simply with, perhaps, a coloured piping, or binding of braid. In navy serge, the slip-on chemise shape, with a belt of coloured patent leather in royal, jade or crimson, looks well. Wool Jersey is still enormously popular for the useful house frock; but it is a material that is far more effective in bright shades, such as tomato, cardinal red, baize green, or the new golden tan.

For chilly little mortals best frocks are often made of velvet in some pale shade, with puffed sleeves. Party dresses of *crêpe-de-Chine*, marocain, taffetas or georgette are trimmed with frills, tucks, pleats or rows of corded pipings, in the same material. Very little lace is used. A delightful schoolgirl's overcoat for the spring term may be carried out in one of the new self-coloured jacquard cloths, or in Paisley velours with a fur collar that will fasten high, when needed. Hats that match the overcoat are a favourite fashion, and they frequently possess a touch of the same fur that trims the coat.

As to colours, shades of brown and red are those which are most sought after. The pleated or plain skirt of serge or suiting, worn with a washable jumper-blouse, is an essential part of the school trousseau. Deep hems are a point that must not be overlooked when making dresses for the growing girl.

Underclothes for the Schoolgirl

There is no reason why the schoolgirl's dressing gown because it has to be plain should not be attractive. The one shown below would look delightful made in sky blue flannel scalloped in silk of a deeper shade, and tied at the side with blue ribbon. Navy blue scalloped in red is another charming effect if the pale blue is considered too light.

Nightdresses designed for the schoolgirl must be dainty and pretty and at the same time simple and hard-wearing. There is little to tear or get out of order in the nightdress shown below. Made of fine nainsook trimmed with pin tucks it is finished with a small collar of Swiss embroidery which also finishes the sleeves.

No. 6,987.
Age, 10–16 years.

Nearly all schoolgirls now wear pyjamas, and although they can never be quite as pretty as a nightdress, yet they are delightfully comfortable and practical. Those shown above are loosely cut; they look best made in a broad striped flannel or silk.

No. 9621.
Age, 10–16 years.

No. 6788.
Age, 8–14 years.

Perfectly plain but attractive in its simplicity is the petticoat on the right. Made of good quality longcloth it will wash and wear excellently. The beading may be bought ready to insert and makes a pretty finish to a plain garment.

Cami-knickers have now almost entirely replaced knickers and camisole, and in the case of the schoolgirl it is particularly a practical garment.

No. 7,482.
Age, 8–14 yrs.

No. 6,062.
Age, 10–16 yrs.

Christmas Cakes for the Children

By C. J. ROBERTSON

THE ordinary rich and solid Christmas cake is not for children.

Something light and digestible is needed that will not have injurious results if the little ones " cut and come again."

Layer cakes, Swiss rolls, sponges, dough cakes and fairly plain loaf cake mixtures can all be used, and iced and decorated in a novel manner to make them look Christmasy.

Three Cakes from One Recipe.

A useful cake mixture that is not too rich can be made with 1 lb. of butter and caster sugar, 1½ lb. of self-raising flour and 8 eggs.

This makes two good-sized cakes or three rather small ones. To make it into three quite different cakes, 6 oz. of cherries can be put into one, ½ lb. of sultanas into another, and ¼ lb. of walnuts into the third.

The butter and sugar are best creamed by hand ; it is less work that way than using a wooden spoon or turning the handle of a patent cake-mixer. The mixture should be creamed till it is quite white and soft, then the eggs are beaten in one at a time, followed by the fruit and flour. A strong wire spoon is the best thing for beating, and makes beautifully light cakes. A good cake mixture should look shiny and smooth ; if it looks rough and curdled it shows that the eggs have been added too quickly and not beaten in sufficiently. A good decoration for a Christmas cake is made by spreading it with Royal icing and roughing it up with a fork. This is dredged with icing-sugar to represent snow. On top can be put a snow-man or a toboggan slide made of almond paste and coated with icing.

Little white china figures for putting on the cake can be bought for a few pence. Or a Father Christmas and a little tree can be used.

An Iced Log.

3 large eggs, 4 oz. of sugar and 4 oz. flour, 1 tablespn. of water and ½ teaspn. of baking-powder. Some hot jam or jelly.

Icing—1 lb. of icing-sugar, 2 teaspn. of lemon juice and the whites of 2 eggs (slightly beaten).

Line a baking-sheet with greased paper and have ready a good hot oven. Whisk the eggs and sugar with an egg-whisk till they are thick, white and full of bubbles. Stir in the sifted flour baking-powder and water, and pour into the tin. Bake on the top shelf of a hot oven for 7 or 8 min. It will not roll up if baked toolong. Turn quickly upside down on to a sugared paper and spread with hot jam, then roll up by means of the paper.

Iced Christmas Log

When cold it can be iced, cutting off two little pieces to represent knots or broken branches. If not considered too rich the cake can be covered with a thin layer of almond paste made by mixing 1 lb. of ground almonds and 1 lb. of icing-sugar with 1 egg and a little lemon juice.

To make the white icing mix all the icing ingredients and beat for 15 min. Lemon juice is essential, as it makes the icing pliable, and the whites of eggs should not be beaten too much or the icing will be hard. Spread it roughly on the cake and sift icing-sugar over. A Father Christmas and a spray of holly add the finishing touch.

Small Swiss Rolls.

These are always liked and they can be made from the same recipe, simply dividing the mixture between two tins instead of pouring it all into one.

Cook for 6 or 7 min. and turn out and spread with jam. Cut the cakes in half lengthways and roll up. When cold cut each piece into three or four small rolls.

Pierrot Tarts.

These are made from bought meringue cases and ice cornet wafers, which can be obtained from many sweet-shops that sell ice-cream.

The tarts can either be bought or home-made. The only part that has to be made is the butter icing used for decorating. Cream ¼ lb. of fresh butter till soft, then work into it ½ lb. of icing-sugar and any colour or flavouring desired.

Pierrot Tarts.

Simply place a meringue case on the tart, which can be filled with lemon curd or jam.

Put the icing in an icing pump with a rose forcer screwed on, and put a line of icing round the meringue, and a line round the bottom of each cornet. Stick the cornets in place and put in the pierrot's eyes, nose and mouth with a few dots and lines.

"Our childhood sits,
Our simple childhood sits
upon a throne
That has more power than
all the elements."

WILLIAM WORDSWORTH.

Further Sayings of the Children

By The Viscountess Grey of Fallodon

(Author of "Shepherd's Crowns," "Sayings of the Children," etc.)

Illustrated by Lewis Baumer

EVERY Mother, even the most careless, will have it in her power to record what Wordsworth calls "rememberable things;" and Mothers owe the exercise of this power to their fellow creatures; because there is often wisdom in what children say, as well as fancy. These "rememberable things" belong to those early years before lessons exert their clamping sway. Before—

> *" those formalities to which*
> *With over-weening trust alone we give*
> *The name of Education . . . "*

have dried the dew upon these young leaves to introduce precision in words, and restraint in self-expression. The child is still an exquisite plaything for its Mother, presenting no problem as yet. Nevertheless these are the years when a Mother may learn a great deal, for the problems are all there, latent; and if she listens she will have a guide to later years; but let her record as well, for she will hear delicacies of diction, little flights of fancy, nascent philosophy, tender turns of phrase, and poetic wisdom that should delight her. A penetrative knowledge, too, of human nature, not always poetic, is sometimes displayed.

He had been thwarted by his nurse and had been rebellious; so he had been put to bed in the day-time for correction. He had evidently spent the time in analysing his own feelings; for when a voice was heard coming from the night nursery, this is what it said:

" I don't love you any more; I've only got used to you." *

An Apollonius this! One who is going to utilise to the full his remorseless vision, so that no illusion, however cherished and fair, shall prevent him unveiling the truth.

An imaginative child can be very ingenious so as to get his own way. He did not like being roused in the morning, he wished to remain in his bed; so when the nurse came to get him dressed, he said she mustn't touch him; it wasn't allowed.

" Why?"

" Because I'm a flower and mustn't be picked."

Next morning the nurse, when she was at the bedside again, said:

" Well, are you a flower again, that mustn't be picked?"

"No," he said, with excellent finality. *" I'm a stamp that's stuck down."* *

The children who will animate these further pages have been given to the world before; their Mother having been taught early in life that if anyone has anything good belonging to them, it should be shared. They were called One, Two, Three, Four and Five, according to their place in their family. Dull names for such radiant beings; but as such, let them figure again here. There will be more about Four and Five in this narrative, for these were so young at the time of the first writing that they had not said so much; but

* D. B.

* The saying of E. A. F. W.

since then whenever there has been a cherishable remark, it has been recorded.

Then open the nursery door once more and hear them speak.

"*There was once a woman who had two daughters* (Five is telling a story here) *and one daughter was very lovely and very good, and she was called Rose-Bud. But the other was nasty; she wasn't at all lovely and she wasn't at all good* (his voice gets very strict and earthy at this point), *and* she *was called Toad-Bud.*"

NOW here one feels the nasty daughter had really got what she deserved. Not so Five, however, for his sincere love and admiration for toads made him most regretful and apologetic whenever he found one in the garden; and he would loudly recant and say they were much too good for the nasty daughter.

It is easy to trace here the story of the two maidens, of whom one reads that from the lips of one fell rubies and precious stones whenever she uttered, whereas the words of her sister turned to toads and vipers as she spoke. Children constantly plagiarise boldly; they will openly say they have made the story themselves. This is no lie; it means to them that they have assimilated the tale and re-phrased it, and made it their own by selection. Children are often thought to lie when they have no intention to be untruthful. People around them should be very careful to draw a distinction between inaccuracy and a definite attempt to deceive. They should always make clear to a child its own inaccuracy or plagiarism, but without any censure beyond explanation; and moreover, with a word of praise that they should have remembered it so well, to tell the story again clearly.

Five was so enchanted by the story of "*The Taming of the Shrew,*" when his Mother read it aloud to him, that he immediately began writing it out in his own laboured, printed, large and misspelt handwriting; then he gave it to his Mother, with a beaming face, signed with his own name. This meant taking a great deal of trouble; but when he was much younger and was in the very early stages of learning to read, he provided an amusing instance of "taking the line of least resistance." It was a little lesson his Mother set him from "Reading without Tears," to use the words he had just newly been learning.

"*I am in my gig. It is great fun. I am enjoying it.*"

But the words *great* and *enjoying* presented difficulty, so he swung the sense round completely, and wrote words he knew how to spell. So that, in time, when the lesson was brought to his Mother, she found this written:

"*I am in my gig. It is bad fun. I am hating it.*"

Five was almost certainly the best baby of all. Five and Three their Mother gives the highest praise to. Invariably happy, sweet-tempered, contented, gentle and amused.

When Five was two years old he cried because he had stepped on the dog's foot, and he thought he must have hurt it. "What a soft-hearted baby!" exclaimed the Irish cook, who had witnessed the happening, and she added she had not known "a baby could be pitiful." How different to Four, who dropped the black cat out of the window of the second story. But then his Mother thinks he did not know how high the window was. The cat was not at all hurt, but none the less, Four must have been haunted.

Was it by the incensed spirit of the mother of the creature? For he maintained he had met a "*D'agon cat in the bathroom with oranges eyes.*"

His family never knew if he meant eyes the colour of an orange, or eyes as large as that fruit. Whichever it was, it clearly figures something horrific.

Five was counting one day.

"*Three is a much lotter than one, isn't it?*" This question must have been asked in the days when he was very little; on one of those days on which he once made a most pleasant suggestion.

"*Let us walk down this lovely path,*" he said to his Mother, "*and sing about ourselves.*" She agreed: "*Only you begin,*" she stipulated. "*You do it first, because you thought of it.*"

Who more ready than he? At once he started in a fine wavering thread of sound, incredibly high, like an audible gossamer, his hands weaving the air, his white-socked strap-shod feet treading a graceful measure. He always danced as naturally as he breathed.

Bedtime is a solemn time for most children; to some an unspoken agony.

"*There was once a Mother and a baby in a garden . . . .*
And they walked down a green path.
They saw daisies and buttercups—
Only little buttercups because of the mowing-machine,
And trees, and lovely parsley; and there were no nettles.
No nettles at all."

THEN something caught his volant fancy, and this pretty and most innocent song ceased. With all its simplicity it gives, none the less, excellent evidence of a bit of true observation at first hand. That of the buttercups on the lawn being shorter in stem than the field buttercups; and the reason for this.

One day Five was on the Downs in early summer. The grass, the undulating scented turf enamelled with flowers warm in the sunshine, stretched around him. Bird's-foot Trefoil, Yellow Cystus, delicate Squinancy, Drop-wort-filipendula, Milk-wort, Burnet, and Early Purple Orchis, made up the living garment of the earth; and here and there, scattered wind-sown, haphazard, grew the resinous Juniper. The yellow flowers were growing in masses making pools of colour on the wide green space about him; they were short stemmed, close-growing, as is the flora of the chalk.

"*What is this?*"

"*That is a rock-rose.*"

He sprang from one flowery mass to another, and as he danced he sang—

"*I'm in golden gardens*
With two roses in my hand."

The poetry of earth is never dead.

Five was so enchanted by the story of "*The Taming of the Shrew,*" when his Mother read it aloud to him, that he wrote it out in his own laboured, printed, large and misspelt handwriting.

One day he said to his Mother: "*I saw a great old barn, and the door was wide open, so I went up to it quite close: and I smelt its ghosts.*"

What may be self-centred in later life is prettily cloaked in childhood.

"*While I was running fast over the Downs, I heard all the flowers saying, 'Stephen, Stephen.'*" The name was uttered in a whisper, soft as thistle-down.

YET just because nothing is thought out in children's parlance, he can be equally prosaic. He was looking at a picture in his Mother's room, that represented Christ at the Well, and the Woman of Samaria.

"*It's very dark,*" he said. "*I can't see her bonnet.*"

He was always very concerned about thieves and robbers. Somebody trebled his anxiety by observing they would be very difficult to recognise; they looked so much like anyone else. This little seed, dropped casually, into the already highly-tilled soil of his apprehension, was to swell and multiply into a troubled harvest indeed. The room was still, the bedclothes folded, the nightlight keeping its tiny vigil, combating the dark. Then a voice lifted in true agony from a little bed—

"*Oh—if I saw a lady thief—would she look like you?*"

One day Two was unusually tardy in recognising someone he had seen but a short time past. His Mother was surprised. He was usually so quick.

"*That was Mr. Fawkes who spoke to you.*"

"*I know.*"

"*But you appeared not to recognise him.*"

"*I didn't.*"

"*But I wonder why?*"

The reason given was as unexpected as it was unanswerable.

"*I didn't remember him because he had got a new face.*"

Another child had, on one occasion, an equally decisive reply.

"*I don't like Mrs. Brown.*"

"*Why don't you like Mrs. Brown?*"

"*For a reason.*"

This was sufficiently intriguing; so much so that his Mother felt she must probe for the cause.

"*What is the reason?*" she asked; and he said: "*Mrs. Brown is the reason.*"

Four was modelling one day in plasticine.

"*O! I've spoilt my elephant. Yes, I've spoilt his trunk.*" Then, *sotto voce*, in thoughtful further explanation, "*the bun end of it.*"

One day he told his Mother: "*You know I often say 'How-do-you-do' to people when I don't know them. When I see them in the drawing-room or in the garden. Your friends, you know. I'm nice to them, though I don't know them. I do it for your sake.*"

Another time he said: "*I always tell God the people I love when I say my prayers, and then as I can't ever get to the end of them I just say, 'You know,' because I know God knows everything.*"

One day listening to reading aloud he swiftly anticipated. With glowing eyes he told the others what the hero was about to see.

"*I know what he saw! I expect he saw a great deep hole, and a lot of rocks and smoke, and Hell-people climbing up out of it.*"

All these children have ever found great ease in verbal expression. Five said one day: "*She had on one of those very evening dresses, you know; just a bulge of illusion and a rose.*"

Another time he was telling a friend of an unexpected frustration. "*And I thought I was going to have a long quiet time with Mummie, when a whole rumple of visitors came strampling in.*"

Again, he was describing a message being brought from the house to a party of happy pike-spearers, away in the water-meadows in April, among the streams. It was brought out by one of the maid-servants. "*She came running towards us, she didn't know it was so marshy, and she looked so glad, jumping all the little water-cuts and laughing—her eyes in happy slits.*"

The children's Mother had a maid at one time who was a Pole. Four heard someone speaking of this maid's nationality, and he raised a face filled with sudden interest.

"*Then does Sipek come from the Zoo?*" he asked. The only place which he knew of, where poles were in use combined with habitation (which conceivably, might be known among grown-up people as Pole-land), was the bear's pit at the Zoo. Apparently he could reasonably figure to himself a human being clinging to a pole, and calling it home. One, however, while those around were still puzzling over what Four could possibly mean, provided another construction.

One day Five said to his Mother: "I saw a great old barn, and the door was wide open, so I went up to it quite close; and I smelt its ghosts."

"YOU *mean she comes from the North Pole?*" she asked.

"*No. She comes from a country called Poland,*" she was told.

"*Where 'Poleon came from?*" suggested Two.

Nothing ever came to an end with these children. The way subjects branched and flowered under their touch continually astonished their Mother.

But when children are very young it must be principally by oral deduction that their conclusions are arrived at, hearing conversation about them that is so often beyond their grasp. For instance, Two was one day describing ecstatically, something very small.

"*You don't know how small it was,*" he said; "*minute!*"

And Four, who was playing upon the floor, looked up and said:

"*Where is Two's newt?*" The family live by a river.

Once Four asked: "*When shall we die?*"

It was said in just such a voice as who should say: "When shall we have dinner?"

The Mother was so constantly reduced to saying she didn't know, and feeling ashamed of not knowing, that she quite welcomed a question to which she could blamelessly confess ignorance.

"*Couldn't we all die together?*" he went on.

These thoughts on death are nearly always suggested by bedtime. It is a solemn time for most children; to some, an unspoken agony; and it should have every amelioration that companionship, and lowered, not extinguished, light may give. For darkness and silence, so grateful to older senses, are abhorrent to children; and probably justifiably so. For children may be unconscious media; channels to influences alien to their nature, and darkness facilitates the manifestation of forces hidden and unknown. But also stored away in their cell-memory, dating from primitive ancestry, is the knowledge deeply set, that to be in darkness is to be vulnerable to attack.

They cannot explain their dread. They only feel profoundly uneasy about something they can hardly formulate, even to themselves.

Therefore until the deep sleep of childhood falls upon them, children should never be left alone in the dark. It is a matter in which the children of the peasant class are more happily placed. The houses are smaller, and so even if they are in a room by themselves they probably can hear their parent's voices, reassuringly, in the room below. Or more often the child is in a cradle in the comfortable kitchen, and is taken upstairs with its mother when she goes to bed, so that these get the sheltering comfort that animals and birds are so unremitting in giving their young.

One child used to think that her nurse turned into a wolf in the night; and so, even if not alone, a light in the room is of real importance, for if this child stirred in her sleep and the gripping thought occurred, and if she could not instantly turn and see the well known face she so dearly loved, then the stress of soul became excruciating. Darkness ill suits these tender years. Let them have open-air and gladness in the day-time, and at evening, quiet light.

The Starfish

Stranded!

WHEN the tide has turned and the waves are receding, leaving a wide expanse of smooth, pale, damp sand, many little creatures of the shallow waters are left stranded on the shore.

It is easy to recognise the Starfish with his pale red star body and his hundreds of little feet. He has many accomplishments, although he seems so unadventurous. If he loses a ray, for instance, he can easily grow another. You may see some Starfish with one ray shorter than the rest, growing again.

Inside-out to Eat

At the tip of each ray there is a lighter spot which is called the "eye-spot." Starfishes have no eyes, of course, but these spots are sensitive to light. But the strangest accomplishment the Starfish possesses is the power of digesting his food outside his own body! If anything is too large to be taken in by the little round mouth (you will see it on the under surface of the body), the Starfish turns himself inside-out! He passes his stomach through his mouth to his food, surrounds it, digests it, and returns it in a fluid condition to his inside!

The young Starfishes have a very adventurous life. In many families of Starfish they are born from eggs, and develop into free-swimming larvæ inside which the true form of star is gradually developed. Like the insects, who are first eggs, then caterpillars, then cocoons or chrysalids, and then perfect butterflies or beetles or flies, they go through several phases of existence.

A Garden Hat-Shop

Tree-Planting

A Sewing Machine

THE Forestry Department of the United States Government has just accepted from an inventor the plan for a wonderful tree-planting machine. It will soon be in operation, and it will plant ten thousand seedlings a day. The United States will be very rich in wood in the future.

The machine digs a furrow, plants the seedlings, applies a small quantity of fertiliser, and packs the earth. The machine is drawn by two horses, and as one row is planted the outer wheel marks out the place where the next furrow is to be dug, so that one man can plant hundreds of trees in a day.

Railway Clocks

Time-piece without Works

Have you ever noticed that the minute-hand of most railway clocks drops one minute all at once and then keeps still till it drops again?

Railway clocks are not like ordinary clocks. Most of them have no works! You will wonder how a clock can go without the wheels inside. This is due to the fact that railway clocks are controlled by electricity. In any station where there are a large number of clocks, you will probably see a wire coming down to each. This conducts the electricity from the central works, and so all the clocks keep the same time and many can be provided for passengers anxious to catch their train.

Playing Shops

A Garden Hat-Shop

AUGUST is a month of much foliage and some flowers. If we are keeping a toy milliner's shop, it is time to be getting out the new autumn models. It is a good plan to choose a quiet corner of the garden for your shop, partly because the fresh air is very good for girls and boys—yes, boys, too, for there are man-milliners nowadays, you know!—partly because all your material is right at hand in the garden, hanging on bushes and trees and growing in the garden beds.

The shop counter for making out bills and putting the hats into bags may be made from a sugar-box, turned upside-down and covered with a few yards of butter-muslin, which is cheap enough to buy. Green is a good colour to choose and fits in well with the general colour-scheme around you in the garden. The hats themselves may be placed on stands made from the green garden-sticks the gardener keeps for tying up his plants. If you look at a real milliner's shop, you will notice that some stands are tall and some are short, the tall ones standing at the back and the shorter ones in front, so that all the hats can easily be seen.

New Hats from Old

Most households have plenty of old hats which are no longer needed. Straw hats can be brushed over with ammonia and gum arabic, both of which are bought quite cheaply from the chemist. This restores the colour and shine and makes them look fresh again. Felt hats can be well brushed and shaken and ornamented with the first hips and haws of the year.

You can supply your sisters and brothers with new garden hats, and even the dollies can be fitted with tiny models, cut out in cardboard, covered with silk or some other material and well trimmed with leaves or flowers or berries. Virginia creeper leaves make beautiful trimmings at this time of the year, and there is plenty of scope to make tasteful trimmings well suited to the special kind of hats you have in stock. Well pressed leaves can remain as trimmings on a hat for quite a long time, and berries of all kinds may be freshened up by moistening them sometimes to prevent cracking.

Things You Don't Learn At School

A Traveller's Tale

The Fairy of Fortune

ONCE upon a time lived two men. There is nothing strange in this. The curious thing about these two men was that one was extraordinarily lazy while the other was just as wide awake. They were great friends, and they decided one fine morning to spend the day out-of-doors.

As they set out from the valley in which both lived, the sun shone out on the mountains. "Look," said the industrious man, "how brightly the sun shines." Then as he looked he gasped. Rising through the clouds on the mountain-top stood a beautiful castle with golden roof and diamond windows. Neither noticed that a little fairy dressed in rainbows was rolling towards them on a golden ball. They started as they heard her musical voice. "Well-a-day, Travellers," she said. "See on the mountains the Castle of Fortune. If you can reach the castle before midnight, it shall belong to you. Inside the castle a princess clothed in silver awaits you, and fairy-attendants shall serve you. Set out at once and lose no time." Then the fairy vanished.

The Journey

"Let's start at once," said the industrious man, trembling with eagerness to be off. "Time enough," drawled the lazy one. "We shall walk all the better for a little sleep first." And he settled himself comfortably under a tree. But the industrious man set off at once, eyes fixed on the castle—walking, walking in the hot noonday sun.

When the lazy man awoke it was past three o'clock, but the castle of Fortune was still visible. "It is no dream, then," he said, and jumped up quickly enough. There by his side was a little brown horse!

"This is better than walking," said the lazy man. He jumped on the horse and before long he overtook the other traveller.

But as the evening shadows crept over the grass, the lazy man slept again. He was quite near the mountain. What was the hurry? He slept till the moonshine woke him. Jumping up in a hurry, he looked round for his horse, but the horse was nowhere to be found.

At the Castle

The Tale Continued

NEAR by he heard a rustle, and, putting out his hand, touched a queer hard saddle. "Aha," said the lazy man, "another steed." And he jumped on the queer hard back. But when the moon shone down he found he was astride an enormous crab!

So he had to be content. "I must try my luck," said the lazy man. "Hurry up, hurry up." As he spoke the Castle clock struck the first chime of midnight. The crab moved forward. At the second chime the crab stood still. At the third chime,

he started going backward. "Hi! hi!" said the lazy man. "Let me go!" But he could not get off the giant crab's back, so fast was it moving. The lazy man saw his industrious friend slowly and painfully climbing the Castle steps. The fourth chime sounded! The door opened, the princess clothed in silver came out to greet the tired traveller. Five! Six! The castle blinds went down. Seven! Out went the lights. Eight! Nine! Ten! The gates clanged.

The industrious traveller lived happily in the castle for ever. But as to what became of the lazy man and his enormous crab, why, no one knows!

Ginger-Beer

A Cool Summer Drink

THE ginger-beer bought in stone bottles at the sweet-shop is full of gas and bubbles. Another kind you can make quite cheaply at home is much nicer to drink and easy to make.

These are the materials you will require to make 4 pints of home-made ginger-beer:

A quarter of an ounce of bruised ginger; 6 ounces granulated sugar; a pinch of cream of tartar; the rind and juice of quarter of a lemon; 4 pints of boiling water and a quarter of a cake of yeast.

The skins must be cut as thinly as possible from the lemons and then squeezed into an earthen bowl. Next the yellow skins must be put with the cream of tartar and sugar into the lemon-juice, and the 4 pints of boiling water poured over them.

When to Bottle

This should be allowed to stand until it is lukewarm, and then the yeast which has been stirred to a thick cream with a little sugar should be added. The whole must be stirred well, and the pan covered with a cloth and left in a warm place overnight.

The yeast must be skimmed off next day and the liquid poured off into a clean vessel, leaving the sediment behind. The liquid should then be bottled, the corks tied down, and in three days it will be fit to drink.

You must be particularly careful with the cream of tartar and the yeast, since cream of tartar, if taken in large quantities, *can be poisonous,* and yeast will make ginger-beer too bubbly if you put in too much.

New Jumpers for Little Girls

Brown Bunnies march around this Blue Slip-on Jumper.

For each jumper the directions tell how many stitches and rows are worked to a one-inch square. As no two people knit alike, find out first whether the size needle mentioned will produce the right number of stitches and rows. As a test, cast on about 20 st, and purl every alternate row.

Abbreviations Used.

K = knit; **p** = purl; **st** = stitch or stitches; **o** = over (put the wool over to make a st); **n** = narrow (knit 2 st together).

A diagram for working the Bunny is shown on the next page. Follow the block pattern by working backwards and for wards (p every alternate row), make 1 st for each space (in background colour) and 1 st for each block (in pattern colour). When k, follow block pattern from right to left; when p, follow next row of pattern from left to right. As soon as the first block appears drop background colour and introduce pattern colour, leaving an end of about 2 in., which may be fastened securely later, k 1 st for each block, then drop thread and pick up background colour which has been carried on wrong side, being careful that it is not drawn too tight or it will pucker the work, nor yet too loose or it will loosen in the first st and spoil the evenness of the work.

An Openwork Design.

A Jumper with a Striped Border.

The Bunny Jumper.

Materials Required.

4 oz. blue, 1 ball tan "Beehive" zephyr wool. Use a pair of bone knitting-

New Jumpers for Little Girls

needles No. 9, and a pair of steel needles No. 12 for cuffs.

The jumper measures 15½ in. in length and 23 in. in girth. Seven st and 9 rows make a 1-in. square.

The Back.

With blue wool cast on 82 st and k 10 rows (5 ridges). Then follow block pattern. For the 4 rows of spaces k 1 row, p 1 row, k 1 row, p 1 row.

5th Row.—Following pattern from right to left, k 8, * with tan k 1, with blue k 3, with tan k 6, with blue k 17, repeat from *, ending with 10 blue st.

6th Row.—Following pattern from left to right p 7, * with tan p 2, with blue p 2, with tan p 3, with blue p 5, with tan p 1, with blue p 14, repeat from *, ending with 8 blue st.

7th Row.—K 8, * with tan k 1, with blue 3, with tan 11, with blue 12, repeat from *, ending with 5 blue st.

8th Row.—P 5, * with tan 11, with blue 3, with tan 1, with blue 12, repeat from *, ending with 8 blue st.

Continue k odd rows from right to left and p even rows from left to right. When the last row of pattern is made (purled) break and fasten off tan wool. Then k 1 row, p 1 row until work measures 15 in., ending with k row.

* In next row p 24, k 34, p 24. K 1 row. Repeat from * twice (3 ridges).

The Front.

In next row p 24, k 6 (slip these 30 st on to a safety-pin), cast off 22 for neck, k 6, p 24. On these 30 st continue for right shoulder, work 11 rows (ending with k row), k the 6 st at neck edge in every row. Break wool. Slip these st on to a safety-pin and make 11 rows for left shoulder, starting at neck edge and ending with k row.

In next row p 24, k 6, cast on 22, and, joining to right shoulder, k 6, p 24. Work 6 rows, k the 34 st in centre in every row. Then k 1 row, p 1 row until border is reached, ending with p row (2nd ridge made for shoulder should form top of jumper). Reverse block pattern and start with the ears of the bunnies.

1st Row.—K 5, * with tan k 1, with blue 3, with tan 1, with blue 22, repeat from *, ending with 18 blue st.

2nd Row.—P 17, * with tan p 2, with blue 2, with tan 2, with blue 21, repeat from *, ending with 5 blue st.

3rd Row.—K 6, * with tan k 2, with blue 1, with tan 2, with blue 22, repeat from *, ending with 17 blue st.

4th Row.—P 17, * with tan p 2, with blue 1, with tan 2, with blue 22, repeat from *, ending with 6 blue st.

5th Row.—K 6, * with tan k 5, with blue 22, repeat from *, ending with 17 blue st.

6th Row.—P 17, with tan p 4, with blue 23, repeat from *, ending with 7 blue st.

Continue to end of pattern. For the

4 rows of spaces (k 1 row, p 1 row) twice, then k 10 rows and cast off.

The Sleeves.

Mark 4 in. on each side from top of shoulder and pick up 54 st (27 st in back and in front of jumper). K 1 row, p 1 row for 2 in. Then decrease 1 st at beginning and at end of every 5th or 6th row (by k first 2 and last 2 st together) until there are 36 st left. When sleeve measures about 8 in. change to steel needles and k 2, p 2 for 2 in. Cast off.

Press jumper on wrong side, stretching the border slightly in shape, and sew up seams on wrong side.

This design would fit a child of from four to five years of age.

Jumper with Striped Border.

Materials Required.

5 oz. tan " Ladyship " Shetland floss, 1 ball brown. Use a pair of bone knitting-needles No. 10, and a pair of steel needles No 12 for cuffs.

The jumper measures 15½ in. in length and 29 in. in width.

The Back.

With brown cast on 72 st and k 10 rows (5 ridges). Introduce tan and k 1 row, p 1 row. Drop tan, pick up brown and k 1 row, p 1 row. Repeat these 4 rows 3 times, making 4 tan and 4 brown stripes. Fasten off brown. Continue with tan and k 1 row, p 1 row until work measures 14 in.

The Neck Border.

In next row (on right side of work) k 21 st, drop wool and introduce brown, k 30 st, drop brown and take a second ball of tan, k 21 st, turn. With tan p 21, drop tan, pick up brown, crossing the thread just dropped, to form joining, k 30, drop brown and pick up tan, crossing the thread just dropped, to form joining, p 21, turn. Repeat the 2 rows 3 times (always drop yarn on wrong side and join by crossing threads).

The Front.

In next row k 21, with brown k 5, cast off 20, k 5, with tan k 21. On these 26 st work left shoulder and slip 26 st for right shoulder on to a safety-pin.

Make 11 rows (ending with p row) k the 5 st for neck border in every row. Break brown and tan at neck edge and slip st on to a safety-pin. Make 11 rows for right shoulder, starting at neck edge and ending with p row. In next row k 21, with brown k 5, cast on 20 (joining to left shoulder), k 5, with tan k 21.

Work 9 rows, k 30 st in centre of every row with brown. Then (starting on right side of work) continue with tan and k 1 row, p 1 row. Work border to correspond with back and cast off.

The Sleeves.

Make 4½ in. on each side from top of shoulder and pick up 50 st (25 st in back and in front). K 1 row, p 1 row for 1 in. (about 6 rows), then decrease 1 at beginning and at end of every 6th row by k first 2 and last 2 st together until 36 st are left. When sleeve measures about 8 in. change to steel needles and k 2, p 2 for 2 in., then change to brown, k 2, p 2 for 1 row and cast off loosely. Make other sleeve the same way and sew up seams.

The directions are for a child of from six to eight years of age.

An Openwork Design.

Materials Required.

4 oz. Paton's " Pearl Crochet " wool. Use a pair of bone knitting-needles No. 7, and a pair of steel needles No. 11 for cuffs. The jumper measures 21 in. in length and 29 to 30 in. in width. Five st and 7 rows form 1-in. square (in the pattern)

The Back.

Cast on 72 st and k 10 rows. K 1 row, p 1 row, k 1 row, p 1 row. In next row (on right side of work) begin pattern. K 6, o, n, 30 times in all, k remaining 6 st.

2nd Row.—P 72 (each o makes 1 st).

3rd Row.—K.

4th Row.—P.

5th Row.—(Second row of holes) k 6 (o, n) 30 times, k 6.

6th Row.—P.

7th Row.—K.

8th Row.—P.

9th Row.—K 6, * o, n, k 2, o, n, k 12, repeat from *, ending with k 6.

10th Row.—P.

11th Row.—K.

12th Row.—P. Repeat from 9th row twice.

21st Row.—(Repeating row of holes) k 6 (o, n) 30 times, k 6. P 1 row, k 1 row, p 1 row. This finishes the first row of squares. (Work should now measure about 4 in.) Repeat from 5th row 3 times,

New Jumpers for Little Girls

making 4 rows of squares. For next square repeat from 5th to 12th row inclusive, then repeat from 9th to 12th row inclusive, once only. Repeat 9th row again and cast on 42 st for left sleeve. P 1 row and cast on 42 st for right sleeve. K 1 row, p 1 row. For row of holes k 6, * o, n, repeat from * to within 6 st, k 6. P 1 row, k 1 row, p 1 row. Repeat row of holes, then p 1 row, k 1 row, p 1 row. Repeat 9th row, k 12 instead of 6 at beginning and at end of row. Continue in pattern for 2 squares (making 7 rows of squares for back), ending with 1st row of holes.

In next row p 66, k 24, p 66. K 1 row, P 66, k 24, p 66. Make 2nd row of holes, k 24 st in centre.

The Front

P 66, k 6 (slip these 72 st on safety-pin), cast off 12 st for neck, k 6, p 66 Continue in pattern on these 72 st, always k the 6 st at neck edge until one square and first row of holes are made. In next and every 4th row increase 1 at neck edge by k first the front and then the back of 7th st from neck edge. Work the new st in pattern. When 6 st are increased in this way, make 2nd row of holes, turn, k 6, p 72 and slip st on a safety-pin.

Make left shoulder and sleeve to match, then join both fronts and continue in pattern. Finish the square just started (5th square of sleeve) and make the 2 rows of holes (with 3 rows between). P 1 row. In next row cast off 42 st for right sleeve, k to end of row and turn. Cast off 42 st for left sleeve and p remaining 72 st for front. Finish front to match the back.

The Cuffs.

Pick up 40 st along end of sleeve and k 2, p 2 on steel needles for 2½ in. Cast off.

Sew up seams.

This would be suitable for a girl of from eight to ten years of age.

A Crocheted Frock for the One-year-old

Materials Required.

8 oz. Knox's "Falcon" Jumper Floss, size "BC"; 1 bone crochet-hook No. 9.

The Tension.

With moderate working, and a No. 9 hook, you should get 6 stitches to the inch on width.

Abbreviations Used.

Ch = chain; **tr** = treble; **sp** = space (2 ch, 1 tr over 3 ch).

The Front.

Make a foundation of 110 ch.

Miss 3 ch, 107 tr (108 tr in all, counting 3 ch as 1 tr).

2nd Row.—3 ch (for 1 tr), then 1 tr into the back of each tr of the preceding row.

3rd Row.—Work as in the 2nd row.

4th Row.—4 tr, * 2 ch, 1 tr, space of 2 ch, 1 tr, 2 ch, 1 tr, 2 ch, 1 tr, 2 ch, 4 tr; repeat from * until end of row.

5th, 6th, and 7th Rows.—Same as 4th row.

8th Row.—Work tr for 110 st.

Then make pattern as from 4th row; work this pattern until you have four patterns in all.

Now work 7 rows all tr. Then 1 tr, 1 sp, 1 tr, 1 sp, to end of row.

Three rows tr. Then 1 tr, 1 sp, 1 tr, 1 sp, to end of row.

Three rows tr. Then 1 tr, 1 sp, 1 tr, 1 sp, to end of row.

The Sleeves.

Now work tr, but cast on 10 ch to each side, this forms small short sleeve.

Now work tr for 3 rows. Then 1 tr, 1 sp, 1 tr, 1 sp, to end of row.

Now work 21 tr (2 ch, 1 tr) for sp. Make 16 of these sp, 21 tr, and turn.

Next row, 21 tr, 16 sp, 21 tr.

Next row 21 tr, 16 sp, 21 tr.

Work 10 sp.

Turn with 6 ch, 1 tr, 1 sp, 1 tr, 1 sp, 21 tr. Work this for 4 rows. This brings you up to the shoulder.

Work other sleeve exactly the same way.

The back of frock is worked in exactly the same manner as the front.

Press with a damp cloth and hot iron. Then sew up the side seams.

A Child's Knitted Play Suit

WORKED in the popular dice pattern this makes a most attractive little garment. It slips on over the head and has a flap closing at back. The garment is knitted in one piece, commencing at the upper edge of the back flap, and working right over.

Materials Required.

1 lb. saxe blue, and ¼ lb. putty "Falcon Floss," size B.C., 1 pair each knitting-needles, sizes 9 and 10, a No. 11 crochet-hook, 4 crochet-covered buttons, and ¾ yard of narrow elastic.

The Lower Front and Back.

With the No. 9 needles cast on 110 st with blue "Floss."

K 5 plain, 5 purl (p) for 5 rows, then reverse, *i.e.*, 5 p, 5 plain for next 5 rows, and so on for 13 in.

Cast off 40 st at the beginning of each of the next 2 rows for the leg openings.

Work 9 more rows on the 30 st in the centre of the needle.

Cast on 40 st at beginning of each of next 2 rows, and work for 13 in.

The Upper Front and Back.

Now to work front waistband. Use the putty thread and the No. 10 needles: k 1, k 2 together, and repeat to end of row, and so reduce to 74 st. K in garter-stitch for 6 rows. Then k 4 st in garter-stitch each end of row in putty, and the rest in blue in stocking-stitch for 4 rows. (To join edge of putty and saxe loop one colour round the other each time when changing thread.)

Finish band with 6 rows of garter-stitch with putty.

Then increase to 75 st, and k in pattern with No. 9 needles for 2½ in., *i.e.*, 20 rows. Cast on 40 st, k to pattern right across row, and cast on 40 st for second sleeve.

K to pattern 125 st, turn.

K to pattern 95 st, turn.

K to pattern 103 st, turn.

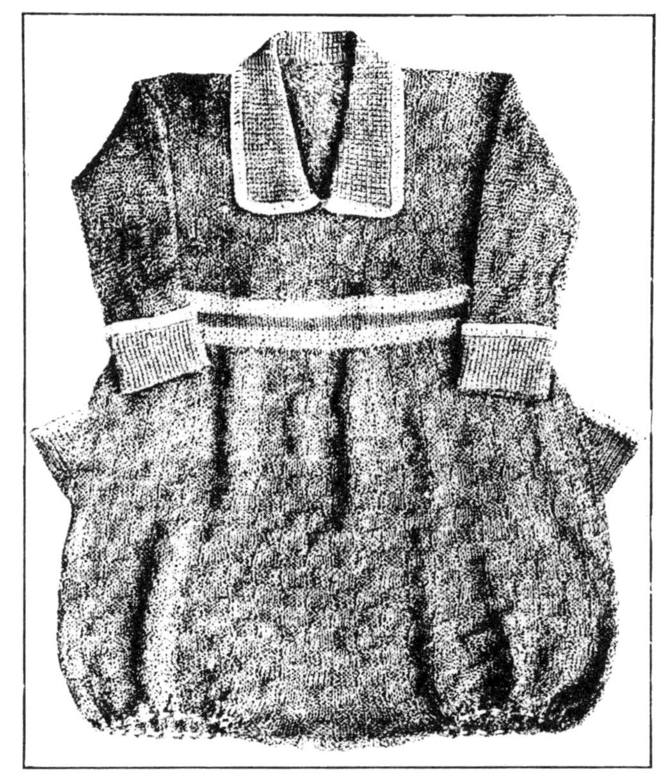

This would fit a child of from four to five years.

K to pattern 111 st, turn.

Take 8 st more on each row to shape sleeve until all are being worked, then divide for neck opening. K 76, k 2 together. Put other st on an odd pin. K 3 rows to pattern on the 77 st, decrease again on the 3rd row and side of opening, and repeat the 3 rows until there are 68 st on this half, and continue in pattern until work measures 6 in. from the division for neck opening.

Work the other half the same, and there will be 67 st only on this half.

Join the work again by casting on 20 st for back of neck, making 155 st. K until end of sleeve measures 8 in. from the cast on st, then leave 8 less at end of each row until the 40 sleeve st are left; cast these off, and work 2½ in. more, *i.e.*, 20 rows.

Join on putty thread, and with the No. 10 needles k 2, k 2 together all across row, reducing to 57 st. K 5 more rows.

Work next 4 rows with 4 st each end in putty, and the rest in blue.

Then 6 more rows in blue in garter-stitch, and cast off.

With the No. 10 needles and putty thread pick up and k the 110 st cast on at the beginning to form back belt.

2nd Row.—K 1, k 2 together, and reduce to 57 st. K 4 more rows. Then k 4 st in putty each end, and the rest in blue, but do not loop the thread as before, as it will form a button-hole each end.

11th Row.—K 20, cast off 4, k 20, cast off 4, finish row.

12th Row. Putty floss only. K 24, cast on 4, k 20, cast on 4, k 24. K 4 more rows, and cast off.

The Collar.

With crochet-hook make 16 ch and work to and fro in tricot for 19 in. Then crochet round edge in tr.

The Cuffs.

Make ch of 16, and tricot for 7½ in. Finish edge with tr, as collar.

The Gusset.

With No. 8 pins and blue thread cast on 1 st; k 2 into it by taking first the front and then the back thread.

2nd Row.—P 2 into 1st st, p.

3rd Row.—K 2 into 1st st, k 2.

4th Row.—P 2 into 1st st, p 3.

Continue making 1 extra st each row until 22 st are made. Join on putty, and increase 1 st on each of the next 2 rows (making 24 st in all), k 2 rows, cast off.

Sew up leg seams 8 in. from bottom edge where st were cast off and on. Then sew in side gusset to give more spring.

Sew collar to back of neck, leaving sides free to be attached with press-fasteners after garment is slipped over the head. The sleeves are slightly fulled into the cuffs. Add 4 buttons to correspond with button-holes.

Crochet 1 d c and 2 ch all round the edge for threading the elastic at knees.

FOR THE YOUNGEST MEMBER OF THE FAMILY

The Coat is Such a Soft Little Garment and with Our Directions You Can Make a Cap or Bonnet to go with it. For Boy or Girl.

BABY'S FIRST COAT

MATERIALS.—2 oz. of 2-ply Scotch Fingering, 2 tubes of Clark's Scintilla artificial silk for crochet edges, 1¼ yards of ribbon, a pair of long bone knitting needles No. 9 and a spare needle, a steel crochet hook No. 1.

SIZE AND TENSION.—Working at a tension of 7 stitches to the inch in width, the following measurements will be attained after light pressing : Length of coat from shoulder to edge, 10½ inches ; width all round coat, 25 inches ; length of under-arm seam of sleeve, including cuff, 6½ inches.

ABBREVIATIONS.—K., knit ; p., purl ; tog., together ; d.c., double crochet ; tr., treble ; ch., chain.

BEGIN at lower edge of coat with wool, casting on 168 stitches for the full width of back and fronts. Knit 5 rows plain, working the first row into the back of the stitches.

The Open Pattern

1st row : K. plain.

2nd row : K. 3, p. until 3 remain, k. 3.

3rd row : K. 3, * k. 2 tog., repeat from * until only 3 st. are left, which k. plain.

4th row : K. 3, * pick up the straight strand of wool before the next st. and knit it, k. 1 ; repeat from * until 3 remain, k.3.

5th, 6th and 7th rows are the same as 1st, 2nd and 3rd rows.

8th row : K. 3, * k. 1, pick up one as in 4th row ; repeat from * until 3 remain, k. 3.

Repeat these 8 rows until the 19th ridge is just completed.

Next row (5th row of pattern). With right side towards worker, k. 44 for right front and slip remaining 124 on spare needle. Work right front in pattern exactly as before, until there are 10 ridges from under-arm.

At the beginning of next row at neck end, cast off 14, work on remaining 30 stitches for 2 more ridges. Either cast off these sts. or slip them on a spare needle, afterwards grafting to back shoulder stitches.

The Back

JOIN wool to spare needle stitches at right under-arm. With right side towards worker, k. 80 sts. for back and slip remaining 44 on spare needle.

Work in pattern until the 12th ridge from under-arm is completed, then cast off, or if you intend to graft shoulders, work 30 sts., cast off 20 for back of neck, work 30.

The Left Front

JOIN wool to 44. spare needle stitches at left under-arm. With right side towards worker, k. 1 row and continue in pattern to match right front.

Now sew shoulder cast-off edges together, or graft stitches together.

BABY'S FIRST COAT

The Collar

WITH wrong side of coat towards worker, pick up 78 st. round neck (one for every cast-off stitch and one for every row over shoulder). Work the 2nd pattern row and continue until the 4th pattern ridge is completed, k. 5 rows and cast off.

The Sleeves

FOR cuff edge, cast on 38 sts. and work as for lower edge of coat, but all through the sleeve k. 1 edge stitch only instead of 3. After the 4th pattern ridge is completed, with right side towards worker, p. 1 row.

Next row: With wrong side of cuff towards worker, k. 1, pick up 1, * k. 4, pick up 1; repeat from * until 1 st. remains, k. 1.

Now work the second pattern row and continue in pattern until 14 ridges are completed for sleeve (without the cuff); cast off.

The second sleeve is exactly the same.

Sew the cuff and sleeve seams. Sew sleeves to armholes, which should fit straight in, putting the seam in the centre of the division of back and front sts. at under-arm.

The Edging

JOIN silk to cuff and work 1 d.c., * 3 ch., work 3 tr. into the d.c. just worked, miss 2 sts. on the knitting, work 1 d.c. into next st.; repeat from *.

Work the same edging all round coat and collar and press lightly.

A Bonnet to Match the Little Coat

MATERIALS: ½ oz. of 2-ply Scotch fingering, ½ tube of Clark's Scintilla, a pair of No. 9 knitting needles and a steel crochet hook No. 1. Jap silk for lining and 1½ yards of ribbon.

SIZE AND TENSION.—Worked at a tension of 7 stitches to the inch in width, the model illustrated measures 13 inches round the front edge, after light pressing. The depth of bonnet from edge of brim to centre back of head can be worked any size from these directions.

ABBREVIATIONS.—K., knit; p., purl; tog., together; ch., chain; d.c., double crochet; tr., treble.

CAST on 82 stitches for front turn over, and k. 5 rows plain, knitting the first row into the back of the stitches.

Now work open pattern as follows.

1st row: K. plain.

2nd row: K. 3, p. until 3 remain, k. 3.

3rd row: K. 3, k. 3 tog. all along the row until within 3 st. of end, which k. plain.

4th row: K. 3, * pick up the straight strand of wool before the next st., and knit it, k. 1; repeat from * until 3 remain, k. 3.

5th, 6th and *7th rows.* Same as 1st, 2nd and 3rd rows.

8th row: K. 3, * k. 1, pick up 1 st. as in 4th row; repeat from * until 3 remain, k. 3.

Repeat these 8 rows twice more, then work the 2nd row, omitting the 1st row to change the side of work, so that the right side of the flap will be uppermost when it turns over. Finish this pattern, and work 5 patterns more.

In the next pattern work 1st row as usual.

2nd row: Cast off 2, k. 3, p. 14, p. 2 tog., (p. 4, p. 2 tog.) 7 times, p. 16, k. 3.

Work next 3 rows in pattern, casting off 2 at the beginning of each row.

Next row: Cast off 2 st., k. 3, p. 10, p. 2 tog. (p. 3, p. 2 tog.) 7 times, p. 11, k. 3.

Work next 3 rows in pattern, casting off 2 at the beginning of each row.

Next row: Cast off 2, k. 3, p. 5, p. 2 tog. (p. 2, p. 2 tog.) 7 times, p. 7, k. 3.

Work next 3 rows in pattern, casting off 2 at the beginning of each row.

Next row: Cast off 2, k. 3, p. 1, p. 2 tog. (p. 1, p. 2 tog.) 7 times. p. 2, k. 3

Work next 3 rows in pattern, casting off 2 at the beginning of each row, when there should be 18 stitches left.

Next row: P. 2 tog. 9 times, break off wool, leaving enough to sew up back. Thread in a darning needle and slip through the 9 stitches, fasten firmly and sew down back seam of bonnet.

The Edging

WITH right side of turnover towards worker, join on silk and work 1 d.c., * 3 ch., 3 tr. into d.c. just worked, miss 2 st. along the knitting, 1 d.c. into knitting; repeat from * all round.

Press lightly and finish with jap silk lining. Sew ribbon ties at sides.

BABY'S BEDROOM SLIPPERS.

These were designed to fit a Baby of 1-2 years.

MATERIALS: One ounce of "Sirdar" ruffle wool in white, half an ounce of "Sirdar" super knitting in rose pink, two bone crochet hooks Nos. 9 and 12, one yard of narrow pink ribbon and a pair of second size fleecy slipper soles.

DESCRIPTION: *The slipper is worked in double crochet, with looped trimming round the ankle.*

COMMENCE at the toe with the ruffle wool and No. 9 hook and make 8 chain.

1st row—Miss the first 2 ch., 1 d.c. in each remaining ch., 2 ch., turn. **2nd row**—The 2 ch. stitch turning stands for the first stitch, work 1 d.c. into each remaining stitch, 2 ch., turn.

Continue repeating the 2nd row until there are 16 stitches in the row. Work 2 more rows without increasing; this finishes the toe. Now work on the first 8 d.c., without shaping a sufficient piece to measure round the sole to the other 8 toe stitches (29 rows in the model). Fasten off and sew the last row neatly to the toe stitches.

With the pink wool and No. 12 hook, work round the ankle thus: 1 treble in the first stitch, * 1 ch., miss a stitch, 1 tr. in the next; repeat from * all round.

2nd row—* 1 d.c. in the first hole, 2 d.c. in the next hole; repeat from * all round.

These Bootees for Baby combine comfort and daintiness.

Still using pink wool and same hook, make the looped trimming. Make 5 ch., work 4 d.c. over this ch., turn, 1 ch.

Next row—Hook into first stitch, wind wool over hook and first finger of left hand four times, draw through hook and then through hook again to form a d.c. and work each st. the same, turn, 1 ch.

Next row—1 d.c. into each of the 4 stitches.

Continue these 2 rows until long enough for top of slipper. Join the ends together and sew to slipper. Then sew the slippers to the sole, easing the crocheting a little round the toe.

Thread ribbon through the holes at ankle and tie in a bow. If liked, brush up the ruffle wool with a wire brush until it has a fluffy appearance.

INDOOR GAMES FOR THE CHILDREN

WHETHER you are giving a Christmas party, or whether the children are getting a little cross and fidgety on a wet afternoon, you will be wise to have ready a list of good indoor games that can be started in a minute without preparation or special apparatus. Much, of course, will depend upon the age of the children you have in mind; for instance, games that require a knowledge of spelling or of the multiplication table are no use if a five-year-old wants to join in, and games that demand much going out of the room and waiting behind doors are not to be recommended if the day is bitter and the hall a cold one.

The games I am going to suggest, however, are all of the kind that can be played inside an ordinary room and that are quite simple enough for the youngest child to enjoy.

Floating Feathers.—A light fluffy feather that will float in the air is needed for this game. The players sit in a circle, rather close together. The leader then throws the feather into the air, and everyone tries to prevent it from falling on any player by blowing it upwards. If it touches a player, that player is "out," and the game goes on until only one child is left.

Hat Quoits.—Spread a newspaper on the floor, and place on it a hat upside down. A man's high hat used to be the correct thing for this game, but such an article will probably be unobtainable, so the hat that comes nearest it in size and shape should be chosen. Divide the children into two sides, and take twelve playing cards from an ordinary pack. Let the children stand at a suitable distance from the hat, then, one from each side in turn, let them try to throw the twelve cards, one by one, into the hat. You can score points like this: Three points for every card that falls into the hat, two points for every card that lodges on the brim, and one point for every card that falls on the newspaper. When all the players have had a turn, the side with the highest score wins.

Hunt the Hanky.—This is a most simple and harmless game, but it is wonderful what fun small children get out of it. Sit them in a circle round a player standing in the middle, and let them throw a handkerchief from one to the other; the standing child attempts to catch it all the time, and as soon as he has done so the child who threw it takes his place. This must be played quickly, and, needless to say, the handkerchief must be a clean, unused one!

Invisible Cats.—One child, blindfolded, sits on a chair in the middle of the room, while the others walk round him *à la* Felix, at a little distance, one at a time. The blindfolded child summons each cat by calling out: "Pussy, pussy, come here to me!" and as the cat reaches the chair, it says "Mew!" If the blindfolded child can recognize the owner of the voice, he is released and his place is taken by the detected "Felix."

Flying.—The children sit round the room, resting their right hands on their left arms. The leader then tells them that he is going to relate some wonderful adventures, and that whenever he mentions the name of an animal that can fly, the right hand must be held up, but that if the hand is held up at the mention of any animal that doesn't fly, the player will be "out." This sounds a very easy game, but at the words "spider," "penguin," ostrich," and so forth, you will be surprised to see little hands shoot up before their owners have had time to think the matter over.

You Mustn't Laugh, or The Solemn Donkeys.—This is a most ridiculous game, but it proves a very good recipe for cheerfulness on a wet day. The children all sit in a row and look solemn. Then the first player says "Hee-haw!" which is repeated all down the line, one after another. Those who can't do this without laughing are declared "out," and the game begins again until only one donkey is left.

Change My Leader.—This game is best played to the music of a piano or gramophone. The children march in single file round the table, and, according to the actions of their leader, they tiptoe, hop, run, walk with arms stretched above the head, do the goose-step, and so on. But the fun consists in the fact that the leader of the party is at one moment the foremost of the file, at the next minute the hindmost. This is contrived by the leader suddenly facing round on the child behind him, when she must at once face round too, and so on with all the children, the march continuing with the erstwhile "last man" as leader. These changes must be made as unexpectedly as possible, so that the children are kept in constant suspense as to which way they will have to go.

DODIN

Try to suit your games to your little guests' ages.

GUARD YOUR TREASURES.

The kiddies are treasures to you, aren't they? So I do hope that if ever you're puzzled or worried over any little ailment or characteristic you'll let me try to help you. I have a family of my own, so you can be sure that my advice comes from practical experience of children.

My address is, care of Lady's Companion, *18, Henrietta Street, Strand, London, W.C. 2. Please enclose the correspondence coupon on page 167, and a stamped addressed envelope if you'd prefer a private reply.*

An Everyday Mother

A cosy dressing-gown in sizes to fit a child of 4 to 10 years

WISE OLD OWLS

Thinking Their Thoughts In The Moonlight

BEDTIME comes and the owls begin to wake up from their sleepy hollow trees! We have captured some of them for baby's dressing gown—and here they are!

A circle of yellow linen, 3½ inches across, represents the moon. Tack this into position on the dressing-gown, and then trace the owl on to a scrap of brown linen, using a piece of carbon paper under this page. Cut out friend Owl, and tack him in place on the Moon.

Work the eyes in cream wool buttonhole-stitch, and sew a brown boot-button in the centre of each. The Owl's body is worked in stem-stitch with dark brown wool, and the same wool suggests the breast markings. Orange wool in fishbone-stitch fills in the beak, black satin-stitch the branch and orange his claws.

Finally appliqué the Moon to the background with yellow wool buttonhole-stitching.

A row of these delightful owls should be worked all round the dressing-gown, which requires 1¼ to 1⅝ yards of 54-inch-wide brown material, and ⅜ yard extra of contrasting material for the collar and cuffs, which might be yellow to match the Moon. The dressing-gown will fit a child of 4 to 10 years.

Little brown felt bedroon slippers each appliquéd with the Owl in the Moon would be a delight to a child's heart.

FOR THE NURSERY CURTAINS

Snow-White Geese Among Green Rushes

APPLIQUÉ-WORK, quickest of all embroideries, trims these nursery curtains of butcher-blue linen. Trace the plump goose on to white linen, using a piece of carbon paper under this page, cut out, and applique two geese on to each curtain.

Cut out several "rushes" in green linen and in sizes varying from six to four inches high, and applique them between the geese. It enhances the decorative effect if you allow the rushes to overlap the geese, so that the birds seem waddling behind them.

Work each goose's beak and feet in orange wool, and add a few stitches to represent eyes and feather markings.

When you've done one curtain, trace the goose on to paper, cut out, and reverse for the second curtain, tracing round it.

The same motif may be used to trim the pocket of a pinafore or the front of a romper suit, if you prefer.

BABY NOTES AND NOTIONS

Contributed By the Matron of a Big Welfare Centre.

Helpful Little Suggestions For Baby's Development.

(Photo by Mabel Robey.)

A Delightful Camera Study of Cathleen Nesbitt with her Baby

Safe Toys

How exciting it is to buy toys for babies. Toys which can bring them to no harm. Bright coloured, soft woolly, washable toys: wooden toys, proof against the paint coming off when they are carried to baby's mouth: rubber toys that can be scrubbed, or will swim in the bath.

I would ban the noisy toy, or one with a tinkling bell, for everyone's peace of mind as well as baby's.

It is a wise aunt who puts in a few extra stitches to hold Jumbo's gay beads of eyes securely, or the buttons on a coat of many colours before the gift is made. Safety first!

"My Own Cup, Please!"

After a romp in the park, most children long for a good drink of water, and nothing could be better for them.

The water so conveniently provided by the public drinking fountains is safe enough, but it's the *cup* that raises suspicion, however thoroughly we may rinse it out.

"Prevention is better than cure," so we carry our own cup, all the year round on our daily outings.

A good stand-by on these occasions is a thermos flask. Filled with delicious home-made orangeade, or even Nature's own provision for thirsty folk, good drinking water, it will banish many a little cross mood when the children are tired and there is a long walk home.

A Place for the Medicine Chest—

It is not decorative, but it is what every home with a happy nursery needs, and it certainly does look efficient.

The best kind of medicine-chest is that with three shelves, and a key kept well out of reach of enquiring young minds.

A safe place is a bare wall in the bathroom, or the light part of a passage. Even mother's bedroom is better than hanging it in the nursery.

This is just as a precaution against the unexpected accident.

—And Everything in its Place

A well thought out system of arranging the shelves helps wonderfully in times of emergency. Applying the right remedy, without loss of time, may save many after-effects of pain.

So we will imagine the top shelf stocked with all things that need a red label (the warning of poison) or not for internal use.

By putting solid and dry articles on the second shelf we get a clearly marked division from the third shelf which might be arranged to take the household medicines.

For instance, the second shelf could have a roll of absorbent white wool, bandages, safety-pins, a roll of white lint, another of "pink" lint (boracic lint) and some oiled skin.

On the easiest shelf to reach, in readiness for baby, among the household medicines, there should be a small supply of castor oil, olive oil, and liquid paraffin.

The Nursery Thermometer

A great saving of arguments is effected when a room thermometer is used in the home. Let it hang on an inner wall, on the opposite side to the fireplace. You can buy one for a shilling or two.

All the rooms into which baby is likely to be carried should be kept at a temperature of 60 degrees (Fahrenheit). This will help very considerably to ward off possible attacks of bronchitis and chest troubles generally.

To be kept in an even temperature is a sure means of bracing the little one's constitution.

Another Thermometer

A clinical thermometer becomes of great value if illness overtakes a member of the household, especially when the little person is still in the nursery and cannot explain her symptoms.

These little instruments are not, however, the easiest things to read without a little practice. So it is a good plan to make oneself accustomed to reading a clinical thermometer, and to the little knack of shaking down the mercury—before an occasion for its use arises.

In taking baby's temperature, the safest place is in the groin, carefully wiping the folds of skin before putting the thermometer in position. Hold the little person gently but firmly still, to be sure of a truthful reading at the end of the time.

Baby's Morning Bath

Heat affects various people very differently. Some cannot stand their hands in water that feels barely hot to another person.

That is the very reason why it is so necessary to have a bath thermometer to test baby's bath water.

There are such handy ones to be had, mounted in cork, which makes a buffer to prevent the glass breaking should the thermometer accidentally strike the side of the bath.

Clear markings easy to read should be the first consideration. A practical test in warm water before finally making the selection, is a good plan.

A Good Tonic

It is a very old-fashioned remedy, and yet it can never be out of fashion.

Try it when your appetite is inclined to fail, and perhaps feeding baby begins to feel rather an effort:

A fresh egg well beaten into about half a pint of well warmed milk. Sweeten to taste as the cookery books tell us, and drink it slowly.

If you want to vary the flavour, a teaspoonful of any one of the well-made essences will make it more interesting.

Through the Eyes of a Child

A Child's Reality

By Mary Chadwick

MUMMY was getting very much worried about Sybil. It seemed to her she was beginning to be a very untruthful little girl, and that since the baby had come, she had altered a great deal, and in many ways not for the better. She couldn't understand it and it puzzled her.

Of course, Sybil had wanted to know where baby Peter had come from, and she, following traditional lines, had told her the doctor had brought him. The child had gone away and asked no more, but not long afterwards she had been heard playing at "Doctor's Shops" with a little friend. The friend had come in and asked for a baby. Sybil, as the doctor, had replied urbanely, "I'm very sorry, madam, I'm out of stock just now. You see, the last lot I had got so stale because nobody wanted them. I just had to send them back again. I couldn't keep them all myself, or I should have had such a large family, and they're not in fashion now. Not like the pictures on the tombstones. Then you got a lot and sent back the ones you didn't like."

Mummy had been not a little surprised when she overheard this conversation coming from her little daughter, for it showed her that Sybil thought more about things than she imagined.

It was true that they had taken the child with them sight-seeing last summer to an old church, where there was a monument showing a knight and his lady, with six boys arranged behind the father, and seven girls behind the mother. They had read from the epitaph that nine of them had not survived infancy, and she remembered that Sybil had asked what this meant, adding quickly after the explanation, "Mummy, couldn't we send Peter back, too, then, it was so much nicer before he came." Someone standing near had made a remark about large families being unfashionable. How children remembered!

The Beautiful Fairy

THE little girl never seemed to want her mummy either now. She was always running about after her daddy trying to help him, pointing out things that "We" had done, or generally that she, Sybil, had made. This wasn't true either, for the child had only looked on, as a rule, her father said.

She was often overheard, too, telling little friends of wonderful adventures she had, of cream-coloured ponies that she kept in the nursery cupboard, that took her to fairy-land whenever she wanted, and the beautiful fairy who lived in a cave, who sometimes sang to her and on whose lap she sat to look at picture books, how she kept a school, where she had only little girls.

Were these dreams, wondered Sybil's mother? If so, surely the child was old enough now to know the difference between what *really* happened and what she *thought* happened. She had once tried to argue it out with Sybil, but the child had only become confused and merely contradicted herself over and over again.

Grown-ups can Say Anything!

BUT, Mummy, things I do at night are just as real, *realler* sometimes than all the dull things, walks and dinners, we have in the day. What I see in my head is real, just as real as me, 'cos it is me. P'raps you can't see it, so you say I'm pertending.

"But it's real my side.

"I don't understand what you mean by real; what do you mean?

"What's telling stories? You tell me stories and say they're true. Then I tell you stories and you say I mustn't; it's naughty to say what isn't true. When one's grown-up one can say anything, and it's true, and things grown-ups do are real. Only when you're little, people say your thinks are only pertending, and what you do's not real. What makes things real, anyway?"

Here mummy didn't know what to answer. But an idea was beginning to glimmer into her mind. Could it be possible that to the child-mind *real* things were anything that was wished for, desired, in fact, like the cream-coloured ponies and the fairy who sang to her? While you tried to pretend things that you didn't want—like that little brother of hers—were not really true.

She was wondering, too, whether she could have been partly to blame for some of Sybil's confusion over the real and true things. She herself had not given her a *real and true answer*, by any means, when the child had asked about Peter.

Was this what the child had meant when she said, "Grown-ups can say anything and it's true"?

Could it be that the beautiful fairy on whose lap Sybil sat in her dreams was a fairy mummy, who loved her best and sang only to her, as she herself had done before Peter came?

Real as Real Can Be

WAS the child inventing a phantasy world, according to her own taste, to establish as her *own reality* instead of an outside world that was proving so disappointing to her.

Daddy only laughed when he was consulted about it and said she would grow out of it. But he asked her about it all the same one evening, when he went up to see her after she was in bed.

"Come now, old lady, you know when you're pretending and when you're not, don't you? You're worrying your mother with all your ridiculous make-believe, you know."

"Sometimes I do, when I really pertend. But Mummy doesn't understand, and often tells me I'm pertending when I'm not, when it's real as real can be, and I *am* the little girl that was stolen away by the wicked witch, and given to other people to bring up, and one day they'll fetch me home to the king and queen, who are my real Mummy and Daddy, and they'll be so awfully pleased to see me. You'll come with me, of course, and I'll tell the king how good you've been, and we'll leave Mummy with Peter at home here, for she won't want to come to my beautiful country, because she says it's silly and only pertending."

Tiny Hands and What They Tell

Most Mothers Wonder What Will Be Their Children's Chief Characteristics When They Grow Up. This Tells You Certain Indications You May Read in Their Tiny Palms.

TWO LINES TO STUDY

By NOEL JAQUIN

TIME was when the birth of a Princess caused a flutter in the dovecotes of the fortune-tellers. Before the physician had left the palace the magician had entered, bearing the " fate " of the Royal infant.

To-day we know that many things which the ancients regarded as miraculous are only the workings of natural laws, of which they knew nothing, mystery is born of ignorance.

" Fate " is but a combination of our health, character, and mental " make-up." These are all marked in the hand, for the human hand is the material, physical expression of the soul. The lines are not chance creases but are formed by nerve action.

A scientific survey of a child's hand shows its latent talents and its potentialities for good and evil.

Palmistry has acquired, through the fraudulent pretensions of unscrupulous charlatans, the reputation of being foolish, silly, and superstitious nonsense. But, eliminating all superstition and everything that is not reasonable and logical, the result is a valuable medical and psychological science.

It is of some interest to observe the hand of the little Princess Elizabeth. The fingers are fairly short, indicating mental quickness and, being rather fleshy at the base, show the possession of intuition. Later in life she will very quickly take likes and dislikes to personalities; her intuition will enable her to see people as they are, not as they appear to be. Also, you will note that the fingers are a combination of the thoughtful type of finger possessed by her father, H.R.H. Duke of York, and the sensitive, intuitive type possessed by H.R.H. Duchess of York.

Glance at the hand of your own child and, by noting the marking of the main lines of the hand, you will be able to detect characteristic faults which by training you can correct.

(*Marcus Adams.*)

The hands of the Princess Elizabeth show that she will have mental quickness and intuition. The fingers are a combination of the thoughtful type possessed by H.R.H. the Duke of York, and the sensitive, intuitive type possessed by H.R.H. the Duchess of York.

When Confidence is Lacking

MANY a clever man has failed in life because he had little self-confidence. Lack of confidence in self is shown by the joining of the two main lines of Life and Head at their beginning. *The Life line is that line which runs from between the thumb and first finger round the base of the thumb towards the wrist, the Head or Mental line runs from the same position but* OUT *into the palm.* The more closely joined at their commencement the greater the lack of confidence in self.

But if the " junction " is open then confidence is shown, and should the space be very wide this confident rashness, which it then indicates, must be checked.

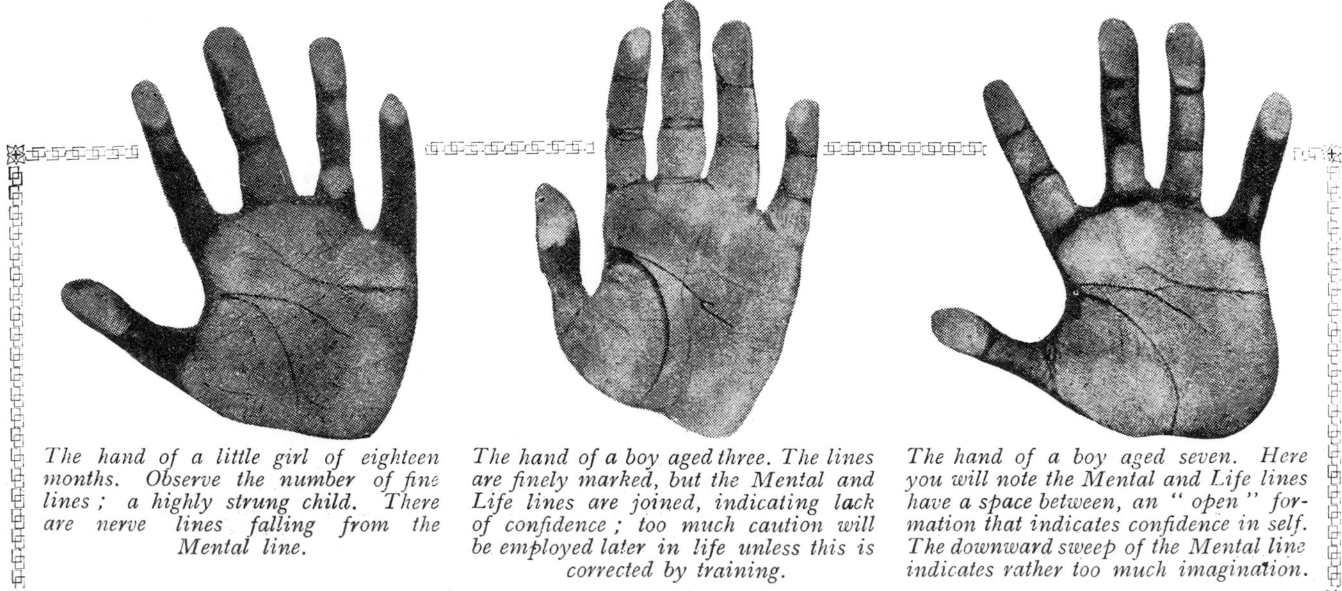

The hand of a little girl of eighteen months. Observe the number of fine lines; a highly strung child. There are nerve lines falling from the Mental line.

The hand of a boy aged three. The lines are finely marked, but the Mental and Life lines are joined, indicating lack of confidence; too much caution will be employed later in life unless this is corrected by training.

The hand of a boy aged seven. Here you will note the Mental and Life lines have a space between, an " open " formation that indicates confidence in self. The downward sweep of the Mental line indicates rather too much imagination.

Study the Mental Line

OFTEN the mental line is chained for a space at its beginning, this indicates a lack of concentration. If the Mental line is clear, later there will be no need to worry, as concentration will be acquired later in life. At school such a child would be anything but brilliant, but in life she should with energy and application be quite successful.

If the Mental line is fretted by a number of small lines which seem to fall from or through it, then it is an indication of an active brain. This marking is found on the hands of highly-strung or " nervy " type of child. If the lines are very numerous, it is a sure indication of such a condition existing, and such a child should not be allowed too much excitement.

When the lines are normal in number, but at the same time thin and clear (that is, free from any lines dropping from or through them), then this indicates merely nerve or mental force more than physical strength; such children possess great vitality.

Where the lines are few and deeply and broadly marked, it indicates more physical strength than nerve force; such children feel emotion very keenly, but they do not show it as the more finely lined type of hand.

Left and Right

IN the case of children, one of the most important lines in the palmar surface is the Mental or Head line.

Great attention should be paid to this, as it indicates the type of mentality inherited by the child. Especially is this the case with the left hand ; the right changes as the mentality conforms to training and circumstances.

If the Mental line is long, straight, and clear, it indicates a business type of mentality, the thoughtful, calculating type.

If it travels in a gentle curve down towards the wrist, then imagination is indicated ; the greater the curve the greater the imagination, so should the line curve down nearly to the wrist, the child's training should be as practical as is possible.

Sometimes you will observe that this Mental line is forked at its end : this indicates even strength and quality of the practical and imaginative aspects of the mentality. The result of this formation is that the child will develop indecision. Where thoughtful consideration is necessary to find the solution to any problem the two traits will oppose a definite decision being quickly arrived at, and so the mental training must be quite practical to prevent the development of this harmful hesitancy.

What the Fingers Indicate

WHEN considering the Mental line, glance at the fingers ; the fingers, if bearing out the indications of the Mental line, accentuate those traits, but if they oppose, then they detract, and the indications shown in the palmar surface should be developed.

Long fingers, especially if the joints of the fingers are at all prominent, indicates the naturally thoughtful disposition. Short fingers indicate quickness and mental " grasp " ; such children will quickly seize an idea, they have the ability to visualise, but often they are unable to concentrate for very long. Detail rather annoys short-fingered people—they like to get things done quickly. Short-fingered people make, as a general rule, better managers than workmen.

So, by closely observing your child's hand, you may be able to detect some slight defect which, if allowed to develop, would minmise her chances of success later in life. For " Fate " dwells within, and Maeterlinck, the sage, very aptly says : *" Let us ever remember that nothing befalls us that is not of the nature of ourselves. If Judas go forth to-night, it is towards Judas his steps will tend ; let Socrates open his door, and he shall find Socrates asleep on the threshold before him."*

Making Toy Harness

Lillie has eight toy horses, and she can't bear to think that the shop harness cannot be taken off at night, so she is going to try to make movable harness.

She has bought some black and brown American cloth, some tiny buttons, and a little glue. She cuts out strips of American cloth and uses the shop saddles and shop bits when she can. She fits the reins on carefully and fastens them with buttons.

Style C 307 **8/11**

Corselette for average figures. Pink Broche on White ground. Hooks and eyes at side front, 2 spiral steels at back and special diaphragm supports. Bust sizes : 30 to 42 ins.

Corsetry for 1927

All the " S & S " Models are scientifically made to give comfortable support. They are *very* stylish, and demonstrate, beyond all doubt, that fashionable corsets need *not* be expensive.

Ask for " S & S " and look for the label. Every Ladies' Outfitter either stocks or can get " S & S " for you. Write to address below for Booklet No. S.68, which illustrates many styles from our 1927 range.

Every S & S model is guaranteed unconditionally

Stapley & Smith, Ltd., 128, London Wall, London, E.C.2.

Style B 215

Wrap-round Girdle for medium figures. Strong Coutille. Supple waistband and three elastic panels. Spiral steels. Hooks and eyes above and below busk. Sizes : 22 to 30 ins. In White or Pink.

BABY'S mother studied big books and trained him scientifically, but . . . she did not love him.

Children We Pity

By Muriel Wrinch

Intuition, which is based on love, is essential for the true understanding of Children

ONCE there lived a baby who had everything possible done for his health and his comfort and his correct development. His mother consulted big books and read the wise treatises on education and child-rearing. Every detail of his training was correct, and in every respect it was up-to-date. No effort and no expense was spared to provide the best—yet he missed something that is the right of the poorest child. We pitied this baby, because he was not loved. He was studied carefully, even experimented upon, because his mother was intellectually interested in children, but even the baby must have felt the lack of something his instinct led him to expect in the woman who had brought him into the world. He did not look to her to be played with or cuddled. He was serious and calm and seldom naughty, but he showed none of the joyousness of the normal baby. He was scarcely ever played with because, said the mother, "Baby must learn from the first to rely upon himself and provide amusement for himself." He was not even spoken to much because "Baby must learn that he is of no more importance than others"—both excellent and true ideas if not carried to extremes.

And so there grew up a child, model in some respects, strangely deficient in others. He had a splendid digestion; he had most orderly habits; quite early he developed the habit of self-reliance and seldom called on grown-ups for assistance in his play. But his personality lacked warmth, he showed little interest in others, not much of that feeling and sympathy for other people which is so strong in the normal child, not much desire for the friendship of other children. He has always remained to some extent isolated from his fellows. She who should have taught him, through love, fellow-feeling with all men, failed him because she did not really love him.

This is a very extreme instance of misplaced, wrongly-developed maternal feeling. But in these days of much child-study, let us remember that love still has its most important place in the scheme of things. Intellectual curiosity — even reverence — for developing life cannot take its place. Intuition, which is based on love, is essential for the true understanding of children.

But very often we go too far in the other direction. More children are loved foolishly than loved too little. And the effects of each extreme are so disastrous that we do not know which type of child is most to be pitied.

Audrey, aged four, was the only child of wealthy parents, who were determined to shower every advantage upon her. Her nursery was marvellously furnished and equipped; every square inch of wall was covered with hand-painted pictures of nursery-rhymes people; chairs and tables were of the most up-to-date design; heating arrangements were of the most hygienic and modern. Poor Audrey! with a fully equipped nurse and a fully equipped nursery, she had little chance to develop normally. Her toys were so elaborately finished that no opportunity was given for her own creative efforts. Her recreations were so carefully supervised that she could not possibly develop any initiative or originality. Her life was so minutely ordered that there was no chance for developing will-power. Not a wish remained ungranted, not a book or plaything for children came out but found its way to Audrey's nursery.

And, of course, the child grew up with a totally incorrect idea of her own importance. When children had been brought to play with her and had displeased her, they had always been sent away. When visitors came Audrey was always on view, beautifully starched and frilled, and admiring comments on her appearance were made in her hearing. Who can wonder that when the child grew up and went into the world, the valuation other people set upon her was an immense shock? At fifteen years old she began to find out that no one can have everything she wants, that she herself was quite an ordinary child with no particular claim to notice. Who can wonder that henceforth she felt a

Healthy Children Like—

A CERTAIN amount of freedom.

Bodily activity – swimming, climbing, rowing, running. These things may cause you slight anxiety and inconvenience, but if you forbid them you arrest the growth of your child's mind as well as his body.

A certain amount of attention—but be careful to give your attention to the right things, not to the wrong.

A feeling of power. Give them the satisfaction of achieving things for themselves and overcoming difficulties without too much assistance from you.

grievance against the rest of the world for not recognising her beauty and importance ?

Both the children we have taken as examples were to be pitied, because their parents did not realise at all the need to educate them as potential members of the human society. What was needed in both cases was a loving comprehension of the needs of the child, and a determination to fit him to take his place in the world. The child's personality must be respected and cultivated in an atmosphere of wise love, and the needs of his nature must be met.

Half the difficulty in bringing up children lies in our failure to understand child - nature. Often children are expected to behave as miniature adults. Clare, aged six, is much to be pitied on this account. She is an unusually bright, good-tempered little girl, even after years of mishandling, but in the end she must be ruined, for her mother seems to concentrate on all the inessentials in training her. Clare must be tidy always, she must not romp noisily, nor tear her frocks, nor make her knees dirty. She must not indulge, in fact, in any activities normal to children. No word is said as to the necessity for always telling the truth, of being kind to others, of being generous in sharing toys and sweets ; no games are planned to give outlet for her animal spirits. Clare is merely being made to conform to the social usages of adult life. Soon all her originality and initiative and spontaneity must disappear.

The harm done here is great. Clare has already learned to regard her mother as a spy watching to prevent her most delightful pastimes. She has already learnt to prevaricate, and she has missed all the good that comes to a child from being allowed to plan and think for herself. She is aware that her mother regards her as something of a nuisance, and she is—all unconsciously—receiving the idea that the lot of mother is a somewhat ungracious one. When she grows up, if she has children of her own, she will probably treat them much as her mother treated her. Or she may swing to the other extreme and indulge them foolishly, remembering her own youthful sufferings.

John is another type of unfortunate child. His mother, far from regarding him as a miniature adult, delights in all he does and cannot be persuaded to take him seriously. John, like all normal children, has immense powers of concentration, but he is seldom allowed to use them. He is watched and applauded and laughed at in his play, until he loses his childish unself-consciousness and *poses* as a child. Too many children, aware of the amusement they excite in their elders, early become buffoons. They retain childish tricks they should drop, and make their youth and ineptitude at various tasks the excuse for attracting notice. This is a serious obstacle to normal psychological growth.

Healthy Children Hate—

CONSTANT needless restriction. Just as adults resent constant interference and criticism of their plans, so children are irritated by over-zealous direction and unsympathetic advice. As far as you are able, leave your children alone, and avoid saying "Don't."

Fussiness. If your home is right in atmosphere, you need not worry about small difficulties and naughtinesses. In the right environment your children cannot help growing rightly.

Being made unlike others. Do not forbid your child the pursuits allowed to his companions ; do not dress them conspicuously better, even if you can afford it, and try not to dress them worse.

AUDREY, bestarched and frilled, was always on view when visitors came.

CLARE regards her mother as a spy who is always behind the door, watching to prevent her pastimes.

There is nothing the ordinary child loves so much as to be the centre of attention. Some children achieve this by being persistently naughty. If they behave well, those in charge pay no attention to them, but any prank attracts immediate reproof. We all know the unfortunate child who is invariably in "hot water." He is much to be pitied, because he relies on bad behaviour to bring him the attention he craves. When he grows up, unless his mother realises in time that efforts towards right should be the efforts to attract her attention, and determines to overlook small naughtinesses, he will enter the ranks of those who are foolhardy, or unconventional, or violently anti-social, merely in order to be different from other people. He will esteem oddity more highly than sincerity, and he can never form a serviceable philosophy of life, because his ideas are built on the wrong foundation.

If only all mothers and nurses recognised the importance of the early years, if they fully understood that impressions received in the nursery must have their effect on the whole of life, there would be fewer unfortunate children and fewer unhappy people in the world. Your child's body, we know, must be carefully tended ; his mind needs equally careful nurture. Protect him from forming wrong impressions, treat him with love and with understanding and with care, and in mature life he will call you blessed.

IT IS EASY TO WEAR BIBS

You won't have to tell them to take care of their clothes if their feeders are provided with these jolly insets

The Chicken Design

MATERIALS:

Worked with Coats' Mercer Crochet No. 70, and a crochet hook size $6\frac{1}{2}$, the insertion measures 3 inches wide by $7\frac{1}{2}$ inches long.

GENERAL CROCHET ABBREVIATIONS:

Ch., chain; s.s., slipstitch; d.c., double crochet; s.tr., short treble; tr., treble; l.tr., long treble (thread 3 times round hook); d.tr., double treble (thread twice round hook); sp., space, consists of 2 ch., miss 2 stitches, 1 tr. in next stitch, and take note that the tr. finishing a sp., bar, or lacet before a group of treble stands as the first tr. of that group, but as it completes the sp., bar or lacet, it is not counted in the group.

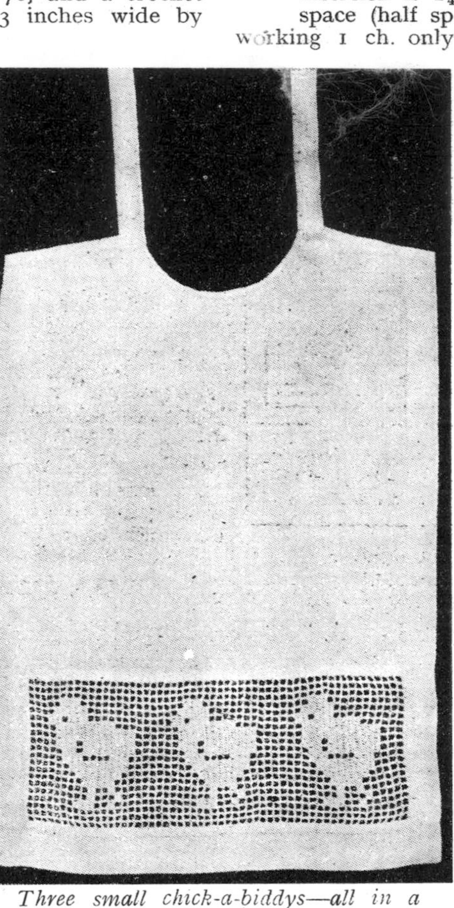

Three small chick-a-biddys—all in a row. An easy design to follow.

TO WORK:

BEGIN with 70 ch., and work 1 tr. into the 5th ch. from hook, 65 more tr., 3 ch. Turn. (This turning ch. forms the first tr. of next row).

2nd, 3rd and 4th rows: Miss the first tr. over which the 3 ch. stands, 3 tr., 20 sp., 3 tr., 3 ch. Turn.

5th row: 3 tr., 14 sp., 3 tr., 5 sp., 3 tr., 3 ch. Turn.

6th row: 3 tr., 4 sp., 15 tr., 11 sp., 3 tr., 3 ch. Turn.

7th row: 3 tr., 9 sp., 15 tr., 1 sp., 6 tr., 3 sp., 3 tr., 3 ch. Turn.

8th row: 3 tr., 3 sp., 27 tr., 8 sp., 3 tr., 3 ch. Turn.

9th row: (3 tr., 3 sp.) twice, 9 tr., 2 sp., 15 tr., 3 sp., 3 tr., 3 ch. Turn.

10th row: 3 tr., 4 sp., 18 tr., 1 sp., 9 tr., 2 sp., 3 tr., 3 sp., 3 tr., 3 ch. Turn.

11th row: 3 tr., 3 sp., 18 tr., 1 sp., 12 tr., 6 sp., 3 tr., 3 ch. Turn.

12th row: 3 tr., 6 sp., 12 tr., 1 sp., 9 tr., 6 sp., 3 tr., 3 ch. Turn.

13th row: 3 tr., 6 sp., 9 tr., 1 sp., 12 tr., 6 sp., 3 tr., 3 ch. Turn.

14th row: 3 tr., 6 sp., 27 tr., 1 sp., 3 tr., 3 sp., 3 tr., 3 ch. Turn

15th row: 3 tr., 4 sp., 3 tr., 2 sp., 18 tr., 7 sp., 3 tr., 3 ch. Turn.

16th row: 3 tr., 7 sp., 15 tr., 8 sp., 3 tr., 3 ch. Turn.

17th row: 3 tr., 10 sp., 9 tr., 7 sp., 3 tr., 3 ch. Turn.

This finishes the chicken pattern.

Work five open rows as at beginning of insertion, then begin another chicken at 5th row, and repeat for width of bib, finishing with three open rows and final treble row.

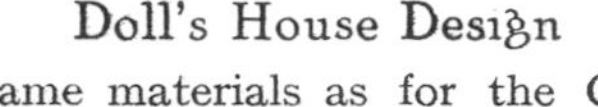

Doll's House Design

USING the same materials as for the Chicken design, the insertion is $2\frac{3}{4}$ inches wide by $8\frac{1}{2}$ inches long. A half space (half sp.) is used in this design, and is made by working 1 ch. only between the trebles, and missing one stitch below.

TO WORK:

Make 64 ch.

1st row: 1 tr. into the fifth ch. from hook, 59 more tr., 3 ch. Turn.

2nd row: 3 tr., 18 sp., 3 tr., 3 ch. Turn.

3rd and 4th rows: The same.

5th row: 3 tr., 7 sp., 9 tr., 8 sp., 3 tr., 3 ch. Turn.

6th row: 3 tr., 6 sp., 15 tr., 4 sp., 3 tr., 2 sp., 3 tr., 3 ch. Turn.

7th row: 3 tr., 2 sp., 3 tr., 4 sp., 21 tr., 4 sp., 3 tr., 3 ch. Turn.

8th row: 3 tr., 2 sp., 42 tr., 2 sp., 3 tr., 3 ch. Turn.

9th row: 3 tr., 2 sp., 3 tr., 4 sp., 21 tr., 4 sp., 3 tr., 3 ch. Turn.

10th row: 3 tr., 6 sp., 15 tr., 4 sp., 3 tr., 2 sp., 3 tr., 3 ch. Turn.

11th row: 3 tr., 7 sp., 9 tr., 8 sp., 3 tr., 3 ch. Turn. (This row finishes the tree.)

12th, 13th and 14th rows: 3 tr., 18 sp., 3 tr., 3 ch. Turn.

15th row: 3 tr., 11 sp., 3 tr., 6 sp., 3 tr., 3 ch. Turn. (This is the first row of the house.)

16th row: 3 tr., 5 sp., 6 tr., 1 half sp., 22 tr., 3 sp., 3 tr., 3 ch. Turn.

17th row: 3 tr., 3 sp., 9 tr., 3 sp., 4 tr., 1 half sp., 15 tr., 2 sp., 3 tr., 3 ch. Turn.

18th row: 3 tr., 4 sp., 9 tr., 1 half sp., 4 tr., 3 sp., 9 tr., 3 sp., 3 tr., 3 ch. Turn.

19th row: 3 tr., 3 sp., 22 tr., 1 half sp., 9 tr., 4 sp., 3 tr., 3 ch. Turn.

20th row: 3 tr., 4 sp., 9 tr., 1 half sp., 7 tr., 7 half sp., 1 tr., 3 sp., 3 tr., 3 ch. Turn.

21st row: 3 tr., 3 sp., 1 tr., 3 half sp., 2 tr., 3 half sp., 7 tr., 1 half sp., 9 tr., 4 sp., 3 tr., 3 ch. Turn.

This is centre row of house. Work rows back from 20th to 15th rows inclusive, which will complete the house. Work three open rows and begin another "tree" at the 5th row. Continue for length of insertion required, finishing with three open rows and a final row of solid trebles, after the last design, whether it is a house or a tree.

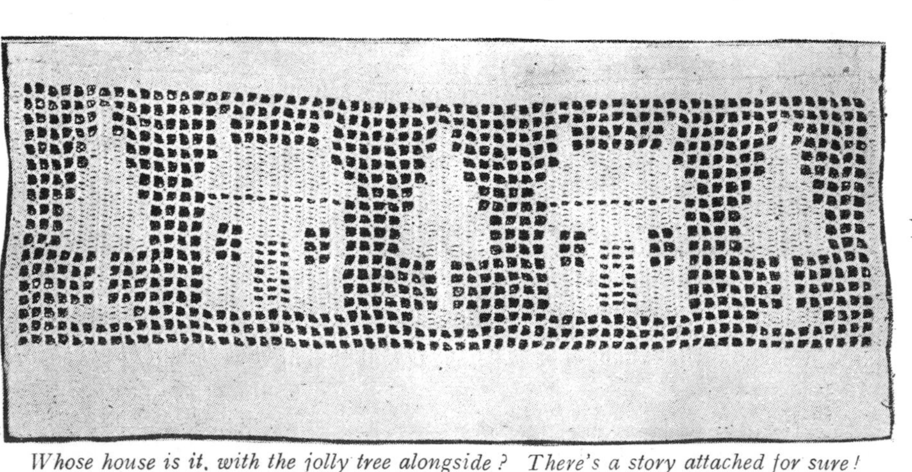

Whose house is it, with the jolly tree alongside? There's a story attached for sure!

Mounting Crochet

SOME crochet workers, who do most beautiful work, are afraid of the last stage—mounting the crochet on linen, yet a little care and patience will produce the work of an expert.

LIKE THESE!

You couldn't call it a hardship to wear anything so decorative.

To Mount.

Turn a hem at edge of bib about one inch wide and tack down. Tack lower edge of crochet strip over this hem on right side of material, so that the row of trebles covers the tacked hem. Tack opposite edge on the linen. Hem outside edge of trebles to right side of linen, cut the latter away at the back, leaving about quarter of an inch, which turn under half-way on wrong side and hem to trebles on back of crochet. Press well on wrong side.

This is the ordinary way of mounting an inset, but by the following method, however, even a neater effect can be obtained on both sides of the linen. It is particularly suitable for an inset such as that on the chicken bib where the crochet does not fit right across. It is also the best way to mount insets, triangles, etc., on teacloths and bedspreads.

The Prize Method.

Spread the linen out flat on an ironing board with a thick blanket over it, or on an old chair seat that will take pins. Pin the crochet in position at all edges, and see that the linen is straight. Now follow round the edge of the crochet with a soft lead pencil, following the same thread of the linen all the way. Remove the crochet, and mark the fifth or sixth thread above the pencil line all round. The number of threads depends on the fineness of the linen. Now draw this thread from the linen to the extent of the crochet inset and five threads beyond, for the side drawing, snipping it at the corner where it meets the thread to be drawn at the side, so that there will be a thread drawn all round. Now work embroidery buttonhole-stitch, putting the needle down at the drawn thread line, and bringing it up at the pencil line, so that the purl edge will be just under the latter line. Work from left to right, putting a stitch about every sixteenth of an inch.

The inset is the all-important feature. Who knows, it may be the little house they built for Wendy!

When finished, cut away the material under the purl edge, and there should now be a space exactly the size of the crochet inset. Fold the inset exactly in half to find the centre of the longest side, place this to the centre of the corresponding buttonholed edge, tack in position, taking care to fit the corners, then sew on the wrong side, taking one stitch of crochet and a buttonhole-stitch together. Finally press, when the sewing stitches will be invisible, and the work will be as neat on the wrong side as on the right.

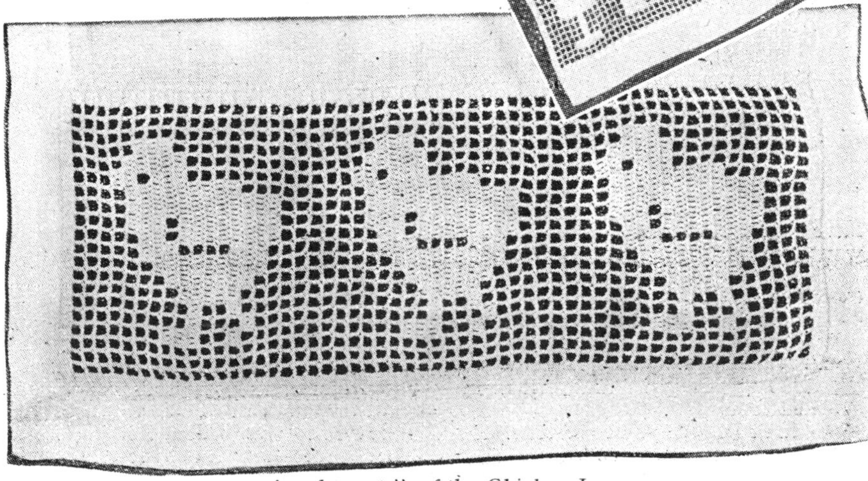

To Avoid Cockling.

The above method of mounting does more to prevent cockling of the linen after washing than any other method, but for a large piece of crochet it is a good plan to soak it in cold water for an hour or so, then place it in a Turkish towel and partly dry by patting between the hands. Pin out on the ironing board, placing all edges quite straight first, and leave it to dry. Pressing will not be necessary, as it can be gently pulled in place with the fingers if not quite straight when dry. This will prevent any further shrinkage of the crochet and prevent the cockling of the linen, which does not shrink. For exhibition purposes, however, the crochet should not be shrunk before sewing in.

A "close-up" of the Chicken-Inset.

A SOLDIER

For The Very Good Little Boy

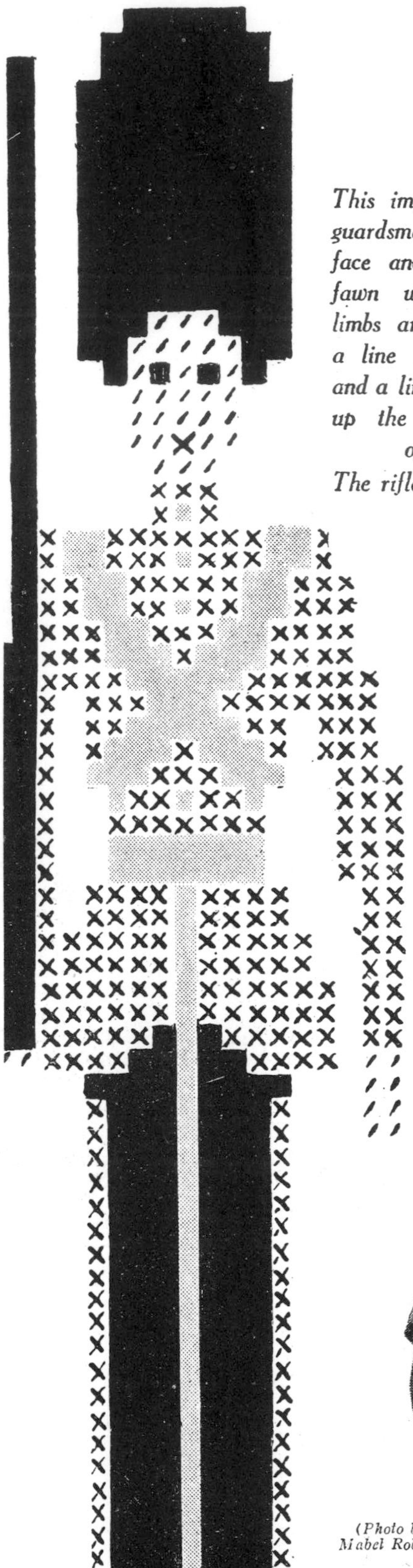

This important cross-stitch guardsman must have hands, face and feet worked in fawn wool. The lower limbs are navy blue with a line of red each side and a line of black stitches up the centre as a line of separation. The rifle is brown, the coat red, with white strappings. The eyes are blue, one red cross represents the mouth and the busby is black.

HERE is a romper that will delight the heart of any child, and it's the easiest thing in the world to knit. The toy soldier is worked in cross-stitch.

MATERIALS.—Four 2-oz. balls of Columbine 3-ply lustre wool in grey, ½ oz. of 4-ply fingering in red, and a few threads of white, black, brown, and fawn for the cross-stitch soldier; a pair of long bone knitting-needles, No. 9, and a spare needle or stitch-holder.

TENSION AND MEASUREMENTS.—Worked at a tension of 6½ stitches to the inch in width, the following measurements will be attained after light pressing: Length, 19 in.; width all round chest, 23 in.; length of sleeve at underarm seam, 2½ in.

ABBREVIATIONS.—*K., knit; p., purl; tog., together; s.s., stocking-stitch (k. 1 row and p. 1 row alternately); d.c., double-crochet.*

To Work

FIRST make the pocket linings. Cast on 19 sts. and work s.s. for 3 in.; after a purl row, cut the wool, leaving about 18 in. Slip these stitches on a spare needle. Work another lining the same, also slipping these stitches on a spare needle.

Begin the romper at the lower centre-front by casting on 37 sts. with grey wool.

Work the first row into the back of the stitches, and continue in s.s., casting on 5 sts. at the beginning of every row for 12 rows, making 97 sts. altogether. Work s.s. until there is 6½ in. from the first row of 37 sts., finishing with a knitted row when the pocket row will be reached.

Pocket Openings

Next row: P. 15, cast off 19, p. 29, cast off 19, p. 15.

Next row: K. 15, k. 19 pocket lining sts. from spare needle, k. 29, k. 19 pocket lining sts., k. 15, making a complete row of stitches again all on one needle.

Continue s.s. until the work measures 9 in. from first row, finishing with a purl row. This brings the work to the waist-line, and the work is now decreased for the bodice.

The Waistline

K. 2 tog., (k. 2, k. 2 tog.) 10 times, k. 13, k. 2 tog., (k. 2, k. 2 tog.) 10 times, reducing the sts. to 75, on which work

(Photo by Mabel Robey.)

ROMPER

Who Loves His Toys

4 in. of s.s. or more, according to length required up to armhole.

The Sleeves

At the beginning of each of the next 6 rows cast on 5 sts., making 105 sts. for front and sleeves. Continue in s.s. for 2¼ in. from sleeve-edge, finishing with a p. row.

Next row: K. 39, and slip these on a stitch-holder for left shoulder; cast off 27 for front neck. On the remaining 39 sts. work 10 rows in s.s.

In the next row the shoulder opening is made. Cast off 18 sts. and on the remaining 21 sts. work 4 rows. Cast on 18 sts. again at neck end, and on these 39 sts. work 4 rows. Cut the wool which is at neck end of row, and slip these sts. on a stitch-holder.

The Left Shoulder

Join wool to the 39 sts. for left shoulder at the neck end of a p. row, and work 10 rows. Cast off 18 at neck end, and on remaining 21 sts. work 4 rows.

Cast on 18 at neck end and work 4 rows. Cast on 27 for back of neck and, on the same needle, k. the 39 sts. from first shoulder; 105 sts. now on.

Work 3½ in., then cast off 5 at the beginning of every row for next 6 rows to finish the sleeves.

There are now 75 sts. on which work 4½ in. in s.s., when back waistline will be reached.

This is an increase row to restore the sts. that were decreased at front waistline.

Next row: * K. 2, k. 1 into the front, and k. 1 into the back of next st.; repeat from * 24 times, when 3 will remain; k. 3. This gives 99 sts. altogether.

Here some short rows are worked for the back shaping, which makes the centre of the row longer than the sides.

Next row: P. 63, turn, k. 27, turn, * p. for 12 sts. more than on last row, turn, k. for 12 sts. more than on last row; repeat from * until all are worked into one row again.

Work 8 in. in s.s., then cast off 5 at the beginning of every row for 12 rows. Cast off remaining 39 sts.

The Crochet Trimmings

With a No. 1 steel crochet-hook, work 3 rows of d.c. in grey on the 39 sts. of first and last rows, putting 1 d.c. in each knitted st. on first row. Work 3 similar rows of d.c. in red at sleeve edges and pocket tops. Work 3 rows of d.c. in red all round neck and shoulder openings. At outer corners work 3 d.c. into same st., and at inner corners of neck miss 1 st. on each side of corner.

The Cross-stitch Soldier

Before making up the romper, work the soldier in cross-stitch on front. He is nearly 10 in. tall, and if a tacking thread is run across front 3 in. below the neck border, this will mark the line for the top of his helmet, and put him in the right position. Also mark the stitch that comes at the centre of front neck, as the centre st. of top row of helmet should be worked on this line. There are 5 sts. across top of helmet.

"They're changing the guard at Buckingham Palace, Christopher Robin went down with Alice."

(Photo by Mabel Robey.)

The easiest way to do cross-stitch is to hold the work with the lines of knitting horizontally before the worker, then put one cross-stitch over each knitting st., treating the four corners of the stitch as the four meshes of canvas in which to place the needle. To get even work, cross each stitch both ways before proceeding to next stitch. The hands, face, and feet are in fawn; the lower limbs navy blue, with a row of red each side and a line of black sts. up centre as line of separation. The rifle is brown, the coat red with white strappings, buttons, and belt, the eyes blue, one red cross representing the mouth, and the busby black.

To Make Up

First press all pieces on the wrong side, putting a thick blanket underneath the embroidery. Sew pocket linings, sleeve and side seams, and work 3 rows of d.c. in red at edge of leg openings. Fasten lower edge and shoulders with snap fasteners.

THE SOLDIER IN SATIN STITCH

Some of you might like to carry out the soldier design in ordinary embroidery stitches, particularly as these bold lines are excellent for satin stitch, either straight or

oblique. Many workers, however, do not like sewing over knitted fabric owing to the movement of the stitches when the needle goes in, resulting in uneven work. There is a special method, which makes it just as easy as embroidery on cambric.

First trace the soldier from page 16 on a piece of fine material, such as book muslin, using a piece of semi-carbon paper thus:

Place the carbon ink side downwards on the muslin, then the soldier design over the carbon. Hold down firmly while you follow all the outlines with a lead pencil. Now tack the muslin on the knitting in the desired position, then work through the two materials together.

Straight satin stitch, just going over from line to line, will do for some parts, such as across the simulated trousers, in which case the centre line marked for black cross-stitch on the first design will be omitted, as the line of knitting will separate the two. Work straight across the rifle in brown and across the hands and feet shortways in fawn. Work in the same direction across the belt in white, but work the strappings in white oblique satin stitch, beginning at a small corner.

The other sections of the coat are worked in red in oblique satin stitch, beginning at the corner of the coat and at a corner of the cuffs on the sleeves. The buttons are all represented by white French knots, the face in fawn sloping satin stitch, the mouth with a small ring of red chain-stitch, and two small blue beans in the centre of the eyes would add to the picture.

66359
Frog
4-12 yrs.

74147
Spring
Chicken
2-8 yrs.

74359
Puppy or "Pip"
2-10 yrs.

39235
White Rabbit
6-16 yrs.

64518
Penguin or
"Squeak"
2-10 yrs.

66361
Bird
4-12 yrs.

77869
Monkey
6-14 yrs.

39228
Teddy Bear
4-16 yrs.

64460
Bat
2-12 yrs.

41564
Tabby Cat
4-16 yrs.

50035
Robin
Redbreast
6-14 yrs.

63892
Wolf
4-16 yrs.

77545
Umbrella
8-16 yrs.

77539
Fairy Sunshine
8-14 yrs.

77511
The Mustard Club
8-14 yrs.

77520
The New Health
10-16 yrs.

77515
Mexican or Spanish Dancer
10-16 yrs.

77543
Queen of the Fairies
10-16 yrs.

75638
Buy British Goods
10-16 yrs.

77550
The Desert Chief
10-16 yrs.

77518
Merrie England
10-16 yrs.

77512
In Nelson's Days
8-14 yrs.

77549
Parcel Pos
8-14 yrs.

Some things for the children

They look elaborate but they are quite easy to prepare. And they will taste "so different" because they have been made at home.

Pineapple Gateau

Wouldn't this be a surprise for the family tea-table? It is a delightfully light cake, spread with apricot jam, to which the almonds adhere. The centre is of crystallised pineapple with a cherry.

Jack-in-the-Box Cake

INGREDIENTS:

1 lb. flour, ¾ lb. margarine, ¾ lb. castor sugar, ½ lb. sultanas, 2 oz. candied peel, 4 eggs, 1 teaspoonful baking powder, a little milk, 4 oz. glace cherries.

A little jam, 2 oz. desiccated coconut, ½ lb. ground almonds, and icing sugar, 1 small egg, 1 dessertspoonful lemon juice.

METHOD:

GREASE a deep square cake (or biscuit) tin, and line it with greased paper to come just above the edge.

Clean the sultanas, chop the peel, and cut the cherries in half.

Cream the margarine and sugar till soft.

Add the eggs (unbeaten) one at a time, and beat the mixture for 5 minutes between each egg.

Stir in the fruit and add a very little milk.

Sift the flour and baking powder, and stir in lightly.

Turn into the lined tin, and hollow out the centre to make the cake flat when it rises.

Bake about 2 hours in a moderate oven.

When cold brush over with jam and sprinkle with coconut.

Make a hole in the top and put in a serviette ring or cork covered with greaseproof paper. This will form the neck of the Jack-in-the-Box.

Put the icing sugar through a hair sieve, mix it with the ground almonds. Beat the egg and add it, also the lemon juice. Mix and knead till smooth. Use a little of the paste to cover the "neck" and make the rest into a ball for the head. Put it in place and make the eyes with bits of cherries or currants, and the mouth with a piece of peel.

A foolscap sheet of paper is used as a cap and the lid of the box is made of thick cardboard covered with white or silver paper.

NO MORE HOLES

A Pair of One-Piece Socks In Simple Knitting Prevents Those Tiresome Holes

THESE little socks serve a double purpose; they prevent holes in the stockings caused by rubbing on the lining of Wellington boots, and they keep little feet very warm. They are worked straight down in one piece, so are quite simple.

Materials: One ounce of 4-ply Fingering and two knitting needles No. 16 will make socks that will stretch over a child's foot 5½ inches long. As this is close knitting they can be enlarged with advantage by using No. 14 needles for a bigger size, say average 6 years.

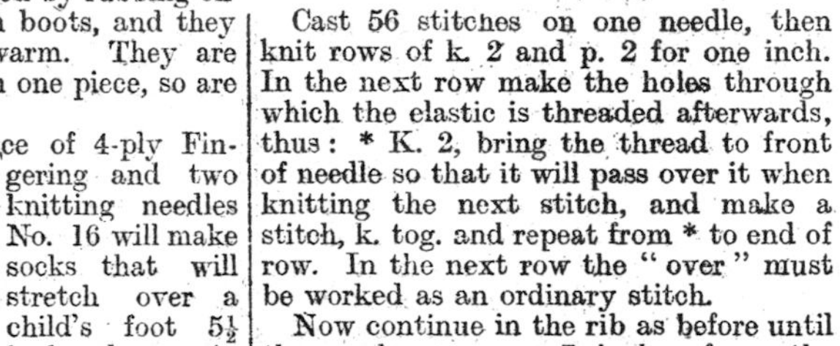

Cast 56 stitches on one needle, then knit rows of k. 2 and p. 2 for one inch. In the next row make the holes through which the elastic is threaded afterwards, thus: * K. 2, bring the thread to front of needle so that it will pass over it when knitting the next stitch, and make a stitch, k. tog. and repeat from * to end of row. In the next row the "over" must be worked as an ordinary stitch.

Now continue in the rib as before until the work measures 7 inches from the beginning, then make another row of holes and again continue for 1 inch, and cast off loosely.

Double the knitting so that the first and last rows are together and sew down each side. Put elastic through the holes so that the socks will stay in position round the ankles, and the work is finished.

What They Ask The Matron

We have persuaded the Matron of a big Welfare Centre, whose homely advice brings solace to dozens of mothers every week, to let us publish some of the queries just as they were brought to her, and the advice she gave the anxious mothers. That those who have little ones of their own will find this information valuable we are confident.

THE EDITRESS

THUMB SUCKING !

Can you suggest a way of curing a boy of over three years of thumb sucking? Correcting him has no effect, and I am afraid to do it so frequently that it will appear just "nagging."

I have tried gloves at night and out-of-doors. I have also threatened him with bitter aloes on his fingers, but he is just too young to use this as a reminder to keep his hands down.

What can I do about it?

I AM afraid that many children want to do just the opposite of what "grown-ups" wish them to do!

I am going to tell you of a way I once heard of, or read about, which was used by a mother who had also reached the point of despair over this disfiguring habit.

She instituted, with all seriousness, "a thumb-sucking drill" three times a day. Within a week the cure was effected. The little boy had no excuse for being contrary!

* * *

AN OLD WIVES' TALE

Is there any truth in the idea that children must go through all the so-called "catching" illnesses, like measles, mumps and chickenpox sooner or later?

THAT is an old wives' tale that should be banished from every household. There is no reason why any child should have any of the contagious or infectious diseases.

The great thing is to learn how we can best protect children against these and similar illnesses. Some illnesses are swift in setting in, like scarlet fever, and others long in showing that trouble is brewing, as in the case of mumps.

We do know that the very best way of avoiding all these troubles is to keep children in such a good state of health that their constitutions can resist the infection if it chances to come near them for a short time.

Fresh air in rooms day and night to keep a sweet atmosphere, good dieting without richness, and as much time out-of-doors as can possibly be arranged, even at the cost of some sacrifice of other things. These are the strongest safeguards.

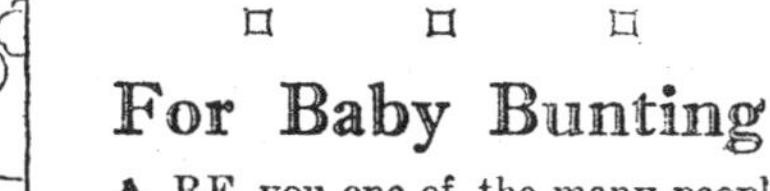

For Baby Bunting

ARE you one of the many people who find it difficult to draw? You will be glad to know that you can buy delightful little bunnies, cats, puppies and ducklings all made in woolly stockinette and cut to shape ready to sew on to your needlework.

This pram-cover, which would be very expensive to buy ready-made, can be made at home at very little cost. You will need ½ yd. of 50-inch-wide monkey-cloth, folded double for warmth, 2½ yds. of white satin ribbon for binding, and a white bunny costing 2/11¾.

The bunny looks better if he is stuffed with cotton-wool before being stitched down. Place him a little on the slant so that he gives the appearance of running for his carrot, which is placed a few inches away.

Satin stitches in red wool form the carrots, and also the green leaves.

TREES ON THE HILLTOP

Two Little Pine Trees Worked In Simple Stitches

THIS little overall has an inverted pleat at each side of the front, which continues right up to the shoulder seam.

The front is embroidered with two little pine trees in two shades of dark green for the spiky foliage and deep brown for the trunks.

The little trees are set in a few blades of grass in a lighter shade of green.

Use straight stitches for the tree tops, and running-stitch for the trunks.

This overall requires 1¾ yards of 35-40-inch material.

* * *

This design has been drawn full size for tracing. Place a piece of carbon paper under this page, and with a sharp pencil trace the trees straight on to the material.

A Cosy Helmet In Felt

Decorated With A Miniature Aeroplane.

A charming helmet for the " Junior Flying Ace."

YOUR wee girlie or her sturdy small brother will be delighted with a helmet like this for motoring and windy days. It is made of soft felt in a delicate shade of pastel blue, decorated with a tiny aeroplane of grey felt.

You will require the following materials :

One 18-inch square of felt.
One 3-inch square of felt in contrasting shade.
A length of soft silk for head lining.
A skein each of White Heather Embroidery Wool in shades of pale yellow and leaf green.
Two press-studs or a length of ribbon according to the way in which you fasten the helmet under the chin.

Arrange pieces of felt like this for the aeroplane.

First cut a pattern from the scale diagram given below, then fit it on the little one's head and make any necessary alterations.

The pattern drawn to scale of one square to an inch.

Should the pattern be too deep, decrease the depth on either side of the dart at the top of the design on a curved line ; if too wide, alter at back. Fold your large square of felt from corner to corner and, placing A—A to the fold, cut out the pattern and also cut two straps measuring 5½ by 2 inches.

Put the pieces together as follows : Seam up the side darts and press them. Then seam the helmet from front to back, taking care that the side seams exactly face each other at the top, and then press. Make up the head lining in the same way. Turn up, press, and slip-stitch the lower edge, making sure that no stitches show on the right side.

To ensure that the ear lapels lie quite flat, it is a good plan to run round these curves and gather them slightly before stitching. Next fit a straight strip (5½ by 2 inches) just above the brow, so that the face is snugly framed, slip-stitch neatly in, turn up and press the lower edge.

Cut out the aeroplane in grey felt, fitting the pieces over one another as shown in the diagram, and stitch down with silk. Add a few simple daisies on the forehead piece in coloured wools. Work two more sprigs two inches from the front edge of the lapels towards the back, as shown in the photograph.

Stitch the lining in position, press the chin-straps, and slip-stitch the edges. Finish off with a press-stud on each side such as those with which gloves and leather goods are fastened. If you have not the tools to fix these yourself, you can easily get them fitted at your local trunk and leather store for a few pence.

The felt can be obtained in a variety of colours. Fawn and blue, red and grey, Air Force blue and grey, orange and fawn, brown and orange, light green and dark green, mauve and grey, etc.

Daisy sprays decorate the helmet as shown in this photograph. A ribbon tie could be used instead of the chin-strap.

STRAIGHT TALKS *from* MRS. MARRYAT

MOTHER'S DARLING

Favouritism Is Bad For The Favourite—But A Thousand Times Worse For The Child Who Is Ignored

I AM going to be very straight in my talk to-day, and say right out that there are few things which can prove a greater curse in a family of growing up children than *favouritism.* The making a special favourite of one child more than another, and letting everyone know the fact, and have no doubt at all about it.

Favouritism is, in my opinion, not only a thing that can be very cruel in its effects, especially on a sensitive child, but it can be like a poisonous weed in the Garden of Life, and stretch its roots far and wide and deep, even into old age. It can poison happiness, not only of the children when young, but when they have left childhood far behind, and their parents are long dead.

I can speak with experience in this matter, for I knew intimately a case where there were two daughters. The mother loved one, who was very pretty, far more than the other who was good-looking, but not beautiful. Money was not plentiful with them, but the favourite got all the best that was going—pretty dresses, and everything else. She was taken out and went to all the parties. The other, only a very little younger, was left at home to help the maid with the housework. She was never taken anywhere. And, not only this, but the fact that she was far inferior to her elder sister in beauty, and in everything else, was rubbed into her constantly by her mother, and, I believe, by her sister, too

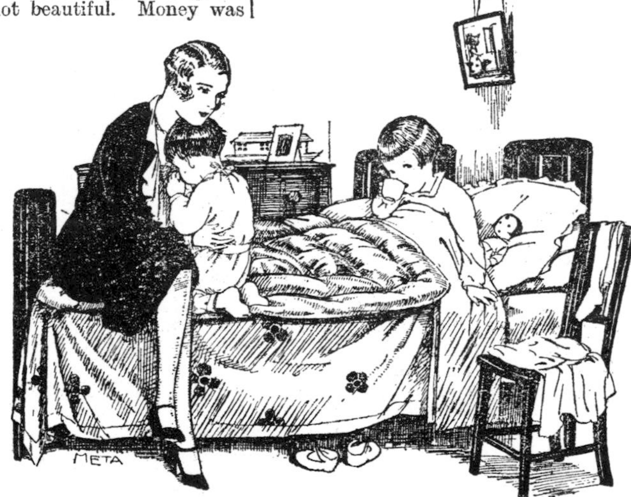

Is it any wonder there was no love lost between these girls? Any wonder that a lifelong antagonism grew up between them?

Now mark the result, and, remember, that this story is absolutely true.

That beautiful sister married a very poor man. She had good "chances" but, somehow she missed them all, married badly, and had a struggling life.

The other, her despised sister, married also. But, such is the whirligig of time which, as has been truly said, "often brings strange revenges," her husband throve and she became very well-to-do. She helped the poorer one to some extent, but there was never any affection between them.

How far different it would have been if their mother had never sown that poisoned root, and made one a favourite, and the other a neglected child. That poisoned root never died. It infected their whole lives, its venom flourished and embittered them. I have often thought how different they may have been—for I knew them both personally—if they had been differently treated by their mother when they were growing up together.

WHEN A CHILD IS IGNORED

FATHERS are sometimes the makers of favourites, too. One daughter is petted and pampered, perhaps for no apparent reason, but just from caprice. It may be that she is prettier, or a bit cleverer, or she may have a more amiable disposition. Therefore, she becomes first favourite.

Now what I would like to point out to parents in such cases is this: Do you ever consider the effect on the characters of your children when you make a favourite of one, and almost ignore another? The one ignored may not be so attractive, or good-natured, as his or her brothers and sisters. Should the other children, therefore, be neglected, ignored, put in the background, made to feel small? Is that the right kind of treatment for a parent to adopt? Is it likely to make a child grow up more amiable, more kindly, with a better disposition, and more attractive, if it is treated in that way? Would it make you, or me, a pleasanter person, or nicer to live with, if we were treated like that?

If it would not make us, the older folks, more amiable always to be kept in the background, snubbed, slighted, and plainly shown we were of no account at all, while another, just on a par with ourselves, was hoisted on to a pedestal, admired, petted, and set forth as a shining example—if this would not improve our tempers, or make our dispositions more lovely, then how can it do anything but injure a child?

And remember that impressions in early youth cut very deep. They often last for the rest of life.

Read these lines written years ago by George Romanes, a great teacher of Physiology. Every parent should take them to heart.

"*No change in childhood's early day;*
No storm that raged, no thought that ran,
But leaves its track upon the clay
Which slowly hardens into man."

Next Week Mrs. Marryat is giving an honest, straight-from-the-shoulder talk on the madness of saying bitter things in the heat of the moment

WHAT THEY ASK THE MATRON

We have persuaded the Matron of a big Welfare Centre, whose homely advice brings solace to dozens of mothers every week, to let us publish some of the queries just as they were brought to her, and the advice they gave the anxious mothers. That those who have little ones of their own will find this information valuable we are confident.

THE EDITRESS.

WAKING UP TIME

My toddler of two-and-a-half has got into the habit of waking at 4 a.m., and then there is no peace for the household till his breakfast-time. How can I change this to induce him to wake later?

HERE are a few suggestions which, if practised without a break, will make waking-up time less of an ordeal.

Let him see you put near his cot one or two of his reigning favourites from among his toys, also an orange all ready to eat, but covered with a glass finger-bowl inverted, or anything that shape. Tell him these things are for him at 6 o'clock, and cannot be had beforehand.

When he wakes at 4 a.m., lift him out of his cot to make sure he is comfortable in every way, then put him back under the bedclothes. Tell him the time will pass much more quickly if he sleeps until he can have the orange. But if he prefers to stay awake he must play to himself quiet quietly, because he will wake his daddy, who has to get up later and do a hard day's work to earn money for more oranges!

He will soon get the idea if you are firm at the beginning, and feel he is taking a hand in helping his father!

* * *

THE SIGN AND SEAL OF GOOD HEALTH

What sign in a child's face is most indicative that the health is all right?

THE eyes give the truest indication of good health. This is a guide even from babyhood.

Bright eyes that shine with light and a clear skin around the lids points to a sound constitution.

Dull eyes with heavy lids, with or without dark rings, are very indicative of a run-down state of health.

It is as well to begin as soon as possible to trace the cause, and this is more quickly solved with a doctor's advice.

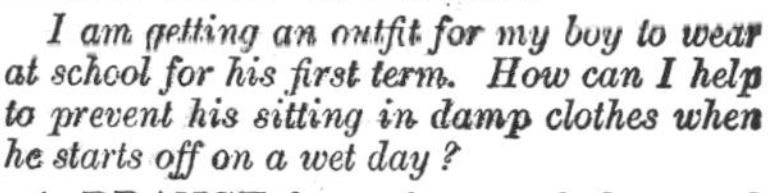

AVOID DAMP CLOTHING

I am getting an outfit for my boy to wear at school for his first term. How can I help to prevent his sitting in damp clothes when he starts off on a wet day?

ARRANGE for a change of shoes and stockings to be kept in his own locker at school. It would be just as well to make inquiries at intervals to know that he makes use of the change you provide.

Outside clothing is simplified nowadays with light-weight mackintoshes and sou'westers for children. And how they love to fancy themselves dressed up as seafarers! It lends quite a fascination to stepping out for school on dull, wet mornings!

Mackintoshes should always be removed as soon as possible, as they are neither healthy nor pleasant for walks of any distance.

This is an argument sometimes used against providing children with rubber boots, but for short distances "gum-boots," as they are sometimes called, can prove very practical.

A LITTLE HOUSE WITH SAILS!

All Small Boys Are Interested In Things Like Windmills!

A WINDMILL is just the kind of thing to work on a small boy's tunic suit. Here is one in very simple embroidery. The sails are filled in with blanket-stitch. Work first one edge, then work the other, taking your stitches between those on the opposite edge. The diagram shows you how this is done.

The roof, the two windows and the door are filled in with satin-stitch.

The windmill is drawn full size for tracing on to your material

First one edge of the sail is worked, then the other

BESTWAY
LEAFLET No. 604
3d.

Little Red Riding Hood

MATERIALS

A large ball (over 1 oz.) of 3-ply wool in mid-blue, and a smaller ball each of scarlet and white ; a pair each of Nos. 9 and 12 knitting pins ; a medium crochet hook ; 1 yard of red ribbon.

MEASUREMENTS AND TENSION

The clothes were made to fit a 17-inch doll (*dress length*, 12 ins. ; *chest*, 11 ins.). The tension is 8 sts. to the inch on No. 12 pins and 6½ sts. to the inch on No. 9 pins.

The Frock

WITH No. 9 pins and white wool, cast on 108 sts. and knit 4 rows in garter-st. Change to blue and work 6 rows garter-st., then work 4 more rows in white.

Change to blue wool and st.-st. and continue for 6½ ins. On next k. row, k. 3 tog. all across, making 36 sts. on pin, then work 1½ ins. straight.

Cast off 6 sts. at beginning of next 2 rows, then work 5 rows straight. Work 10 rows straight on first 6 sts. only. Cast off. Now cast off centre 12 sts. for neck and work on last set of 6 sts. for 10 rows. Cast off. Work another piece to match.

THE SLEEVES

WITH No. 9 pins and blue wool cast on 36 sts. and work 18 rows in st.-st. Change to No. 12 pins and k. 2 tog. at both ends of next row. Change to garter-st. and k. 4 rows white, 6 rows blue. Change to white again and k. 2 tog. at each end of row. K. 3 more rows, then cast off.

TO MAKE UP

PRESS the work, join the shoulder seams, then sew in sleeves and join side and sleeve seams.

With white wool crochet round neck as follows :

1st round : S.-st. in first st., * work 4 ch., miss 1 st., s.-st. into next and repeat from * all round.

2nd round : 3 tr. in first 4 ch. loop, * 4 ch., miss the next 4 ch. loop, 3 d.c. in next loop and repeat from * all round.

Work a length of chain to thread through this edging and tie at back.

The Apron

WITH No. 9 pins and white wool cast on 40 sts. and work 36 rows in st.-st., then cast on 36 sts. at beginning of next 2 rows.

Next row : K. 36, * k. 3, k. 2 tog. ; and repeat from * till 36 sts. remain, k. 36. Work 4 more rows without shaping, then cast off.

For the pocket cast on 10 sts. and work 8 rows in st.-st. Cast off. Crochet a picot edging round apron and pocket as follows : s.-st. in first st., * 3 ch., miss 1 st., s.-st. in next st. ; repeat from * all round.

The Cloak

WITH No. 9 pins and scarlet wool cast on 108 sts. and work 10 rows in moss-st.

Next row : Moss-st. 10, k. 88, moss-st. 10. Keeping a border of 10 moss-st. at each end and the remainder in st.-st., continue straight for 5 ins.

Next row : Moss-st. 10 (k. 2, k. 2 tog.) 22 times, moss-st. 10. Work 3 rows without shaping.

Next row : Moss-st. 10 (k. 1, k. 2 tog.) 22 times, moss-st. 10. Cast off.

For the Hood cast on 70 sts. and work in moss-st. for 1 in. Now keeping a border of 10 sts. in moss-st. at each end of pin and the remainder in st.-st., continue straight for 2½ ins. or depth required to fit the doll's head. Cast off. Press the work carefully.

Fold the hood in half and sew up the back seam (the first inch of moss-st. forms the border which goes round face). Sew the side edges of work to neck edge of cloak. Catch the ribbon to the neck and arrange to tie in front.

RAINBOW BALL

THE CROCHET COVER.

COMMENCE with 67 chain.

1st row—Miss 1 ch., 3 s.s., 4 d.c., 5 s.tr., 6 tr., 30 l.tr., 6 tr., 5 s.tr., 4 d.c., 3 s.s., 1 ch., turn.

Next 35 rows—3 s.s., 4 d.c., 5 s.tr., 6 tr., 30 l.tr., 6 tr., 5 s.tr., 4 d.c., 3 s.s., 1 ch., turn. Press crochet under a damp cloth with a hot iron. Make a ball with sateen and fill with kapok, then place crochet cover over ball and sew last row worked to foundation chain.

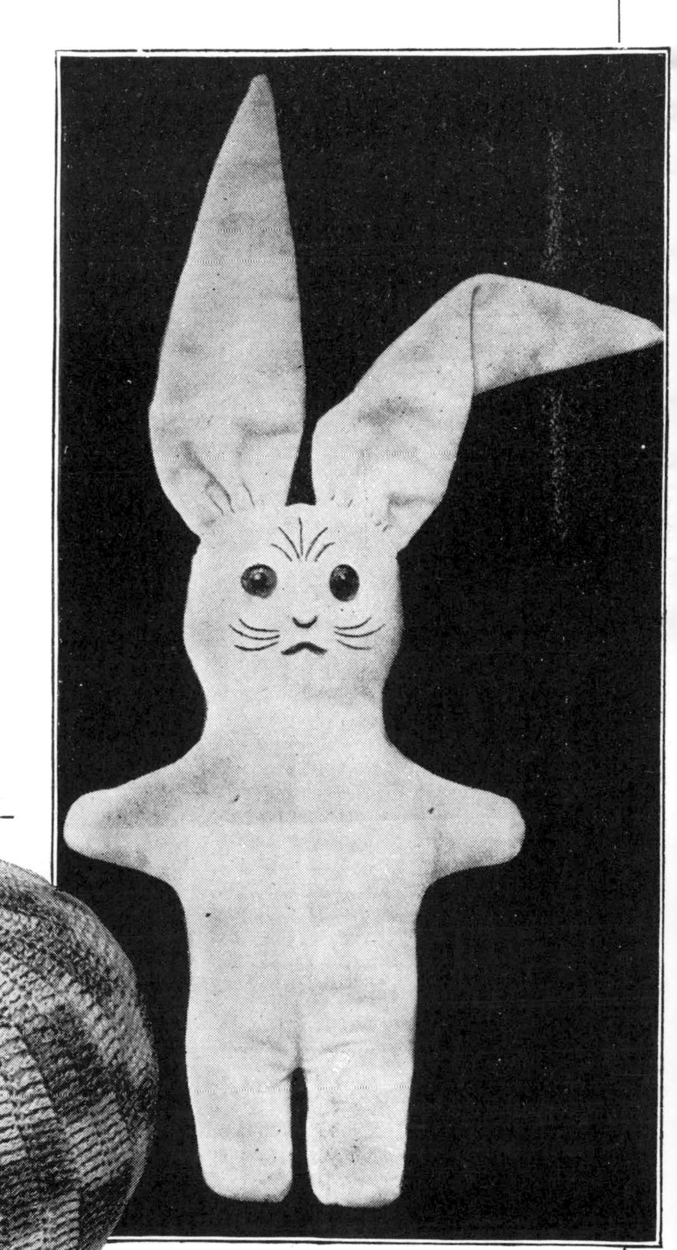

Baby will love this Bunny made in white velveteen.

TEA at Buckingham PALACE!

Marcus Adams.

The most delightful mother and child in the Kingdom—H.R.H. The Duchess of York and Princess Elizabeth.

IN the blue and cream boudoir of her Majesty the Queen in Buckingham Palace there is a piece of furniture that is always an object of curiosity to visitors to the Palace.

It is a very delightful little Louis Quatorze chair, but its distinctive feature lies in the fact that it is a perfect miniature of a real chair and is much too small for any grown-up to sit in.

It is the special chair belonging to Princess Elizabeth, replacing the high baby-chair that used to stand there in the days when the Duchess of York was in Australia and her baby daughter was under the special care of her Majesty the Queen.

It was after Princess Elizabeth's third birthday that she decided that she was now too grown-up to sit in what she called "baby-chair," and her Majesty obtained this delightful miniature in an antique shop especially for her "grown up" granddaughter.

It is one of the features of the present House of Windsor that in spite of the calls of public duty the private ties of family are not allowed to languish, and indeeed, it is probable that Princess Elizabeth sees more of her grandparents than most children.

Nearly every week that the Court is in London little Princess Elizabeth goes over to Buckingham Palace to take tea with her grandmother, a meal at which the King is often present also.

These teas are looked upon by Princess Elizabeth as a great treat, and she has evolved a little ceremonial that always takes place when she is there.

When Elizabeth is at home her tea is what would generally be called a "nursery tea," but at Buckingham Palace she insists that she should be treated as grown-up, and her tea is served on a little stool by the side of her chair.

At first Elizabeth had one invariable plea.

"Please, Granny, can I put my cup on my knee like Mummy does?"

But that method has not proved so successful as might have been expected, and so the stool has been introduced!

There are, too, special cakes which are particularly favoured by Princess Elizabeth, little tarts with lemon cheese fascinatingly concealed within, and these always appear on the afternoon that she is at the Palace.

At one time her Majesty was afraid lest her little granddaughter should be so tempted by these delicacies that tea would become an unsuitable meal for her, but it is now an invariable arrangement that Princess Elizabeth should have one cake and then one extra as a treat.

It is rather delightful the way in which Princess Elizabeth asks for her second cake. Her Majesty had explained to her that polite little girls do not eat more than one specimen of each cake, and this advice made a great impression on the little Princess.

To-day when she wants another cake she always asks for it in a particular formula! "Granny," she says, "*please*, need I be polite this afternoon?"

HER SPECIAL TOYS

THE Queen, who has not forgotten the days when she too, had a large family of children to bring up, has also provided a number of toys which her little granddaughter only plays with when she visits the Palace.

Not very long ago her Majesty found a delightful series of clockwork toys made in the shape of various animals and insects. When these are wound up they crawl across the floor going through the usual motions of the animals that they are supposed to represent.

There is, for instance, a large highly-coloured lady bird that crawls across the floor with a great buzzing and moving to and fro of feelers, and the greatest favourite of all, there is a large and fearsome blue-bottle, very highly coloured, which flaps its wings and buzzes as it progresses with short jerks. For some unknown reason the little Princess Elizabeth has christened this toy Wilfred, and she is extremely fond of it, and during tea time it always makes a hearty meal off lumps of sugar presented to it by its young mistress.

LITTLE WHITE MICE!

On A Dear Little Dressing-Gown Which Is Cosiness Itself

WHITE flannel is used for the appliquéd mice which decorate the pocket of this cosy dressing-gown.

Place a piece of carbon paper under this and outline the mice with a sharp pencil straight on to the flannel. Cut them out and buttonhole-stitch in position.

A little pink French knot marks the eye, and the nose is pink, too

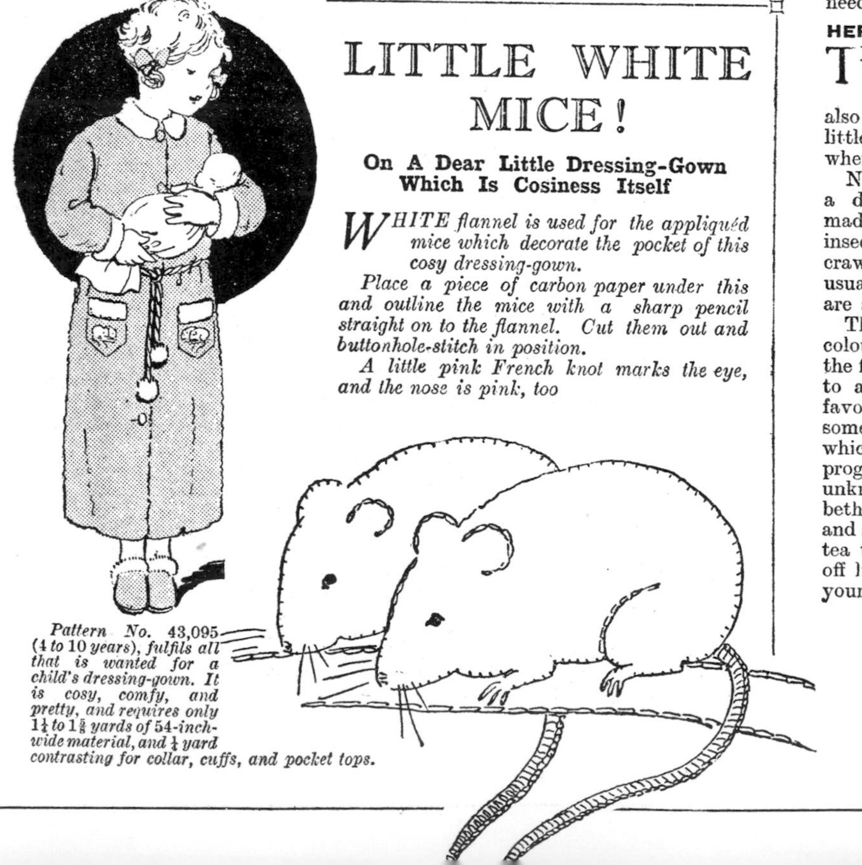

Pattern No. 43,095 (4 to 10 years), fulfils all that is wanted for a child's dressing-gown. It is cosy, comfy, and pretty, and requires only $1\frac{1}{4}$ to $1\frac{5}{8}$ yards of 54-inch-wide material, and $\frac{1}{4}$ yard contrasting for collar, cuffs, and pocket tops.

1930

The Royal Babies

A Series by:

EVELYN GRAHAM

Here, in this series of intimate articles, interesting facts about the daughters of the Duke and Duchess of York are told for our readers entertainment. The material contained in these articles has been gained at first-hand

Photo by Marcus Adams

H.R.H. Princess Elizabeth of York, whose greatest friend is His Majesty the King!

IT is now four years since the birth of the elder daughter of their Royal Highnesses the Duke and Duchess of York, and those four years have constituted what cannot in any sense of the term be called an adventurous or even an eventful life!

Yet the fact remains that at four years old Princess Elizabeth is one of the most popular persons in the land, although soon she will have to share this popularity with her baby sister, Princess MargaretRose.

In part, of course, her popularity must be due to the fact that for those four years she has been the final heir presumptive to the throne of England, and that is a position that would ensure notice for any baby. But it cannot be pretended that the little Princess' popularity rests on so slender a foundation as that.

She may be only four years old, but she has already found time to show that she has a very determined character of her own, as I hope to indicate in the articles that will follow.

When the whole nation was waiting anxiously for the arrival of the Duchess' second baby, there was the possibility that Princess Elizabeth might be called upon to relinquish her position in the direct line of succession to the throne, but since she has been given a baby sister instead of a small brother, her position as a possible Queen of England remains the same.

She was born the Nation's baby, and what was hers by birth, she has made doubly hers by her own dawning character. Her popularity is founded upon the firmest rock of personal charm, which even Princess Margaret Rose will be unable to eclipse, I am sure.

If anyone should be so rash as to doubt whether a child of four years old may be said to have personal charm, I have only one reply to them—*Ask any mother, and they will tell you!*

If anyone doubts that the Princess Elizabeth has personal charm at the age of four years I have a similar answer. Ask anyone who has met her, from the Duchess of York herself to the photographer who takes the Princess' photograph and they will all tell you the same story!

Never since the birth of the present Prince of Wales, over thirty years before, had the hopes of the whole nation been so fixed upon an event that was taking place in Bruton Street, that was at that time the London residence of the Duke and Duchess of York.

HEIR TO THE THRONE OF ENGLAND

THERE were several reasons for this interest that kept crowds of men and women standing anxiously outside the wrought-iron palings of that quiet Mayfair House, watching the coming and going of the doctors, the arrival of nurses, the hastening of messengers to the various members of the Royal Family.

In the first place the Duchess ever since her marriage had been the idol of the country. There was in her wedding to the Duke that element of romance that has in the past been at times rather lacking from the marriages in the Royal Houses of Europe.

There has thus been a purely personal interest in the birth of both Her Royal Highness' children, due to the popularity of the Duke and Duchess themselves.

But there was more than that.

The children of the Duke and Duchess of York whether boy or girl must by the laws of precedence be heir presumptives to the throne of England.

Small wonder that the Nation should wait patiently, that the reporters should be standing by their proofs, that the telegraph wires should be buzzing with messages as to the progress of the Royal mother, on each of the two notable occasions.

The scene at the births of Princess Elizabeth and Princess Margaret have been closely similar.

Within the house all was carefully controlled. At no time was there need for anxiety. The Duchess of York before the birth of both her daughters had taken very great care of her health for the months that preceded the happy event.

THE QUEEN AND THE DUCHESS

It was during that period, just before the birth of Princess Elizabeth, that the Duchess of York and the Queen first came closest together in companionship.

Her Majesty, as is well known, is an excellent needlewoman and, what is perhaps not so well known, her favourite work is the making of baby garments. Even to-day, in a drawer in the Queen's boudoir, there are some clothes that she sewed herself in preparation for the coming of the Prince of Wales.

The imminence of a happy event in the family of her second son gave her a new opportunity of returning to her old occupation, but this time she did not sew alone. Quite a large part of the time that the Duchess took off from her public duties was spent with the Queen in Buckingham Palace, making the clothes for her baby.

The Duchess is not quite so fond of sewing as her Majesty, though she makes a large number of Princess Elizabeth's clothes even to-day, and her laughing account of the afternoons spent in sewing at Buckingham Palace was, "I felt like an old-fashioned grandmother sitting in front of the fire and sewing all day long."

Yet in spite of that comment there can be no doubt that the Duchess enjoyed those long quiet days, sewing and talking with her mother-in-law, in which she reaped the experience of the mother of the most popular family in England.

Such a darling! Princess Elizabeth with her cousin and her nurse

It is the only thing that H.R.H. has ever allowed to interfere with her official duties, and those who may have been disappointed personally at their inability to secure the presence of the Duchess at a public function were, nevertheless, delighted at the reasons for that absence.

Perhaps one comment of an East End mother will do for all. "Eh, I was looking forward to seeing the Duchess," she said with a little sigh, "but I'd rather she stayed at home to look after herself, though I may never get the chance of seeing her again."

At any rate, it says much for the industry of Her Majesty and the Duchess that for the first few months of Princess Elizabeth's life she wore no garment that had not been made personally by her mother or her grandmother.

AN ANXIOUS TIME FOR THE FATHER

The birth of a first baby must present much the same experience to the father whether he be a prince or whether he be a commoner.

Certainly H.R.H. the Duke of York spent an anxious wearing morning in the dining-room of No. 17, Bruton Street, waiting for the first news to come to him from the room above.

His remark to a close personal friend of his, who was himself about to become a father, perhaps throws the best light upon his feelings.

"It's all very well knowing that nothing dangerous is likely to happen," he said, "but all the same you'll find when the time comes that you'll be more frightened than you've ever been in your life before."

As a matter of fact at the births of both Princess Elizabeth and Princess Margaret there was at no time any need for anxiety—and very shortly the Duke was released from his vigil, and allowed to take just one peep at the baby.

The Duke has often said afterwards that Princess Elizabeth did not burst into tears when she saw him for the first time, but gave him that sunny smile that has since become famous in her photographs all over the world. But then fathers are notoriously inexact over their first encounter with their offspring!

After the Duke had seen Princess Elizabeth in the afternoon of April 21st, the watchers outside the gates had their first real thrill of the day.

Their Majesties the King and Queen motored over from Buckingham Palace to see their third grandchild. Her Majesty the Queen hurried quietly up to the bedroom of her daughter-in-law, while the King stayed downstairs to offer his congratulations to his son.

By that time it was decided that the Duchess had seen sufficient visitors for one day, and accordingly the King and Princess Mary, who later arrived with a large bunch of beautiful pink roses, did not see Princess Elizabeth until a day or two later.

The Prince of Wales, who was abroad at the time and who had been informed of his niece's birth by telegram, sent a long wire of congratulation to his brother by return. In fact, apart from the visits of their Majesties and of Princess Mary, the chief excitement for the watchers was the coming and going of the telegraph boys, who wore an air of importance befitting the public interest in the occasion.

THE BABY HEROINE HERSELF!

And what of the centre of interest upon this great occasion?

Princess Elizabeth at the age of one day was exactly like any other baby at that age. Her head was covered with soft black down, without a sign of those golden curls that are the envy of half the mothers in the kingdom to-day. The Duke of York always says that the only way in which he could recognise her to-day from his recollections of her in the first few weeks of her life is by the twinkling smile that lurked in her blue eyes even then.

One of the nurses who was in attendance upon Her Royal Highness tells me that Princess Elizabeth was a sunny-tempered baby. She was less prone to crying than many children, and when she did cry she had very excellent reasons for doing so, all of which has been remarked about thousands of babies born every week!

But little Princess Elizabeth early showed that she had a character of her own and a determination to get her own way.

In spite of the attentions of the nurses

she soon showed that she preferred to be looked after by her mother, and when the mood was on her the Duchess was the only person who was able to pacify her little daughter.

"WHAT NAME SHALL WE GIVE HER ?"

THE problem of finding a name for each new member of the Royal Family has been one that has always presented many complications.

With Princess Elizabeth there seemed from the very beginning to be only one possible choice. For the name Elizabeth, besides being that of the the Duchess of York and therefore the most suitable to give to her daughter, was also that of the most famous Queen of England, and as there was at the time, and indeed there still is, a possibility that Princess Elizabeth should succeed to the throne, there could be no better omen than calling her Elizabeth.

Elizabeth, too, presented another advantage shared, I believe, by no other name. In itself it is as good as several different names, because it has a large number of diminutives. Immediately that she was able to say a few words Princess Elizabeth christened herself Lisabet, that being the nearest approach that she could get to the proper pronunciation of her own name, and it is as "Lisabet" that she is known to her father and her mother.

With regard to the naming of Princess Margaret there has been even more discussion and suggestion amongst the various members of the Royal Family. Many names were suggested, including "Ann," by the Prince of Wales, and "Angela" from Princess Mary The final choice has given everyone pleasure, however. Margaret is an old Scottish Royal name and Rose is taken from the name of the Duchess' beautiful sister, Lady Rose Leveson-Gower.

The actual nursery consists of three rooms, the day nursery at No. 145, Piccadilly, itself is a cheerful room, decorated with a frieze of all the favourite animals and characters of the fairy stories going in a long procession round the wall.

These little figures on the frieze are great favourites with "Lisabet," and she knows the names and histories of all of them.

Often when the Duchess comes up to the nursery to spend an hour or two with her little daughter she is met with the demand for a fairy story.

Her favourite story is that of "Goldilocks and the Three Bears," and this she knows almost by heart, echoing the words with her mother, and always insisting on taking the part of the "little bear."

Her greatest treat is when the Duke of York comes up as well and then the Three Bears is told with its full dramatic value! The Duke, of course, has to take the part of the Big Bear, the Duchess of the Middle Bear, and Princess Elizabeth is a most confusing mixture of the littlest bear and Goldilocks herself.

There is a story that the Duchess tells which shows that Princess Elizabeth is herself a story-teller of some merit.

On one occasion she had been naughty and as a punishment the Duchess refused to tell her the usual bedtime story.

Lisabet pleaded for a little and then, with a little sigh, she said, "All right, mummy, Lisabet will tell you a story."

She trotted over to the frieze and pointed out the picture of Goldilocks.

"Once there was a little fairy princess called Lisabet," she began, "and she asked her mummy-dear for a story, an' her mummy-dear wouldn't tell her a story, an' so she ran away into a great big wood, and a great big bear came along and said 'Who's been eating my porridge?' an' he gobbled Little Lisabet right up, so that her mummy-dear didn't never see her any more, an' her mummy-dear did wish she'd told Lisabet a story so that she wouldn't have been all gobbled up," finished Elizabeth hastily, overcome with the pathos of her history.

As the Duchess said, when describing the incident to a friend afterwards: "It may have been bad for discipline, but I'm afraid that Elizabeth got her story that evening, after all!"

The Royal baby has a smile for the footman as she returns to No. 145, Piccadilly

"Goldilocks and The Three Bears" is Princess Elizabeth's favourite fairy story

A Series
by
EVELYN
GRAHAM

who has written biographies of H.R.H. The Prince of Wales and several other Members of the Reigning Houses of Europe

A snapshot of Princess Elizabeth taken by her father, H.R.H. The Duke of York.

Pricess Elizabeth out for an airing with her nurse in the park

The ROYAL BABIES

Pretty Little Stories About The Children of H.R.H. The Duke and Duchess of York

Her favourite toy is a little white rabbit—

—And his name is Peter

PROBABLY no child has ever possessed such a large store of toys as Princess Elizabeth.

They have come to her from all parts of the world, there being several hundred from Australia, where many of those who met the Duke and Duchess on their tour wished to send some little token to the baby of whom they had heard so much.

But though Princess Elizabeth possesses a great many toys, her mother has made a very salutary rule, that only a reasonable number of them should be used, and the great majority are stored away in cupboards and only appear on special occasions.

Elizabeth herself seems to agree with this rule, for certainly her favourite toys are those which she has had longest.

In her nursery, occupying pride of place, is a large dolls' house which was given her by her grandmother, Queen Mary, and in this Elizabeth takes a constant delight..

Recently whenever one of her uncles gives her a present it is some piece of furniture for this doll's house, and by now each room is fully filled.

The last present that the Prince of Wales gave his niece, when he returned from his recent tour in Africa, was a set of miniature native weapons, which were specially made for him by a native craftsman in Tanganyika, and these Princess Elizabeth has hung up in the hall of her doll's house, where they are said to be the trophies of Mr. Milton, for Princess Elizabeth has invented a family to live in the doll's house, consisting of Mr. and Mrs. Milton and their little daughter Lisabet.

These characters Elizabeth herself adopts at will, sometimes being the little daughter Lisabet, but more often pretending to take the part of Mrs. Milton, especially when she has been naughty.

One of her nurses tells me that whenever Lisabet has been in trouble, which occurs occasionally, for she is a high-spirited child, she can be heard in the nursery, playing with her doll's house, and administering rebukes to Lisabet Milton in the character of Mrs. Milton.

"No," she has been heard to say, "you can't sleep in a bed to-night, 'cos you've been very naughty, Lisabet. You've got to sleep in that horrid old cot again."

"MY HORRID COT"

THAT is another characteristic of Princess Elizabeth. She has been longing to sleep in an ordinary bed instead of the cot in which she sleeps at present.

Many a time has she tried to persuade her mother to allow her to be promoted to an "ordinary bed," but at present to the cot she is condemned.

A few months ago she managed to achieve her ambition to sleep in a bed, by an ingenious means. She was a little feverish one afternoon, and the Duchess decided that it would be safer for her to go to bed and sleep it off.

Elizabeth promptly pleaded to be allowed to go to bed in her mother's room, and as a special treat she was allowed to do so. Later on, when her usual bedtime came Lisabet was told that she was being sent back to her own room to sleep. She protested fiercely.

"But, mummy-dear," she said, "I shall be wide awake all night in my horrid cot, can't I stay in your lovely bed?" Alas for her hopes, she was promptly packed off to the night nursery where, in the 'horrid cot,' she slept the sleep of the just and the very young.

PETER RABBIT

THERE is one toy that always shares Elizabeth's cot with her. It is perhaps an incongruous choice for her to take to bed with her, but the likes and dislikes of childhood are difficult things for a grown-up to fathom. She has a choice of some of the most delightful dolls in England, of the most cuddly teddy bears and woollen toys that are made.

And each night she takes to bed with her, sleeping under the pillow of her cot, a small white rabbit, about two inches long, which could not have cost a greater sum than a few pence.

Yet Princess Elizabeth and this toy rabbit, which is known as "Peter," are quite inseparable. During the daytime Peter lives in the pocket of Elizabeth's overall, during the night he spends his time under her pillow

At meal times great care must be taken that he is not forgotten, his staple food being lettuce, of which Princess Elizabeth provides him with a mouthful whenever there is any at her meal.

It is a remarkable thing how one finds unexpected subtlety in almost every action of a child. It might be thought that there was nothing but sheer delightful baby imagination in Princess Elizabeth's affection for Peter, yet even Peter has been used in a method that in an older child would bear the strongest marks of subtlety!

At one time of his adventurous career Peter showed an extraordinary taste for prunes, which his mistress very strongly disliked. His taste for prunes was even stronger than his taste for lettuce, and at every meal where prunes appeared he was presented with a large helping from his little mistress's plate.

The nurse suggested that perhaps Peter might be served from the dish direct, but Lisabet insisted that he couldn't eat his prunes unless he had them from her plate The nurse therefore made it a rule that when Peter was provided with prunes Princess Elizabeth had an extra helping to make up for the number that she had given away.

Perhaps it was only a coincidence that Peter's liking for prunes stopped from the very first day that the new rule was introduced.

PRINCE GEORGE'S WOOLLY DOG

PETER, too, has been used to administer a rebuke to Prince George.

Prince George is a great favourite with his little niece, and is always finding some little present to give her.

One day he arrived at her nursery with a delightful woolly dog, with an ingenious device that enabled him to bark most realistically, under his arm. This he gave to Elizabeth, and suggested that perhaps she might find him as jolly to play with as the little bunny rabbit Peter.

Princess Elizabeth thanked him, and for a while played happily with her new toy.

A few days later, however, when Prince George arrived again he inquired after the new toy that he had given his niece. With a great air of mystery Princess Elizabeth led him to a dark cupboard just outside the nursery. Inside was the woolly dog that Prince George had presented with so much pride a few days before.

"I had to put him there," said Elizabeth, in explanation, "he used to frighten Peter with his 'bow-wowing.'"

It is rather charming to find Princess Elizabeth so faithful to an old friend like the little woolly rabbit.

It shows, at any rate, that she has not been spoilt by all her toys and all her opportunities of being spoilt. Though so many of her toys have been put away lest she should become blasé about them, yet even of those that are left she has enough to be the envy of any other child.

It is her affection for Peter that shows that there is no reason to fear that a surfeit of good things is likely to spoil her charming, sunny character.

SIXPENNY DOLLS

Dress Them in Pink or Blue Silk and They Will Find a Ready Sale at a Bazaar.

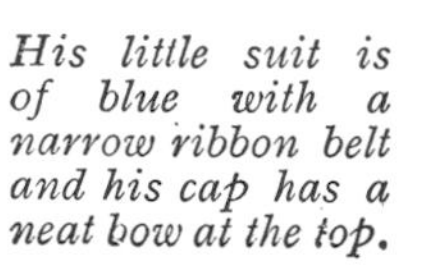

His little suit is of blue with a narrow ribbon belt and his cap has a neat bow at the top.

THESE little dolls cost sixpence each before they were dressed and found a ready sale at one shilling and sixpence each at a church bazaar.

The little girl is dressed all in pink. Her frock, which is finished at the waist with a ribbon sash, is up-to-the-minute with its tight fitting bodice and frilly skirt. Her bonnet matches, and with a dainty set of lingerie in Shetland wool her outfit is complete.

The boy's tunic suit of blue is finished with a narrow blue ribbon belt and his cap has a neat bow at the top.

The Little Girl Doll

ONE ball of Ardern's Star Sylko No. 8 and half an ounce of Shetland wool will dress two little girl dolls, using two bone needles Nos. 10 and 12. About $1\frac{1}{2}$ yards of narrow ribbon for waists and bonnet strings to match the Sylko in colour.

Begin at the neck making 26 ch. with the No. 12 hook. Join into a round by slipstitching to first st., after which mark the first stitch of the round with coloured cotton, so that the rounds need not be joined up.

Do two rounds of 1 d.c. in each st. taking up both loops at the top of each st.

3rd round : 6 d.c., 4 ch., miss 2 d.c. along the row, 10 d.c., 4 ch., miss 2 d.c., then d.c. to end of round.

4th round : 1 d.c. in each st. all round, putting 6 d.c. in the 4 ch. loops for armholes.

Do three rounds more of d.c.

8th round : 1 tr. in each st. all round.

9th round : Change to No. 10 hook, and work 2 tr., 2 ch., and 2 tr. (making a shell), all into the sp., after first tr., * miss next

(Continued on page 71)

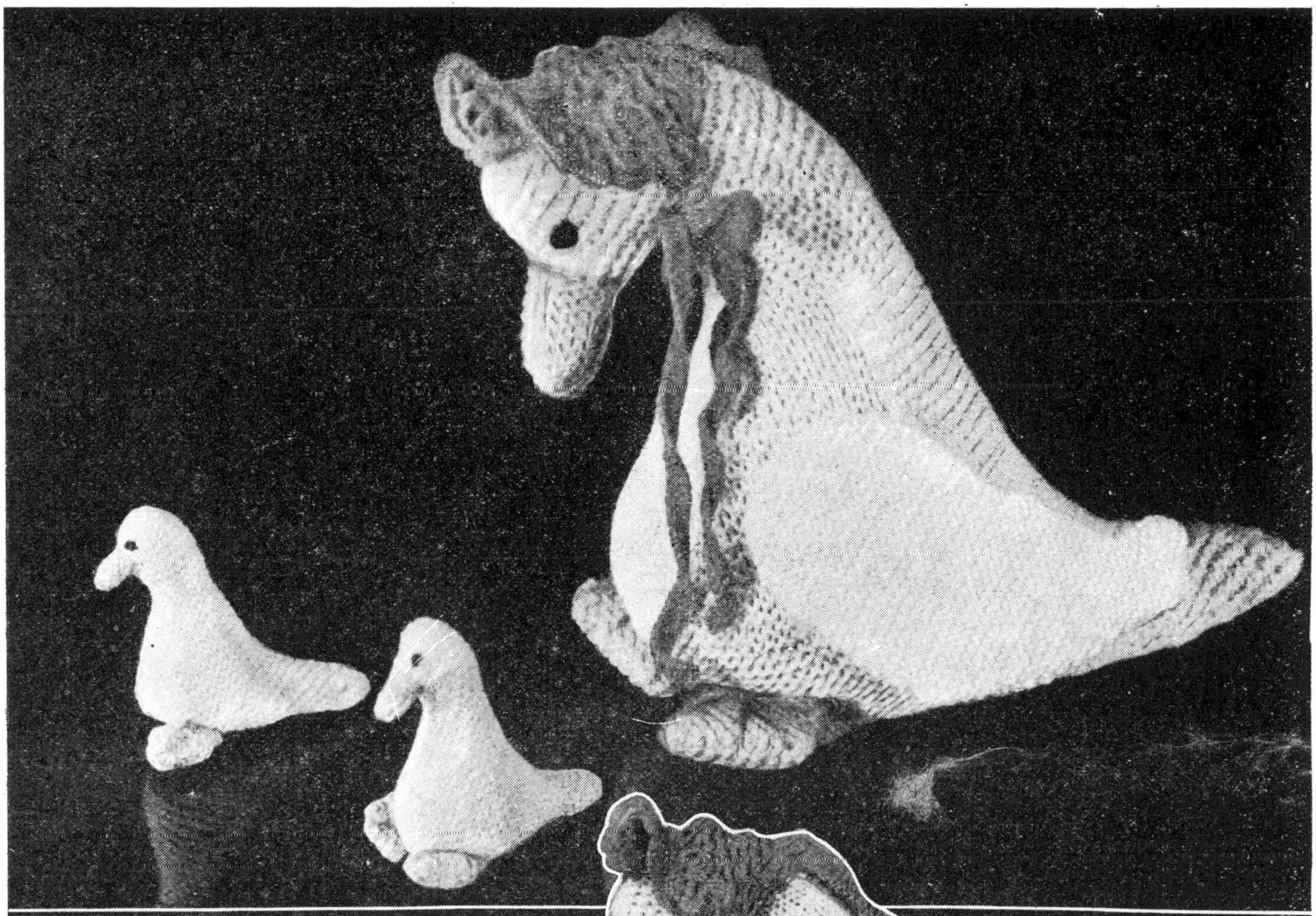

MRS. PUDDLEDUCK AND HER LITTLE ONES

A Happy Family Sure of a Hearty Welcome From The Children.

Made from Soft Wool and Stuffed with Down, They are the Most Cuddlesome Little Creatures.

HERE is a cosy, cuddlesome family that can be made at home at little cost in comparison with the ready-made toy. The wool and woolly down for stuffing only costs 4/4d., and, using up oddments of wool, it can be cheaper than that.

ABBREVIATIONS: K., knit plain; tog., together; inc., increase; dec., decrease; sl.st., slip-stitch; ch., chain; dc., double crochet; tr., treble.

Materials

THREE ounces of 4-ply Fingering in white, 1 ounce of the same wool in orange colour, and 1 ounce of yellow. A few yards of brown wool and less than half an ounce of cherry wool for the bonnet. A pair of No. 8 bone needles for the mother duck, and a pair of No. 14 steel needles for the ducklings; a No. 10 bone crochet hook.

The ducklings are of yellow wool with orange bills and feet.

To Work Mrs. Puddleduck

BEGIN at the top of the head and with No. 8 needles and white wool, cast on 12st. Work plain knitting throughout.

K. 3 rows.

4th row: Inc. in first and last st. by knitting in the front and back of the st.

5th row: K. 14.

6th row: Inc. in last st.

7th row: K. 15.

Repeat last 2 rows 3 times.

K. 12 rows on these 18 st.

26th row: Here begin to shape the neck. K. 2 tog. at beginning of row. *27th row:* K. 17.

Mrs. PUDDLEDUCK— and HER LITTLE ONES

Repeat last 2 rows 3 times more. K. 6 rows on 14 st.

40th row: Inc. 1 at beginning of row.

41st row: K. 15.

Repeat last 2 rows 4 times more.

50th row: Inc. 1 at each end of needle.

51st row: K. 21.

Repeat last 2 rows twice more.

56th row: Inc. 1 in first st.

57th row: K. 26.

Repeat last 2 rows 10 times more. K. 14 rows on 36 st.

92nd row: K. 2 tog. at beginning and inc. 1 in last st.

K. 3 rows on 36 st.

Repeat these 4 rows twice.

104th row: K. 2 tog. at beginning and inc. 1 in last st.

105th row: K. 36.

Repeat last 2 rows 5 times more.

116th row: K. 2 tog. twice at beginning and inc. 1 at end of row.

117th row: K. 35.

Repeat last 2 rows twice more.

122nd row: Cast off 9 st., inc. 1 in last st.

123rd row: K. 25.

Repeat last 2 rows once.

126th row: K. 2 tog. twice at beginning. K. to end of row.

127th row: K. 15.

128th row: K. 2 tog. 3 times. K. to end of row.

129th row: K. 12.

Cast off. Knit another piece like this.

The Wing

Cast on 12 st.

1st row: K. into back of st.

K. 2 rows plain.

4th row: Inc. at each end of row.

5th row: K. plain.

Repeat last 2 rows twice more (18 st. now on).

10th row: Inc. in last st.

K. 3 rows plain.

14th row: Inc. 1 in first st.

15th row: K. 20.

16th row: Inc. 1 at each end of needle. K. 40 plain rows on these 22 st.

57th row: K. 2 tog. at beginning of row.

58th row: K. plain.

Repeat the last 2 rows twice more, then k. 2 more rows plain.

65th row: K. 2 tog. at beginning of row.

66th row: K. 18.

67th row: K. 2 tog. at beginning of row.

68th row: K. 17.

69th row: Inc. 1 in last st. (18).

70th row: K. 2 tog. at end of needle (17).

71st row: K. 2 tog. at beginning of row (16).

72nd row: Inc. 1 at beginning of row and k. 2 tog. at end of row (16).

73rd row: K. 16.

74th row: Inc. 1 at beginning and k. 2 tog. at end of row (16).

75th row: K. 2 tog. at beginning and inc. 1 at end of row (16).

76th row: K. 2 tog. at end of row (15).

77th row: K. 2 tog. at beginning of row (14).

78th row: K. 2 tog. at end of row (13).

79th row: K. 2 tog. at beginning and inc. 1 at end of row (13).

80th and 81st rows: K. 13.

82nd row: K. 2 tog. at each end of needle.

83rd row: K. 2 tog. at beginning of row.

Next 3 rows: K. 2 tog. at each end of needle.

87th row: K. 2 tog. twice.

Cast off. K. 3 more pieces like this.

The Bill

Join the orange coloured wool on 5th ridge down from the top on the straight side of the head. Pick up 9 st. K. 14 rows on these 9 st.

15th row: K. 2 tog. at each end of the needle.

16th row: K. 7.

Repeat last 2 rows once. Cast off.

K. the same on the other half body.

The Feet

Cast on 7 st. in the orange coloured wool and k. 8 rows plain.

9th row: Inc. at each end of needle.

10th row: K. 9.

Repeat last 2 rows 4 times more.

K. 3 rows on 17 st.

22nd row: K. 2 tog. at each end of needle.

23rd row: K. 15. Repeat last 2 rows until only 5 stitches remain.

Cast off. K. 3 more pieces like this.

The Bonnet

With the No. 10 bone hook make 12 ch. and sl.st. into first st. to form a ring.

1st round: Work 10 d.c. into ring.

2nd round: 5 ch. and 1 tr. into first d.c., * 2 ch., 1 tr. into next st. and repeat from * all round.

3rd round: 3 d.c. in each sp. all round.

4th round: 5 ch., 1 tr. into the middle d.c. of first sp.,* 2 ch., 1 tr. in middle d.c. of next sp. and repeat from * all round.

5th round: 5 ch. and 1 tr. in first sp. of last row, * 2 ch. and 1 tr. into next sp., 2 ch., 1 tr. into next sp., 2 ch. and 1 tr. into the same sp., repeat from * all round.

6th round: As 5th round.

Now form the frill. 1 d.c. between the first 2 tr., 2 ch. and 1 tr. in same place, then repeat from first * in last row until half-way round the circle, when finish with a d.c. in one sp. Turn and work another row in the same way. For the last row put 1 d.c. between first 2 tr., * 5 tr. into next sp., 1 d.c. into next sp., and repeat from * ending with a d.c.

Across the back on the row that was left unfinished work 2 d.c., 5 ch. and 2 d.c. in each sp. all round.

The tie strings are made by working a ch. 16 inches long and then working 1 tr. in each st.

Make another ch. 25 inches long and put 1 tr. into each st. Thread through the holes of the bonnet and tie at the back, fitting the bonnet to the head.

The Ducklings

Using No. 14 needles and the yellow wool, cast on 5 st. and k. one row plain.

2nd row: Inc. 1 at each end.

3rd row: K. 7.

4th row: Inc. 1 in last stitch.

5th row: K. 8. Repeat last 2 rows twice more. K. 6 rows on the 10 stitches

16th row: K. 2 tog. at beginning of row.

17th row: K. 9. Repeat last row once and then 2 rows on 8 stitches.

21st row: Inc. 1 in 1st stitch.

22nd row: K. 9. Repeat last two rows once.

25th row: Inc. 1 at each end.

26th row: K. 12. Repeat last two rows once.

29th row: Inc. 1 at beginning of row.

30th row: K. 15. Repeat these 2 rows 4 times. Now k. 8 rows on 19 st.

47th row: K. 2 tog. at the beginning and inc. 1 at the end. K. 3 rows on 19 st.

51st row: K. 2 tog. at beginning and inc. 1 at end of row.

52nd row: K. 19. Repeat last 2 rows twice more.

57th row: K. 2 tog. twice at beginning and inc. 1 at end of row.

58th row: K. 18. Repeat last 2 rows once.

61st row: Cast off 4. Inc. 1 in last stitch.

62nd row: K. plain. Repeat last 2 rows once.

65th row: K. 2 tog. twice at beginning of row.

66th row: K. Repeat last 2 rows once. Cast off. K. another piece like this.

The Bill

Count four ridges down from the top of the head on the curved side of the body, and pick up four st. down from this point.

K. 7 rows plain.

8th row: K. 2 tog. twice. K. the 2 remaining st., then cast off.

Knit a corresponding piece on the other side of the body.

The Feet

Cast on 4 st. and k. 4 rows.

5th row: Inc. 1 at each end.

6th row: K. 6. Repeat last 2 rows twice more, then k. 1 row.

12th row: K. 2 tog. at each end of needle.

13th row: K. Repeat last 2 rows twice more. Cast off. Knit 3 more pieces like this.

Making up the Duck

Sew up the body from the bill over the head down the back and a short way under the tail with white wool. Sew the bill with orange. Then with white wool sew up the body from the bill until within 2 inches of the other white sewing—this leaves a hole for putting in the woolly down. Stuff the duck so that she is firm and shapely. Be careful not to put too much down into the bill. Sew up the part left for filling. Sew the feet together and put a little stuffing into each. Sew to bird in position seen in illustration. Make the wings by sewing two portions

(*Continued on page 71*)

Three White Seagulls

A Simple Appliqué Which Will Make All The Difference To a Little Girl's Frock

HERE is a most unusual embroidery of seagulls appliquéd in white on a little girl's frock. The wings are worked in grey wool, and the beaks and legs in yellow wool.

You can trace the gulls by placing a piece of carbon paper under this page over your material, and outlining with a sharp pencil.

This pattern includes frock and knickers, to fit a child of 2 to 8 years. You will require 1⅞ to 2⅜ yards of 36 to 40-inch-wide material, and ½ yard of contrasting for the collar.

The gulls are drawn full size for tracing

(*Continued from page 70*)

together and sew the broad end to the sides of the duck two inches away from the middle front line.

The markings on the feet are made in brown wool and consist of long stitches taken from the points to the centre, where they are caught down. The division of the upper and lower part of bill is also made with long brown stitches, extending from the middle of one side, round front of bill to the corresponding position at other side. The eyes are made with black wool in satin-stitch, laid one over the other so that they are raised in the middle.

The ducklings are made up in the same way.

SIXPENNY DOLLS

(*Continued from page 68*)

sp., and work a shell as just described into next sp., and repeat from * all round.

Work two more rounds of shells, putting them into the middle of shells on previous row and fasten off. Thread ribbon through the tr. row at waist.

Her Petticoat

WITH No. 10 hook and Shetland wool, make 30 ch., and join into a round.

Do one round of d.c. and one of tr., then finish like the frock with three rounds of shells. Thread ribbon through the tr. at the waist.

The Combinations

WITH Shetland wool and No. 10 hook make 20 ch., join and work two rounds of d.c.

3rd round: 5 d.c., 4 ch., miss 2 d.c., 7 d.c., 4 ch., miss 2 d.c., then d.c. to end of round.

Work 12 rounds more of d.c., putting 1 d.c. in each of the ch. on the first round. After the last round sl.st. to the middle stitch of the round, which will divide it into two smaller circles for the legs Work one round of d.c. on each leg, and fasten off.

Her Bonnet

WITH the No. 12 hook and Star Sylko make 3 ch, and join into a round. Work rounds of d.c., increasing by working 2 d.c in alternate st. until there are 24 in the round. On these st. work 10 or 12 rounds of d.c. according to fit of head. Sew ribbon at sides with small bows and tie.

The Boy's Jumper

WITH the No. 12 hook and the No. 8 Sylko make 30 ch., join into a round, and do 3 rounds of d.c., marking the first st. with coloured cotton.

4th round: 1 d.c. in each of 7 d.c., 6 ch., miss 3 d.c., 13 d.c., 6 ch., miss 3 d.c., then d.c. to end of round.

Work 16 rounds of d.c., then work another row on top of the last one to give a firm edge.

The Sleeves.—Work 14 d.c. round armhole, then 3 rounds more to complete.

Thread ribbon through 2 d.c. at left and cross over to right where secure with Sylko.

His Knickers

MAKE 36 ch., and join round, do 15 rounds of d.c., then sl.st. to the four middle st. of round to form legs. Do one row of d.c. round each leg. Make a crochet chain of Sylko to thread through top of knickers and tie.

The Cap

MAKE 3 ch., and join into a round, then continue working in rounds without joining, increasing in each alternate st. until there are 22 st. On these st. work rounds of d.c. until there are about 15 rounds altogether. Finish off the top of the cap with loops of ribbon.

The undergarment is worked in Shetland wool from the directions for the girl's combinations.

The Story of The Old *Who never*

Illustrations by Elsie

BEYOND the furthest mountain that you can see there lies a country, which is perfectly flat, except for one mountain in the middle of it (which was not always there), and a small hill. On that small hill there is a palace, and in the palace there lives a queen. She is so old that none can even remember when the king, her husband, died. She just goes on reigning and reigning. This is the story of why she never dies.

Once upon a time a very long while ago when the Queen was young, she was walking with the King, her husband, in the garden of the palace.

"Let me give you a present," she said. So she picked an apple and gave it to the King.

"Now *I* must give *you* a present," said the King: and going to the chicken run he took out of it the only egg that was there.

"Here is my present," he said to the Queen.

"That is a nice present," said the Queen: "I will keep it next my heart."

So the Queen took the egg, and put it down the front of her dress to keep it warm. And at night she took it to bed with her; and in the morning when she put on her clothes she put it in the front of her dress again. And so at last the egg was hatched: but instead of a chicken the most marvellous bird came out of it: its feet were grey, and made of stone, and its feathers were green, and made of leaves: and its beak was shining and see-through like water. So the Queen took it to show the King.

"That is the greatest wonder in my kingdom," he said.

"It all comes of your giving me that egg," said the Queen.

"And that came of your giving me the apple," said the King.

"And that came of our walking in the garden," said the Queen.

"So let's walk there again."

So they went out into the garden, with the bird perched on the Queen's shoulder. When it felt the sunshine it began to sing, and its song was like all

Told for the children by RICHARD HUGHES

Author of "A High Wind in Jamaica"

the rivers in the world falling off all the rocks in the world. To hear it made the King and Queen so happy they said:

"Let's go and ring the church bells."

So they went to the church, and began to pull the bell-ropes: but however hard they pulled, not a sound could they hear.

"That is funny," said the King; and looked up to see what was wrong. And to his surprise he couldn't see the top of the steeple at all: it was stretching up high into the sky, right out of sight.

"They must be so far off by now that we can't hear them."

"When I was a little girl," said the Queen, "my nurse told me that if I pulled a bell-rope, and then when the bell began to ring I hung on, it would lift me up and up into the air. Let's try and see what happens." So they each gave a good tug to their bell-rope and then instead of letting go they hung on, and the bell-rope lifted them up into the air.

"Let me give you a present," the Queen said. So she picked an apple and gave it to the King. "Now I must give you a present," said he, and gave her an egg

Queen *dies*

Harding

But instead of going down again it carried them on, up and up, and all the while the wonderful bird flew round them singing its song, now round their heads and now round their feet, though they were three hours altogether going up.

First they could hear the bells faintly ringing, in the distance.

"We are getting near them," said the King.

Then as they got nearer the sound got louder and louder, till at last it was so loud they couldn't hear their lovely bird sing, and that though when they were on the ground they couldn't hear the bells at all. Then they reached the bells themselves, and they climbed out on to the tip-top of the church steeple. They were so high up they couldn't see their country at all: it was all blue down below like the sky, and far down there were clouds floating under their feet.

The point of the steeple was sharp as a pin, but on top was a weathercock. So the King sat on the arm which said West, and the Queen sat on the arm which said East, and the bird on the arm which said South.

"I wish there was someone to sit on the arm which says North," said the Queen: and no sooner had she said it than, lo and behold, there was a fairy sitting on it as if she had been there all the time. And the fairy was green, and shiny and see-through like the bird's beak.

"Come and see my country," said the fairy.

When she said that, one of the clouds which were far under their feet began to rise up, till soon it was close under them: and then they found that though it looked like cloud it was as solid to walk upon as ground. So they walked with the fairy till they came to her house: and the house was made of green cloud, and inside was a hearth, but the fire, instead of burning yellow or red, burnt a bright blue.

"Now," said the fairy, "I am going to make for each of you a magic robe, so that once you have worn it you will never die. (*Continued on page 74*)

The bell-ropes carried them on, up and up, and all the while the wonderful bird flew round them. At last they could hear the bells, faintly ringing in the distance. "We're getting near," said the King

The Old Queen

(Continued from overleaf)

But while I do it one of you must be blowing the fire."

"*I* will," said the Queen: and took the bellows. Now the curious thing about these bellows was that, when you blew with them instead of air coming out it was water; and yet instead of putting the fire out it only made it burn the brighter.

"But someone must help me with these scissors," said the fairy. "They are far too large for me to manage alone."

And so they were; for each blade was as long as a tall man.

"*I* will," said the Queen. "I understand scissors better than he does."

"Then he must blow the fire," said the fairy. "I can only work while it is being blown."

So the King took the bellows, and began to blow the fire, but not looking what he was doing, watching the Queen and the fairy instead. Then the fairy took off a peg a piece of stuff so magic I mustn't describe it; and the Queen took hold of one handle of the scissors and the fairy the other and they made a robe for the Queen and she put it on.

"Now let's make one for the King," said the fairy.

And they began to do it. But now for the first time the King began to look at what he was doing; and when he saw water pouring out of the bellows, "Good gracious!" he thought: "that will put the fire out"—so he stopped blowing.

No sooner did he stop blowing than the cloud broke under them, and both he and the Queen began to fall.

"Don't be afraid!" said the bird, flying under them: "You sit on my back." So they did; and when they did, the bird changed into a mountain, the mountain that is there now; his feathers became trees, and his feet became rocks, and his beak became a waterfall.

As the King and Queen were walking down the side of the mountain she said to him: "Now I will never die and you will: and that is the saddest thing that has ever happened to either of us."

But every year they climbed the mountain, and planted flowers on the top in memory of their lovely bird. Forty years went by, and the King grew old, and the Queen grew old, and the King at last died: but the Queen didn't, she just went on getting older and older: and she is still alive now.

THIS IS SAD

I have been keeping company with a young man now for about twelve months. I am nineteen and he is twenty-five. We love each other, and he asked me to marry him a month ago. I consented willingly, knowing how he loved me, but since then he has been thrown out of work—temporarily, I think.

Do you think it would be advisable for me to marry him now? We were to be married shortly.
—WONDERING.

I AM very sorry for you, my dear, but it certainly would not be advisable to marry him while he is out of work. If he is only "out" temporarily it is far better to wait until his work begins again—and I hope it will soon. Do write and tell me how things go, won't you?

This beautiful little song has been specially written and composed for readers of WIFE and HOME.

OUR CRADLE SONG

Words by Muriel A. Grainger — *Music by Gwladys Jones*

KEY D.

VOICE. PIANO. *Tenderly.*

The wind is rock-ing the trees to sleep, And the flow-ers have closed their eyes,— While snug and warm 'neath the count-er-pane In his cra-dle my ba-by lies.—

So soon the Lady of Dreams will call
For my drowsy wee sleepyhead;
With arms outstretched, she will whisper, "Come,"
As she stands by his little bed.

The whole night through, she will croon to him,
And so mother will have no fear;
She knows her darling is safe from harm
While the Lady of Dreams is near.

A PARTY for the LITTLEST ONES!

Joan Gaiety is always pleased to help you with your Entertainment Problems. Write to her c/o "Woman's Weekly," The Fleetway House, Farringdon Street, London, E.C.4, enclosing a stamped, self-addressed envelope for a personal reply

I have been elected secretary for a children's party fund. Their ages are between eight and four years. Could you give me any advice about the games to play, and what to get them for little gifts, and also a pretty way of distributing them? Would you also please tell me what are my duties as secretary?—INEXPERIENCED.

YOUR duties would be to keep the minutes of any meeting in connection with the fund, and all records. You must be careful to keep an exact account of the money received and spent. To you will fall the task of organising the party, and on the day to see that all goes well.

There are firms who make a speciality of party novelties and toys which would serve as inexpensive little gifts for your children's party. They will make up parcels of assorted toys, dolls, caps, balloons, streamers, etc., suitable for various ages. Another inexpensive source would be the sixpenny bazaar.

A party of tiny children is perhaps one of the most difficult to organise. Some of the children are so shy that it is not easy to draw them out of themselves and into the fun.

Begin with very simple games which most of the children will know, like "Ring o' Roses," "Nuts and May," "Tom Tiddler's Ground," "Hunt the Slipper" variation of "Hunt the Thimble," "I Sent a Letter to My Love," "Blind Man's Buff," "Oranges and Lemons," and so forth.

Here are some more which will not be so generally known:

"TINKLE BELL"

THIS is a pretty variation of "Blind Man's Buff."

A small bell is passed from one child to another, and the blind man has to catch the child who is actually holding it.

"CAT AND THE MOUSE"

TWO are chosen—one as the cat and the other as the mouse. The rest of the children form a ring, holding hands, and the cat chases the mouse round and round, in and out, and under the children's arms. When the mouse enters the circle the children close up to prevent the cat from coming in, and they open out when there is danger of the cat forcing her way in. If the cat does get inside the ring they may try to prevent her from getting out again. When the mouse is caught the cat becomes the next mouse and another player from the ring is chosen as the new cat.

PAPER BAG COMPETITION

THE children specially enjoy this game, because it involves the bursting of paper bags. Get some small paper bags from the stationer. Place some in a row at one end of the room. The same number of children as there are bags will stand in a row at the other side ready, at the word "go," to race across and seize a bag. They must sit on the floor (or chairs if you desire), each blow up his bag and burst it, then race back. The first back wins.

THE BALLOON WOMAN

WITH balloons you can make a very pretty scheme for giving away little gifts.

Someone dressed as an old lady comes in with a big basket to which are attached a bunch of balloons. Each balloon has a number. The old lady seats herself in the middle of the room and, to a gay tune, the children all march round her and are brought to a standstill in a circle round her. One by one they choose a number and a balloon which tallies with it is presented to the child. On pulling it out of the basket it is discovered that a parcel is attached to it.

MUSICAL BALLS

THIS is played in much the same way as Musical Chairs, only instead of chairs a number of tennis balls are placed in a row down the centre of the room. The players march round them to a gay one step or march, and when the music ceases all make a dash for the nearest balls. Those failing to pick up a ball drop out, as in musical chairs

At the end of each turn one or more of the balls are removed.

As the music ceases each child grabs a ball

Christmas Joys for Girls and Boys

ALL BRITISH BOOKS FOR BRITISH CHILDREN

Easy to Pack—Cheap to Post—Certain to Please!

GIVE the children books this year—they are the best gifts and never fail to please. Here are books for children of all ages—from six to sixteen—beautifully illustrated, stoutly bound, and packed from cover to cover with lively fun in picture and story. Most of them contain beautiful coloured plates and many pages printed in colour. If you want a present that will keep the children happy during the long winter evenings you cannot do better than to choose one of these famous "All British" Annuals. Your newsagent or bookseller will be pleased to show you any of these jolly gift books.

A book for the manly boy between 10 and 15 years. Thrilling adventure stories, interesting articles, and eight beautiful plates. **6/- Net.**

For girls who are still at school. Full of adventure and school tales, also entertaining articles. Lavishly illustrated. **6/- Net.**

Tiger Tim's own book. Stories and pictures of the famous Bruin Boys, fine school and adventure stories, fairy tales, etc. **6/- Net.**

For girls between 10 and 17 years. Delightful stories of school life, sport and adventure. Also entertaining and useful articles. **5/- Net.**

School and adventure stories; also interesting articles, and 250 illustrations in colours and black and white. **5/- Net.**

Charming adventure, fairy, animal and humorous stories, and dainty verse. Delightful colour plates and black and white illustrations **5/- Net.**

Pages of pictures of Tiger Tim and the popular Bruin Boys. Scores of adventure stories, fairy tales, jokes, and riddles. **6/- Net.**

A novel book for little boys and girls who are just beginning to read. Pictures to paint. **3/6 Net.**

A wonderful all-story gift book for girls, contains well-illustrated stories of absorbing interest. **2/6 Net.**

A delightful book for children of all ages. One hundred large pages of entertaining features. Many illustrations in colour. **3/6 Net.**

For boys and girls up to eight years. Cheery stories with an abundance of pretty and amusing pictures. **2/6 Net.**

832 pages of reading. Stories of school, footer, mystery and adventure. Splendid articles. Pages of photographs and 12 colour plates. **12/6 Net.**

1931

A MOTHER'S PROBLEM

I have become a bad sleeper since my baby came. At first it was an effort to wake to feed him, but now he sleeps all through the night.

I keep on waking up just the same, and cannot get to sleep again. Can you give me some advice?

THIS often happens, but if you are careful and firm with yourself, time will soon put this right.

Don't fly to stimulants when you feel tired during the day.

Take your tea not later than four o'clock, and very weak. No coffee. Go to bed early and try reading a pleasant book for an hour before turning out the light.

Have a drink of hot milk, or one of the cocoa-flavoured foods. Some people benefit by having a thermos flask with hot milk beside their bed which they drink when they wake up in the small hours.

Others find sipping a glass of hot water helpful, while others find a dry biscuit suits them better. A few of these can so easily be kept in an air-tight tin within reach of you.

Above all, don't worry about this condition. It will pass.

TWO FOR MIRTH!

A Jolly Appliqué To Make Your Little Boy Happy.

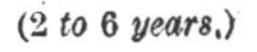

(2 to 6 years.)

You remember the old country rhyme about the magpies:

One for sorrow,
Two for mirth,
Three for a wedding,
Four for a birth,
Five for silver,
Six for gold,
Seven for a secret,
That's never been told.

Isn't it a pretty notion to appliqué two of these most decorative birds on a small boy's tunic suit? Trace the magpie with carbon paper under this page on to a scrap of black cloth, and then trace the wing part and the underside on to white cloth and appliqué them with buttonhole-stitch into position. The beaks are worked in white wool satin-stitch, and four long straight stitches form each little leg. A white French knot indicates the eye.

The twig can either be outlined with small black running-stitches or filled in with grey wool satin-stitch.

To make the neat tunic suit you will require 1¼ to 1½ yards of 36-inch-wide material and ¼ yard extra of contrasting material for the strappings. For long sleeves you will require about ¼ yard extra.

WHEN TO WEAN BABY

I want to continue feeding baby myself as long as I can. What is the correct age for weaning?

IT is a good English fashion to wean a baby at the age of nine months, as up till then a mother's milk contains everything that is necessary for a baby's welfare.

If the ninth month should fall in the hottest months of the year, it is sometimes advisable to lengthen the period a little; but that should depend on your own health and strength.

By the sixth month baby should be given a hard, well-baked crust or rusk, with a smear of fresh butter on the end, while fresh fruit juice with water can be added from the second month.

* * *

NO HIGH HEELS

I have always been accustomed to wear rather high heels on my shoes, but now that I am looking forward to a happy event my mother says I ought to put them aside for a few months. Is she right?

YES, high-heeled shoes should not be worn, particularly during the last few months. It is easier and safer to preserve a good balance with low-heeled shoes. In high heels there is always more danger of a fall going down steps, so put your pretty shoes away for a time.

I am sure you will find low heels more comfortable because you must take all the brisk walking exercise you can. It will keep you in good health, and daily exercise is the right preparation for the time baby comes.

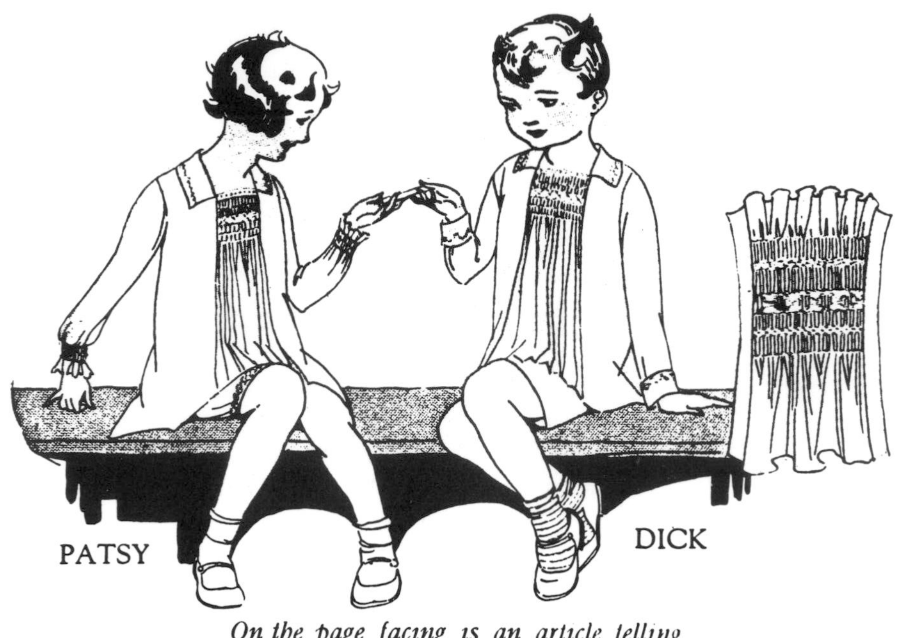

On the page facing is an article telling you how to smock. It is really very simple

HERE is quite a novel Painting Competition for you this month, and I *shall* be disappointed if you don't like it and if I don't get entries from the whole 800 odd of you!

First paste the picture on thick paper or thin cardboard. Prick each dot with a pin, then sew along the lines with brightly coloured wool, silk, or cotton—blue for the clouds, gold for the sun, red and blue for the parrot.

When you have done these outlines, paint in the rest of the picture. First prize, £1. 1s. 0*d.*; second, 10*s.* 6*d.*; third, 5*s.*; and ten beautiful consolation prizes.

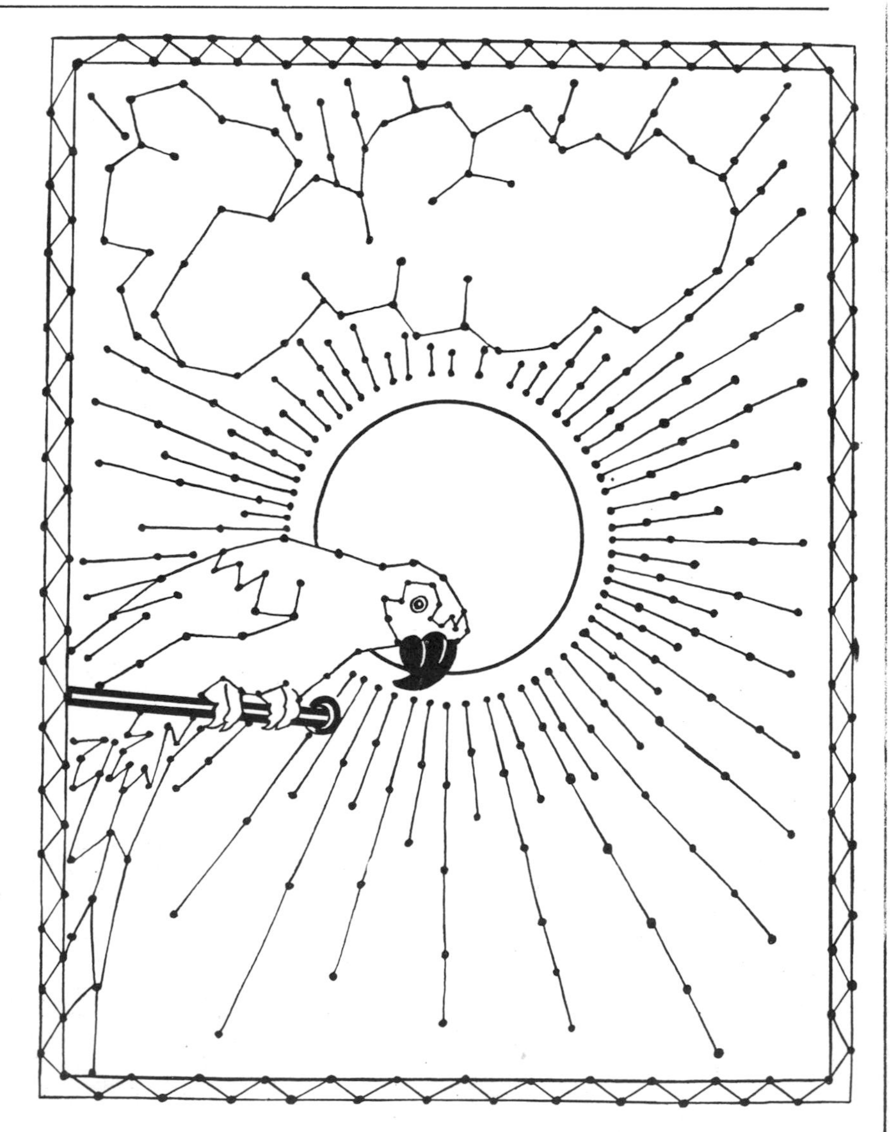

SMOCKING—MADE EASY!

With Our Special Transfer and "What-to-Do" Diagrams

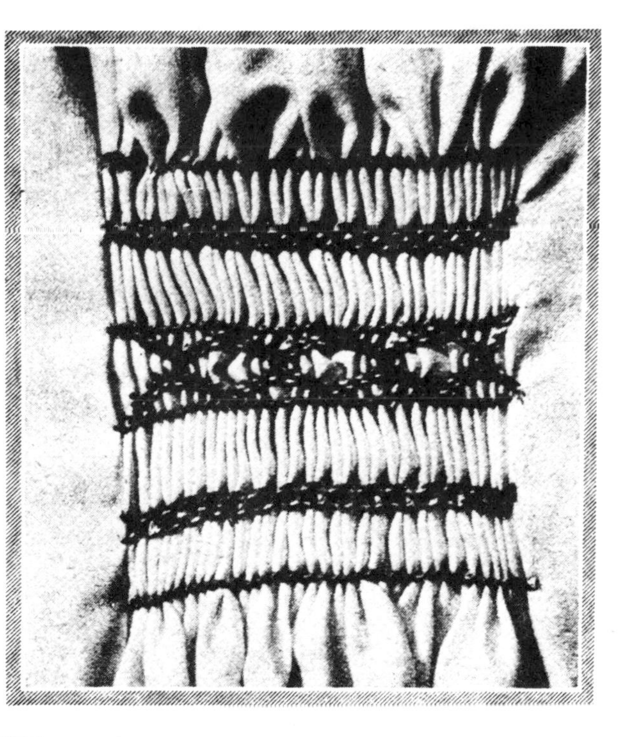

SMOCKING is one of the easiest kinds of stitchery, although it looks so elaborate when it is finished. With the help of our special Smocking Transfer (No. 70) you can work the two delightful little smocked frocks shown on the opposite page.

(The transfer sheet has different strips for frocks of different sizes.)

Transfer the size required on to your material.

You will find that the transfer has a number of tiny crosses down one side at intervals three-eighths of an inch apart (Diagram 1).

Take a length of white cotton and run along the lines *with the crosses*, bringing the cotton in and out just each side of the dot (Diagram 2). (Use a fresh thread for each line.)

When all are complete draw up the gathers fairly closely all to the same width, and finish off each thread (Diagram 3).

Now you can begin the embroidery part. The lines of dots indicate where to embroider, so that you will have no difficulty in keeping your embroidery even.

Turn the gathered part horizontally and work along the first line a row of stem-stitch (with embroidery cotton), taking one stitch over each pleat (Diagram 4). Work a second line of stem-stitching along the second line, but instead of holding the cotton on the same side of the needle each time, put it first to the left and then to the right all across the line. Work a second line similarly next to it (Diagram 5).

Next work a line of ordinary stem-stitch, then a zigzag line, taking the cotton four times to the left of the needle, four times to the right, and following the zig-zag line of spots on the material (Diagram 6).

Work another line beside the last (Diagram 7). Now reverse the whole of the rows from this point out to the last line on the transfer.

When the embroidery is quite complete, pull out the tacking threads.

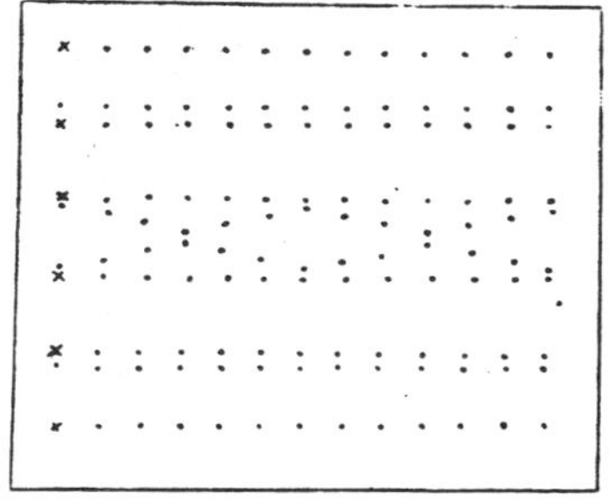

1 *This is what the transfer looks like when ironed on to the material.*

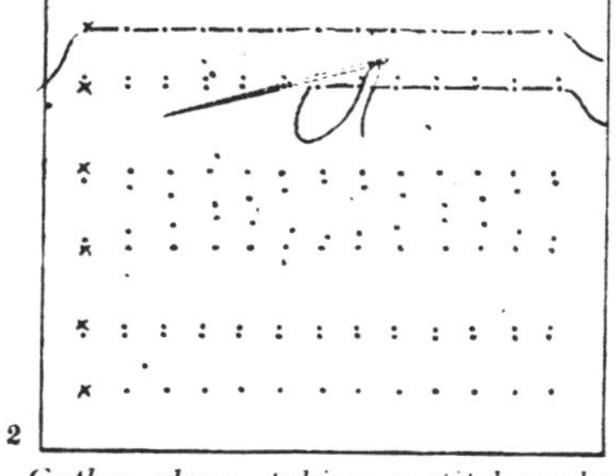

2 *Gather along, taking a stitch under each dot.*

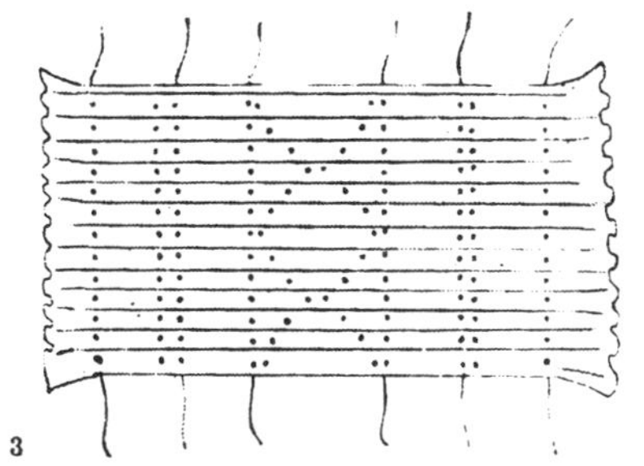

3 *When complete, draw up all the gathers evenly and fasten them off*

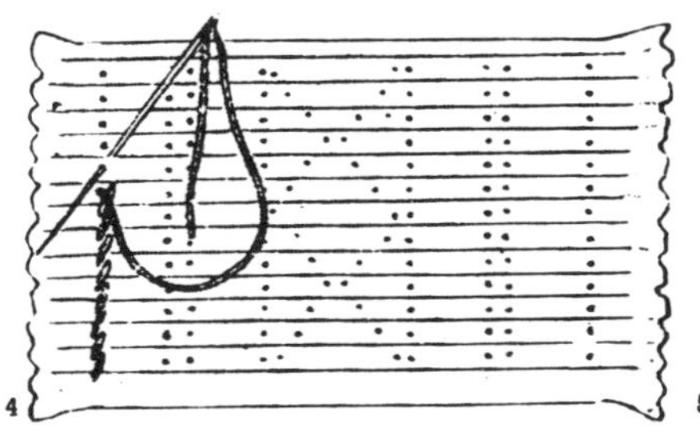

4 *Work along the first line of dots in stem-stitch, taking one stitch over each pleat.*

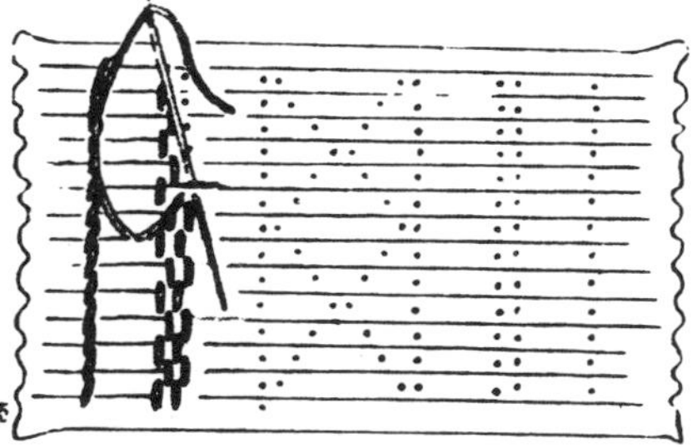

5 *Two lines of stem-stitch follow, taking the cotton first on one side of the needle and then the other.*

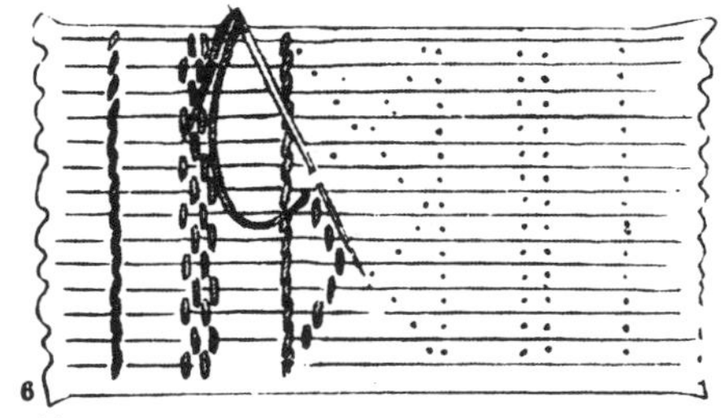

6 *Next comes a plain line of stem-stitch and a zig-zag line.*

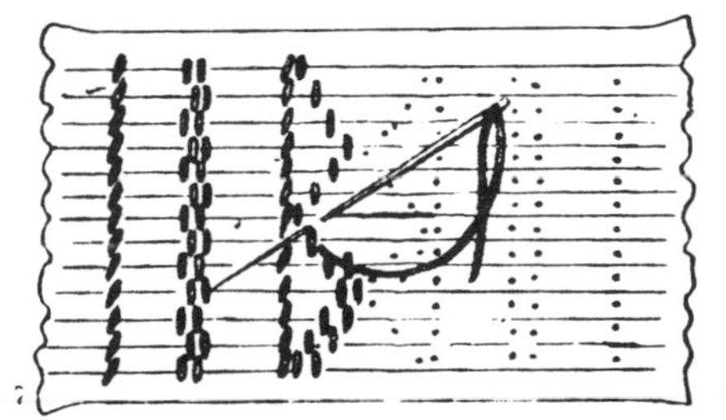

7 *A second zig-zag line comes next close to the last one.*

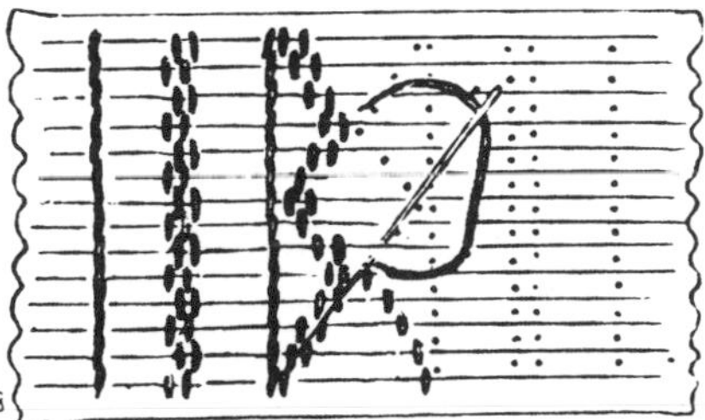

8 *A reverse line of zig-zags meet the last line in the centre of the points.*

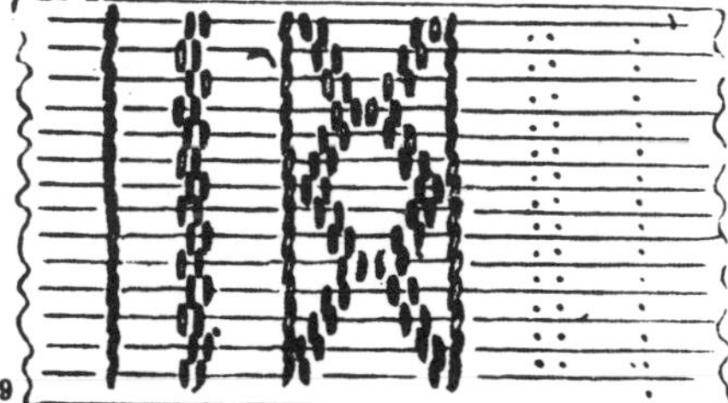

9 *This shows the centre zig-zags completed.*

This Month Our Hundred Guinea Cookery Course Reveals the Secrets of Making a Mushroom Cake. It is Most Delicious to Eat and Most Decorative to Behold—the Perfect Tea-time Delicacy.

A Mushroom Cake Looks So Pretty!

The cool October days bring us once again to fireside teas.

This "mushroom," which consists of a light cake mixture moulded with almond paste and topped with chocolate icing, is most interesting to make.

INGREDIENTS:

2 *eggs.*
Their weight in flour (or the same amount of self-raising flour, when no baking powder will be needed).
1 *level teaspoonful baking powder.*
3 *oz. castor sugar.* 2 *oz. margarine.*

FOR THE ALMOND PASTE:

¼ *lb. icing sugar.*
¼ *lb. castor sugar.*
6 *oz. ground almonds.*
Egg white or whole egg to mix.
Flavouring.

FOR THE CHOCOLATE ICING:

2 *oz. butter.* 2 *oz. plain chocolate.*
About 1 *tablespoonful water.*
¼ *lb. icing sugar.*
¼ *teaspoonful vanilla flavouring.*

To Make the Cake Mixture.—Beat the sugar and fat to a cream. Add the eggs separately, stirring each one in quickly and beating it well before adding the next one.

When both the eggs are well beaten in, stir in the flour sifted with the baking powder. Mix these ingredients together lightly before turning the mixture into a buttered pie tin. This is a

(Below) The sides and base of the cake must be brushed with melted jam to make the almond paste adhere.

A Daintily Served Tea We Can All Offer to Our Friends—and This Attractive Mushroom Cake Would Add Charm to the Prettiest Table.

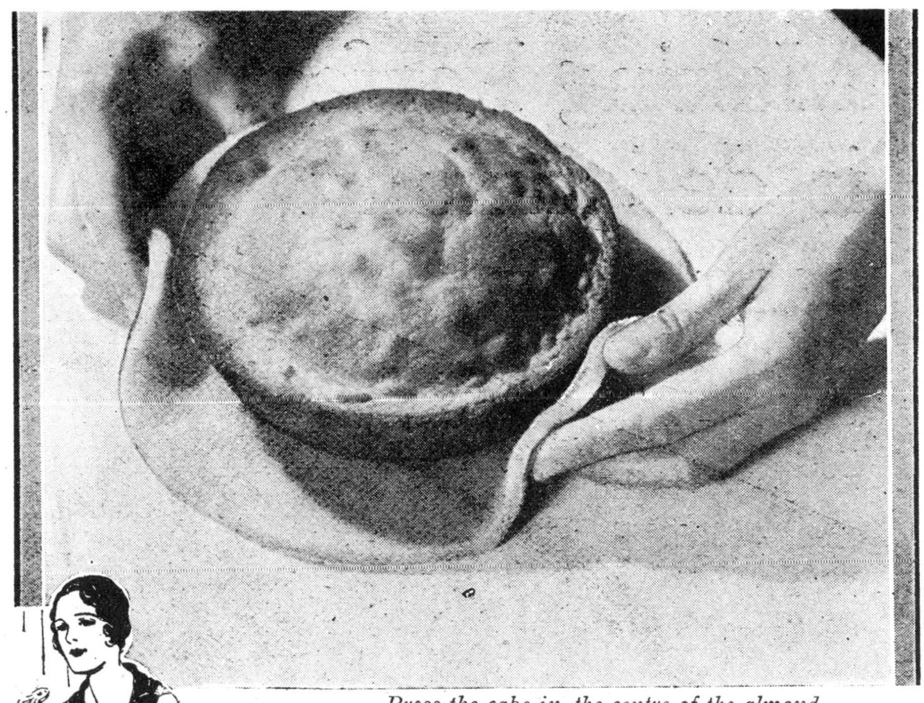

Press the cake in the centre of the almond paste and mould the paste round it.

round tin rather deeper than a sandwich tin, with sloping sides.

Put the cake into a fairly hot oven to bake. It will take about twenty-five minutes. Place it on a sieve to cool.

To Make the Almond Paste.—Rub the icing sugar through a sieve. Then mix it with the castor sugar and ground almonds.

Make them into a stiff paste with lightly beaten egg white or a beaten whole egg.

Flavour the paste with a few drops of vanilla. The white of egg will make a more real-looking mushroom, as the whole egg gives the paste a yellowish tinge.

One egg white may not be quite sufficient to mix the paste, but to save breaking another egg just a little water may be added to make up the amount of moisture.

If liked, a teaspoonful of orange flower water may be used to flavour the paste instead of vanilla.

Put a small piece of paste aside for the stalk and roll out the remainder to a round.

Brush the base and sides of the cake with melted jelly or jam. Then place it in the centre of the rolled-out paste and mould the paste round it. If the cake has risen in the centre it must be cut level before finally moulding the paste just over the top edge.

To Make the Chocolate Icing.—Break up the chocolate and dissolve it in a saucepan or basin, standing it over a pan of hot water. Stir in about a tablespoonful of water, then let the chocolate cool. Rub it through a hair sieve.

Beat the butter to a cream, then gradually beat the sugar into it. When it is soft and creamy, stir in the dissolved chocolate. Add the vanilla flavouring and mix the icing well.

If it seems too stiff, a little more water or milk may be added. Or the beaten yolk of the egg serves very well if it has not been used for the almond paste. If the icing is too soft, add a little more sifted sugar.

Put the icing into an icing pump with a shell-patterned tube affixed, and force it on to the top of the cake. Work from the edge almost to the centre, as shown in the photograph, and fill it in completely. Finally, form the remaining piece of almond paste into a fat stalk and stick it in the centre of the mushroom.

Force the icing on to the top of the cake, working from the edge to the centre and filling it in completely.

What Shall We Do at the—

Here are Some Jolly Games to Play Out-of-Doors.

THE CAT AND THE MICE

One of the children is chosen as "cat," and the others are all "mice." The mice are divided into groups of three or four. Each group chooses a "hole." Joining hands, they all dance round the cat, and while they dance they sing "Three Blind Mice."

Suddenly the cat pounces and catches as many mice as she can before they reach their holes. Those caught must then stay in the centre with the cat and help her catch more mice.

They must keep in the circle.

"LEGS"

The children are divided into two groups, three in each is a good arrangement. A circle is drawn on the ground and two groups (six children) stand inside. The other children stand around and with a tennis ball try to hit the legs of those standing inside the circle. These jump about to avoid the ball, but they must keep inside, and if even one foot goes over the edge of the circle that player must come "out."

Anyone hit below the knee is "out." If the ball stays in the circle it is kicked out as far as possible.

Two minutes are allowed for the bombardment, and then the other side goes in. The team to bowl out the largest number wins.

The one to keep up longest wins.

PRICKED BALLOONS

The children sit in a row on the ground, legs stretched in front of them. Somebody blows a whistle and they all take a very deep breath. The whistle goes again, and they let out their breath in a long sustained note. When all breath is gone they collapse on the ground. The one to keep up longest wins.

—Birthday Party

THE BOOK TEAM RACE

This is a relay race, a member from each team racing to a given mark and back, balancing a book on her head.

If the book drops, a bad mark is counted against the team.

The team to finish first gains ten good marks, which must be balanced up against the bad ones.

THE STOCKINGS

The little guests are divided into two or three teams of about five or six. The children of each team are numbered 1, 2, 3, 4, 5, 6, and stand in files. Some way off hang stockings, one of which is allotted to each team. These are filled with a large collection of small articles: one of each kind in every stocking.

The organiser, who holds a list of the articles, calls a number and names one of the articles in the stockings. All those who bear that number race to their particular stockings, and produce the article named. The

A stocking for each team.

The Stockings (continued)

quickest player wins, and scores a point for her team. The game then goes on with another number, and another article, and so on.

THE TORTOISE RACE

This is a good game to play after a fast one. The race is to the slowest, and the last in at the winning-post wins.

No one must actually *stop* during the race. They must keep moving on the track, and several umpires should be elected to watch for defaulters.

The race is to the slowest.

BABY'S "CHARACTER"

HERE are photographs of twenty-four little members of our Babies' Club, and a clever character-reader's delineations from them.

Yours is a very sweet nature, Baby Maude Wahltuch (of Fleetwood), but you are apt to be over-sensitive. You will develop a gift for understanding others and a great desire to help those in trouble.

Catherine Smyth (of Devonport) has great courage and will show determination in accomplishing an object. She is full of high spirits, and needs plenty of physical exercise, taken as much as possible in the fresh air.

Great opportunities lie ahead of thoughtful little Jean Strange (of Reading). As she grows up she will be keen to learn, and should develop the gift to instruct. Her nature will influence others for good.

Baby Alma Thompson (of Oldham) will probably grow into an imaginative little girl, perhaps rather too sensitive. She will be very generous-hearted, but a little difficult to convince that she is not always right.

There should be great things in store for you, Graham White (of Newport), in the artistic side of life, for already you show every sign of the artistic sense and a great love of all things beautiful.

You already have a sympathetic nature, Frederick Davies (of London), and an unusually quick understanding. As you grow older you will show a strong desire for knowledge, and should do well in life.

Jeanne Woods (of Ipswich) will be a great lover of the open air, and should, when she grows older, work out of doors as much as possible. She will develop a keen sense of humour, and will always be busy.

Isobel Ferguson (of Kilsyth) should do well in all pursuits which require a quick, active mind. Nevertheless she is apt to be rather restless, and should be trained to finish one task before starting another.

Yours is a nature which is strongly influenced by your surroundings, Eileen Orames (of Australia). As you grow up you will show a placid disposition, loving peace and happiness, and disliking quarrels.

You are a thoughtful little man, John Horne (of Bath), and gifted with an excellent memory. As you grow older you will be happiest when working with other people. You should be shielded from unnecessary worry.

Yours is a delightful, sympathetic nature, Eileen Marchant (of Westbury). As you grow older, the troubles of others will be your greatest worry, and you may be almost too generous in your response to their difficulties.

Baby Norman Thomson (of Norwich) should do well in life, as he possesses tremendous perseverance. He will probably like to work with method rather than with a rush and bustle, and will prefer action to words.

You have a very affectionate, self-sacrificing disposition, Beryl Jones (of Hayes), and should be happy and successful, but as you grow up you will need to guard against lack of concentration and perseverance.

You have great strength of character, Baby Rosemary Oakley (of Hurst Green), and as you grow older you should have much influence over others. Be careful, however, not to let your ideals run away with you.

Little Thelma Ross (of Belfast) shows every sign of being a deep thinker, and capable of intense feeling. She is already very determined, and should do well in pursuits that need great skill and care.

There is a strong originality and love of freedom in the temperament of Roland Ross (of Ilford). He has artistic ability, and should cultivate this as he grows older. He should develop an excellent memory.

You have the making of a very fine man, William Alington (of New Zealand). Resolute and level-headed, you will be capable of steady and sensible action in time of trouble, and you have great courage.

Here's a smile that tells a story! Yours is a very trusting nature, Colin Cleave (of Wadebridge), and you are almost too generous. You may be apt to take life a little too easily, however, and should guard against this.

Ideals, thoughtfulness, and originality will probably shape the life of little Josephine Bogussz (of Andover). She will show a strong sense of justice and much determination, but she should not be allowed to get too excited.

You will become an ambitious little fellow, Frank Edge (of Birkenhead), persevering and unwilling to let difficulties get the better of you. You may be rather keen to have your own way, however.

You are, I think, a doer, not a dreamer, Lloyd Barber (of Fareham), and should do big things in life, but you may be impulsive and inclined to rush headlong into risks without first thinking them out.

What a thoughtful little face, Baby Ernest Bowen (of Blandford)! You have an extremely sensitive nature and a keen imagination, which, as you grow up, may make you moody and a little difficult to understand.

Derek Spencer (of Derby) should accomplish great things in life, as he has an alert mind and great courage. He should be taught, however, to exercise self-control, as he may be impulsive, and apt to act too quickly.

And what's in store for you, Brian Berridge (of Leeds)? I think you will show great sincerity and perseverance and a gift for designing things. You may, as you grow up, be apt to take life a little too seriously.

HULLO, TWINS!

Twins have a great interest for us all, not merely on account of their birth, but because of the striking likeness that often exists between them, the similarity of character and tastes, and the mysterious link that often binds them in an affection and understanding far deeper than that usually shared by ordinary brothers and sisters. All the darlings on this page are members of our Babies' Club, the world-wide membership of which is growing every day.

Here are a soldier's twin sons—PETER and GERALD LITCHFIELD, of Tidworth. We wonder if they will become soldier boys, like daddy, when they grow up?

If you know any interesting stories of wonderful understanding between twins, the Editress would be glad to hear them.

This is a "pigeon pair"—GRACE and PETER GRIFFITHS, of Plymouth. One twin is often physically stronger than the other, and in this case the girl looks the more lively one, doesn't she?

Here you see JEAN ELIZABETH and MARGARET SALLY RHODES, of Waddon, bonny little lassies who look full of life and energy. We wonder what the photographer showed them to attract their attention so eagerly?

Here we have REGINALD and LESLIE DORE, of Gosport, a bright-eyed little pair. Although there is a strong likeness between them, they look as if they differed in character and disposition, don't they?

Very striking is the likeness between these two sturdy little girlies—JOYCE and BERYL COLEMAN, of Salisbury. Their mummy, like the mothers of the others, dresses them alike—but we are sure she always knows which is which!

And here are KATHLEEN and SYLVIA PICKLES, of Colne. Here again we see an unmistakable difference in character already developed, young though the little darlings are.

Keeping Them

Even if you have only a little bit of garden, your children may play happily in it all day long through the fine weather, in the health-giving air and sunshine, if you give them a little help and encouragement.

(*Photo: Ruth Alexander Nichols.*)

CHILDREN love playing with water, and there is no reason why they should not, if suitably dressed—or in hot weather undressed !—in the garden.

AT this beautiful time of the year there is no more delightful sight than a group of children happily at play in a garden, with the glow of health in their little cheeks, the sparkle of fun in their clear, bright eyes, and joy ringing in their shouts of laughter. I really believe that the kiddies find more enjoyment in garden games than in indoor ones. They are out in the open air and sunshine ; and, moreover, they are out of mother's way while she gets on with the work of the house, and yet safely under her eye.

(*Kodak snapshot.*)

A GOOD-TEMPERED dog is a splendid playmate in the garden, especially for an only child.

Some of us, of course, who live in towns are not fortunate enough to possess gardens for our little ones to play in. All we can do in the way of giving them open-air games is to make the most of the parks and open spaces that lie within our reach. And even those of us who have gardens do not always find that our children will play happily in them for long. After a little while we find they become discontented and restless, and come bothering at the back-door. Yet in most cases this is not the fault of the children, nor even of the garden, however small a plot it may be. The trouble is usually one that we parents can put right.

First of all, we must admit that the garden is the children's, as well as ours. I am sorry to say I know a young father, a very keen gardener, who not only "shoos" his small son away from the neighbourhood of the flower-beds, but will not even let the little fellow play on the grass, "because he would spoil it". No doubt he would, and it is beautiful grass ; but I think—and I am sure all you mothers will agree with me—that a little child's health and happiness are worth more than the most velvety turf. I know another father who goes to the other extreme and has sadly given up any attempt to grow anything at all in his garden, because he grew tired of telling his tiny daughter not to pick the flowers. This, of course, is absurd.

As in most things, the moderate, middle course is the wise one and the right one. Children *can* be taught not to pick the flowers or trample on the vegetable plot, and the mere fact of having to remember, in their play, to keep to the ground that is theirs, and keep off that which is daddy's, is good training for them. If your children will grow flowers for themselves in a little

IN parks where there are paddling pools, let the children use them to their hearts' content.

THE simplest toys often give children the most pleasure—particularly in their garden play.

(*Photos: H. Armstrong Roberts.*)

Good in the Garden

plot of their own—not all children will take this interest, I admit—your task is easier, for they soon learn how much work and care go to the tending of a garden and the growing of flowers, and will be as mindful to avoid spoiling daddy's garden as they will their own.

And if, now and again, in the excitement of a game of "touch", a small person *does* cut across the rose-bed and leave a few footprints in the mould, or knocks off a few blooms, or snaps a shoot or two, does it really matter so dreadfully much, after all ? And do, please, let the children have the grass plot as their playground; and if there is scarcely a blade of grass left by the end of the summer, the joy their garden play will give them, and the health it will bring them, are well worth the sacrifice of turf.

Well, there is the first thing towards happy garden play : let the children feel that at least one little bit of the garden is their own, and that they can play as they please in it. The second thing is that we may have to provide them with materials and suggestions. I do not mean that we must try to "organise" games for them, or that we need provide expensive and elaborate toys. We all know that children get the most fun out of the simplest toys, and even make-believe toys ; and even if we mothers had the time to arrange games for them, they would still be happier playing the ones they invent for themselves. But they do sometimes need just a suggestion or two.

So let them loose in the garden, give them such simple oddments as you can spare as playthings, suggest something amusing that they can do with them, and leave the rest to the bairns themselves. You will find that they will play happily for hours, and if they should tire of one game and be unable to think of a new one, another little suggestion from mummy will start them off again.

I have been astonished sometimes at the *very* simple games that will keep small kiddies amused for hours on end. I have seen toddlers of three or four delightedly practising walking along a chalk line drawn along the path, placing one foot exactly in front of the other and finding it tremendous fun. And it is a good game for them, because it teaches them balance.

I heard of another good idea the other day. A friend of mine puts an old mattress down in a sunny spot, and her tiny boy and girl roll about on it for hours. She tells me that they love it, and I can quite believe it, can't you ?

My own children have spent many hours happily racing up and down the garden astride their "hobby horses"—ordinary hedge sticks—shrieking with delight the while, and whipping their steeds with home-made whips. Even the tiny of two-and-a-half would gleefully toddle on in the wake of her elders, crying "Gee-up !" as she ran. I remember, too, how upset John was last summer when I unwittingly threw away "Bess", which he had left lying outside the back-door, and which I didn't recognise as his trusty steed !

I used to be almost distracted on washing-days when my two small girls kept on begging me to let them help, until one day I hit upon the idea of giving them some washing to do. Since then, many, many times, they have occupied themselves delightedly for hours in the garden with a bowl of water, a tiny piece of soap, some clothes-pegs, a few dolls' clothes, and sometimes I have even risked one or two of the family handkerchiefs.

(*Photo: Wilkinson.*)

Even the tiny crawler can be happy in the garden with a few simple playthings.

(*Kodak snapshot.*)

Imagination plays a great part in children's games ; give them suggestions for "pretending".

(*Photo: Ruth Alexander Nichols.*)

Pets will keep the tinies happy for hours, and teach them love of animals.

For those of us who have no gardens, the public parks provide splendid playing grounds.

(*Central Press photo.*)

Some things for the children

Keeping Them Good in the Garden

They have washed and re-washed these articles, hung them on the garden fence—which in our case happens to be of twisted wire—and then commenced making inquiries as to when they could begin ironing! And, actually, this does teach little girls to like washing. You will be surprised, too, to find that they have watched you so closely that they really have quite a good idea of how to do it.

On wash-day, too, it is quite an easy matter to give the children some soapy water and some clay pipes. They will thoroughly enjoy blowing bubbles and seeing whose efforts will fly the highest.

And, by the way, doesn't every child simply love to play with water? I remember, when I was small, the tremendous delight we used to get on hot days from two or three baths full of cold water in the garden. We put on our bathing costumes, and then the fun began!

A favourite amusement of my tinies when they return from their annual holiday, is to play "seaside" with a bath of water. In this they float their boats, celluloid ducks, and any other similar toys which they may have collected while they were away. If you have space for a sand-pit in your garden, do buy a sack or two of sand, for little ones never tire of playing with this.

It is really wonderful how inventive quite small children can be in their "make-believe" games. I have watched my tinies playing quite happily and industriously for an hour or two with nothing more than small stones and bunches of wild flowers and greenery. They will make an enclosed space with the stones, about five feet square, and this they call their "shop". The flowers and greenery are placed in disused jam jars ready for "sale". Sometimes the "shop" is a grocery one, when the jam pots hold "sugar" in the form of dock seeds, "rice" (tiny stones), or "flour", which is usually earth!

A variation of this game is to make the enclosure into a "house", and in this case it is divided into "kitchen", "scullery" and "living-room", and the doors and windows are marked out with spaces. This forms a foundation for the game of "Mothers", which is played all the world over.

Then remember, won't you, that the small boy of the family, who rather turns up his nose at the idea of playing "girls' games" with his sisters, will find entire satisfaction in a box on wheels.

We must not forget the youngest member of the family, however. He also will play quietly in the garden without bothering mummy. If you haven't a play-pen, get the largest box you can. Set this in a shady spot, put the little man in it, and he will amuse himself for a long time. A few cotton reels on a string will hold him fascinated. My baby is very fond of bricks, of which he has a great number. He also gets great amusement from chestnuts, fir-cones and such-like treasures collected for him by the elder children.

To talk of having a "gymnasium" in the garden sounds extravagant, but actually daddy can often contrive simple things that will give the kiddies endless delight and really good, muscle-developing exercise.

If two strong wooden bars are fixed, horizontally, one near the top of the garden fence, and the other about six inches from the bottom, the children will enjoy travelling sideways along it, hands grasping the upper rail, and feet supported by the lower one.

A swing is always a great favourite, and can, of course, be made by daddy. A see-saw is also easily improvised from a log of wood and a plank, while the plank can afterwards be made to serve an additional purpose: Raise one end a few inches from the ground and the children will soon walk up and down this quite easily. Then gradually raise the end higher and higher until they are able to walk up a steep incline without falling. This is a splendid exercise for learning balance and giving an easy, graceful walk.

I have yet to meet the boy or girl who doesn't like climbing! If you possess a short ladder, just place it at a slight angle somewhere in your garden, and the children will amuse themselves for a considerable length of time in simply getting to the top and down again. Then, if you have a stout rope or clothes-line which you can spare, do let them have this, too. Knot it at intervals of about a foot, and hang it from a tree or beam, with a large loop at the end nearest the ground.

Children will generally play quite happily out of doors with their pets; the older ones often become particularly interested in looking after rabbits, or even a tortoise. It is a good plan to keep a dog where there are little ones and, personally, I think that a medium-sized one is the best kind to choose.

I spoke at the beginning of this article of the mothers who have no gardens, and send the children to the parks and commons during the fine weather. The little ones cannot take all their toys with them—but mummy can suggest games that only need things they can carry easily.

A very good game of quoits can be played with the aid of a clothes peg stuck in the ground and some wooden curtain rings. Then there is battledore and shuttlecock, which is not so much seen now, but which all children enjoy.

Balls are always popular, and quite a number of pleasant games can be played with them, including the old favourites "Rounders" and "Stool Ball".

"Wandering Ball", however, is not so widely known, and it is an excellent game for a large number of children on a warm day, when they have become too hot for more active games. The little players form a circle with one in the middle, and the ball is thrown across from one player to another, the one in the centre trying to intercept it. Of course, the great thing is to deceive the middle player, by pretending to throw the ball in one direction and actually sending it in another. When the child in the middle catches the ball, he changes places with the one who threw it.

One great advantage of the park as a playground is that the children meet their friends; and so games requiring larger numbers of players are possible. "Mother Bird" is one of these. One of the number is chosen to be the Hawk. Another is the Mother Bird, and she divides her children into groups, each bearing the name of a different bird. The groups scatter and the Mother Bird and the Hawk go to their respective "homes". Then the Mother Bird calls each group to her and, whilst they run, the Hawk has to catch as many as he can, and take them as prisoners into his "home.

Another favourite is "Three Blind Mice". In this, the children form a ring, with one kneeling down in the middle, and they dance round singing "Three Blind Mice". The child in the centre thinks of a certain word in the song, and when that word comes, he jumps up and chases the others, who run away in all directions. Those caught then come into the ring, kneel down together, and the whole is repeated.

After such games as these, the children will welcome one or two with less movement, which will enable them to get cool, and "Quick Jack" is excellent for this purpose. Quick Jack himself stands close to and facing a wall, and the others line up about fifteen to twenty yards away. The object of the players is to creep up and touch the wall, or slap Jack on the back, without his seeing them in the act of moving; for he is allowed to look round suddenly at any minute. Those seen moving have to go back and start again. They can vary this by "bunny jumping" or hopping up towards Jack.

No, it isn't difficult to keep the children good out of doors. Give them, as far as you can, plenty of scope for doing things for themselves. Let them imitate if they wish; let them construct at will; let them "pretend" to their hearts' content; and in such a way, not only will they keep themselves constantly happy and amused, but their play will be valuable in character-building and mental training.

THE END

"Where's mummy gone?"
—Why, to the newsagent's, of course, to get her copy of WOMAN'S COMPANION, your Editress' twopenny weekly

The Margaret Rose Frock

This delightful little Frock won the First Prize in our Knitting Competition

Original Design Sent in *by* Miss J. Clowser

MATERIALS : OF PATON & BALDWIN'S Ladyship " Babyship " 3-ply Wool : 3 ozs. White, 1 oz. Pink. 2 pairs of No. 9 Knitting Needles, and 1 Crochet Hook No. 15. 4 Pearl Buttons.

MEASUREMENT : Length of dress from shoulders, 16 inches.

TO KNIT : COMMENCE at lower edge of FRONT by casting on loosely 158 stitches in pink wool.

1st row.—Knit plain into back of stitches. *2nd row.*—Purl. *3rd row.*—Plain.

4th row.—JOIN ON white wool. Knit 1 *, knit 2 together, knit 4, make 1, knit 1, make 1, knit 4, slip 1, knit 1, pass slipped stitch over knitted one. Repeat from * to end of row, knit 1.

5th row.—Purl.

6th row.—REPEAT 4th row. *7th row.*—Plain. *8th row.*—Purl. *9th row.*—Plain.

10th row.—REPEAT 4th row. *11th row.*—Purl.

12th row.—REPEAT 4th row.

13th row.—Plain. *14th row.*—Purl. *15th row.*—Plain.

16th row.—REPEAT 4th row, omitting to " make 1 " wherever instructed, thereby decreasing the number of stitches on your needle to 134.

17th row.—* Knit 1, purl 1. REPEAT from * to end of row.

FOUNDATION PATTERN :

18th row.—Knit 1, purl to the last stitch, knit 1.

19th row.—Knit 1, purl 1. REPEAT to end of row.

REPEAT these last two rows for a further depth of $2\frac{1}{4}$ inches. The work is now ready to have the SECOND FRILL joined on. This is worked as follows :

SECOND FRILL : With the second pair of needles cast on 158 stitches in pink wool and proceed EXACTLY as at the commencement of the work, from the 1st row to the 17th, inclusive.

Now place the needle holding the frill stitches on top of the needle holding the first piece of knitting, and holding the two together—right sides towards you, purl all along the row, taking two stitches together—one from each needle.

CONTINUE for $2\frac{1}{4}$ inches on these 134 stitches the 2 rows of FOUNDATION PATTERN, i.e. knit 1, purl 1 on wrong side of work, and knit 1, purl 132, knit 1, on right side of work.

THIRD FRILL : Now the THIRD FRILL must be made and joined on in the same manner as described above, and the FOUNDATION PATTERN continued for $1\frac{1}{2}$ inches only.

WAIST : The number of stitches must now be reduced for the WAIST. With the pink wool and right side of work towards you ; knit 1, knit 2 together, and repeat to end of row, then work 3 rows plain in pink.

*1.—Join white wool. Knit 1 row plain, 1 row purl.

3rd row.—Knit 1*, make 1, knit 2 together, and repeat from *.

4th row.—Purl.

5th row.—Knit 2*, make 1, knit 2 together, and repeat from *.

6th row.—Purl.

JOIN ON pink wool and knit 4 rows plain. CHANGE to white wool and knit 1 row plain.

2nd row *.—Knit 1, purl 1, REPEAT to end of row.

3rd row.—Knit 1, purl to last stitch, knit 1.

CONTINUE these last two rows for 3 inches, then cast on 12 stitches at each side for the sleeves and continue right across in pattern for a further depth of $1\frac{3}{4}$ inches, then JOIN ON pink wool and knit 4 rows plain, CHANGE to white wool and work same pattern as at waist from *1 to the end of the 4 rows plain in pink wool. CAST OFF.

BACK : Work exactly the same as at FRONT.

CUFFS : Cast on 48 stitches in pink. Knit 4 rows plain. JOIN ON white wool, and work 1 row plain, 1 row purl.

3rd row *1.—Knit 1 *, make 1, knit 2 together, repeat from * to end.

4th row.—Purl.

5th row.—Knit 2 *, make 1, knit 2 together, repeat from * to end.

6th row.—Purl.

JOIN ON pink wool and work 4 rows plain, change to white wool and work 1 row plain and 1 row purl.

Then work another 2 rows of holes as above (*1), ending with 2 rows plain. CAST OFF.

PRESS WELL with a hot iron over a damp cloth. Sew shoulder seams together 4 inches from each end. Sew cuffs to sleeve edges and buttons on shoulders. Crochet loops on opposite side to correspond. Decorate with crochet roses.

The "Margaret Rose" Frock

(Continued)

CROCHET ROSES TRIMMING: With pink wool and Crochet Hook commence with 5 chain—join into ring.

1st round.—6 ch. 1 tr. into ring (3 ch. 1 tr.) 4 times into same ring.

Join every round with a slip-stitch.

2nd round.—1 d.c. 6 tr. and 1 d.c. into each ch. space.

3rd round.—1 d.c. between each group with 4 ch. between—join. Bend petals forward so that chain is at the back.

4th round.—1 d.c. 8 tr. 1 d.c. into each space.

FASTEN OFF.

THE LEAVES: COMMENCE with 14 ch. and 1 extra ch. to turn.

1st row.—Make 1 d.c. into each of the first 2 ch., then 1 tr. into the next 8 ch., and 1 d.c. into each of the last 2 ch.

Turn work and repeat row on the other side of foundation ch. FASTEN OFF.

Sew into position as in photograph.

TO KEEP LITTLE ONES AMUSED. All kiddies love jig-saw puzzles, and they will spend hours putting the different pieces together. I, myself, have a weakness for this sort of puzzle, and I'm not the only grown-up, either!

It's an expensive business buying new puzzles, however, so here's a hint I'm passing on to all mothers and aunties. Gather all the covers and coloured illustrations from magazines you can find, and paste them on to thin cardboard. Now place each picture under the needle of the sewing-machine, and mark them off into designs. These will tear apart easily and neatly. The children will delight in putting these "home-made" pictures together again.

At a party this is a game that always goes down well. Give each child the pieces to make a complete picture, and offer a small prize for the one who gets his or her picture finished first.

How I Made my Baby's Chair

By a "WIFE and HOME" DADDY

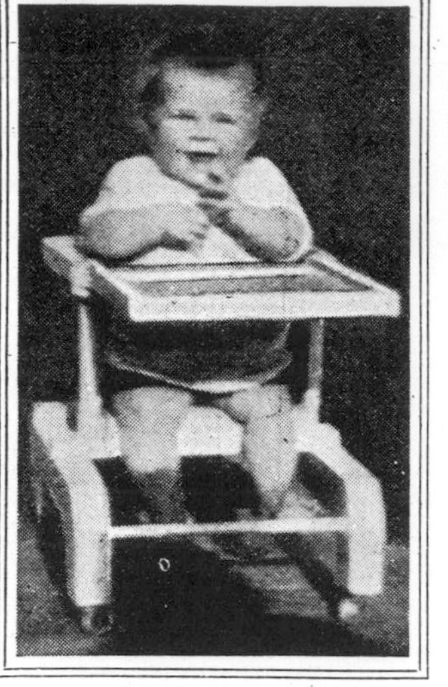

Doesn't baby look happy in the chair that daddy made?

WHEN the little lad or little lass has reached the crawling stage, a baby chair is so useful that it is almost a necessity, but they are rather expensive things to buy. Any father who is at all handy with tools, however, can make one himself. I made the one my small son uses every day, at the cost of a few shillings, and I think other WIFE and HOME daddies may be interested to know how I did it.

The materials I used were merely these:

1 piece of wood (deal, pine, whitewood or something similar), 11 inches by 9 inches by 1 inch.

3 feet of $4\frac{1}{2}$ inch by $1\frac{1}{4}$ inch.
9 feet of $1\frac{1}{4}$ inch by 1 inch.
2 wooden rods, fourteen inches long by $\frac{1}{2}$ inch in diameter.
1 large tea chest.
1 set of 4 castors.
3 bolts, 3–16 inch diameter.
Sundry screws.
1 tin white paint.
1 tin white enamel.

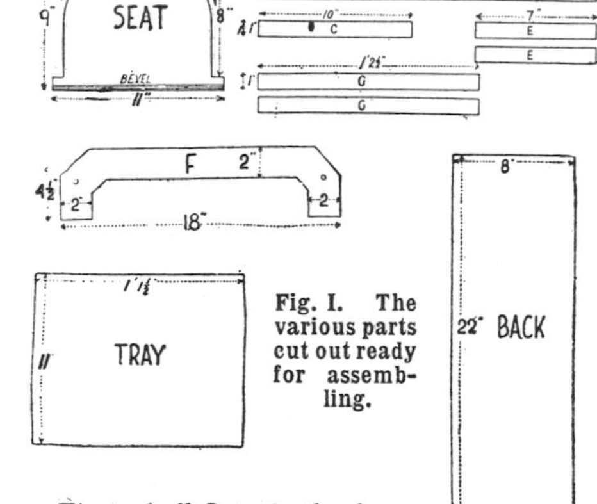

Fig. I. The various parts cut out ready for assembling.

First of all I took the large piece of wood and with a small saw cut it to shape for the seat, as shown in Fig. 1, saving the pieces A, A that I had sawn off, and bevelling the front edge with a plane. From the $1\frac{1}{4}$ by 1, I cut two lengths of 1 foot 10 inches each, and out of each of them cut a piece $\frac{1}{2}$ inch by 10 inches, as shown. This gave me the pieces B, B and D, D. I also cut piece C, 10 inches long, pieces E, E each 7 inches long, and pieces G, G each 1 foot $2\frac{1}{2}$ inches long. The $4\frac{1}{2}$ inch wood I sawed into two lenths of 1 foot 6 inches each, and cut them to the shape F. Taking the plywood tea-chest to pieces, I cut one piece 1 foot $1\frac{1}{2}$ inches by 11 inches for the tray, and one 1 foot 10 inches by 8 inches for the back.

Then I began to assemble the parts. I did the tray portion first, laying the pieces B, B parallel and screwing C into place at the back and D, D (with the pointed ends cut off), as shown in Fig. II. The tray I fixed underneath the frame with small screws, screwing them well home so as not to leave any projecting heads to catch baby fingers. I then put in the pieces A, A with screws through B, B and C.

Next I took the piece of plywood for the back, and screwed the centre of the bottom to the centre back of the seat. Then I bent it round the seat, putting in screws every 3 inches until it was firmly secured. I then inserted the top of the back into the tray frame and screwed it up in the same way, starting in the middle with a screw into C and then screws round into A, A and B, B at 3-inch intervals. The stiffeners E, E were then screwed into place as shown in Figs III and IV.

This completed the upper section. I then assembled the undercarriage. I laid the two pieces F, F parallel, a foot apart, bored holes in the inner sides and inserted the tie-rods, securing with glue, and screwed the bearers G, G into position across the top as shown in Figs. III and IV. The upper and lower sections I then fastened together with the bolts let in through the seat — one at centre back, and the other two in front—and the bearers G, G. I was careful to sink the heads of the bolts well into the seat. I then fixed the castors.

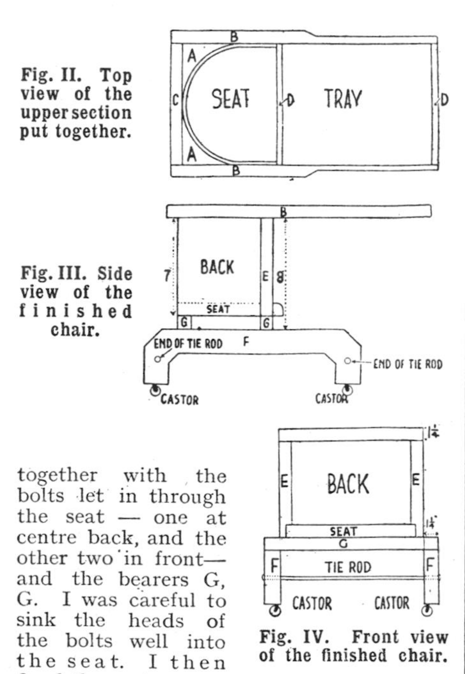

Fig. II. Top view of the upper section put together.

Fig. III. Side view of the finished chair.

Fig. IV. Front view of the finished chair.

Only the finishing touches remained. I went over all the sharp edges with an old file and sandpaper and gave the chair two coats of white paint and one of enamel (easy to keep clean). And behold, my small son had, as you will see in the photograph, a really useful little chair, as good in many ways as any I could buy. In this he will sit happily for hours, playing with toys on the tray, while his mother is busy with her housework.

THE END

The first article of a very interesting new series that will help every father to be a "pal" to his children, and to answer some of the countless questions they ask.

YOUNG George Farman is one of those fathers who believe in being their children's best friend. Although he can be stern when necessary, his girl and boy look upon him almost all the time as a big, splendid pal, whose knowledge of things is wonderful and who is *always* right. Mrs. Joan Farman calls them her three D's—Daddy, Doris and David.

George is anxious to give his children the best general education he can manage, and he is not content to leave the job entirely to their school teachers. The fact that the children began to ask him countless questions almost as soon as they could talk, showed him that their little minds were hungry for knowledge—often the kind of knowledge that is not dealt with in school lessons. He made up his mind to supply this himself so far as he could, to learn about the subjects that interested them, and resolved to be patient with their questions, curious though some of them were; and to be in complete sympathy with their eager desire to learn things about the wide world round them.

In the garden, for example, he did not give the kiddies the shady, dust-dry patch against the brickwork of the house, where nothing of any worth would grow. He set aside for them a bright, sunny spot with good, deep soil, and dug it over himself to get it into really good condition. Their garden is a real joy to the Farman children, for they were not discouraged at the beginning by failures due to causes they could not cope with. Sometimes the children bring home wild plants for their garden, and it is daddy's rule that the plants must be dug up complete with a trowel, and carried in a little basket instead of in hot, clammy hands.

"Plants are real, living things," he says, "and it's wrong to uproot them roughly and then let them wilt and wither in the sun."

On Saturday afternoons, when the weather is fine, George will often take the youngsters for a ramble, showing them some of the simple wonders of nature that are to be found in the fields and woods and hedgerows. They live on the fringe of the suburbs of a city, and just beyond their home a bridge carries the main road over a stream. One of their favourite walks is to cross the bridge, turn to the right, and follow the stream through some open parkland until they reach a wood. They like to go through the wood, climb the hill on the other side and wander over the heath, down into a valley, and so back to the high road at a point not far from the tram terminus.

THE STICKLEBACK'S NEST

"OH, do look at those little fish!" said Doris, on one of these walks, as they stood where a back-water of the sluggish stream made a pool.

"Yes," daddy explained, "those are what little boys call 'tiddlers'. You can catch them with a net and keep them in jam jars, but it's not very kind to do so, and they'd be

An American (grey) squirrel eating a nut. (*Photo: Tom Taylor*).

Sticklebacks, male and female, with their under-water nest.

A skylark's nest with eggs. The nest is a very simple affair of grass, hay and rootlets, but is so cleverly hidden that it is very hard to find. (*Photo: Tom Taylor*).

A British (red) squirrel. These pretty little animals are dying out, because the greedy American ones have over-run much of our country-side.

A young skylark that has just left the nest. Skylarks always nest on the ground and seldom even perch in trees. (*Photos: Frances Pitt*).

Nature Walks with Daddy

[*Continued*]

far happier in a small aquarium. Their real name is Stickleback, from the prickles that grow along the top of their spines, and they're hatched out in nests."

"*Nests?*" demanded David, eyes wide with wonder. "Not nests like birds make?"

"Not altogether unlike those of some birds," explained dad. "First of all, the father fish fixes some lengths of straw among sand and pebbles in shallow water, and then attaches to them pieces of grass, roots, hay, and so on, which he finds floating by. He fastens them with gummy threads from his mouth, after the style of a spider making his web. Presently he has built quite a pretty enclosed nest, something like a long barrel or cask in shape, with a hole at either end. He then goes off and finds a mother fish and coaxes her to come into the nest and lay some eggs.

"Now the curious and unusual part is that once the eggs have been laid the mother fish goes away and it is the father who takes charge of them. The eggs hatch themselves—the fish don't have to 'sit' on them as a hen does on hers—but he guards them like a sentry, scarcely ever taking his eyes from them, and fighting off all intruders, using his sharp spines as weapons if there's need. By and by, the eggs or 'spawn' turn into wee fish, and the father, who has been such a stern policeman, now becomes a tender nurse. He breaks the top part of the nest away, till the lower half lies like a dish-shaped cradle, in which the babies live and grow until they are large enough to swim away and take care of themselves in their under-water home."

Leaving the stream at this point, they walked across the open field in the direction of the wood, when a small bird seemed to rise from the strong-growing spring grass at their very feet and went soaring into the air, singing as it flew as if its throat would burst.

"A skylark!" cried David, knowing already the warbling of the songster and the flowing, liquid stream of his trills.

"Right, old chap," agreed daddy. "Notice that he keeps on singing all the time he is climbing towards the sky. In May, skylarks sometimes stay in the air twenty minutes, singing all the while."

Doris wanted to know something about the lark's nest, and daddy explained that it is always made on the ground.

"You'll usually find skylarks either on the ground or in the air, dearie," he said, "for they very seldom perch. The nest is rather a poor affair of bits of grass and hay, roughly arranged among the dense spring herbage of a meadow, in a field of growing corn, or on some common. Mother Lark lays four or five eggs at a time, greyish-white, tinged with green and mottled with brown."

MR. SQUIRREL AT HOME

The cheery little party had not gone far into the wood before daddy said, "S-h-h-h!" and touched David, who was leading, on the shoulder. When they had all stopped short, he pointed along a glade to where a saucy squirrel was sitting bolt upright, bushy tail in the air, picking seeds from the cone of a fir tree, and eating them eagerly, with a paw that served as thumb and fingers. The next moment the squirrel sensed their presence, for the breeze was blowing from the humans towards him, and he went straight up the trunk of a tree like a flash, jumped sheer through space to another tree, tail spread out astern like a sail, and disappeared from view.

"He is a grey squirrel," said daddy, "and has not long wakened from his snooze all through the winter. Probably on a few sunny days he roused, felt hungry and came to ground, where he would have had a store of food near the roots of the tree—a larder which he had thriftily prepared in the autumn. So long as the weather was bleak, though, he would have slept quite soundly and not wanted anything to eat."

"It's funny," said Doris, puzzled, "but in my picture book the squirrel is reddish. Why is this one grey?"

Daddy explained that the red squirrel is the British kind, the only kind found in this country till a few years ago, when some grey squirrels were brought from America, and some of their babies, when they grew up, were let loose in London parks. So contented were the animals in their new land that they spread far and wide—and are gradually making it impossible for our more timid native red squirrel to live at all, simply because they steal his food.

BLUEBELLS

They saw no more of Mr. Squirrel, but at the other end of the wood, where the path drops, was a wonderful carpet of bluebells, spreading away to left and right till it tailed off into violet haze, and swayed like waves in the breeze.

"Only gather just as many as you think mummy would like, dears," said daddy; "and then wrap dock leaves round the stems to keep them cool until you get home and can pop the flowers in water with a pinch of salt to make their freshness last. Take care not to pull up the bulbs.

"If you want a few bulbs to plant in your own garden you must get permission, and come with a trowel at the end of the school summer holidays. You'll be surprised to find how deeply they grow, but they are well worth the trouble of digging up. Half a dozen bulbs planted in the late summer will go on increasing season after season till you have a big patch."

As it was getting on for teatime, they went home, happy and hungry, chattering about the things they had seen and that mummy would be so interested to hear about.

"*Oh, the little birds sang east, and the little birds sang west.*"

Elizabeth Barrett Browning

Baby's Dainty Christening Set

By

Honor Tuite

In this, her latest original design, I think our Needlework Expert has excelled herself in creative daintiness. All readers who decide to make this Robe, Cap, and Matinée cannot fail to be delighted with its delicate, lacy charm.

THIS set is designed to fit a baby from birth to three months.

MATERIALS REQUIRED: Of Copley's "Excelsior" Baby wool, 4 ozs. in white and 1 oz. in blue. $2\frac{1}{4}$ yards of $\frac{1}{2}$-inch wide satin ribbon. 1 pair of Stratnoid Knitting Needles, No. 8, and a Stratnoid Crochet Hook, No. 15.

ABBREVIATIONS: k. = knit; p. = purl; m. = make; dec. = decrease; inc. = increase; tog. = together; st. = stitch; d.cr. = double crochet; ch. = chain.

ROBE: The back and front are worked exactly the same. Commence at lower edge of back by casting on 90 stitches in white wool, and always working in stocking-stitch (i.e. one row plain, one row purl alternately), work ten rows white, two rows blue, ten rows white, two rows blue, ten rows white, two rows blue. On the next row, which is a knit row, change back to white again and commence web pattern, as follows:—

1st row.—Insert right-hand needle into first st., and wind wool three times round needle instead of once. Repeat to end. *2nd row.*—Insert right-hand needle into first st. *purl-wise*, and pull off st. together with the other two loops, thus making one long st. Repeat to end of row. You should now have 90 stitches on needle again.

Repeat the last two rows twelve times more, or add a few extra rows if a very long robe is desired. Now work two more rows in stocking-stitch in blue, two more white, then commence to make holes at waist-line, thus: k. 5, m. 1 (by putting wool over needle), k. 2 tog., and repeat to end of row, ending k. 4. Purl the next row, then knit one more in white. Change back to blue wool, and decrease stitches to 60 by taking every second and third st. together to end of row. Work one more row in blue, then break off and continue in white only until bodice is complete.

Work four rows more, then commence to decrease for arm-hole by casting off three stitches at the beginning of the next two rows. Then continue to decrease by knitting 2 st. tog. next to the edge st. at beginning and end of every knitted row until stitches number 44. On the next knit row, k. 12, cast off 20 for neck, k. 12. Continue on the last 12 stitches only for eight rows more. Cast off. Join wool to other shoulder, and work to match first. Work another piece exactly the same for front.

Press well with a hot iron over a damp cloth, being careful to pull web stitching as tightly as possible from top to bottom, otherwise the whole effect will be spoilt. Sew up shoulder seams, then with right side of work towards you, pick up 8 stitches down the side edge at each side of shoulder seam (16 stitches in all), p. back, increasing by working twice into every stitch, thus increasing number to 32. Now work four rows of web stitching. Cast off. Work other sleeve to match.

All round the neck edge, work two even rows of double crochet in blue wool, and all round lower edge of robe also work two rows double crochet. Then edge with the following fancy edging: * 5 ch. miss 3 stitches of previous row, 1 d. cr. into the fourth stitch, 3 ch. 1 d. cr. into the same stitch as before, and repeat from *. All round epaulette sleeves, work one row of double crochet, keeping the tension very loose, then work edge row as for bottom of robe. Cut off $1\frac{1}{2}$ yards of blue ribbon, thread through holes at waist, and tie in front.

CROCHET EMBROIDERY. THE FLOWERS: In blue wool make 5 ch., join to ring with a slip-stitch, * 5 ch., 1 d. cr. into ring, and repeat from * four times more. Break off wool, leaving sufficient length to sew flower to frock. You will require thirty of these flowers for the frock. Sew on as shown in photograph between the sets of blue lines at bottom of robe. If liked,

a French knot in yellow may afterwards be embroidered in the centre of each.

THE CAP: Commence with 4 ch., and join into a ring. *1st round.*—6 d. cr. into ring. *2nd round.*—2 d. cr. into each d. cr. of previous round. *3rd round.*—As 2nd round (24 stitches in all). *4th round.*—Increase by making 2 d. cr. into every third stitch all round. *5th round.*—Work without any increasing. *6th round.*—Increase by making 2 d. cr. into every fourth stitch. *7th round.*—Increase by making 2 d. cr. into every fifth stitch all round. Continue thus, always allowing one extra stitch between each increase in each successive round, or, should the work commence to flute a little, work a round occasionally without any increasing, until you have a circle measuring 4 inches across.

Work three rows plain, join on blue wool. Next row, 3 ch. (to stand for the first treble of row), 1 tr. into every stitch of previous row. Join with a slip-stitch, break off blue wool, and continue in white. 5 ch., miss 3 tr., 1 tr. into the third, * 2 ch., miss 2 tr., 1 tr. into the third, and repeat from * all round. The next row is worked the same as the last row, only the trebles are worked into the spaces. Work two more rows as last row. Join on blue wool, and work 2 tr. into every space. Work one more row, stitch into stitch. Fasten off. Decorate crown with five blue flowers made as for robe.

THE MATINÉE: With white wool cast on 60 stitches, and work ten rows stocking-stitch, two rows blue then six rows web-stitching. Change back to stocking-stitch and work four rows more, then at the beginning of the next two rows, cast on 15 stitches for the sleeves. Work for 2½ inches more, ending on a purl row. Next row, k. 35, cast off 20 for back of neck, and knit over remaining 35, leaving the first 35 stitches on a stitch-holder until the first front has been completed. At the end of the next purl row, cast on 10 stitches (these form revers at neck edge), then continue in stocking-stitch for another 2½ inches, ending on a knit row. At beginning of the next purl row cast off 15 stitches, then work four rows over remaining 30 stitches. Work five rows of web-stitching, then change to blue and work two rows of stocking-stitch, and ten in white. Cast off. Join wool to other side, and work right front to match left, always reading knit for purl and purl for knit for all shapings.

Press with a hot iron over a damp cloth. Sew up sleeve and side seams. Work the three rows of blue round edge of coat as given for bottom of robe. All up the front of the right side of the coat work a row of double crochet, and carry this round neck edge and down to extreme point on left side. Work one row double crochet round cuff edges. Cut remaining blue ribbon in half, and sew on as ties in centre front. Sew ten flowers round edge of coat, placing them at equal intervals apart, and one flower at each lapel. Press seams and the little set is complete.

Baby's Dainty Christening Set

(Continued)

NIGHTLIGHT TALES

What happened next to *JACK and JILL*

ONCE, Jack and Jill went up the hill—all children know the rhymes—and Jack fell down and broke his crown. (It was in fairy times!) But do you know what happened next? Or why their mother was so vexed?

I'll tell you why. Hard times had come, and she was very poor. The landlord was a surly man, and always at the door, asking for rent she could not pay, saying he'd turn them out next day!

"What *shall* I do?" their mother sobbed. Jack and Jill, at the well, were wondering what they could do to help. That's why they fell. They missed their footing, for they were thinking what mother had to bear.

"If only fairies helped," sighed Jill. Then down she fell. You see, she didn't guess that fairies had arranged that carefully. A fairy seed lay there, you know, which needed watering, to grow.

Jack didn't know, Jill didn't know, nor did their mother sad, that, by upsetting their big pail, quite by mistake, they had watered that seed. But fairies knew! And poor Jill's wish was coming true!

"Why, look!" said Jack, next morning, when they both went up the hill. "I've never seen that plant before." "No, nor have I," said Jill. "Let's give it water every day. Or else perhaps 'twill fade away."

So up the hill they went again, and with the greatest care, they gave the little plant as much as it had need of. "There!" said Jack, "I hope it will not die!" Said little Jill, "And so do I!"

Well, listen. When they woke next day a tall tree stood quite near their cottage, waving branches green. "What *do* I see and hear?" said Jack. "I think I'll climb that tree. I must find out the mystery!"

So up he climbed, with Jill behind, right up into the clouds. And there they found a little house where elf-workmen, in crowds, were singing, while they worked away: "This house must ready be to-day!

"It is for Jack and Jill," they sang. "And for their mother, too. They took care of a thirsty plant, until it grew and grew up to the clouds, and here's their prize. A fairy home up in the skies!"

So down the children hurried fast. This time they didn't fall. Up climbed their mother, too, to see, when she'd heard of it all. And there they lived for many a day, with never any rent to pay!

On the Amusing Sayings of Children

THE other day I was amused to hear a child of five staidly remark: "Children do say very pecoolable things." They certainly do. They also say lovely things.

A child's capacity to restore tired words to their pristine freshness, by an instinct for the exact epithet, is often so surprising that it raises high hopes for his future; but alas, freshness of style dries up with the loss of wonder, and in a few years the tongues of angels settle down to the use of an utterly commonplace vocabulary.

Often a child's gift of expression does not long survive his lisp. Babyhood holds practically no pledge for maturity, and entrancingly quaint children grow into irretrievably normal men. All the more reason to enjoy and remember their delightful early phrases; and I think every mother should keep a book in which all funny or pleasing sayings are set down.

For such a book to seem worth while, you need cherish no illusions about your children. However normal they are, you may be sure they will say things you will be glad to remember.

Very likely you are so amused by them at the time that you cannot believe they will ever escape your memory, but often will you find yourself wondering what it was one of your children said the other day. In vain you ransack your own, and other people's, memories. The delicious absurdity, the lovely phrase, is irretrievably lost.

Later on, such a book will be a great delight to the children themselves. "Tell me about when I was little" is a reiterated demand. I know a rationalist of nine who smiles indulgently at the two-year-old self who refused to have a fire lit on Christmas Eve for fear Father Christmas should burn his toes as he came down the chimney!

A friend of mine who has kept a children's chronicle showed it to me yesterday, and I found it well worth reading. I quote from it at random:

Six Years Old: "Mother, I think I should understand if only you wouldn't explain."

Six Years Old (a disappointed angler): "The little fish ran away thinking he wasn't mine!"

Four Years Old (whose dressing up has fallen flat, in pathetic reproach to preoccupied parents): "I was a Giant, but nobody noticed."

Four Years Old (to a brother who has spoiled a sand castle): "Oh! you naughty, naughty Liberty boy!"

Three Years Old: "What is Daddy *for*?"

(How ably this expresses the bewilderment of the puzzled little egotist as to the *raison d'être* of anyone whose function towards himself is not apparent. It is easy enough to see the object of Nannie and the cook. Mother is either a makeshift for Nannie or a standing treat, but what and why is this strange being who is neither child nor servant?)

Three Years Old (in first sailor suit): "Now I am the beginning of an Admiral!"

Six Years Old (aware that some explanation is due): "If I'm not naughty sometimes, I shall never get emptied of my naughtiness!"

Six Years Old (advised to propitiate a disagreeable governess with civil words): "Oh, no! it's no use talking flowers to her!"

Six Years Old (on his promotion from pencil to ink): "Mother! I've gone into ink!"

Six Years Old (told to watch how his father holds a cricket bat): "I'll nail my eye to Daddie with the hammer of my brain."

Six Years Old (describing the expression in a poet's eyes): "Oh! I *did* like that man! He looked at me just as though a thousand theatres and circuses were going on in my face!"

Four Years Old (presented by waitress with a macaroon instead of an éclair): "Oh! that isn't the cake I invited!"

A mother who decides to keep a children's chronicle should enlist their nurse as an ally, for she will often be the only witness of memorable conversations.

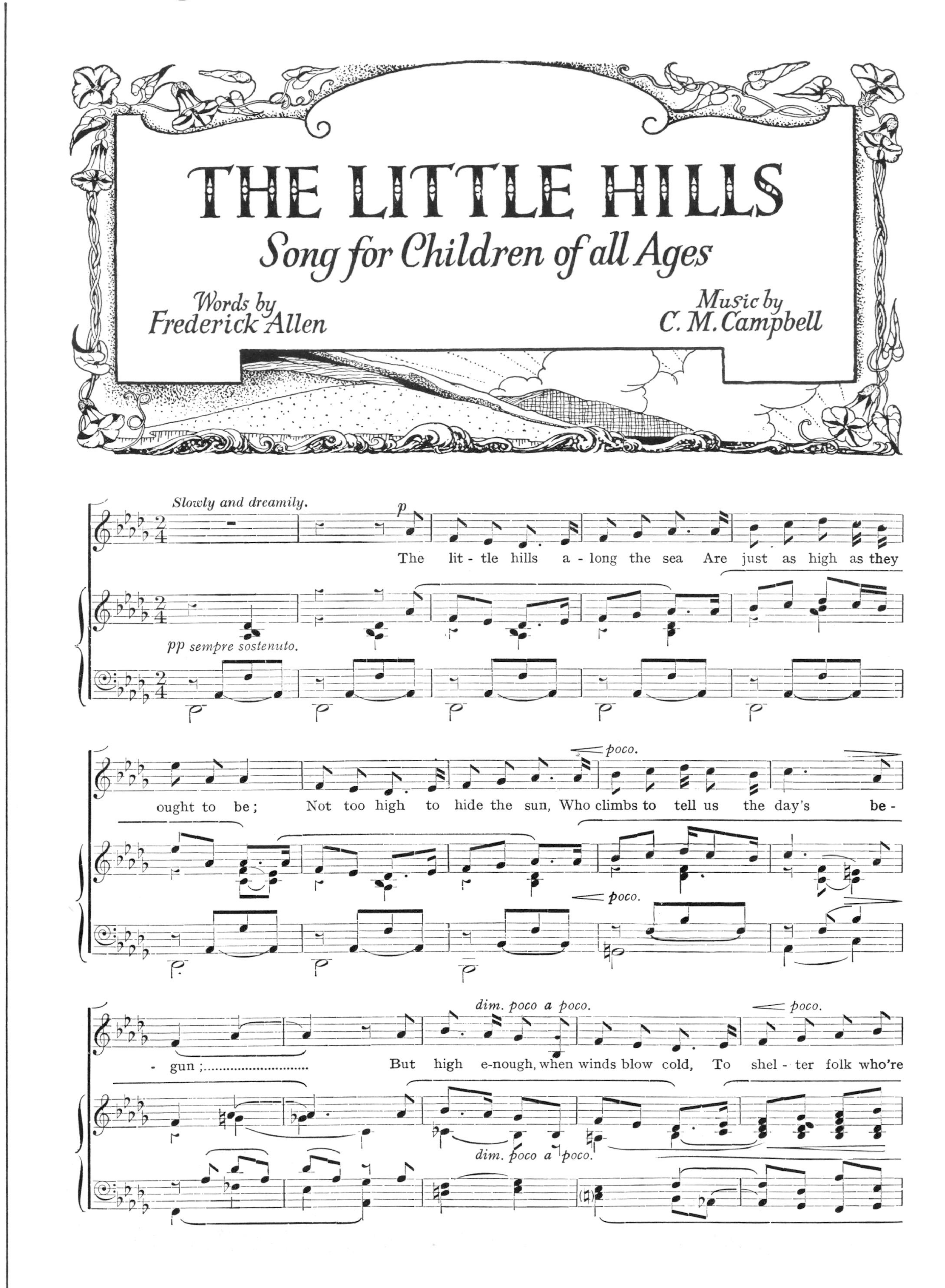
THE LITTLE HILLS
Song for Children of all Ages
Words by
Frederick Allen
Music by
C. M. Campbell
Slowly and dreamily.
p
The lit - tle hills a - long the sea Are just as high as they
pp sempre sostenuto.
ought to be; Not too high to hide the sun, Who climbs to tell us the day's be -
poco.
- gun ;
dim. poco a poco.
But high e-nough, when winds blow cold, To shel - ter folk who're

The Little Hills
molto rit.
molto meno mosso.
a tempo, ma poco ritardando.
pp
grow - - - ing old. I'm sure the hills a - long the sea Are
ppp
sempre molto legato.
just as high as they ought to be.
p più rit.
dim. e rall.
L·R·STEELE

Space-Saving in the Nursery

By

Rosamund Martin

In small nurseries, where space is precious, it's an awfully good plan to make a series of big pockets that can hang on the wall, and will form a home for the children's soft toys. Teddy-bears, rag-dolls, and the like can all be stowed away tidily; and yet they'll be instantly accessible should their little owners want them for a game. If mother or nurse make it a rule that every toy is popped back into the pockets so soon as the games are over at night-time, then the nursery will keep tidy, and the actual work of clearing-away will be reduced to a minimum.

The ideal plan, of course, is to make a pocket for each child, with its own name worked along the bottom. And if you decorate them with quaint Noah's Ark folk, like the ones pictured here, the pockets will add a truly attractive note to the wall. We have christened our family the " Binks Family"—there's Mr. Binks, Mrs. Binks, and Miss or Master Binks, with their neat little cottage and prim, pointed tree ! You can trace over their outlines, and transfer them to the material you're embroidering very simply ; to do this, lay a sheet of red carbon paper, greasy side facing the material, under the tracing, and go over the lines with a steel knitting-needle. When you remove the papers, you will see the pattern clearly outlined on the material in red ; it's a good plan to pin the stuff and the tracings to a drawing-board, or smooth-topped table, so that you are sure to get the outlines on straight.

Use Old Bleach Linen for making the pocket ; this is splendid for working on, and washes beautifully. The natural cream shade makes a good background for embroidering with Dewhurst's " Sylko Mouliné "—this is a six-stranded cotton, which you can divide up into different thicknesses, or use complete, just as the embroidery demands.

The size and number of the pockets will depend, naturally, on the size of the family ! Our example, for three children, takes one-and-a-quarter yards of 36-inch wide linen ; this gives you a piece of material 36 inches long and 45 inches wide. Lay it flat on the table, and pull threads and cut along the two 45-inch edges, to make sure that you have a perfectly straight edge along the top and bottom ; the selvedges will form the sides of the pockets. Measure 17 inches up from the bottom, and fold over, to get the pocket, as you can see if you look at the diagram ; then divide this folded edge into three, by ruling lines down, 12 inches apart. Trace the designs on to these three divisions, arranging Mr. Binks and Co. as you think best ; one pocket will have, perhaps, two children and a tree, another Mr. Binks and his house, and so on.

Outline the figures with four strands of " Sylko Mouliné," in the following shades : Mr. Binks's hat, his shoes, and buttons in black, No. 808 ; his hat-band in red, No. 796 ; his coat in blue, No. 883 ; and his trousers in green, No. 889. His face and hands and feet are worked with two strands of flesh, No. 878. His hair is brown, No. 779. Use back-stitch for the outlining, with satin-stitches for the hat-band and shoes. Mrs. Binks has a yellow hat, No. 758, with a gay red flower ; her hair

As you will see by these diagrams, the stitches are quite easy to work and the little figures very simple to trace

is brown, her blouse green, her skirt blue, and her apron red! Miss or Master Binks has a black satin-stitch cap with a red pom-pom on top, a green dress with red buttons, a blue collar and socks, and black shoes.

The house-roof is red, the sides and bottom line are black, the windows blue, and the door red. The green tree has a brown trunk, and the little flowers which are dotted about round the figures' feet are worked in gay mixed shades, with bright green leaves. The petals are lazy-daisies, and so are the leaves, while the stems are worked with stem-stitch.

Draw each child's name along the lower edge of each pocket, and outline with stem-stitching, as shown in diagram. Press embroidery under a wet cloth with a very hot iron.

To make up the pockets, bind the top edge with green wool tape, and machine down the pencil lines between each pocket. Bind the sides, and make a deep hem along the top, through which you must push a cane, 36 inches long. A bone ring fastened to each end of this will enable you to hang up the pocket, as the rings will fit over ordinary brass dresser-hooks screwed into the nursery wall, 35 inches apart.

11" 17" 12" 12" 12" FOLD 36"

The diagram showing pocket measurements

A "Woolly" For Baby.

This adorable little matinee coatee would be an enchanting wee garment to give to Baby to keep her cosy and warm. It is crocheted in a most attractive wavy design, which is very simple to do.

Materials required.
Two ounces Beehive Shetland; Crochet Hooks No. 13 and 7.

* * *

STARTING at neck with 75 ch., miss 3, then * 1 tr., 3 tr. in 1, 1 tr., miss 1. Repeat from *, end with 2 tr., 18 scallops.

2nd row: 3 ch. to turn, * miss 2, 1 tr., 5 tr. in 1 tr. Repeat from * end 2 tr.

Repeat these 2 rows, working 3 tr. in 1 and 5 tr. in 1 in the next until 13 rows are finished.

14th row: Work 3 scallops, 7 tr., 5 tr. in 1, miss 2, then miss 4 scallops, putting hook into work ready for the next scallop, this makes arm-hole; work 4 scallops across the back, then miss 4 more scallops for other armhole, and work the 3 scallops left. Turn. Work the 10 scallops until 19 rows are done; last row should be 10 tr., 3 in 1, 10 tr., turn.

With large hook along bottom, 3 ch., turn, miss 3, then * 4 L. tr., miss 3, 1 tr., miss 3 again. Repeat from * at end of row, turn. 3 ch. * 4 tr. in centre of four and 1 tr. under 1 of last row. Repeat from *.

Work *3rd row* the same as last, and fasten off.

1 tr. in every stitch along neck, turn 3 ch., 1 double in every 3rd st.

Work along neck in first hole, * 4 tr., then 1 tr. in next, 4 tr. in next. Repeat from *.

At side miss 1 hole, then work as before 1 row along bottom and up other side.

Sleeves: 2 rows of the tr. and join round.

3 rounds * 4 tr., miss 3, 1 tr., miss 3. Repeat from * until 12 patterns. Then 2 rows more as before.

Thread a ribbon through each 2 tr. at the neck, tie in a pretty bow in front.

1932

BABY'S OWN DRESSING-TABLE

A Hint from Holland, by an Anglo-Dutch Mother.

Here is the actual dressing-table as used in Holland: any handy British husband should be able to contrive one out of a cheap second-hand chest of drawers.

EVERY self-respecting Dutch baby has a dressing-table of his own, that solves the problem of where to put baby while he is being washed and dressed, and leaves mummy with both hands free.

As the illustration shows, it is really a small chest of drawers, about thirty-two inches high. The top is flat and railed off on three sides. On this flat top lies a mattress made to fit, and covered with a gaily-patterned bath towel.

This is an ideal place to put baby while you are attending to his wants; it is most comfortable for him—and for you. It is just the right height for the average mother, so that there need be no stooping or stretching.

The dressing-table has plenty of other uses. It has a little cupboard for toilet accessories and four drawers, two large ones and two small, where the greater part of the layette may be stored conveniently at hand.

The dressing-table has a towel-rail on one side and a pull-out shelf on the other. This shelf is particularly useful for putting bottles and basins on while baby is being washed, and it should be covered with oil-cloth.

The table continues to be of use when baby is older. It is always tiring to dress a small child, as it involves much stooping, and cannot always be done satisfactorily while sitting down. When, however, the child is lifted on to the table the task becomes easy.

It should not be difficult for a handy husband to contrive something on these lines from a solid and not too high chest of drawers, such as can be picked up quite cheaply at a second-hand furniture shop. One that is a little too high could be lowered by taking off the feet. It would be a boon to a busy young mother.

THE END

A Fleet of Wooden Battleships

Nothing Could Be More Simple To Build.

The lower deck and masts are bright red and the rest blue.

These realistic-looking ships painted in red and blue with blue and white funnels are the easiest things to make and cost practically nothing. They float beautifully or will stand on the floor.

Materials Required:

A few pieces of wood, about ⅜-inch thick; a white enamelled 1d. curtain rod for the funnels; a pennyworth of gold gimp pins; some yellow sewing silk; blue and red paint; paper for the flags and some thin sticks for the masts.

Cut out the boats in three sizes, the largest 7½ by 2½ inches, the second 6½ by 2⅛ inches, and the third 5½ by 1¾ inches.

Shape them at the ends as in the photograph.

Next cut three oblong pieces to take the funnels and masts, 3¾ by 1¼ inches, 2¾ by 1⅛ inches, and 2½ by 1 inch respectively.

Cut the funnels, 1½ inches long for the bigger boats and 1¼ for the smallest. Nail these on the top deck, three for the biggest boat, two for the middle size, and one for the small one. Then nail the top decks to the lower ones with a couple of gimp pins at each end. Make holes for the masts at each end of the upper deck and glue them in. Paint the lower decks bright red, the top ones blue. The edges of the boats and the bands on the funnels and the tops of the funnels should also be blue.

The next day, when the paint is dry, put in the gimp pins, all round the edge of the lower deck—eight to each ship.

Paint a wee flag and gum it to one of the masts on each boat.

Then wind the yellow silk round the pins and up to the top of the masts from each end and across from one to the other.

The fleet is then ready to set sail for foreign parts!

Neapolitan Blancmange has three colours and flavours. They are poured alternately into the mould to set.

NEAPOLITAN BLANCMANGE

A Delicious Sweet Served in a New Way which Will Prove a Sure Favourite

DELICIOUS, creamy blancmanges are very simple to prepare, provided just a little extra care is taken. The chief faults which lead to failure are making the sweet too stiff in consistency, insufficient flavouring, lumpy, insufficient boiling.

Neapolitan Blancmange

INGREDIENTS:

FOR THE WHITE:

¾ pint milk, barely 1 oz. cornflour, 1½ dessertspoonfuls sugar, ½ oz. butter, few drops of pineapple or orange essence.

FOR THE PINK:

¾ pint milk, barely 1 oz. cornflour, 1½ dessertspoonfuls sugar, ½ oz. butter, few drops of rose essence, cochineal.

FOR THE CHOCOLATE:

¾ pint milk, barely 1 oz. cornflour, 2 ozs. cup chocolate, ½ oz. butter, vanilla flavouring, sugar if required.

PUT the three quantities of cornflour into three separate basins. Mix them to a smooth paste with half a gill of milk taken from each three-quarters of a pint of milk. Then pour the remainder of the milk into three separate saucepans, adding the sugar to the pink and the white mixtures, and the chocolate to the third.

Heat the three pans of milk, then pour them, one at a time, on to the mixed cornflour. Return the separate quantities of mixed cornflour to the pans and bring them to the boil, keeping them stirred.

It is better to add hot, but not boiling, milk to the prepared cornflour, as it is less likely to form lumps, but when once the hot liquid has been added to the cornflour, it must be returned *at once* to the pan and *stirred until it boils.*

Let the pans of cornflour boil gently for ten minutes and add a lump of butter to each pan and stir them alternately.

Flavour one of the white portions of cornflour with orange or pineapple essence, remembering that only a few drops are necessary. Flavour the other white mixture with a few drops of rose essence, and colour it pink with cochineal. Add some vanilla essence to the chocolate mixture, and some sugar if required.

Take a quart mould and rinse it with cold water. Then pour in the three mixtures, adding them alternately.

Let the Neapolitan Blancmange set then turn it on to a glass dish.

AND HERE IS CONTRARY MARY—

A Charming Little Lady to Delight the Heart of Any Small Miss Who Finds Her Tucked in the Top of Her Christmas Stocking

The doll is 15 *inches high—she is dressed in crisp printed cotton.*

MARY, Mary, Quite Contrary is made of scraps of material, stuffed with bran or rags. The Transfer, No. 630, includes the shapes of the body and the clothes, with the exception of the skirt, petticoat, bodice and apron, which are straight strips.

The body and legs are of white cotton, and arms and head of pale pink.

Printed gingham, with an inch-wide pink frill at neck and hem makes the dress, and the petticoat and "pantalettes" are of white zephyr edged with narrow lace.

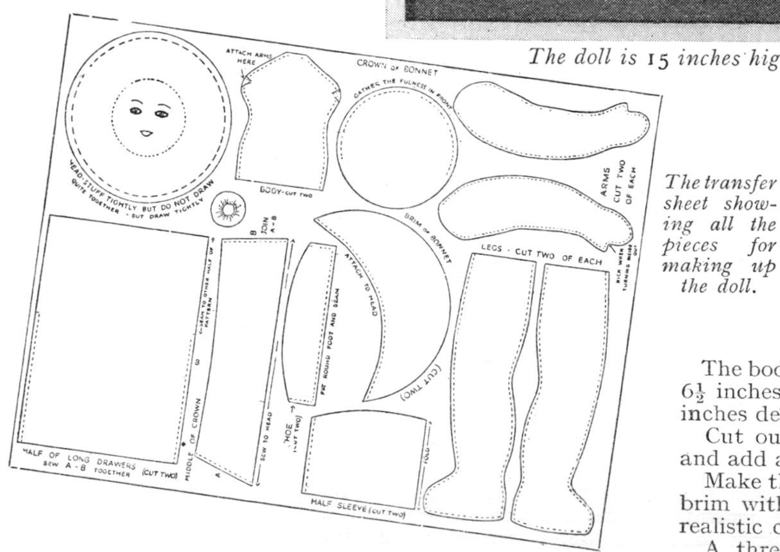

The transfer sheet showing all the pieces for making up the doll.

The shoes are black velvet, and the mittens scraps of black lace.

Iron off the transfer of the body and legs on to white cotton, and head and arms on to pink. Machine the pieces together, leaving openings for the stuffing. Stuff them well and sew the limbs and head to the body. Paint the face, using the brush as dry as possible.

The petticoat is a strip of material 20 inches wide by 7½ inches deep, and the skirt is a strip 27 inches wide by 7½ inches deep.

The bodice is a strip of material, doubled, 1¼ inches wide by 6½ inches long. The muslin apron is 4 inches wide by 5½ inches deep edged with narrow lace.

Cut out the shoes in black velvet, sew them on the feet and add anklets of black thread.

Make the bonnet of pink sateen, and stiffen the crown and brim with buckram. Black rug wool combed out makes realistic curls.

A three-inch circle of raffia worked in double crochet edged with blue raffia is doubled in half and filled with a few artificial flowers to make the flower basket.

A safe place for Baby

Play-time "when we are very young" can be a perfect delight when Mother gives Baby such a cosy, safe "Play-house" in which to spend his waking hours

The Happy Kick Box

By Mary Cranfield

A FREE kick constitutes Baby's idea of perfect happiness, besides being one of the things he needs for perfect health. The question is where to put him so that freedom and safety are combined. Unless his age is still being counted in weeks, he can't be trusted to find out how not to roll perilously near the edge of a sofa or big chair, and the floor is a draughty place, even on a cushion.

For his indoor play-time, however short it is, he wants something to lie in that can be moved anywhere, that is big enough to give room for a really satisfactory kick, and where he will be protected from draughts, and be perfectly safe if left alone for a few minutes.

"A babe in a house is a well-spring of pleasure."

Martin F. Tupper

Here is one solution of the problem: Go and look amongst the family trunks and boxes, and see if there is not an old cabin trunk that could not fairly be asked to stand another journey. Take off the lid and remove the locks and hinges, and see that no nails or splinters are left. A little roughness won't matter, as it will be safely covered in decorating the box.

Buy some coarse, cheap crash, costing about sixpence or tenpence a yard according to the width, and cut lengths of this to cover the panels between the wooden bands. On each of these embroider a large, simple design in bright-coloured Viyella wools. Flowers were chosen for the box illustrated, but animals or figures could be used equally well.

The ends are covered in one piece with a hole cut to leave the leather handle exposed, the edges of the holes being turned in and worked round in close blanket stitch in one of the colours used for the embroidery.

When all is ready for covering the box, get some drawing-pins with flat prettily-coloured heads, and a few slightly longer brass-headed tacks for critical corners, and set to work. Before putting on the panels, take a strip to bind over the edge and pin down inside. This will cover the gap left between the crash panels by the width of the wooden bands.

In the illustration a bit of golden-brown linen was used which carries on the line of the yellow wood. Then the embroidered crash is stretched tightly over the panels and down inside the box, the end pieces are fitted on in the same way, a piece of crash is pinned over the bottom of the box, covering all ends and raw edges, and the "happy kick box" is ready for its occupant.

Such a box adds enormously to Baby's pleasure as well as to the peace of mind of everyone concerned.

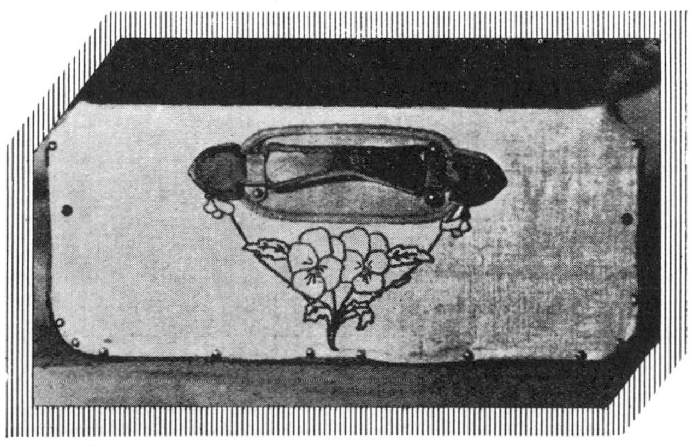

If a suitable design is chosen, the serviceable old leather handles can form part of the scheme of decoration

a delightful party frock

The far photograph shows you how the dress fastens up the back with little buttons and a pompom tie. Diagram of motifs is on page 100. A paper pattern of the shape (Fig. No. 518) can be had price 4d., overseas 7d.

THIS frock is made of motifs in Irish crochet effect, with bands of treble crochet round the waist and connecting armholes to sleeves. A narrow edging to match is worked all round neck and the edges of the back opening, also along lower edge of skirt and sleeves.

Work at an average tension, neither tight nor too loose, and the frock should suit children of 4–5 years. The paper pattern made for this frock shows the approximate size the motifs should be, and gives the approximate shape the skirt, yoke and sleeve should be when all the motifs are made and connected for each part.

MATERIALS REQUIRED: 7 oz. Copley's 2-ply " Excelsior " Shetland Floss in white; one steel hook, size 3.

ABBREVIATIONS: Ch., chain; s.s., slip-stitch; d.c., double crochet; tr., treble; p., picots. (Note: To make a picot, work 4 ch. and slip-stitch back into same ch. from where you started.)

THE MOTIFS

BEGIN at the lower edge of skirt by making a row of 22 motifs.

1ST MOTIF: Make 6 ch., and join into a ring with a s.s.

1st round: * Work 3 ch., 1 d.c. into the ring; repeat from * 6 times more; 3 ch., and join to first d.c. with a s.s.

2nd round: * 1 d.c. and 3 tr. and 1 d.c., all into the first space of preceding round; repeat from * into every space all round, then s.s. to first d.c. of the round.

3rd round: S.s. along to centre of first petal, 1 d.c. into same place; * 9 ch., 1 d.c. on centre tr. of next petal; repeat from * 6 times, 9 ch., s.s. to first d.c. of the round.

4th round: S.s. along to 5th ch. of next loop, 2 p. into same ch.; * 9 ch., s.s. into centre ch. of next loop, 2 p. into same ch.; repeat from * 6 times, 9 ch., and join to beginning of round with a s.s.; fasten off.

2ND MOTIF. Work first three rounds as for first motif. *4th round:* S.s. along to centre ch. of next loop; * 9. ch., s.s. into centre ch. of next loop, 2 p. into same ch. Repeat from * 5 times; ** 4 ch., s.s. to centre ch. of facing loop on previous motif; 4 ch., s.s. into centre ch. of next loop on unfinished motif, 2 p. into same ch. Repeat from ** once; s.s. to centre of 2 p. just made; 9 ch., and join to corresponding 2 p. on previous motif. (See broken line on the right of the * in Diagram 1 on page 100.)

Make the next and each succeeding motif of this row in the same way until you have completed the 22nd.

2ND ROW OF MOTIFS. 1ST MOTIF: Make the first 3 rounds as for the other motifs. *4th round:* S.s. along to centre chain of next loop, * 4 ch., s.s. into centre ch. of facing loop on motif of row below; 4 ch., s.s. into centre ch. of next loop on unfinished motif, 2 p. into same ch.; repeat from * once; ** 9 ch., s.s. into centre ch. of next loop on unfinished motif, 2 p. into same ch. Repeat from ** 5 times, and fasten off.

2ND MOTIF. Work first 3 rounds as for the other motifs. *4th round:* S.s. along to centre ch. of next loop; * 4 ch., s.s. to centre ch. of facing loop on previous motif; 4 ch., s.s. into centre ch. of next loop on unfinished motif, 2 p. into same ch. Repeat from * once (Diag. 2, page 100); ** 9. ch., s.s. to centre ch. of next loop on unfinished motif, 2 p. into same ch.; repeat from ** 3 times; *** 4 ch., s.s. to centre ch. of corresponding loop on motif below, 4 ch., s.s. to centre ch. of next loop on unfinished motif, 2 p. into same ch. Repeat from *** once. Now s.s. to centre of the 2 p. just made; 4 ch., s.s to centre of the 9 ch. connecting 1st and 2nd motifs in row below; 4 ch., and s.s. to the picots in previous motif in row above. See broken V-line below * in Diagram 2 on page 100.

Make the next and each succeeding motif of this row like the second, until 22 are worked. Then fasten wool to picots of one motif at top and make a length of 9 ch. to connect to next motif as shown by broken line on the right of *, Diagram 1, on page 100, doing this all along the gaps at top.

Work 5 more rows like the second. Join the skirt to form a circle by sewing the side loops of one edge at back to the side loops of the other edge, and then fill the gaps with short lengths of chain to match the rest of skirt.

Make the motifs for yoke as follows: Begin at lower edge of front by making one row of 6 motifs. On this work 2 more rows each of 6 motifs.

4th row: Work first 2 motifs, then work a third, but do not join the two lower loops of this one to the row below; instead, repeat the outside loops of 9 ch. and 2 p. for 5 times, instead of 3.

The next motif for third row work entirely separate and complete just as for first motif of first row, then work the two remaining motifs to complete the row, joining each of these to the preceding motif and to the row below. Do not work the connecting loop of 9 ch. along top of third row between 3rd and 4th motifs.

Now on top of each half row work another half row of 3 motifs. Do not work the connecting loops of 9 ch. along top of last row, between one motif and another.

For each sleeve begin by working 1 row of 6 motifs for lower edge. Above this work 1 row of 4 motifs for top edge, starting over

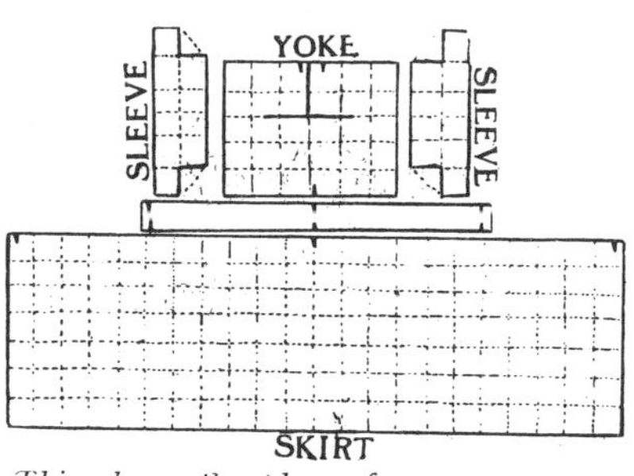

This shows the plan of the child's crochet frock

INSTRUCTIONS FOR MAKING

Very dainty and adorable is this little crochet frock for you to copy. It has a Medici air that is altogether charming!

Continued from page 53

2nd motif of 1st row, so that 1st row has 1 motif extending each end. Do not work connecting loops along top of 2nd row.

Now fasten wool to lower of the two side loops on 4th motif in top row; work 9 ch. and s.s. into centre of upper right side loop in 6th motif of lower row, then s.s. back to centre of this 9 ch., do 4 ch., and join to middle of connecting loop between 5th and 6th motifs in lower row. Repeat this process on the other end of the sleeve, so helping to make the beginning and termination of 4th row less abrupt.

That completes the motifs. Pin out work and press on wrong side over a damp cloth.

The Edgings

Now, starting at lower edge of right back edge of yoke, work a row of d.c. and ch. all up this back, round the neck opening and down the other side of back.

To begin, make a d.c. into centre ch. of the lower side-loop in bottom row of motifs, 4 ch., 1 d.c. into 1st p on side of same motif, 1 ch., 1 d.c into next p., 4 ch,. 1 d.c. into centre of next loop on lower motif, 4 ch., 1 d.c. into each of the next 2 p., with 1 ch. between; 4 ch., 1 tr. into the join between lower and upper motifs, 4 ch., 1 d.c. into each of next 2 p. on upper motif, with 1 ch. between, 4 ch., 1 d.c. into centre of next loop on upper motif, 4 ch., 1 d.c. into each of the middle side p. on upper motif, with 1 ch. between; 4 ch., 1 d.c. into next loop, 3 ch. This brings you to the top of back and you should work the ch. at such a tension that the back edge now measures about 4½ inches. Continue in the same way all along neck and down the other edge of back, always making a tr. where one motif is connected to the other. At end of row make 3 ch. to turn.

2nd row: Work a row of treble all along the left back, the neck and right back edge, but along the neck occasionally space the tr. slightly apart in order to shape the neck slightly. Make 3 ch. to turn.

3rd row: 2 ch., 1 tr. into edge between 2nd and 3rd tr., 2 ch., 1 tr. into edge between 4th and 5th tr., 2 ch., 1 tr. into edge between 6th and 7th tr., 2 ch., 1 tr. into edge between 8th and 9th tr., and continue in this way all along till you reach the top of the left back edge, and down this omit the ch. and set your trebles closely together, to leave no holes, as here the buttons are to be sewn on. Make 3 ch. to turn.

4th row: Work a row of treble up to top of left back, then along neck and down right back work 2 tr. into every hole; fasten off. That completes the neck and back edgings.

Now work a row of d.c. and ch. along each side or armhole edge of yoke, to match right back edge. Start with a d.c. into centre of lower side loop on lowest row of motifs in front, and finish at a corresponding position at the lowest row on back, remembering to do a treble into every join between one row and the next. Work at such a tension that the row, when finished, measures about 10½ inches. On it work 2nd, 3rd and 4th rows as for yoke, just as it comes down right back edge.

Now work a row of d.c. and ch. along one seam edge of sleeve, along the top edge and down the other seam edge. Begin with a d.c. into lowest of the three sets of side picots on end motif. The top of the seam will be the upper side loop on the same motif. In working along the top edge of sleeve, always pick up the two upper *side* picots, as well as the centre top picots of each motif, and only work 2 or 3 ch. into each space. Work at such a tension that sleeve edge measures about 1 inch more than the armhole edge of yoke. Sew up the seam of the sleeve. Along lower edge of sleeve work a round of d.c. and ch., picking up each loop and the lower *side* picots on each motif, as well as the centre ones, and this time omit the 1 ch. over each 2 picots, and only work about 2 ch. in each space. Work at such a tension that the sleeve edge measures about 7 inches. Join end of round to first st. with a s.s., then work rounds of tr. like the rows for right back edge of yoke, omitting the 3 ch. to turn.

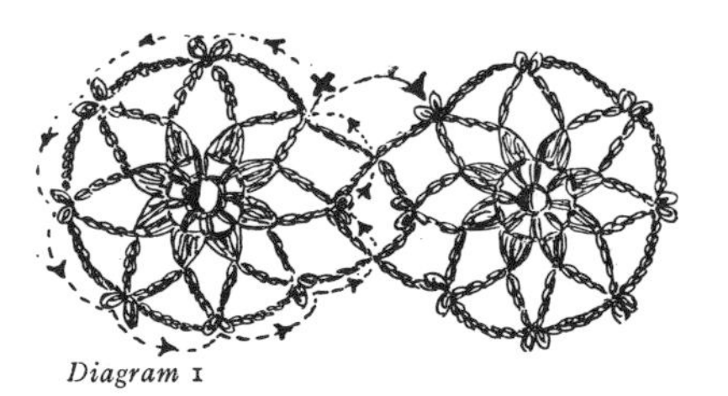
Diagram 1

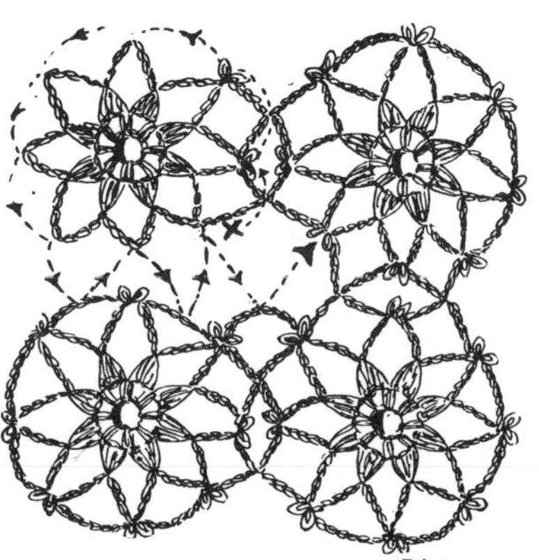
Diagram 2

Sew sleeves to edge of armhole bands on yoke, allowing ½ inch of sleeve to remain detached below bottom of front part of band, and ½ inch below bottom of back, so that the ends of the armhole border do not meet by about 1 inch. This detached part of sleeve is joined to the waistband.

For waistband, work a row of d.c. and ch. along lower edge of yoke. Begin with a d.c. into extreme edge of left back, work d.c.'s right along bottom of back edging, then continue with ch. and d.c. Catch in the lower *side* picots, as well as the centre ones on lower edge, and across the back make fewer ch. into the spaces than across front, so that you add depth to the back, as it were, by drawing the pattern closer together, and so elongate it. This helps to bring the neck opening in the right position instead of too far over towards back. The row of ch. and d.c. across the "lace" part of each back should actually measure about 4½ inches and across the front 11 inches. Remember to do a treble into each join of one motif to the next, and when you reach the commencement of the armhole edging on left side of back, work * 1 tr., 2 ch., and repeat from * all across the base of edging, the detached piece of sleeve and the base of the edging at side of front. After working across front, work in treble and ch. across other side to match left side, and then work across right back as for left back. On this row of d.c. and ch. work 2nd and 3rd rows of crochet as for right back edge of yoke, then join last st. of 3rd row to first st. with a s.s. and repeat 2nd and 3rd rows 3 times more, only this time they will be "rounds," so you omit the 3 ch. to turn; then repeat 2nd row once more, and fasten off. Every time you work the plain rows of treble increase 1 st. occasionally, to give a very slight spread to lower edge, according to taste.

Work an edging of crochet along lower edge of skirt just as down right back edge of yoke, but again you work in "rounds."

Now sew top of the skirt to lower edge of the waistband, catching up each loop and each picot, and setting them closely together, so as to give a gathered-in effect and making the skirt fit the waistband. You can distribute the fullness quite evenly if you mark the skirt into halves and quarters with pins, and also mark the halves and quarters of band with pins, and then set pin to pin.

Fasten back edges of yoke with tiny buttons which will slip through the holes on right back edge, then make a length of chain to tie the neck. Thread through the holes and then finish each end with a wool bobble or pom-pon.

OUT OF THE MOUTHS OF BABES

Half-a-crown has been awarded for each of the following.

TOO GOOD TO BE MISSED

On entering a shop with her mother, a little girl heard an assistant say :

" Pay what you like and have what you like, madam."

The child glanced up quickly.

" Pay a penny, mummy, and get a ham ! " she whispered urgently.

Sent in by M. Dawber, Lilywood, Appley Bridge, Nr. Wigan.

POOR BIRDS

Auntie took little Mary for a walk, and they came upon a notice-board which read : *"Bird nesting strictly prohibited."*

Mary sighed.

"It's a pity the poor little birds can't build where they like," she remarked.

Sent in by Mrs. A. Smith, 87, North Road, Bourne, Lincs.

NOT JUST YET!

Wee Rosemary was having a little party for her third birthday.

" Three years old ! My word, you're getting very old ! " exclaimed one visitor, on arrival.

Rosemary looked wistful, and, edging nearer her mother, whispered anxiously :

" I'm old, but I'm not shabby, am I ? "

Sent in by Mrs. Watson, Carrigheg, Kilmacanogue, Bray, Co. Wicklow.

A GOOD GUESS!

The teacher gave a lesson on money-values to a class of five-year-olds, and, later, tested their memories.

" And what is a florin, John ? " she asked.

John thought for a moment.

" I know—a flower shop," he answered brightly, at last.

Sent in by Mrs. Bennett, Foxhangers, Devizes, Wilts.

SHE KNEW

Before he went off to work daddy always had a word of warning for little three-year-old Betty.

One morning he called her as usual.

" Yes, daddy ? " Betty answered.

" You must be a good girl while I'm away," he said.

Betty looked up expectantly.

" And don't what ? " she asked mischievously.

Sent in by Mrs. Parkes, 109, Constitution Street, Cape Town, South Africa.

GRANNY MISUNDERSTOOD

While he was away on holiday, sonny's granny sent him a postcard, on which she wrote :

" *My word, you will be a little brownie when you return !* "

Sonnie looked up at his mother.

" Granny's got it wrong," he said ; " she means I will be a scout ! "

Sent in by Mrs. Stephenson, 2, Ormskirk Avenue, Withington, Manchester.

A 'FLYING FISH' GLIDER

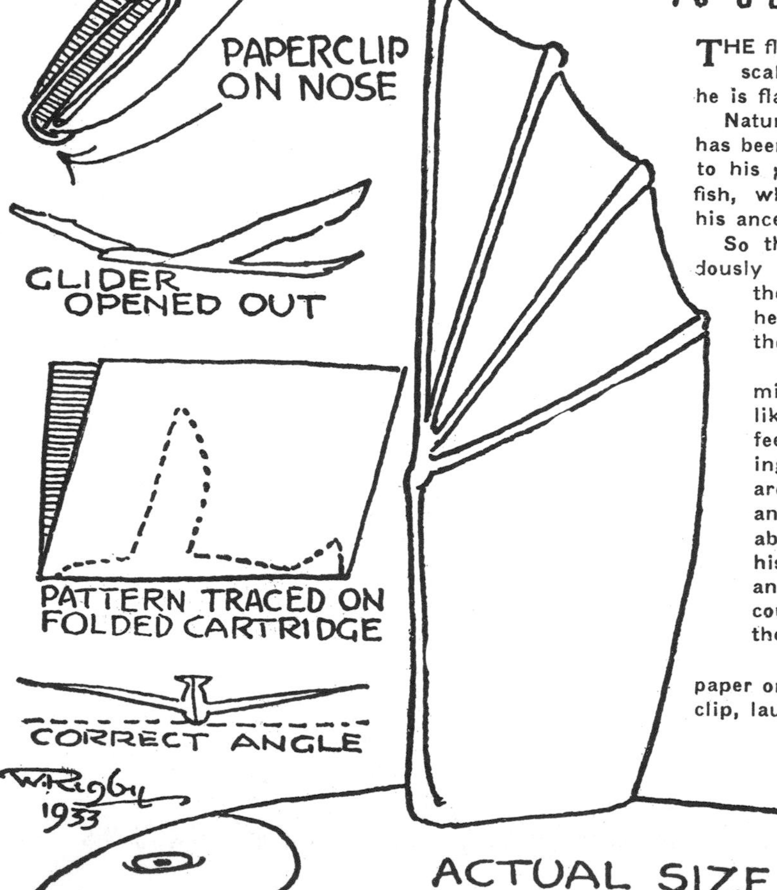

The flying-fish is very like a large mackerel, with a glinting scaly coat which shines all colours of the rainbow when he is flashing over the surface of the Mediterranean Sea.

Nature never intended him to fly ! What has happened has been a gradual enlargement of his main front fins, owing to his perpetual race from death, by being eaten by larger fish, which has been going on for many generations of his ancestry.

So the flying-fish, from first of all becoming a tremendously rapid swimmer, gradually increased his speed and the size of his fins to such an extent that one day he found he had swum so fast that he completely left the water !

So to-day, when being pursued (which is nearly every minute of his life, poor fellow), he leaves the water like a silver flash and rises generally to about eight feet, where he maintains a steady, level course, seeming to glide very fast, but in reality his wings, or fins, are working at about two thousand flaps to the minute, and actually he sounds like clockwork, as he whirrs over about a hundred yards of surface. The tragedy is that his pursuers have also begun to " get wise " to him and simply flash along in the water, under his aerial course, and are ready to attack him when he drops in, thoroughly exhausted.

Trace this glider on to a folded sheet of thick notepaper or thin cartridge, open out and add a large paperclip, launch not too briskly, and a fine glide will result.

PRETEND
I wore my Auntie's summer hat,
With cherries on it and a rose,
And put on Mummy's petticoat—
I looked so fine in grown-up clothes.
I walked downstairs, and didn't smile,
And Gran'ma said I was a minx;
And Daddy grunted, "Run away,
I'm tryin' to get my forty winks."
Our Dickie yelled out, "What a fright!"
He's nine years old and such a tease,
And *he* had jam all down his shirt,
And hadn't washed his face nor knees.
But Mummy said "It can't be *you*,
Oh, Mrs. Top-Lofty, pray how-do-you-do?"
Lucy Betty McRaye
L·R·STEELE·

SAFETY FOR YOUR

One of the Six Rules for Safety in the Street is—" Never chase your hoop, ball or playmate into the roadway." So many children do it, thoughtlessly, and it is very dangerous.

"ACCIDENTS *will* happen," the old saying goes, and it is truer than ever in these dangerous days. No mother can help feeling a little anxious when her children are out in the busy streets, with so much traffic about, yet it is impossible to keep them away from the risks, especially when they are old enough to go to school, or to run errands for mummy.

The only thing is to teach the little ones to be careful in traffic, warn them against the thoughtless, impulsive actions that are dangerous, and tell them of the proper precautions to take when they have to cross the road. Most street accidents are caused by people—either drivers or walkers—being careless or in too great a hurry.

Six excellent Rules for Safety in the Street are given in a little illustrated booklet, specially written for children, which is issued by the National Safety First Association—an organisation whose object is to reduce the number of accidents in the streets, and elsewhere.

Here are the six rules :

(1) Always use the footpath if you can, and cross the road at a refuge, if there is one.

(2) Always look *both* ways before you cross a road, or before you pass in front of or behind a standing vehicle. Never run across without looking.

(3) Never steal rides on vehicles.

(4) Never play dangerous games in the streets ; never throw things at moving vehicles.

(5) Never chase your hoop, ball or playmate into the roadway.

(6) Always play in a playground, park or open space *if you can*, but *never* play in a busy street.

And here are a few other useful hints mentioned in another leaflet :

Always face traffic when stepping off the pavement.

Always look out for motors turning corners.

Always look and listen for warning signals.

Always wait till the bus or tram stops before getting off.

Never throw each other's caps, or push each other, into the roadway.

Never ride on the step of another's bicycle.

Never ride a bicycle that is too high for you.

Very simple rules, but very sensible ones, and if all of us, children and grown-ups alike, learnt them and always carried them out, there would be far fewer accidents in the street, wouldn't there ?

Of course, many accidents are caused by careless or bad driving, and in these cases people on foot are not to blame, but it isn't *always* the motorist's fault when people get run over, and the more careful walkers learn to be, the better.

These are all things that we mothers can tell our children, and impress upon them ; and in addition, much is being done to teach the same rules in schools and elsewhere. In many towns a police inspector, or perhaps the chief constable, visits schools and gives the children simple lectures on the meaning and use of traffic signals and lights, and other " lessons " that will help the little ones to avoid running unnecessary risks in the streets.

On the right : a signal, in London, which a pedestrian herself can work to stop the traffic when she wants to cross the road.

Below : Small school children at Tanshelp, in Yorkshire, crossing a busy main road to school, all holding a rope. The traffic has to stop till they are all over, and there are no stragglers.
(*Photos : Topical.*)

CHILDREN

A police inspector explaining to a class of Bedford school children the meaning and use of traffic lights, with a constable showing the hand signals. (*Fox Photos.*)

German children being shown, by means of an ingenious model, the proper way to cross the street at cross-roads. (*World Wide Photos.*)

An article every mother, and every father, too, ought to read.

The Safety First Association also issue striking posters, which are displayed in schools and on hoardings, warning children against such dangerous actions, as riding on the backs of vehicles, chasing a ball into the road, and so on, pictures that make a real impression on the little ones' minds; it arranges "Children's Hours" at local cinemas, at which a special "Safety First" film is shown—a lesson the children seem to understand very well and thoroughly enjoy! It shows vividly the dangers of playing in the roadway, running into or across it without proper care, and all the other risky things kiddies are apt to do without realising their possible consequences. It impresses upon the children, too, that there is nothing "brave" in running foolish risks, and nothing "cowardly" in being careful.

The "Safety First" people also organise Essay Competitions, and hundreds of thousands of school-children enter for them every year. The essays are on such subjects as:

"How can people walking, drivers of vehicles, and policemen, help each other to avoid accidents in the streets?"

"How would you take care of your little brother or sister, crossing the road, getting out of a tram, playing in the street, or minding him at home when mother is out?"

And so on. In the London area alone, about three hundred and fifty prizes, ranging from five guineas to half-a-crown, are awarded for these essays every year.

To show how successful these various ways of teaching "Safety First" to children are, it is a fact that in one of our big cities, while the

[CONTINUED ON PAGE 112]

STOP! CHILDREN CROSSING

At Oxford, to help the traffic police, a kindly civilian sees parties of school children across a dangerous bit of road, holding up a sign that stops the traffic meanwhile. (*Topical Press.*)

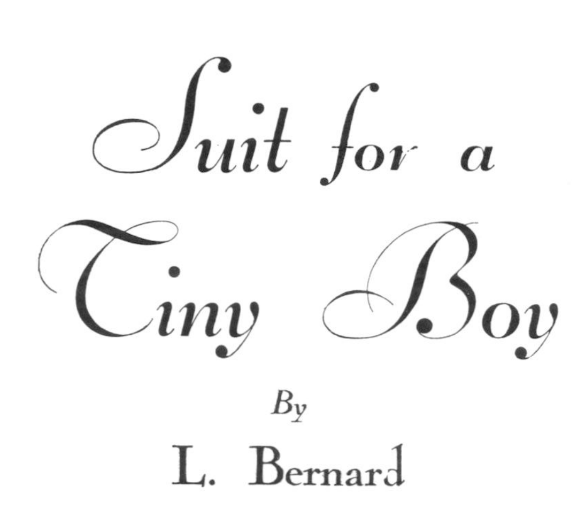

Suit for a Tiny Boy

By

L. Bernard

MATERIALS REQUIRED: 1½ yards of crash, 16 inches wide; 3¼ yards of binding in pale green; 8 large and 4 small green pearl buttons; 1 skein each of red and green embroidery wool.

SIZE: Length, when buttoned together, 19½ inches; can be either lengthened or shortened by altering the position of the buttons on the bodice. Width across the widest part of the knickers, 15 inches. Width across, at waist, 13 inches. Length of sleeve from neck, 6 inches.

Begin by cutting off a piece of crash 24 inches long for the bodice, and fold this over to make the two cut edges meet.

The fold forms the top of the shoulders. Pin the material to keep it in position, then fold across to make all selvedges meet.

Measure 7 inches from the centre fold along the top of the shoulder; mark this with a pin, and pencil a line across.

Measure downwards from this mark for a depth of 5½ inches, and measure downwards from the top of the shoulder along the selvedge edges to a depth of 4½ inches.

Now cut from the lower edges of the material straight up to the mark 5½ inches from the top of the shoulder, then curve outwards to meet the mark 4½ inches from the top of the shoulder on the selvedge edges.

This gives you the side edges and sleeves.

Measure from the sleeve edges along the top of the shoulder and mark at 5¾ inches, then cut a curve from here to the centre to a depth of 1¼ inches.

Open out the work and cut the curve 1 inch deeper on one side for the front, then cut down the centre of this to a depth of 4½ inches for the front opening.

Back-stitch the side and sleeve seams up ½ inch from the edges. Press open the folds of the material and herringbone down on each side of the seam.

Turn up ½ inch to the wrong side on the lower edge and herringbone down. Bind the neck and front opening and sleeve edges.

Sew the small buttons on one side of the front, and work buttonhole loops on the opposite side.

For the trimming work zigzag stitches about ½ inch long with ½-inch spaces between each point, in red round the sleeves.

These stitches are worked close to the binding. Quite close to these work another row of stitches in green, and follow this with another row in red.

The same trimming is worked round the neck and front opening.

The Knickers

Cut two pieces of crash, one measuring 16 inches in width and 12 inches in length and the other 16 inches in width and 11 inches in length.

Pin these two pieces together, level on one cut edge and one edge projecting an inch beyond the other. Fold over, bringing the selvedges together. Measure 6½ inches from the fold at the top—this is the uneven edge—and from this mark cut down the selvedges in a slanting line to the lower edge. This forms the side edges of the knickers.

On the lower edge at the fold cut out a small curved piece for the space between the knicker legs.

Open out the work and cut the upper edge of the large piece—which is the back—in a slanting or curved line, level with the front side edges, but keeping the full size in the centre. Back-stitch the side edges together ½ inch from the edges, then open out flat and herringbone down on each side of the seam.

Bind the lower edges of the legs, after joining the little curved edges in the same way as the side edges, and bind also the upper edge. Open the side seams a little to form buttonholes, and make buttonholes on the front and back, in the centre, and between this and the sides. There will be 8 buttonholes altogether.

Try on the little garment to decide the height for the buttons on the bodice, then sew the buttons in position, press all well with a hot iron over a damp cloth, and the dainty and useful little suit is ready.

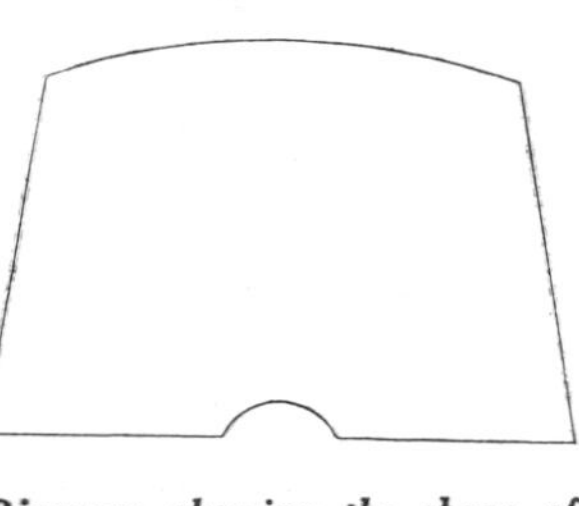

Diagram showing the shape of the knickers. Patterns of this simple Suit are NOT available

Let the Kiddies Dress Up

HOW YOUR LITTLE ONES WILL ENJOY GOING TO A PARTY WEARING ONE OF THE HOME-MADE FANCY DRESSES DESCRIBED BELOW BY MOTHER OF SMALL CHILDREN. A FEW ODDS AND ENDS WILL MAKE A MOST ATTRACTIVE OUTFIT.

This Indian outfit needs only a pyjama suit, a jacket, a gay scarf, and the whiskers.

If you have a little dark-haired maiden, a kimono, a sash and a paper sunshade will make her a JAPANESE LADY.

Perhaps the little Japanese Lady has a brother who would like to dress up as a CHINAMAN? Well, it is easily done.

ALMOST every day now my kiddies say to me, their faces alight with eagerness, "Mummy, what shall we dress up as on Christmas Day *this* year?" You see, last Christmas they had such a perfectly wonderful time doing the thing all kiddies love best of all—putting on fancy dress after their Christmas dinner.

And by fancy dress I don't mean a carefully made, complete-in-every-particular garb that costs a lot in time and money. No small boy, and few little girls, care much for this kind of fancy dress. But they simply revel in our simple, go-as-you-please plan—just dressing up and getting the best result one can with things that are in the house.

The children love this, for it's so much more than merely putting on special clothes. Quite half the fun is in thinking out what you'd like to be and then puzzling and experimenting to get the effect without spending money.

We really achieved some wonderful results last year and mean to surpass ourselves this Christmas.

We were quite a party both of grown-ups and children, for my two sisters, one with three kiddies and the other with one, live near us and they and their families all came to us for Christmas Day. So, with the three husbands and my own two kiddies, Nellie and Dick, we were a houseful, and the six children had a good audience for their dressing up.

We three sisters arranged the idea between us a few days beforehand, to give us time to think things out a little and hunt up anything we should want for the costumes. I said I would lend to the other children anything out of my kiddies' wardrobes or out of the kitchen or linen cupboard, but anything else they wanted they must bring with them. We were not barred from buying little oddments we could not supply ourselves, but it was a point of honour that not more than a few pence should be spent on any child's costume. Actually, several of them cost nothing at all.

I leave you to imagine the excitement, the giggles and the untidiness of the upstairs rooms which the dressing up caused. But oh, it was worth it! It made the kiddies so happy, it amused the grown-ups in the rather sleepy hour before tea, and it seemed to me that it gave the little ones new ideas as to what could be done without spending money.

It is quite easy to make your small boy a PIRATE for the evening. Dress his sister in a GIPSY costume, and they will make a gay pair.

This little bride will capture the hearts of many young "bridegrooms" at the party. Her costume is one of the simplest of all, too.

Dressing up has been one of their favourite amusements since, and now I keep a special "dressing up box," into which I pop all sorts of discarded odds and ends that sooner or later come in useful for some quaint costume.

Just to show you how simple and enjoyable it all is,

Continued overleaf

I'll describe the children's costumes to you. None of them cost more than a few pence yet they provided us with endless amusement.

FROM the beginning, my own small daughter, Nellie, who'd recently been bridesmaid at an auntie's wedding, set her heart on dressing up as

A BRIDE

She wore her white party frock and over it the white voile skirt of a very old summer frock of mine. It came down to her toes, as a bride's dress should. She took the white flower wreath from her last summer's hat.

Her idea for the bridal veil was one of my short cream net curtains from my bedroom. For a bouquet we thrust some artificial flowers through the centre of a paper doyley and tied them with an imposing piece of ribbon.

Dick entered into the dressing-up idea so thoroughly that nothing would do but that he must "dress up" his face, too.

For this I decided to spend sixpence on a stick of brown grease-paint, such as actors use.

This is quick and effective and easy to take off. Remember to rub cold cream lightly into the skin first and work the grease-paint over this; then, as the paint doesn't sink into the skin, it is easily removed afterwards with more cold cream and paper towels.

We decided he should be

AN INDIAN STUDENT

and with a bottle of spirit gum (borrowed from a friend) I rigged him up a short beard and fierce moustache of black darning wool. The spirit gum also came off easily with cold cream.

The rest of his costume was easy. A pair of white flannel trousers and his school blazer gave the student look, and a piece of gorgeous, wide metallic ribbon, which was really a sideboard runner, made him a colourful turban.

MY sister Meg, having three kiddies to costume, gave a good look round her house for ideas, and the gay Japanese pyjamas she wore at the seaside last summer caught her eye at once. One need not be too particular about the fit in Christmas dressing-up. So that three-piece gave her the basis of two costumes, one for Hugh and the other for Margaret.

Hugh wore his own pyjamas trousers (hers were too long and wide) and her Japanese jumper. She intended to make him a round black cap, but found a close-fitting stockinette sports affair of her own that was just right when she'd removed buckle and wrap-round pieces. She just fixed a brown mending plait to this and there was Hugh, the complete little

CHINAMAN

Meg's kimono reached very nearly to little Margaret's ankles. With a broad sash (one of Meg's scarves) it made a realistic Japanese costume, especially when Margaret carried a paper parasol that was also a seaside relic.

Little Jimmie, Meg's youngest, loves nothing better than a fight, and when mummy reads to him, it must be sea stories, if possible. He begged to be

A PIRATE

He wore his own knickers and shirt as a foundation. All self-respecting pirates seem to have worn short striped kilts, like Scotsmen, and Meg made one for her youngster from an odd yard of striped cretonne left over from curtains. It looks elaborate in the photograph, but actually it was all done with a few tackings and a hot iron.

She cut the yard into two widths and joined them with tackings, also tacking a hem round the bottom. Then she simply ironed the pleats (the stripes made it easy to keep these straight) and tacked on to a piece of tape, which was tied round the little fellow's waist. A thick leather belt of his daddy's covered the tape, and into this were stuck paper-knives and kitchen knives, to look like cutlasses.

A striped scarf, gay red and white, was knotted round the boy's head, with loose ends hanging over one ear and almost hiding his ear-rings (large gilt curtain rings tied on with flesh-coloured cotton). The pirate's cocked hat was Meg's chief difficulty, and baffled her rather till she remembered a square of black American cloth left over from covering a table-top.

You remember the cocked hats we used to fold out of paper in our childhood days? Well, that's all it was, folded dull side outwards, with the brim shiny side outwards and secured with a safety-pin or two. Very effective.

Just in case you've forgotten how cocked hats are made, here is the way to fold one:

Take a piece of black American cloth (or stiff brown paper) almost square, measuring about 16 inches by 19 inches. Double it (shiny side in, in the case of American cloth) so that it now measures 16 inches by 9½ inches. Take the two doubled corners and fold them down diagonally till they meet in the centre about 1½ inches above the cut edges. Turn these edges outwards to form the brim of the hat. In paper it is now complete; in American cloth it will need a couple of safety-pins to hold the diagonal folds in place.

MY sister Mary has only one little girl, Mollie. A dark-haired girlie with lovely brown eyes. She looked very pretty and attractive as

A GYPSY.

The costume was very gay and very easy to make. Her mother spent threepence on a roll of scarlet crêpe paper (as the kiddie hadn't any clothes this colour), and made a skirt of it. The photograph gives a very good idea of how it looked.

Mary made the skirt in the same way as sister Meg made the pirate kilt. The width of the paper was just the right length for Mollie from waist to knee and paper needs no hemming, so there was nothing to do but pleat the paper roughly, tacking it as it was pleated to a tape which tied round the child's waist. For an impromptu dress of this sort, you don't even need to bother to sew up the back seam, but just let the two edges of the skirt overlap behind.

Mollie wore a blouse of her own with this skirt, its sleeves short or rolled up, and a green and grey striped scarf of her mother's made her a gay sash. Another large hankie covered her head and she was barefooted in true vagabond style.

If you're thinking of letting your kiddies dress up on December 25th (and you couldn't do anything they'll enjoy more), make up your mind that ingenuity, and not money, shall be brought into play. Start a dressing-up box into which you put discarded clothes and all sorts of odds and ends that may prove useful, not to mention a roll or two of crêpe paper (I find red and white the most useful colours), odd ribbons and plenty of safety-pins and string.

Show the kiddies a picture of the costume they're aiming at, and then let them think out how it can be managed. Make suggestions, of course, but let them do most of the planning and experimenting. They'll love it, and it will teach them, as nothing else could, how much can be achieved with the most everyday clothes and furnishings. You'll be surprised how clever and inventive even small children can prove.

THE END

SAFETY FIRST

[*Continued from page 109*]

number of grown-up people killed in street accidents every year has more than doubled in the last ten years, the number of children who meet with such fatal accidents yearly remains practically the same. Which suggests, doesn't it, that the little ones learn to be careful in the streets better than we grown-ups do! Perhaps, after all, we have less cause to be anxious about them than they have reason to be concerned about *us!*

Of course, it is not by any means always the children, or grown-up pedestrians, who are to blame when accidents happen, and a great deal is being done to teach motorists and drivers to do their "bit" in making the roads safe, by sensible and careful driving. Apart from the work done by the police, the "Safety First" people help.

They issue thousands of posters, intended for drivers. They produce a "Safe Driving" pamphlet, setting out the rules and courtesies of the road, which is given free with every motor-driving licence.

There is also a "Safe Driving" Competition for paid drivers. Every driver who completes a year without an accident is given a certificate; if he goes for five years running without accident he is awarded a silver medal, and if he can show a clean sheet for ten years he receives a gold medallion. This has proved a great encouragement to careful driving, and a help in making the streets safer for our children and the rest of us who go a-foot.

IN THE HOME

APART from the dangers of the streets, there is a real need for "Safety First" in the home. Actually more fatal accidents happen at home and in everyday pursuits than in traffic and industry together! These accidents include falls, burns and scalds, suffocation, poisoning, explosions, and so on, and about one-seventh of the cases are children.

There is a little booklet which gives excellent warning hints to mothers on things that are dangerous for baby, the toddler, the schoolchild, and herself—for instance, that torn or worn carpets, too-highly-polished floors, and articles left lying about, can cause nasty falls, and so can standing on rickety chairs; that clothes made of inflammable material, unguarded fires, naked lights, and the careless use of petrol and other inflammable cleaning liquids may result in bad burns; and so on. Most of these things, we all know, of course, but it is very easy to forget and be careless, isn't it?

Where our children are concerned, "Safety First" should be our motto always, wherever we may be.

1934

All Children Like Pretty Things To Eat And When These Party Goodies Appear On The Table The Faces Round It Will Be Bright And Smiling!

Try these for the SMALL GUESTS

Jelly Meringues

INGREDIENTS:

8 meringue shells.
½ pint packet cherry jelly.
Cream. Hot water.

THIS is quite a good party dish for children, and it is not too rich.

Dissolve the jelly in hot water, making it up to half a pint with the jelly. Let this set firmly, then chop it up and fill the meringue shells.

Whisk up a very small quantity of cream until it thickens, and drop a little on top of the jelly.

Chocolate Sailing Boats

INGREDIENTS:

3 level dessertspoonfuls cornflour.
2 level dessertspoonfuls cocoa.
1 level dessertspoonful custard powder.
2½ gills milk.
2 dessertspoonfuls sugar.
½ oz. butter.
Vanilla flavouring.

FOR THE SAILS:

Rice paper.
Tiny wooden skewers.

MIX the cornflour, cocoa, and custard powder together, and mix them to a smooth paste with some of the milk.

Heat the remainder of the milk with the sugar and butter, and when hot add them to the cornflour mixture. Then return the mixture to the pan and bring it to the boil, keeping it stirred.

Continue to boil it gently for a few minutes to cook the cornflour. Then take it off the heat and add vanilla flavouring to taste. Turn the cornflour into small, boat-shaped tins, which have been previously rinsed with cold water.

Leave the moulds to set. Then unmould them and place the chocolate shapes with the wide side uppermost.

Cut small triangles of rice paper for the sails. Make a slit along the top of each boat, and stick the sails in position with a small wooden skewer in the centre, between the sails.

Sufficient for five boats.

NOTE.—*The boats should be unmoulded as soon as they are set. If the chocolate mixture remains too long in the tin moulds it is apt to discolour.*

If the mixture seems too thick, it may be thinned with a little more milk.

Chocolate Sailing Boats

Marshmallow Soufflés

INGREDIENTS:

¼ lb. marshmallows.
1 gill milk.
1 egg. Water.
Few hundreds and thousands

SEPARATE the egg. Beat up the yolk, heat the milk and add it to the egg yolk. Cook them in the top of a double boiler until the custard thickens, keeping it stirred. Then turn it into a basin and leave it to get cold.

Wash the double boiler and put the marshmallows into it, add a tablespoonful of water, and stir the marshmallows over hot water until they are dissolved. Then mix them with the custard.

When this begins to set, fold in the stiffly whisked egg white and turn the mixture into soufflé cases. Sprinkle a few hundreds and thousands on the soufflés just before serving them.

Sufficient for five or six soufflés.

When Winds Do Blow!

By D. Whitley

This cosy little Outfit is for a Girl of 2 to 3 years old, and is ideal for the treacherous winds of late Autumn

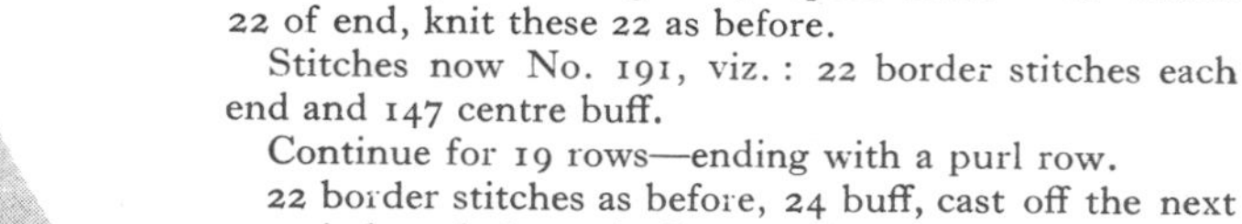

MATERIALS REQUIRED: 6 ozs. 4-ply "Golden Eagle" Merino Wool in buff, 4 ozs. in blue; 4 balls coloured embroidery wool (colours to choice); embroidery transfers (design to choice); pair No. 10 Stratnoid needles; patent fasteners and elastic.

MEASUREMENTS: Coat: Shoulder to hem 17 ins., width round under arms, fastened, 27 ins., width round hem 41 ins., length of sleeve under arm 10½ ins. (or required length). Overalls: Length from waist to instep 19 ins. (side measurement). Hat: Round head 15 ins., stretching to 18 ins. if required.

Directions for Making

COAT :—*Fronts and Back in one.* In blue cast on 240 stitches. 36 rows moss stitch, knitting first row into backs of stitches. (If coat required longer, knit extra rows of moss stitch here.)

10 moss stitch blue (for border), 220 plain in buff, 10 moss stitch blue.

10 moss stitch blue, 220 purl in buff, 10 moss stitch blue.

Repeat last 2 rows once more.

10 m.s. blue, 4 plain buff, 212 blue plain, 4 plain buff, 10 m.s. blue.

10 m.s. blue, 4 purl buff, 212 purl blue, 4 purl buff, 10 m.s. blue.

10 m.s. blue, 4 plain in buff, 2 plain in blue, 208 plain buff, 2 plain blue, 4 plain in buff, 10 m.s. blue.

10 m.s. blue, 4 purl in buff, 2 purl in blue, 208 purl in buff, 2 purl in blue, 4 purl in buff, 10 m.s. blue.

Repeat last 2 rows once more.

10 m.s. blue, 4 plain in buff, 2 plain in blue, 4 plain in buff, 200 plain in blue, 4 plain in buff, 2 plain in blue, 4 plain in buff, 10 m.s. blue.

10 m.s. blue, 4 purl in buff, 2 purl in blue, 4 purl in buff, 200 purl in blue, 4 purl in buff, 2 purl in blue, 4 purl in buff, 10 m.s. blue.

10 m.s. blue, 4 plain buff, 2 plain blue, 4 plain buff, 2 plain blue, 196 plain buff, 2 plain blue, 4 plain buff, 2 plain blue, 4 plain buff, 10 m.s. blue.

10 m.s. blue, 4 purl buff, 2 purl blue, 4 purl buff, 2 purl blue, 196 purl buff, 2 purl blue, 4 purl buff, 2 purl blue, 4 purl buff, 10 m.s. blue.

Repeat last 2 rows 13 times more.

On next row knit the first 22 stitches as before, and then decrease the 196 buff as follows :—

* Knit 2, knit 2 together, repeat from * to within 22 of end, knit these 22 as before.

Stitches now No. 191, viz.: 22 border stitches each end and 147 centre buff.

Continue for 19 rows—ending with a purl row.

22 border stitches as before, 24 buff, cast off the next 12 stitches, knit 75 buff, cast off another 12, knit 24 buff and 22 border as before. Work now divided into 2 fronts and back.

Continue on front to which wool attached, 22 border as before, 24 in buff.

24 in buff, 22 border as before. Repeat last 2 rows 16 times.

At border end cast off 12, knit remainder as before and back again.

At border end cast off 4, knit remainder as before and back again.

At border end cast off 2, knit remainder as before and back again.

At border end cast off 2, knit remainder as before and back again.

24 buff remain. Knit 2 rows (ending neck end of work).

Knit 16, reverse knitting and knit back the same 16.

Knit 8, reverse knitting and knit back the same 8. Cast off.

Knit other front to correspond.

BACK: Join in buff wool and knit in stocking stitch for 34 rows. 6 rows s.s., casting off 8 stitches at beginning of each row. Cast off remainder tightly.

SLEEVE: In blue cast on 45 stitches, 20 rows moss stitch, knitting first row into backs of stitches.

Change to buff and on plain row increase by knitting twice into every 5th stitch. No. of stitches now 54.

Change to blue, 2 rows s.s. Change to buff, 4 rows s.s. Change to blue, 2 rows s.s.

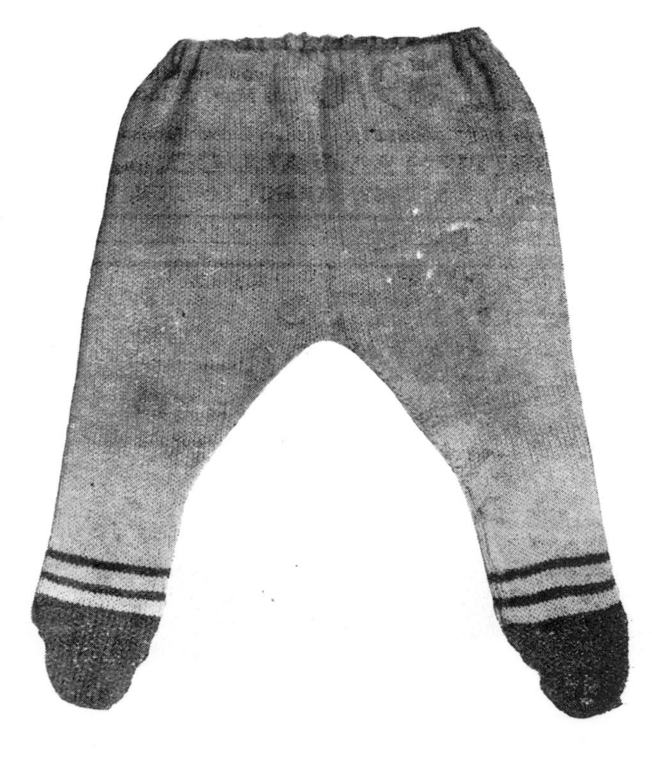

52 rows s.s. buff, making an extra stitch each end of 5th, 11th, 17th, 23rd, 29th, 35th, 41st and 47th rows. (Knit extra rows here if sleeve required longer.) 16 rows s.s., casting off 4 stitches at beginning of each row. Cast off remainder.

COLLAR: In blue cast on 85 stitches, 26 rows moss stitch, knitting first row into backs of stitches. Cast off.

HAT: Cast on 90 stitches in blue and knit in m.s. for 38 rows, knitting first row into backs of stitches.

Change to buff and on plain row knit as follows:—Knit 9, making an extra stitch in the 9th stitch, repeat to end of row. Stitches now 100.

Purl 1 row, plain 1 row, purl 1 row.

2 rows s.s. blue. 4 rows s.s. buff. 2 rows s.s. blue. 4 rows s.s. buff. On next row in plain decrease as follows:—

* Knit 2 together, knit 21, knit 2 together, repeat from * to end of row.

* Knit 2 together, purl 19, knit 2 together, repeat from * to end of row.

Continue in this manner until 12 stitches remain. Knit 2 together 6 times. Cast off.

THE OVERALLS: In buff cast on 90 stitches, 14 rows s.s., ending purl row. On next row plain knit up loops of cast-on stitches to form hem.

Now on purl row, purl to within 20 of end, reverse knitting and plain back.

Purl to within 30 of end, reverse knitting and plain back.

Purl to within 40 of end, reverse knitting and plain back.

Purl to within 50 of end, reverse knitting and plain back.

Purl to within 60 of end, reverse knitting and plain back.

Purl complete row and continue in s.s. for 62 rows.

2 rows, s.s. casting off 2 stitches at beginning of each row.

Knit in s.s., casting off 1 stitch at beginning of each row until 50 stitches remain. Continue without decrease for a further 24 rows. 2 rows s.s. blue, 4 rows s.s. buff, 2 rows s.s. blue, 4 rows s.s. buff. Change to blue, 1 row plain. Knit 1 in. in m.s., ending on front or shorter side. Cast off 3 m.s., knit remainder of row. Cast off 24 m.s., knit remainder.

6 rows m.s., knitting 2 together at beginning of each row.

6 rows m.s. without decrease.

6 rows m.s., knitting 2 together at beginning of each row.

Cast off remaining 11.

Knit other leg for opposite side by purling a complete row after picking up for hem and plaining to within 20 of end, etc.

To Make Up

Thoroughly press each part with hot iron over damp cloth. Press seams in same manner.

Press transfers on coat and hat and embroider.

Fasten coat at front with press-studs. Thread elastic through waist of overalls and sew some under instep.

Make cord in blue and thread at waist, finishing ends with pom-poms.

The measurements stated are only obtained after thoroughly pressing as stated above.

That Old Chest *of* Drawers

A CHEST of drawers that looks most antiquated, and is not wanted in your rooms at all, you'll find will make an excellent toy-cupboard, when it is stood against the nursery wall.

Remove the drawers and inside wooden structures; this gives a large amount of cupboard space; or if you like to use the inner ledges, you'll find for shelves they're in a handy place.

The handles of the drawers should be extracted, the surface then made good and holes filled in, then place your drawers on end and you are ready, your modern unit structure to begin.

Place the long drawers down each side of the carcase, and fit with shelves, or not, just as you please; then if you've room for just the slight addition, place your small drawers quite firmly against these. You'll find it looks, oh, really most attractive; your structure will have just that modern air, which even in the nursery is pleasant, and old wood stands a tremendous lot of wear.

Written by Jean Morton — Pictured by Joyce Plumstead

BATH-MAT *or* SPLASHER!

In White and Green Towelling

THIS bath-mat or splasher is made in two colours and is decorated with an amusing sailing boat scene in appliqué.

You will need: A piece of white towelling, 27 by 18 inches; and one piece of sea-green towelling, 27 inches square; some scraps of red and brown linen for the little sailing boats; and a needleful each of black and white embroidery cotton.

Join the white and green towelling together round three sides, leaving a nine-inch green "flap."

Turn out to the right side and fold up the green "flap," tacking it in position half-way up on the white side of the mat. Make four-inch curves along the green edge, turn under a single fold and hem down invisibly.

Cut out the hulls for the little sailing boats in brown linen, and the sails in red linen. Tack them in position and turn under the raw edges and hem them down.

Work the rigging with black embroidery cotton, and their names in white.

The Progress

The history of baby's "car," how it was invented and improved—and an offer of £10 for

THE mother of to-day wheels her baby out in a nice, deep, roomy pram with ball-bearing wheels and shock-absorbing tyres; *her* mother wheeled her out, when *she* was a baby, in one of the older pattern, with a shallow, boat-shaped body and high wheels; and granny in her turn rode in a pram of a still earlier type. But not many people realise that when *great*-grandmother was a baby, such things were unknown; the pram as it is to-day simply did not exist.

"But whatever did mothers do without prams?" you naturally ask. "Did they carry their babies about in their arms, or slung on their backs as native mothers do?"

Until about a hundred years ago, they did. And then somebody invented the "stick-wagon," which might be called the ancestor of the pram. The "stick-wagon" was really copied from the Kentish "hop-wagon," which was nothing more than a rough box on wheels in which food, cooking pots and the smaller children were taken along when the family went off for a day's hop- or fruit-picking.

The first pram ever made, and the finest. With another somewhat similar, it was built for a tiny daughter of a Duke of Devonshire in 1780. (*Photo: Keystone.*)

"Father Pulls the Stick-Wagon." (*From a magazine of* 1833.)

The "Stick-Wagon"—the ancestor, so to speak, of the pram. (*By courtesy of the "Pram Gazette."*)

The first reversible pram, patented by Dunkley's in 1881. The handle was hinged to the middle of the under-carriage and swung round to either end. (*From an old print.*)

Above: The Bassinette. At first it had no well, and was simply a wicker cradle on a wheeled under-carriage. One of this pattern, patented in 1883, was supplied to the Royal Family. It could be steered by the horn handles. A similar one, with gold-plated springs and a musical-box under the seat, was made for an Indian prince. (*By courtesy of "Solperams."*)

A "Three-Wheeler," at least seventy years old, which can be seen at the Prittlewell Priory Museum. (*By courtesy of the "Pram Gazette."*)

An improved pattern of the "Three-Wheeler" which was in general use, together with the bassinette, in the 'eighties. The first prams were made not for tiny babies to lie in, but for toddlers too heavy to carry to sit in. (*By courtesy of W. J. Harris & Co.*)

of the Pram

suggestions towards designing the WIFE and HOME Ideal Pram

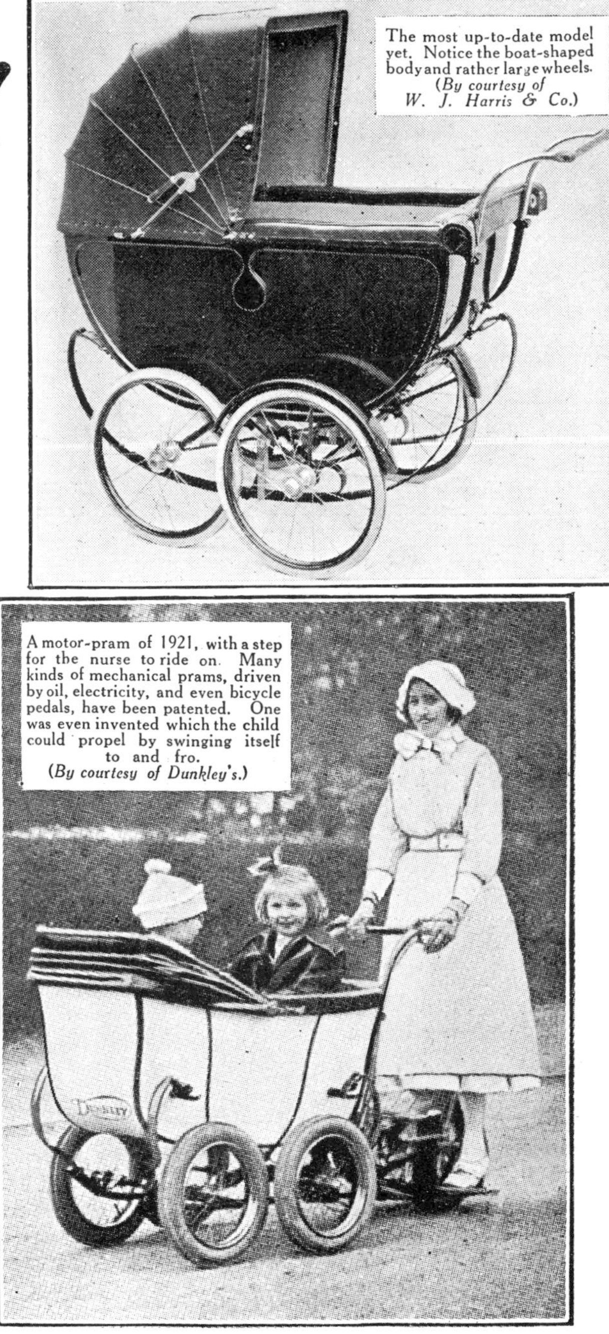

The most up-to-date model yet. Notice the boat-shaped body and rather large wheels. *(By courtesy of W. J. Harris & Co.)*

A motor-pram of 1921, with a step for the nurse to ride on. Many kinds of mechanical prams, driven by oil, electricity, and even bicycle pedals, have been patented. One was even invented which the child could propel by swinging itself to and fro. *(By courtesy of Dunkley's.)*

The "stick-wagon" was, of course, an improvement on this. It was made in a variety of more or less ornamental shapes, and it had railed sides, but it had no springs or upholstery, and no mother of to-day would think of putting her baby into such a thing. It was made to be pulled, not pushed; the mother could not see what the child was doing without turning round, and as nothing in the shape of a safety-strap had been thought of, there was always the risk of a baby who had reached the crawling stage falling out over the low side. The "stick-wagon" was not a great success.

THE FIRST PRAMS

It is rather interesting that the earlier prams were made not for small babies to lie in, but for the bigger children, who had grown too heavy to carry far, to sit in. The very first prams ever made were designed for this purpose.

There were two of them, and they were made in 1780 for Lady Georgina Cavendish, the eldest daughter of the fifth Duke of Devonshire. They were fitted with iron-shod wheels, luxurious upholstery, a leather canopy, and C-springs, and one of them had shafts, so that it could be drawn by a donkey or pony. Mr. S. J. Sewell, the editor of the "Pram Gazette," who, of course, is an authority on the subject, considers these two prams probably the best ever made—from the point of view of material and workmanship. A photograph of one appears on the previous page.

But these two were "special" prams; they were probably never used outside the grounds of Chatsworth House, the ancestral home of the Dukes of Devonshire, and nobody seems to have thought of copying them, at that time. No doubt the rough roads and cobbled pavements of those days were quite unsuitable for pram traffic.

Another early pram has been mentioned by the founder of the well-known firm of Dunkley's. It was made for himself, as an infant, by the village blacksmith, and he has described it as being "like two steel fireguards put together." His mother used to wheel him in it to and from the [CONTINUED ON NEXT PAGE]

A "Hammock Pram"—the first with a suspension body—patented in 1887 by Simpson & Fawcett. *(By courtesy of the Star Manufacturing Co.)*

An ingenious invention of 1895 was a pram that could be lifted off its under-carriage and used as a cradle. Although of the "bassinette" type, it had a well, which remained on the under-carriage. *(By courtesy of "Solperams.")*

The type of pram that was popular from about 1900 to 1914, when the deep pattern with small wheels, much cosier and less likely to upset, was designed. During this period upholstery was much improved, and ball-bearing wheels were introduced. *(By courtesy of W. J. Harris & Co.)*

The mailcart, invented in 1886 and immensely popular for fifteen years, until the folding push-car took its place. The mailcart was first made as a toy, but

mothers *would* use them for real children, and the makers simply *had* to supply full-sized ones. The baby in the mailcart shown above is now associated with the WIFE and HOME Advertisement Department!

Some things for the children

cornfields near Stratford-on-Avon when she went gleaning; he little knew that in the years to come he would start a firm in Birmingham that would make up-to-date prams far in advance of the crude vehicle he shared with the corn-gleanings!

THE THREE-WHEELER

All these early prams were made to be pulled, not pushed. It was not till 1840—sixty years after the Devonshire prams were made—that it occurred to some clever person, whose name has been forgotten, to invent a pram that could be pushed from behind, with the baby under mother's eye.

It was not until the 60's that pram-makers came to the conclusion that mothers might like to wheel out their tiny babies instead of carrying them in their arms, and a sort of cradle on four wheels was produced. This was called a "bassinette," because wicker cradles, called "bassinettes" which French mothers had used for many years, were at first actually imported from France and fixed on to wheeled undercarriages over here. The bassinette pram soon became popular, but the three-wheelers continued to be used for many years—until the 80's, in fact—and then slowly went out of fashion.

The bassinette pram was quite flat; it had no well, but in time it occurred to somebody that a pram in which baby could either lie down or sit up would be an advantage, and then the model with the well became "the thing," and lasted, with little improvement, for fifteen years. About 1900 this developed into the shallow, boat-shaped body with high wheels that lasted until about 1916. Between 1910 and 1912, however, although the actual design did not alter much, great improvements were made in springs, upholstery and general comfort, and in 1914 came ball-bearing wheels, which at first cost £4 extra, but are now included, by one firm, in all their prams without extra charge.

This pattern, although it was popular for so long, had the disadvantage that it was easily upset, and at last the body began to grow deeper and the wheels smaller, until it developed into the deep, well-balanced, small-wheeled pram of to-day. It is interesting, though, that the very newest models show a tendency to go back, slightly, to the boat-shaped body and rather larger wheels. Too great depth, it is considered, keeps the air from baby. On the other hand, there is a drawback about the larger wheels, nowadays. They must be made to overlap, which means a longer back axle that will not go through the narrow doorway of many a modern small house!

MANY INVENTIONS

Of course, as the years went by, and the pram developed, all kinds of improvements were invented—some successful and some not!

There have been many inventions in the way of "convertible" prams—ingenious devices for using the pram body as a cradle, a bath, a trolley, and even a swing-boat! A patent taken out in 1903 was for a kind of hammock that could be attached to the side of the pram to accommodate a second baby, and it is curious that this is said to be the only patent in connection with prams ever taken out by a woman.

As is usually the case with inventions, it is the simple device that is the most useful and successful. For instance, every mother knows how in wet weather the rain collects in a pool on the apron, however tightly it may be stretched, and has to be shaken off. It is only recently that this has been overcome, very simply, by making the apron of such a shape that when it is fastened to the hood a ridge is formed that shoots the water off to either side.

ROOM FOR IMPROVEMENT

Every year the manufacturers bring out new designs, with fresh improvements, but there is still plenty of scope for ideas that will make the pram a more comfortable, more practical carriage for baby, or more convenient for mother who pushes it and looks after it, and probably many of them are things that would only occur to a mother. Haven't *you* ever said to yourself: "I do wish someone would turn out a pram that has a ——" something or other that has not yet been thought of?

If we could collect all these bright ideas and embody them in a pram that has all the other features a good pram should have —the greatest possible accommodation contrived in the smallest outside space, smooth running, perfect protection from weather, lightness combined with strength and durability, and so on—then we should have the Ideal Pram, shouldn't we?

Well, that is just what your Editress would like to evolve, with the assistance of her readers. So here is your opportunity. If you can think of any *original* device, however simple—in fact, the simpler the better—for improving prams in any way, or suggest anything that is lacking in the modern pram, write and tell us about it.

We have arranged to send all the suggestions we receive to Messrs. W. J. Harris and Co., the well-known pram manufacturers, and they have undertaken to build a pram embodying as many of them as are workable; in other words, to produce *the WIFE and HOME Ideal Pram*—and this will be on show at their stand at the Ideal Home Exhibition in April.

Of course, some ideas, however ingenious, are not practicable; others are too expensive to carry out; others, again, may be already patented by somebody else, but you may be sure that any really good, sound, *original* idea will find its way into our Ideal Pram. So send your suggestions, please, to "Prams," WIFE and HOME, 5, Carmelite Street, London, E.C.4 (Comp.), before February 16th. There's a prize of **£5** for the suggestion the Editress considers the best, and five others of **£1** each for the five other most interesting replies. In the event of the best idea being sent in by more than one reader, the prize will be divided between them. The Editress' decision, of course, is final. All rights in the winning suggestion shall become the property of the proprietors of WIFE and HOME.

MAKE BELIEVE

We "make-believe" our little home's a mansion,
Its modest furniture of precious worth,
And we pretend our tiny lawn is spacious,
Our simple flowers the rarest blooms on earth!

We "make-believe" that all our homely makeshifts
Are just a piece of fun (sometimes they are!);
And we prepare for each small jaunt and picnic
With all the zest of those who venture far!

This game of "make-believe" gives endless pleasure,
And helps us smile through many trying hours;
It's easy to pretend, for all life's treasures
Of love and joy and trust are REALLY ours!

SUSAN INCH

The First Prize of £5 has been awarded to:

Mrs. O. CRAWFORD, 214, Haymarket Street, Carntyne, Glasgow;

A photograph of the actual WIFE and HOME Ideal pram, built for us by W. J. Harris & Co. It has many novel features, including transparent panels in the hood, a transparent storm visor, a cupboard for parcels, an attachment for an open umbrella, an ingenious device for cleaning out the well, handles that can be attached to either end, etc. It also has an extension for the growing baby and a detachable seat for the toddler.

The Wife & Home Ideal Pram

Built specially for us and including many clever suggestions sent in by our readers.

OUR recent competition, in which we asked for suggestions for improving baby's carriage, brought letters from hundreds of readers, and many of their ideas were excellent. We submitted them all to Messrs. W. J. Harris & Co., the pram manufacturers, for their opinion, and they found them very interesting.

Many of them, they say, are already included in existing prams, though some, being expensive, are only in the more highly-priced models. Others are not practicable, and others have been tried and not "caught on." But several of the ideas are real practical improvements, and the best have been introduced into the WIFE and HOME Ideal Pram, which will be on view at Messrs. Harris' stands, Nos. 315 and 316, at the Ideal Home Exhibition from April 3rd to April 28th. A photograph of the pram appears on this page.

The suggestion that came from the greatest number of readers is that of a cupboard under the seat of the pram, for carrying parcels, that could be reached without disturbing baby. This idea, as a matter of fact, was tried some years ago, and did not prove popular, but it is so useful that it has been made a feature of our Ideal Pram, which also has a locker under the other seat.

Another very sensible idea that many readers contributed is that of an opening in the floor, to make cleaning out the well easier. The difficulty here is to avoid draughts, but this has been done, we think, in the WIFE and HOME pram.

Another thing for which there is plainly a big demand is a detachable seat for a toddler using the pram at the same time as baby. This is already a feature of many of the new models, and forms part of our Ideal design. Another suggestion that deserves mention is a step that a toddler can stand on for short rides or when crossing the road.

Many mothers ask for some kind of window in the hood, so that baby can see out, on either side, when the hood is up. The difficulty hitherto has been to find a suitable transparent material, but Harris & Co. have discovered one that has stood all tests so far, and the "Sunshine Hood" is a notable feature of our Ideal Pram.

Another good suggestion, sent in by a number of readers, that will be found in our pram is a ventilator in the well, to prevent it becoming stuffy.

Yet another widely suggested improvement is a brake of some kind. Many prams are already fitted with automatic footbrakes, but readers living in hilly districts ask for some kind of brake that can be gradually applied, from the handle, to check the pram when going down hill. As this is not needed by everyone it does not form part of our model, but it can be fitted to any pram as an extra.

A very large number of readers said that pram-handles should be adjustable to suit pram-pushers of different heights. This idea has already been patented, and it is included in the WIFE and HOME pram. Another suggestion is for reversible handles, to avoid the awkward and tiring business of pulling the pram when travelling with a strong wind. In our pram the handles can quickly be detached from one end and inserted in sockets in the other.

Many readers have asked for an attachment for holding an open umbrella over mother, to protect her in rain yet leave her hands free. This is not easy to carry out, but Harris & Co. have arranged with a firm of umbrella manufacturers to supply a special umbrella, included in our model.

Another good suggestion is for a kind of visor to keep rain from blowing into the open front of the hood, without closing it up entirely. This is already covered by Harris' patent "Storm Hood," which is fitted to the WIFE and HOME pram in a transparent material.

Other good ideas that our readers suggested, that are already in many prams, are: A Special Shopping Bag, attached to the handle; a Hygienic Mattress; Seats adjustable to different heights; Umbrella Holders of various types; Aprons with Pockets for various purposes; Washable Linings for hoods; an Extra Detachable Hood for a second child; Grease-packed Hubs to the wheels, etc.

There were many other quite ingenious ideas that we are told could not be successfully introduced into an ordinary pram: Rubber Buffers to protect exposed corners and hubs of wheels not practicable; Pockets in the lining—difficult to keep clean; a Receptacle for Wet Nappies sounds an excellent idea, but has been tried and did not "catch on"—our locker under the front seat would serve the purpose; an Adjustable Back-rest or shaped cushion for when baby sits up also seems a good notion, but we are told that most mothers prefer ordinary cushions.

Other readers suggest various methods of keeping mother's hands warm while she is pram pushing—a "Handle Muff" was tried years ago but was not successful, it got very dirty and wet; methods of warming the handle with hot-water, electricity or chemicals are not practicable. A non-folding, Transparent Hood that slides down inside the pram is also a good idea, but very expensive to construct. A Draught-proof Flap to cover the join of hood and body is also suggested, but we are assured that no properly-fitting hood does let in a draught at that spot. Another idea is for a Summer Hood of light material, made like the ordinary hood and fitting inside it, so that either could be raised as required—possible, but costly, and no great advantage over the ordinary canopy; a Hood that can be raised or lowered by a lever from the handle end—not practicable.

Many readers suggest Steering Devices, but few of these are practicable and all are costly; others ask for a device for raising the front wheels when mounting a kerb—this was tried years ago and found to be impracticable; others ask for Disc Wheels, as easier to keep clean than spoked ones—this has been tried, but was not popular; several suggest Scrapers or Brushes that automatically clean the tyres before the pram is pushed into the house—not practicable; others ask for red reflectors or headlamps for use in the dark, bicycle bells or hooters for warning people obstructing the pavement, and similar things, but these, after all, could be rigged up by any handy man.

At any rate, we feel that with the assistance of our readers we have evolved a really Ideal Pram.

"SHAN'T!"

This Business of Being a Mother

This month our four mothers talk over the problem of the wilful child.

Photo: H. Armstrong Roberts

"WHAT lovely holidays we have had this year," remarked Mrs. Taylor one afternoon, as the four mothers strolled along Lyme Avenue together, enjoying the early September sunshine, their children trotting by their sides.

"Yes, the sea air really did my bairns no end of good, I feel certain," Mrs. Bates said slowly, "but for some little time now I have been worried about Joan. I've not mentioned it before as I thought probably it would all pass off—but it hasn't."

"What is the trouble, my dear?" asked Mrs. Williams, the eldest of the four. "She looks healthy enough."

"Yes, I know," Joan's mother answered. "I am sure there is nothing seriously wrong so far as health is concerned."

"I wonder what the trouble is, then? Is Joan, perhaps, getting a little tiresome?" Mrs. Williams asked tactfully.

"However did you guess, Mrs. Williams?" Mrs. Bates exclaimed. "Yes, that is just what is worrying me. She is inclined to be so contrary. If I want her to do anything she prefers to do just the opposite. It's not like my little girl at all."

Mrs. Williams nodded her head thoughtfully.

"I had just this very trouble with one of my boys," she said. "My doctor said he was inclined to be 'negative.'"

"I've heard about 'negative' children before, but I never quite understood the meaning," remarked Mrs. Perry, who was listening intently.

"Oh, it is not an uncommon problem for a mother to come up against, and I am glad we have a few moments together this afternoon. It gives us a chance to talk the matter over. Now tell me, Mrs. Bates, how does this affect your girlie? I rather imagine you may be having tears and troubles at mealtimes."

"We do, and it does worry me so!"

"I expect, as my boy did, she plays and picks at her food till you feel nearly distracted, wondering whether she has had enough to eat?"

"Yes, and more than that, Mrs. Williams. Joan has taken to refusing so many things. She refuses her food, refuses to come in to meals, refuses to wash her hands, won't eat many of the little dainties I get ready for her. I am so anxious, you see, to ensure that she gets enough nourishment."

"Joan is just like my little son was, I can see. Well dear, as I was saying, I had a talk with my doctor, and he told me first of all not to worry, and not to let my boy see I was anxious about him. The tiresome little mood would soon pass off then, he assured me."

"Really? That sounds simple enough." Mrs. Bates showed signs of relief.

"It *is* simple, dear; and I can assure you that it works wonders. Doctor said I was to treat it all in a very gentle, but quite off-hand manner. I was to pretend that if sonny did not want to eat—well, never mind, perhaps it was best for him to go without a meal. I should explain to him that it would, at any rate, give his tummy a rest, and make no difference to me at all. You'd be surprised at the result. It was not very long before he began to eat heartily."

"How very interesting, Mrs. Williams. Did you ask doctor what was the cause of the trouble?"

"Yes, I did, and to my surprise he told me it was generally the result of the child's parents being over-anxious to bring the little one up properly and also of too many 'do's' and 'don'ts,' and too many 'must's' and 'mustn'ts.' All this puts a check on the little one's activities, and the result is that the toddler takes up the opposite side, as it were. It is a nervous trouble really. The child can't help being like this, and that is how it differs from real deliberate disobedience. I wonder if Joan is showing any of the other signs often seen in negative children? Refusing to go to school is one of them — but, of course, she is too young for that yet. But let me think—not wanting to go to bed—tears and crying at bed-time—that is quite a common trouble."

"Oh, yes, Mrs. Williams. Lately, bedtime has meant such a lot of unhappiness. Once, she went off to bed without any trouble, but now — just the opposite—sometimes she cries herself to sleep. I don't think she means to be naughty. It seems as if she just can't help it."

"No, it is not naughtiness, my dear," the older mother was able to tell her. "With a highly strung, nervous child, like Joan, bedtime will be either all smiles or all tears."

"I'm afraid it has been a series of tears and struggles lately," Mrs. Bates confessed. "But I am sure you will be able to help me, and tell me what to do. I do so want to do the best for Joan, and I know how important it is to get the babies off to bed happily. It makes such a difference to their sleep."

"It does, my dear. Now if I were you, the first thing I should do is to prepare Joan for bedtime very gently. About half-past five—I suppose she goes to bed at six? Yes, that is very wise. About half-past five, then, remind her that it will soon be time to put her playthings away, and prepare her for the next move—going off to bed. You see, to a child, the hour before bedtime is so often the most interesting in the whole day. It is then that we are more free from household tasks and love to talk and play gently with our children.. Daddy generally comes home then, and there seem so many interests about. If, all of a sudden, six o'clock arrives without any warning (kiddies don't watch the clock like we do), resistance and tears are sure to follow. It is very natural, don't you think?"

"Now that I come to consider it, I believe I went through just such a time as that myself," remarked Mrs. Perry suddenly. "I hated going to bed!"

"So did I," added Joan's mother. "I must see what I can do for my little girl. I wonder how I should start? Do you think letting her help to get her supper ready would be a good thing?"

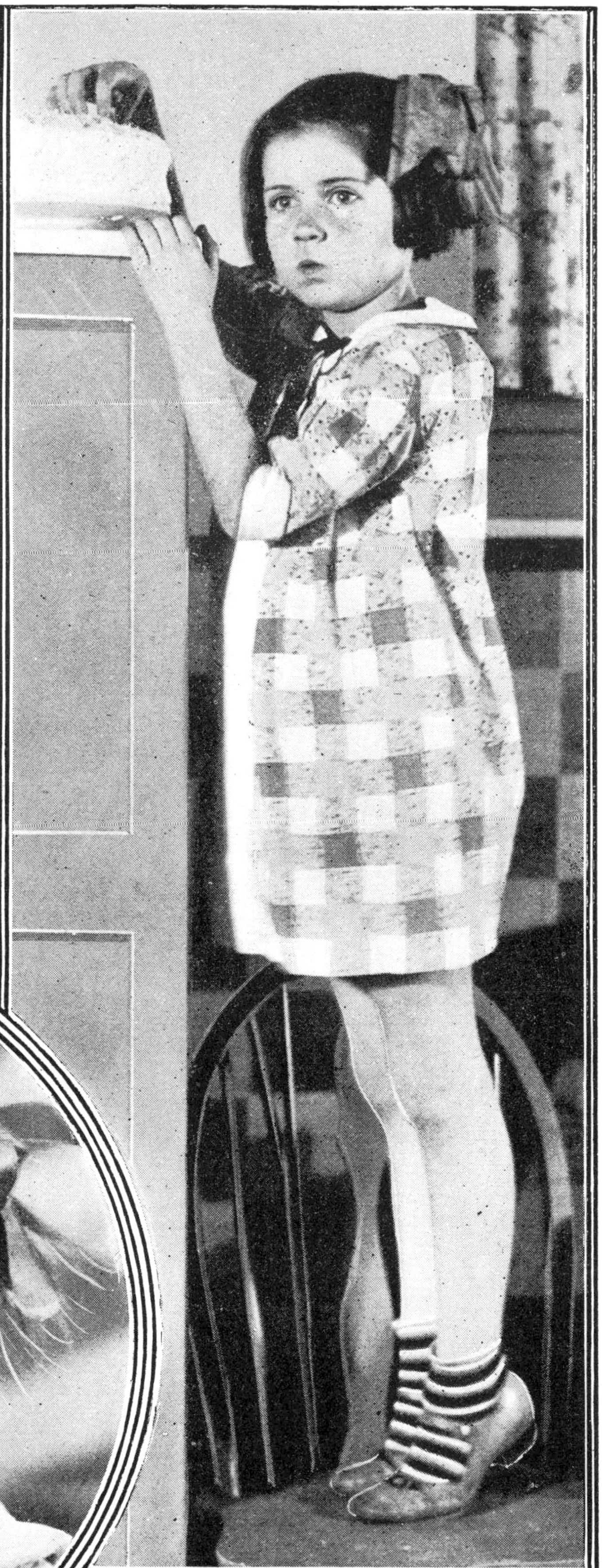

Often a child's disobedience is mere mischievousness, but a busy and harassed mother does not always see the joke! This ill-timed humour, however, should not be dealt with in the same way as deliberate disobedience.

The "motor-minded" child is a puzzle. If you say to her "Leave the cake alone," she will touch it at the first opportunity. This is not wilful disobedience, but the child's mind finding the cake an irresistible attraction because you spoke of it. The only way with a child of this rather unusual type is to be very sparing with "don'ts" and to draw her attention to other things quickly.

OUT of the MOUTHS of BABES

This Business of Being a Mother [continued from previous page]

"Yes, that would be splendid, and then, Mrs. Bates, teach her that upstairs there are new joys to be found. She will love to turn on the bath taps herself, and see that the soap and sponge are ready. After the bathing is over, don't put her straight to sleep, but let her sit up in bed for a few minutes, where she can watch you put her clothes away."

"Supposing she starts to cry after she is in bed?"

"Then pat her quietly on her shoulder for a few moments, saying nothing, and begin to busy yourself about the room, making no reference to the tears, but passing a few commonplace remarks about what you are doing, and you will find that she will gain a lot of confidence from that, and soon settle off to sleep."

"Thank you, Mrs. Williams. I shall try to remember all you have said. I am sure it will be helpful."

"Disobedience is not the same, you say?" Mrs. Bates inquired, after a short pause.

"No, dear. You see, a disobedient child quite deliberately disobeys his parents, and he knows it—only too well." She smiled.

"Jackie has been very disobedient then, lately," sighed Mrs. Bates. "Sometimes he does what I tell him without any bother, but sometimes he refuses. What shall I do about him? It would not do to treat him in the same way as Joan, would it?"

"No, I believe that children must be taught to obey, and I should be quite firm with Jackie about this, if I were you. Children on the whole, dear, are naturally obedient. But sometimes mothers actually make children disobey them, by giving in to them too much, or by making too many laws, so that they themselves find it difficult to remember them all! I think it is best to make as few rules as possible, and always keep to them quite strictly. When it is 'No' once, then it should be 'No' always; not 'No' one day and 'Yes' the next, for no reason at all."

"Don't you think it is a good plan to tell a child the real reason why mummy says 'No'?" asked Mrs. Perry, who always had such sensible ideas.

"Yes; I do. Children see reason very readily, you know. Of course, they all get into mischief"—her eyes twinkled—"but they obey quite willingly when they understand that our commands are just and reasonable. They are far happier doing so."

"Your little ones look happy enough," Mrs. Williams said, turning to Mrs. Taylor. She had just been looking at Elsie and Roger.

But Mrs. Taylor seemed worried.

"I am not too happy about my youngsters," she said at last. "They have been quarrelling so much lately."

"I think most kiddies do, you know," sympathised Mrs. Williams.

"How did you deal with your children's battles?" Mrs. Taylor asked. "I am sure some methods must be better than others."

"I always thought it best to ignore the little upsets, if possible, by starting the children on some other game or interesting occupation. Very often, you know, squabbling shows that children have not enough outlet for their superfluous energy."

"I suppose it's a case of 'mischief for idle hands,'" Mrs. Perry laughed at her own suggestion, and all the others laughed, too. "What is your opinion as to the best kind of toys, Mrs. Williams?"

"Toys ought, I suppose, to be the kind that the kiddies can use and understand without the help of elders?" suggested Mrs. Bates.

"And the simpler the toys are the better, I should say," Mrs. Taylor added.

"Yes, dears, you are both right. Children love the plain, easily-worked toys best. Didn't you, when you were tiny? I know I did. I used to make all kinds of jobs 'play' for my children, as well. They have polished the spoons for me, and taken a great delight in doing it, too. And I often used to let them pick over the currants before I made a cake. They loved helping mummy, and it made useful amusement for them also, and none of it was too difficult for them to do well. Occupations and toys which make a child exert a little real effort are very good, but remember that if these things are *too* hard, the feeling of not being able to succeed simply gives rise to outbursts of temper, and does more harm than good."

Quaint sayings of children, sent in by our readers. Half-a-crown is awarded for each one printed. Address "Children's Sayings", 5, Carmelite Street, London, E.C.4. (Comp).

A PROMPT REPLY

A shopkeeper was giving away toy balloons, and Bobby asked if he might have two.

"I'm sorry," the shopkeeper answered, "but we only give one balloon to each boy. Have you a brother?"

Bobby shook his head.

"No," he replied, "but my little sister has."

Sent in by Mrs. Rellaw, 129, Wickham Street, Welling, Kent.

NOT HIS FAULT

Bertie was sent upstairs to wash his hands and face. When he returned his mother said:

"Your face is still not clean, Bertie."

"Well, it ought to be, mummy," he replied. "I gave it two helpings of soap."

Sent in by Mrs. Slater, Gorsefield, Midway, Walton-on-Thames.

HER ONLY OBJECTION

Joan was out shopping with her mother. "Does God send us all our food?" she inquired suddenly.

"Yes, darling," mother answered.

Joan sighed.

"Then I wish He would stop sending tomatoes," she murmured.

Sent in by Mrs. E. Jewell Layton, 2, Tetherdown, Muswell Hill, N.10.

NO NEED TO APOLOGISE!

I took my five-year-old little boy out to dinner one day, and the lady of the house asked him if he was sure he could cut his meat.

"Oh, yes," John replied, without looking up. "We often have it as tough as this at home."

Sent in by Mrs. Mordey, c/o Stokeld, nr. Station, Cleadon, Sunderland.

A Cardboard Railway

A few cardboard boxes, some corks, and one or two odds and ends that every mother will be able to "dig up," provide the materials for this toy to delight the heart of the small boy.

Left: Here you see how very simple the station is. The bookstall and the match machine give a very realistic touch.

EVERY boy loves playing with toy trains—and so do many little girls!—and the little ones who are not old enough to be very critical about realistic accuracy will enjoy making—with perhaps some help from mummy or daddy—the toy railway, made from cardboard boxes, paper and other oddments, I am going to describe.

The body of the engine is made from an old notepaper box turned upside down. An oblong box of the same length, but of about half the width, will make the boiler and driver's cabin. With a pair of scissors cut the shape of the driver's cabin at one end of the box. Don't forget to provide a nice round "porthole" on each side for the driver to see through without having to put his head out in the draught.

At the other end of the boiler we must draw the "door" which enables the engineers to get to the engine's "works" if anything goes wrong, but as our engine is extra special and won't go wrong, our door need not really open.

If you have any trouble in finding a suitable oblong box for the boiler, one of the chocolate "croquette" boxes, or a cardboard roll such as is used for packing rolled-up photographs, will do equally well. Glue the boiler on to the body of the engine, which now wants a smoke-stack, whistle, steam dome and some wheels and buffers.

A cork will make the smoke-stack (glue it on), and half a cork each will do for the whistle and steam dome. Buffers are easily made from pieces of cork. The body of the engine is hollow, of course, and this is very useful when adding the wheels. Cut pieces of firewood to the right length and fit them *inside* the body of the engine. These form the axles.

The wheels can be made in several ways, or you may be able to get tin ones from the toy shop. Large black buttons make good wheels, if you sever the partition between the holes through which the cotton is meant to pass as a rule. If it is necessary to smooth off the hole in the button to secure even running of the wheel, do it with emery paper. Failing tin wheels or suitable buttons, wooden or cardboard discs will serve quite well. Secure each wheel in place by driving a broad-headed nail through the outer side of the cardboard engine body into the ends of the firewood axles.

To make the tender, cut in half the lid of a box of suitable depth, and, at the division, trim the walls of the box to a suitable curving shape. A strip of white paper gummed across the open end of the box will make the front. Since the lid has to be upside down in order that its walls may form the walls of the truck, we cannot conceal the axles. These should be made of firewood, as before, and gummed on.

Lumps of black paper (or, if mother does not mind, tiny pieces of real coal or coke) will make a fine finishing touch.

For the carriage a fairly deep box is required, which we shall use right way up. A door should be cut in the centre of each side with windows on either side of it. A realistic touch can be added by using a brass paper clip as a door handle. When it is turned, the arm of the clip will keep the door closed.

Seats inside the carriage can be made either from folded paper gummed into position, or by using a portion of the lid of the box cut off to the required length. If one corner of the lid is left intact it will add considerably to the strength of the seat.

WE must now paint the inside of the carriage, as we shall be unable to get at this when we have added the roof. The roof is made by cutting an oblong of white paper wide enough to reach from side to side of the open top of the box in a slight curve, leaving just enough paper to be fixed with gum to the outer side of the box.

The paper should be about three-quarters of an inch longer than the box at either end, so that, by folding in and sticking the overlapping paper, the open space between the curving roof and the top of the wall of the box can be closed. The best way of folding in the paper is first to fold in the corners, and then to [CONTINUED ON NEXT PAGE]

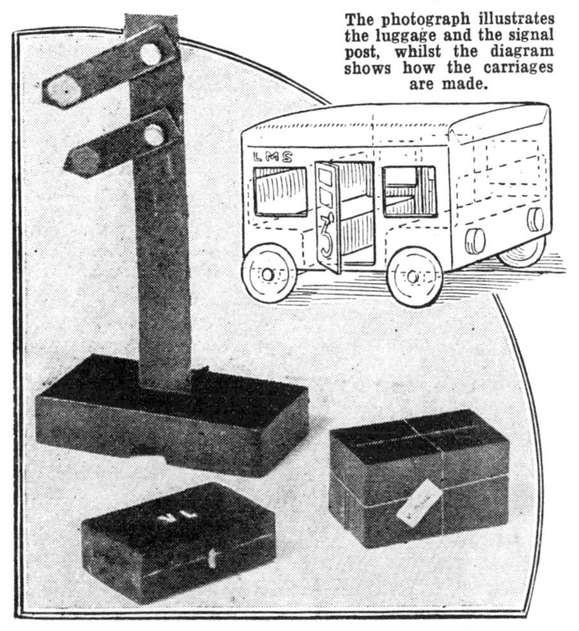

The photograph illustrates the luggage and the signal post, whilst the diagram shows how the carriages are made.

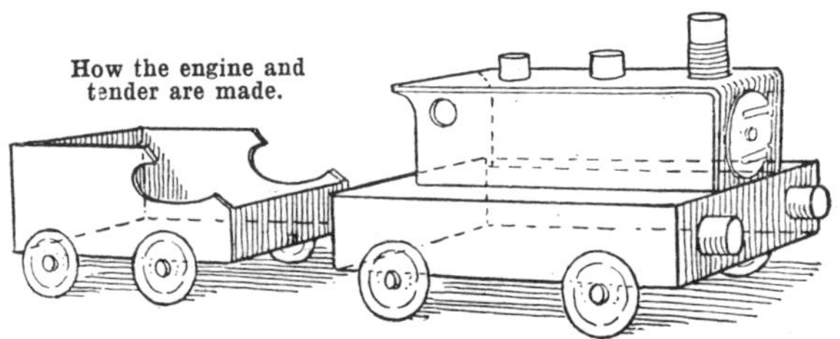

How the engine and tender are made.

A Cardboard Railway [continued]

make three or four cuts at intervals along the ends, and fold it in sections. This prevents any ugly folds.

Axles and wheels are made as for the coal-truck, and buffers can be added as for the engine. The ventilators which are to be seen on the top of all carriages can be represented by little circles of paper painted black and fitted with short paper "tails," which are stuck into thin slots cut with a penknife in the roof.

The luggage van is made in a similar manner to the carriage, but with large double doors in each side instead of the carriage door and windows.

The station is quite a simple thing to make. Fasten together end to end the two halves of a notepaper box (the slight difference in size is not enough to matter). This makes the platform. Along the back stick a piece of thin cardboard or paper with the top cut into a series of V-shaped points.

Next, if you can, find a box such as those in which fountain pens are sold, and cut the lid or the box into halves. These are to be used as the supports for a roof(which is made by cutting V-shapes along the front edge of a small box lid), and should be placed so that the recess in one pillar faces away from the fence and the other faces inwards towards the portion of the platform covered by the roof.

The first pillar should then be fitted up as a bookstall by the addition of a paper shelf across its face. The second pillar can be left untouched.

As finishing touches to the station's appearance, a few small advertisements (cut from magazines and newspapers) can be pasted on the fence, and a "slot machine" can be made by a piece of paper painted red, bent and pasted against the fence. Luggage can be made from match-boxes (one for a suitcase and two glued together for a trunk), fitted with paper handles, painted brown and ornamented by labels cut from coloured paper.

The signal is made by cutting a long, thin, oblong of cardboard for the signal standard, bending over about a quarter of an inch at one end and sticking it to the top of a small box lid. A brass paper clip through the piece bent over adds much to the strength. The signal is fitted with two arms, one above the other, fastened in place with brass paper clips.

Our station and train are now complete, but so far, we have said no word about painting. In the original the engine was painted red with brown smoke-stack and buffers and whistle. Gold rings were added to the smoke-stack and buffers. Everything else on the railway was painted brown except the inside of the carriage, which was red, and the number on the carriage door (gold).

The various parts of the train are joined together with short lengths of string secured to the axles with drawing pins.

Now set up the train on a table and attach a length of string from the front axles of the engine to the rear axle of the last coach, passing the string under the table. By pulling on the string under the table the train can be made to move backward and forward as if under its own steam!

There is no space in which to go into the many other little details that can be added if you have the time—and patience—so in conclusion it is only necessary to suggest that you may be able to find model porters and milk-cans, etc., that would add just one lovely finishing touch. Now, if you have not enough suitable cardboard boxes at hand, get your friends to save them for you.

Good Night Dolly

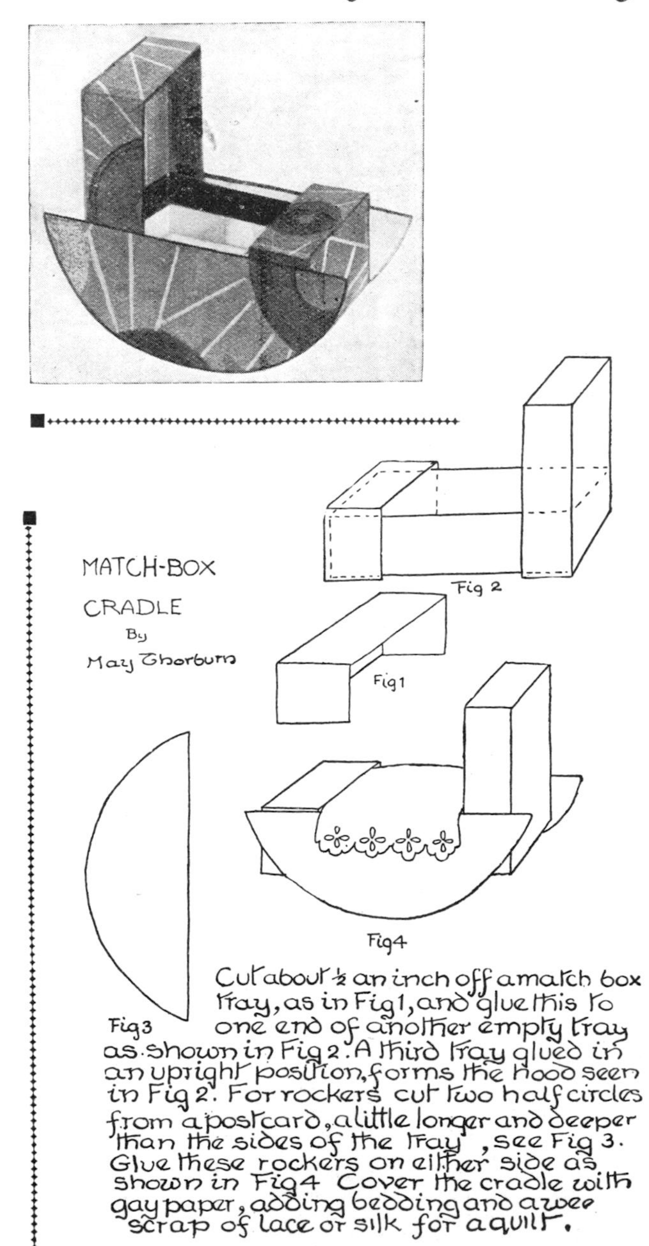

SOMETHING NEW

Thinking out a change of menu is not easy, so this month Mrs. Wise is helping you with some novel suggestions. The dishes shown in the photograph are from some of her recipes, and they certainly look tempting, don't they?

THERE are times when everyone—including the housewife—feels that they would give anything for a change. Meals of meat and vegetables do become dull and uninteresting, and the sight of an unfamiliar dish would be appreciated by all concerned.

This time of the year affords plenty of opportunity for changes. There is an abundance of vegetables, and with these and a few ideas, it will be a very poor cook who cannot make up some enticing dishes. And if she herself does not enjoy the actual making of them, I shall be surprised!

THE USE OF NUTS

NUTS are a very useful food, and, judging by the quantity of shelled Brazils that are on sale at most of the sixpenny stores, it looks as though more people must be eating them.

With the exception of chestnuts, all nuts are rich in proteins (or body-building substance), of which they contain as much as one-fifth. Nuts also contain the very valuable Vitamin B, which is often lacking in our diet and is an important nerve food.

Some of the most useful nuts are almonds, walnuts, filberts, coco-nuts, Barcelonas, Brazils, and peanuts, to name the best-known ones; but besides these there are excellent pinekernels, which may be bought at any of the stores which specialise in food reform goods.

Nuts can be chopped or ground and sprinkled on savouries or salads or into soups, and they can also be used in cakes and various nut roasts, rissoles, and puddings.

NUT SAUSAGES

INGREDIENTS:

2¼ ozs. of pinekernels.
½ pint of brown breadcrumbs.
2 ozs. of ground Brazils.
½ grated raw onion.
1 dessertspoonful of chopped parsley.
1 beaten egg
Salt and pepper.

MIX all the ingredients together and bind stiffly with beaten egg. The grated onion supplies a little moisture and the dryness of the breadcrumbs varies, but one egg is usually sufficient. Shape into sausage shapes and bake in the oven till firm.

TIGER EYE TOAST

INGREDIENTS:

For each rather large slice of hot, buttered toast, allow:
1 dessertspoonful of hot spinach purée or other mashed vegetable.
1 oz. of butter. 1 egg.

HAVE the slices of toast rather thick and well buttered, and lay them on a tin. Beat the whites of the eggs to a stiff froth and place a large spoonful on each piece of toast, then hollow out the centre well and make it round but not smooth.

Into the centre drop a small spoonful of cooked spinach, and put the yolk of an egg in a depression in the centre, and a small piece of butter on top. Bake for six or seven minutes to set the white, and brown it very slightly. Make this dish quickly and have the eggs and purée all ready before the toast is done.

WHOLEMEAL NUT LOAF

INGREDIENTS:

4 ozs. of wholemeal flour.
4 ozs. of white flour.
A good pinch of salt.
A little milk.
1 egg.
2 ozs. of butter or nutter.
3 ozs. of sultanas.
3 ozs. of light Barbadoes sugar.
2 ozs. of coarsely chopped walnuts.
½ teaspoonful of baking powder.

MIX the salt, baking powder and flour, and rub in the fat. Add sugar, cleaned sultanas and the walnuts. Add a little milk to the beaten egg and stir into the mixture, adding more milk as required to make into a paste that is just stiff enough to drop from the spoon. Place in a greased tin and bake in a moderate oven for 1 hour.

Front view of the house and garage.

Match-Box MANOR

A Charming Detached Residence Built Almost Entirely With Empty Boxes. A Large Sheet of Cardboard Fits Over the Back to Close the House at Night.

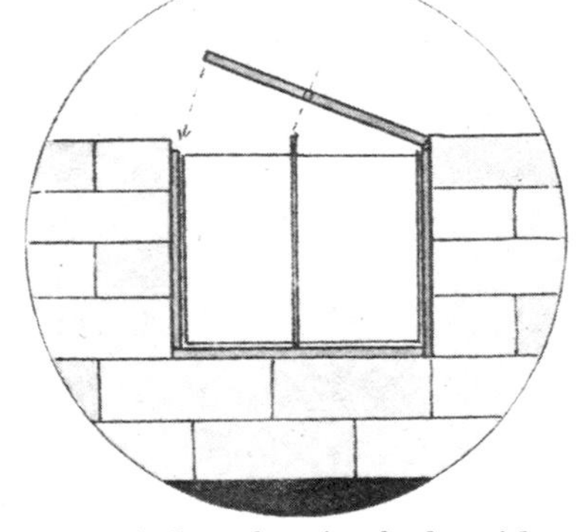

The window glass is of talc, with a piece of wire threaded through the middle so that it can swing open.

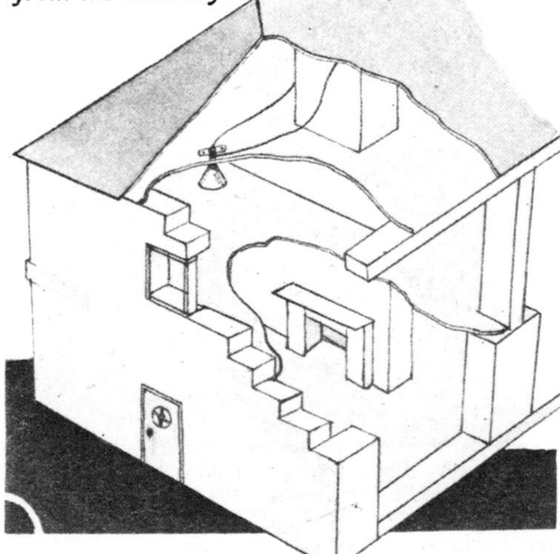

Showing the plan of the house with the door at the side, and the method of lighting from the chimney.

THIS most desirable residence is made almost entirely with empty match-boxes. The furniture, too, is manufactured from boxes and little odds and ends which can be found in most homes.

The first thing to do is to persuade your friends to save all their empty match-boxes for you, and to begin collecting them yourself. You'll need so many.

The House

YOU must have a piece of three-ply wood for the base, about 24 x 20 inches. Strengthen it by wood battens underneath, and this will enable the house to be lifted up easily.

Glue beading around the top edges to neaten them.

Begin building the house in one corner. It is eight match-boxes long by six wide. The boxes are glued together. The trays overlap the joints to link the cases together, as shown in the diagram at the foot of this page.

The house is also strengthened if the joints in alternate courses are vertically above one another. This necessitates the cutting of some match-boxes in half with a razor blade or fret saw at the end of the wall.

The trays of the match-boxes should overlap the joints.

After building up two layers of boxes, begin the front windows. These measure 3 x 3½ inches long.

Cut small strips of three-ply wood about ½ an inch wide for the frame, and stick them to the window opening.

A Lovely HOME

Complete with Garden and Garage.

It has a red roof, cream walls, and window frames painted green.

BUILD the house fourteen match-boxes high, the top windows being made in the same way as the lower ones.

Project the eighth row out a little, to leave a ledge inside for the floors to rest on.

Leave a door opening on the right side of the house, also a window for the top floor. The doorway is towards the front, to allow room for the staircase which comes inside at the back of the house.

The left side of the house has two small windows, one for the ground floor and another for the top floor.

Inside the House

HAVING finished the outer walls, make the inner wall which divides the rooms. The fire-places are in the dining-room and kitchen, and one is shown in the plan on page ii.

When the inner wall is finished it should be papered. A plain cream wall-paper is best. Paper the other walls, also, then put the partition wall in position, glueing it to the floor.

The upstairs floors are pieces of cardboard, brown one side and white the other. Having stained and covered them, they can be slid in on the ledge provided for them, as seen in the picture on page iv.

The dining-room floor is stained dark brown. The kitchen floor is covered with a small checked pattern of American cloth in blue and white.

The ceiling of the top rooms is a large piece of cardboard, white on the underside. This is glued down and pinned on to the three walls and partition. The lower half of the match-box chimney is then built on (see page vi).

The Roof

THE roof is cut out of a large cardboard box (or boxes) in the shapes indicated by the diagram on page vi. If possible, make use of the natural bends already made along the edges of the boxes.

The roof is then fixed by pinning it with large pins all round on to the walls and chimney. Some match-boxes can also be built up inside the roof and the roof pinned on to them.

Paint the roof and chimney a brick-red. The walls of the house should be painted cream and the window frames green.

See page vi for the construction of the chimneys.

The Garage

THE garage is made of a small cardboard box with a roof attached. Two sides of the doorway are cut, and the third is bent so that the door opens and shuts. There is a small window at the side of the garage.

The sitting and dining rooms, kitchen and staircase.

The Inside is So Cosy

Paint a large sheet of cardboard cream to slide over the back of the house, to close it at night. Cut slots in the roof and base for it to fit into.

The Garden

The little garden is built on the wooden base. It consists of broken cork, glued to the base and painted to resemble earth, rock and moss.

The flowers are coloured pins painted green and planted in the corks.

The small yews on each side of the garden are pine cones, painted green and planted in plaster of Paris, in small, cream cartons. These are painted orange to match the garden furniture.

The Windows

The window "glass" is talc, with a piece of thick wire threaded through (an old hat-pin will do excellently); this is put through a small hole in the base of the frame. The top of the frame has a corresponding hole in it and is placed on top of the wire, so the talc should be fitted when building the walls. The window can then be opened by revolving round the hatpin or wire.

The Sitting-Room

The table is made with a circle of cardboard or thin wood glued on to a cotton-reel. This is painted gold and the top of the circle black.

The two armchairs are made of tiny match-boxes, glued together, and one has a little black velvet cushion.

The little chair is a large flat cork with cardboard pinned round it.

The standard lamp is a large match or orangewood stitch stuck in a small cork base, and a little parchment shade is attached with thin wire.

All the furniture, with the exception of the table, is painted green and gold.

The table ornament is a big bead painted gold, with bent pins on which brightly-coloured small beads have been stuck.

The Flower-Pots

The flower-pots can be small cotton reels, large wooden beads or the top of a tooth-paste tube. Press a small bit of cork into the hole and form the flowers by coloured-headed pins or beads with pins through them.

Bend the tops of the pins over with a small pair of pliers to make them look more natural.

Paint the pots in bright colours and the stems of the flowers green.

A touch of glue on the base will keep them permanently in position.

The Garden Furniture

The chairs are corks cut in half, with bits of thin wood stuck in the back. The table is made in the same way as the dining-room table.

All the furniture is painted orange. The lawn between the house and the flower-bed is painted green, and several domestic animals in miniature appear to be having a happy time there!

An interesting collection of these animals can be picked up on your travels.

The sitting-room furniture is in green and gold.

FUN to *Plan these* TINY *THINGS*

Every Room Has Its Own Special Furniture.

The bedroom is also in green and gold.

The Bedroom Furniture

THE dressing-table is made of cardboard, with four tiny match-boxes for drawers. Small red beads are threaded on for handles. The round mirror can be a circle of tin or a small mirror, inserted in a slit at the back of the table.

The bed is the tray of a large match-box with a round cardboard head-board. Four large beads are threaded on for legs. A green silk bedspread, trimmed with rosebud ribbon, completes it.

The cupboard is a large match-box, slit down one side to form a door; the tray of the box is glued inside. Two red beads sewn on and a little wire loop make the fastening.

A small "adhesive plaster" tin makes a good linen box, if painted green with "linen" painted on it in white.

The screen frame is made from four large matches, each with a small red bead pinned to the top. They are glued to a piece of thickish paper, bent to shape.

The dining-room furniture is painted oak brown.

The Dining-Room Furniture

THE table is made from the tray of a match-box, upside down. Rectangular bits of cardboard are glued on the inside for legs. Another piece of cardboard makes the top.

One chair is made of cork, with pieces of shaped cardboard for the back, pinned to the cork with tiny pins. The other is from pieces of tiny match-box trays.

The sideboard is made in the same way as the table, with the addition of a back. It is covered with a piece of oilcloth with large match-sticks stuck round the back and sides, like a beading.

The grandfather clock is made of two tiny match-boxes glued together, the clock face being cut out of a catalogue and stuck on. The rug is of canvas, with a simple cross-stitch design of brown, green and orange.

All the furniture is painted oak brown.

The fire in the fire-place is made of short lengths of twigs, stuck together with bits of red and silver paper between, to represent glowing logs.

The Staircase

THE staircase, which you can see in place in the dining-room on page iv, is made of tiny match-boxes glued one above the other to represent stairs. A piece of ribbon is pinned down them for stair carpet.

A piece of cardboard is glued to one side to hold them together and act as a hand-rail.

A hole is cut in the bedroom floor so that the imaginary occupants may ascend to the bedroom.

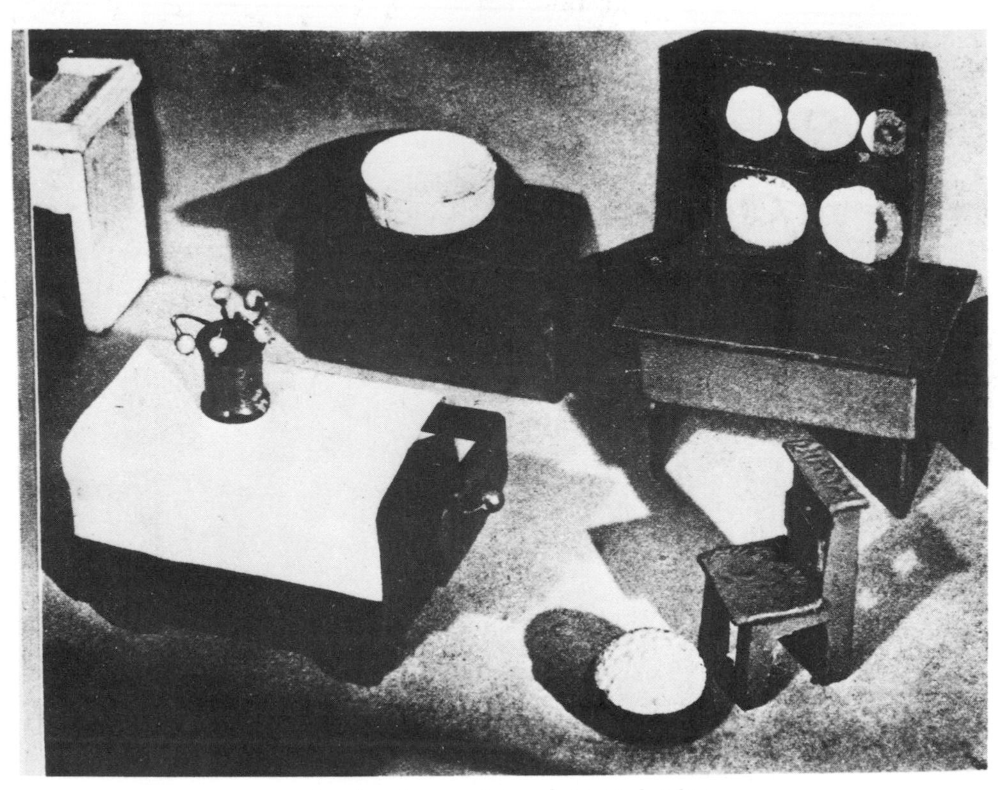

The furniture is stained brown oak colour.

In the KITCHEN

Was Ever a More Fascinating Little Room Planned and Furnished?

Here is the practical side of the little house. How the lighting is installed and the chimney fixed is shown at the foot of the page.

The Kitchen

THE table is made of two match-boxes, glued on top of each other, with beads attached for handles to the drawers. Two strips of wood are glued to the base to raise it off the ground. A small white sheet of American cloth makes the table cover.

The dresser is constructed in the same way as the dining-room table, with the addition of two tiny match-box trays glued one above the other to form shelves. The plates are small painted rounds of white paper.

The side-table is a match-box on edge with a cardboard top. The basin is the metal screw top of a capsule bottle, painted white inside and out.

An old cloth button in contrasting colours makes the attractive footstool.

The chair is evolved from tiny match-boxes.

The cutlery can be cut from the layer of tin which is found protecting the contents of cigarette or tobacco tins. Keep it, of course, in the kitchen-table drawer.

The sink is made by inserting a mixing saucer from a paint-box inside a tiny match-box. One side has the draining board, made of a small piece of wood with matches round the edges. Two square pieces of cardboard make the supports.

The Lighting

THE lower half of the match-box chimney is built on as shown in the diagram on this page. The wiring for the electric light is done before the roof is put on.

Four 2½-volt bulbs (about 1d. each) are required, four bulb holders (1d. and 2d. each), two 4½-volt batteries (3d. each), a small switch (6d.) and some thin wire, all of which can be bought at the sixpenny stores. Fix the wiring as shown in the diagram on this page.

The dining-room light is above the door; the kitchen light above the fire-place. The switch is fixed on the back corner of the house, at the top, with screws.

Cut the corner from a stout card-board box and glue it into the corner of the house, to form a more solid surface to which to fix the switch.

The Chimney

THE chimney contains the batteries (see diagram on this page). This is made of three large-sized match-boxes of which the top one is made to lift off. The lower two are cut, leaving only the sides surrounding the batteries.

The four wires are brought up into the chimney, one in each corner, and wound round the tongues of the batteries.

The chimney-pots are old, inverted anti-splashers sold in the sixpenny stores.

(Below) is the diagram of the roof. This is made from large, strong cardboard boxes.

19½"
12"
11"
10"
15"
9¾"
12"
9¾"
15"
10"
19½"

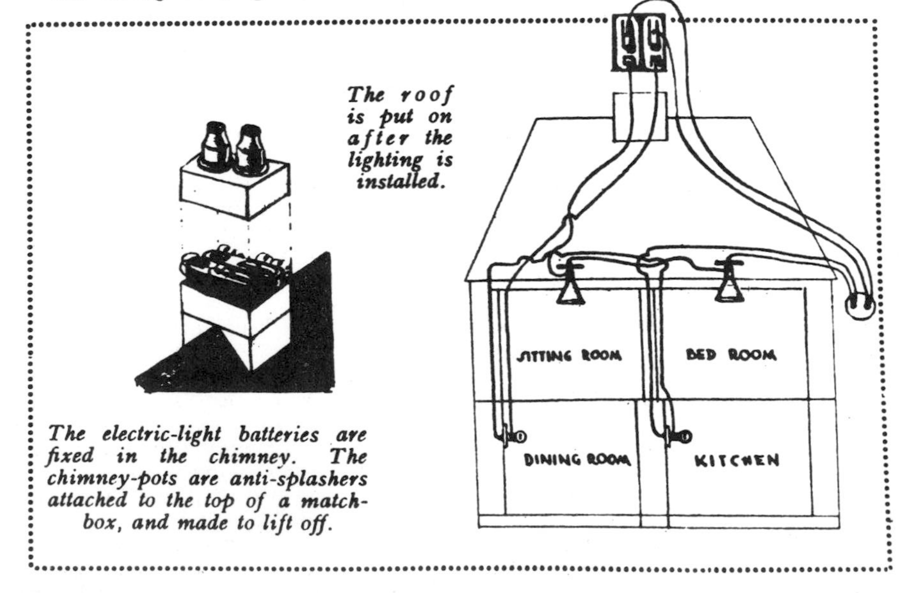

The roof is put on after the lighting is installed.

The electric-light batteries are fixed in the chimney. The chimney-pots are anti-splashers attached to the top of a match-box, and made to lift off.

1935

Children find "Maurice" irresistible. He is so soft and good-tempered!

"MAURICE" *the Monkey*

A Delightful Woolly Toy which can be made for a few Pence

By

MARIANNE RAYNOR

A "close-up" of the simple loop-stitch used

Do you remember the looped knitting which once used to be popular for making bedroom slippers and similar articles? It is a simple and very attractive stitch, and finds a modern use in making the soft animal toys which kiddies always love.

No patterns, and very few directions, are needed for this method of toy-making. All kinds of animals, of which Maurice the Monkey, whom you see here, is an example, can be made from straight strips and squares of looped knitting. The stitch gives a delightful furry surface, and it is so soft and pliable that it can easily be shaped to make the limbs and body of any animal.

Try out the loop-stitch with an odd ball of wool and a pair of fine needles, and you will quickly realise its possibilities. It is worked as follows:—

Cast on 12 stitches, and knit one row plain. Knit the first stitch of the second row in the ordinary way. Put the needle into the next stitch as though to knit it. Pass the wool over the point of the right-hand needle and round the first finger of the left hand. Pass it once again over the needle and round the finger. Then pass it round the needle *only. Note that the wool goes in the opposite direction from that used in ordinary knitting.*

You now have three strands of wool over the needle, and two round the finger. Slip the loops from your finger and complete the stitch in the ordinary way, keeping all three strands on the needle. Knit the rest of the stitches the same way, except the last, which is a plain knitting stitch.

Knit the next row all plain, taking each group of strands together as one stitch. Continue these two rows alternately—one row of loops and one row of plain knitting to hold the loops in place. After each plain row, pull up the previous row of loops, making them as long and even as possible.

You will soon be able to work quite quickly, and as the looped knitting "grows" more rapidly than the usual kind, the animals are soon made.

To make Maurice the Monkey, you need 3 ounces of light grey double-knitting wool, a little dark grey wool for the paws, and a pair of size 12 knitting needles.

There is no complicated shaping to be done, and these are the only directions:

Body.—Use light grey wool. Cast on 24 stitches, and knit 20 rows of loops—that is, 40 rows of knitting in all. Cast off.

Head.—Cast on 20 stitches (light grey), and knit 9 rows of loops. Cast off.

Arms.—Cast on 12 stitches (dark grey). Knit 3 rows of dark grey loops, and then join on light grey wool, and knit 18 more rows of loops. Cast off.

Legs.—Cast on 16 stitches (dark grey). Knit 3 rows of dark grey loops, and then 22 rows of light grey loops. Cast off.

Ears.—Cast on 8 stitches (light grey), and knit 4 rows of loops. Cast off.

Tail.—Cast on 7 stitches (light grey), and knit 42 rows of loops. Cast off.

Stuff Firmly

Seam up the body, head, arms and legs, each one separately, and stuff with soft rags or shavings. Stuff the head very firmly, pushing out the lower part of the face to get the correct profile.

Sew the limbs and head to the body, tucking in the corners of the knitting, and pulling the parts into the right shape.

No stuffing is needed for the tail. Seam it up lengthways, and it will curl round very naturally. Sew to the body.

Sew the ears to the head, pulling them into a rounded shape. Use two buttons, placed rather close together, for eyes, and mark nose and mouth with black wool.

For Father and Son

MATERIALS REQUIRED: 11 ounces of Sirdar 4-ply "Majestic" Wool, shade 230 (maroon), for the father's pullover; 5 ounces of Sirdar 4-ply "Majestic" Wool, same shade, for the son's pullover; 1 zipp fastener, 8 inches long; 1 zipp fastener, 6 inches long; 1 pair of Stratnoid knitting needles, size 6; 1 set of Stratnoid knitting needles, 9-inch length, size 12.

ABBREVIATIONS: k. = knit; p. = purl; sl. = slip; tog. = together beg. = beginning dec. = decrease or decreasing; inc. = increase or increasing.

TENSION: 7 sts. and 8 rows of rib to 1 inch; 9 sts. to 2 inches over fancy pattern, and 6 rows to 1 inch.

MEASUREMENTS: FATHER'S—Width around under arms, 38 inches; length, 20 inches; sleeve seam, 21½ inches; collar stretching to 23 inches. SON'S—Width around under arms, 25 inches; length, 14 inches; sleeve seam, 13½ inches; collar stretching to 20 inches.

What fun to have a pullover just like Daddy's!

The Father's Pullover

Using two of the No. 12 needles, cast on 104 sts. and work in rib of k. 1, p. 1, for 4 inches in depth. Now change to size 6 needles and knit as follows, commencing pattern on wrong side:—

1st row.—k. 1, p. 1, to end of row.
2nd and every row on right side.—Knit.
3rd row.—k. 1, sl. 1, to end.
4th row.—As 2nd.

These 4 rows complete the pattern. Repeat for depth of 9½ inches, making 13½ inches in all from start, including rib.

Then shape for the armholes, e.g. cast off 5 sts. at the beg. of the next 2 rows, then dec. 1 st. at each end of every other row until 78 sts. are on needles. Now continue in pattern until armhole is 7½ inches deep.

Then shape for the shoulders and the neck, e.g. work to the centre 14 sts., place them on a piece of spare wool or cotton, then work to end. Now work back to neck end, knitting tog. 2 sts. at that end of needle.

2nd row.—k. 2 tog., work to 7 sts. from shoulder end. Turn and work back, dec. at neck end as before. Now work a second shaping to 14 sts. from shoulder end and back. Then a third shaping to 21 sts. from shoulder end and back. Then a fourth shaping to 28 sts. from shoulder end and back. Still dec. at neck end on every row. Now cast off right across the shoulder sts.

Work on *right* shoulder to correspond.

The back is worked exactly as the front to armhole shaping. Then cast off 3 sts. at the beg. of the next 2 rows and continue as in front.

Sleeves

Using the No. 12 needles, cast on 60 sts. and work in rib as on body for 4 inches in depth. Then change to pattern and work for 4 inches.

Continue in pattern, but inc. 1 st. at each end of every 12th row until 80 sts. are on needle and seam measures 21½ inches from the start (inclusive of rib). Now shape for armhole. Cast off 3 sts. at the beg. of the next 2 rows, then dec. 1 st. at each end of every row until 32 sts. remain. Cast off.

Work the two sleeves alike.

Collar

Join shoulder seams; pick up the sts. left at neck and, starting from the centre of *front*, add 58 more sts. either side—146 sts. in all. Work on these sts., leaving the opening at centre front for 8 inches in depth. Then cast off loosely and in pattern.

To Make Up

Sew up the side and sleeve seams and press, using a damp cloth and warm iron. Tack the 8-inch zipp under at front of collar opening, and machine-stitch in position; neaten ends. Give a final light press.

Designed by "Dorette"

The Son's Pullover

The Front

Using the same needles as for the father's, cast on 78 sts. and work for 2½ inches in rib, then change to pattern and needles as before and work for 6½ inches in pattern stitch.

Now shape for the armholes, e.g. cast off 3 sts. at the beg. of the next 2 rows, then dec. 1 st. at each end of every other row until 58 sts. are left. Then continue in pattern until armhole is 5 inches deep.

Now work as follows: First work to the centre 12 sts., leave these on a piece of wool, and work to end. Now work back to neck end, knitting tog. the last 2 sts.

2nd row.—k. 2 tog., work to 4 sts. from shoulder end. Turn and work back to last 2 sts., knit them tog.

3rd row.—k. 2 tog., work to 8 sts. from shoulder end. Turn and work back, knitting the last 2 sts. tog. Work a fourth shaping to 12 sts. from shoulder end worked, then a fifth shaping to 16 sts. from shoulder end. Cast off across the shoulder sts.

Work on right side of neck to correspond.

Back

Work exactly as in the front to the armholes. Then dec. 1 st. at each end of every other row until 58 sts. are left, and continue to the end as in front.

Sleeves

Using the same materials, cast on 45 sts. and rib for 2½ inches. Then change to the No. 6 needles and pattern stitch, and work likewise, increasing 1 st. at each end of every 10th row until 65 sts. on needle and seam measures 13½ inches from the commencement of work.

Then shape for the top, e.g. cast off 2 sts. at the beg. of the next 2 rows, then dec. 1 st. at each end of every row until 23 sts. left. Cast off. Work the two sleeves alike.

Collar

Join shoulder seams and pick up the sts., commencing at the centre front, 6 of the sts. off the front at neck, and 40 sts. at each side, making 104 sts. in all. Work on these, leaving the opening at the front for 6 inches deep. Then cast off in pattern and loosely.

Make up exactly as the father's.

Your Daughter's School Frock

MATERIALS REQUIRED: 14 ounces of "Sirdar" Knop Yarn in any colour liked (the original was made in a soft shade of blue, flecked with white and black); 1 pair each of No. 7, No. 9, and No. 10 Stratnoid knitting needles; 1 No. 10 Stratnoid crochet hook; 1 press stud; a leather belt to match wool; and ⅛ yard of plain white neck trimming for a collar.

MEASUREMENTS: Width all round under arms, 30 inches (stretching to 32 inches); length from shoulder to lower edge, 31 inches; length of sleeve seam, 20 inches.

This will fit a girl of ten or eleven years.

TENSION: On No. 7 needles, 5 sts. to the inch; on No. 10 needles, 6¼ sts. to the inch; on No. 9 needles, 5½ sts. to the inch.

ABBREVIATIONS: k. = knit; p. = purl; tog. = together; st. = stitch; sts. = stitches; dec. = decrease; inc. = increase; d. cr. = double crochet.

The Back

With No. 7 needles, cast on 105 sts.

1st row.—k. 5, p. 2.

2nd row.—k. 2, p. 5. Repeat these two rows until work measures 9 inches, then change to No. 9 needles and continue in ribbing for a further 7 inches. Change to No. 10 needles and work 2 more inches (18 inches from start of work).

Work the first row of ribbing, then on the next k. 2, p. 5 row dec. as follows: * k. 2, p. 3, p. 2 tog., and repeat from * to end (90 sts. remain). This brings work to waistline.

From here, work a further 7 inches, working in rib of: *1st row.*—k. 4, p. 2, and repeat to end. *2nd row.*—k. 2, p. 4, and repeat to end.

Now shape armhole, by taking 2 sts. tog. at beginning and end of every row for 12 rows, always being careful to keep the continuity of the ribbing. From here, work without further shaping until armhole measures 6½ inches, then shape shoulder by casting off 7 sts. at beginning of the next six rows.

The Front

Work this exactly the same as back, as far as and including the row of the waist dec., then work as follows:

Rib over 40 sts., k. 8 (for garter stitch panel up front), rib 42 sts. Continue in ribbing, always knitting the 8 sts. for garter stitch on every row, until work measures 7 inches from waistline, but on last row before armhole shapings (a p. 4, k. 2 row on wrong side of work) work the first 42 sts. on to a spare needle. Finish row. Leave the sts. on a spare needle for right front, and continue working on left side thus: At beginning of every *1st row* of ribbing (a k. 4, p. 2 row) and end of every *2nd row* of pattern (a k. 2, p. 4 row) take 2 sts. tog., always keeping the continuity of the ribbing, until you have 12 dec. rows in all. Work five rows without dec., and at beginning of the next row (wrong side of work towards you) cast off 8 sts., then complete row as usual. Now dec. by taking 2 sts. tog. at end of every k. 4, p. 2 row until sts. number 21. Work straight until armhole is same depth as that of back (two rows on original), then shape shoulder by casting off 7 sts. at beginning of the next three rows, commencing from shoulder edge.

Join wool to neck edge of opposite side, and work armhole to match the first, reversing the shapings by dec. at END of every k. 4, p. 2 row, and *beginning* of every k. 2, p. 4 row, until you have 12 dec. rows in all. Work a further six rows, then on next row, starting at neck edge, shape for neck edge as follows:

1st row.—Cast off 5 sts. and complete row as usual. *2nd row.*—Rib as usual. Now dec. by taking 2 sts. tog. at beginning of every k. 4, p. 2 row, until sts. number 21. When armhole is same depth as that of other side, shape shoulder to match the first.

The Sleeves

With No. 10 needles, very LOOSELY cast on 36 sts. Work 2½ inches in k. 1, p. 1 rib, then change to the k. 4, p. 2 rib as used for bodice of frock, and work for a further 3 inches. From here, inc. (always keeping continuity of pattern) by working twice into the first and last st. of every 10th row until you have 45 sts. Work sixteen more rows without inc. (or more or less, if the sleeve is required shorter or longer for individual requirements), then dec. by taking 2 sts. tog. at beginning and end of every row until only 14 sts. remain. Work three rows without shaping, and cast off.

To Make Up

With a warm iron over a damp cloth, carefully press without stretching ribbing over-much. Join shoulder seams and sew sleeves into armholes. Sew up side seams. With right side of work towards you, crochet three rows of d. cr. from neck opening to join on the left-hand side of front. Sew on press stud for closing neck when in wear. Press seams.

Sew collar on to neck, and fasten on belt, using loops of crochet chain to keep it in position at waistline.

By
Beryl Grimsby

Let's Make TRUFFLES *and* FUDGE

Two Recipes for Home-Made Chocolates

THERE is always an element of fun in making sweets at home. Here are two varieties which will be sure to be eaten as soon as they are ready.

Chocolate Truffles

Chocolate Fudge

INGREDIENTS :

¾ lb. sieved icing sugar
3 ozs. almonds, blanched, shredded and baked golden, but not dark
2 ozs. butter *¼ pint cream*
2 ozs. unsweetened chocolate
Vanilla essence to taste

CUT the chocolate up small and put it into a saucepan. Melt it by standing the pan in another pan containing hot water. When the chocolate is melted, stir in the cream and let the mixture cook gently for five minutes, stirring it all the time. Remove the pan from the hot water, then add the butter a small piece at a time. Stir well, and see that each small addition of butter is mixed in before the next piece of butter is added. Then beat in the icing sugar gradually and add the vanilla. Then stir in the almonds and continue beating the mixture until it thickens, then pour it into a well-greased tin.

When it is set, cut it into squares, leaving them on grease-proof paper to dry.

If preferred the almonds can be omitted from this sweet.

Chocolate Fudge

Chocolate Truffles

INGREDIENTS :

4 ozs. grated chocolate
2 ozs. sifted icing sugar
A little thick cream
Vanilla essence to taste
Chocolate powder

MIX the grated chocolate and icing sugar together, adding the vanilla and sufficient cream to make a stiff paste.

Shape the mixture into small balls, and, as each one is ready, drop it into some chocolate powder, covering them all over. Use a spoon for this (not fingers).

Lift out the truffles with a fork and leave them to set, then put each one into a little paper case, or roll it up in tinfoil.

Party Cakes

By LILIAN MATTINGLY

Make this fairy tale house for your next children's party. The kiddies will love its white iced walls and almond paste lawn

JANUARY is the great time for parties, both children's and grown-ups, and new ideas are likely to be welcomed by the givers of them.

The modern child, at any rate, does not seem to like over-rich food, and I have therefore made a point of choosing simple recipes; but children do like amusing cakes, and the little house is really quite easy to make and is sure to be a great success. All the recipes given here are equally suitable for grown-up parties.

Here is a suggestion for a twenty-first birthday party. The problem of how to introduce candles without making a mess of the cake can be neatly solved in the way suggested in the photograph.

Have a ring of wood made and hammer twenty-one nails into it. Then cover it with silver paper or paint it with gold paint. Put twenty-one large candles of as many different colours as possible on the nails, and put the ring round the birthday cake.

As to the cake itself, this is very much a question of the personal taste of the "birthday child." I have chosen for this particular birthday cake an orange flavoured one.

Orange Birthday Cake

8 ozs. butter.
8 ozs. castor sugar.
4 eggs.
Rind of a large orange.
9 ozs. flour.
1 oz. ground rice.
½ teaspoonful baking-powder.

BEAT the butter and sugar to a cream, add the beaten eggs gradually, then the dry ingredients, including the grated orange. Put the mixture into an 8 or 9-in. tin, and bake in a moderate oven. Put it on a rack to get cool.

When cold, cut in half and put in a filling of orange icing (recipe follows), and put together again. Then spread the rest of the icing smoothly over the cake. Decorate with crystallised orange slices and angelica, or split almonds and angelica.

Orange Icing

Juice of 2 oranges.
2 whites of egg.
About 1½ lbs. icing sugar.
Orange colouring.

SIEVE the icing sugar. Put the orange juice sieved into a basin, and add the icing sugar slowly, mixing it with a wooden spoon. When half the icing sugar is in, put in the slightly beaten whites of egg, and continue adding the icing sugar, and beating well, until the mixture is thick and creamy. Colour it with orange vegetable colouring.

For the writing, make a very little water icing, and colour it with green vegetable colouring. Put a thread icing pipe into a forcing bag, fill the bag with the icing and write whatever birthday greeting you like.

Hedgehog cake is another amusing novelty. Mr. Hedgehog has a coat of chocolate icing and blanched almond "prickles"

Our Cookery Expert gives Recipes for Fascinating Tea-Time Novelties

Twenty-one to-day ! says the latch-key on the cake and the candles so cleverly arranged on a silvered ring around it

Chocolate Cake

(for the Little House).

4 ozs. butter.
4 ozs. castor sugar.
2 small eggs.
¾ oz. chocolate powder.
4 ozs. flour.
½ teaspoonful baking-powder.
2 tablespoonfuls warm water.
1 oz. ground rice.

CREAM the butter and sugar, add the well-beaten eggs gradually, and then the other ingredients, adding the warm water gradually at the end. Put the mixture into a square tin (5 ins. across), and bake in a fairly quick oven. Put on a rack to cool.

When cold, cut the top of the cake so that it slopes like a roof. Beat up some white méringue icing (see below) and spread smoothly round the sides. Let this set. Then mix a very little chocolate butter icing (see page 137), put it into a forcing bag with a thread icing pipe, and outline the door and windows with it. Fill in the door, and outline the panes on the windows. Make a tiny door handle of almond paste (see page 137). Stand the house on a small upturned oblong tray.

Having made the almond paste, take three-quarters of it and colour it with cochineal and a little lemon colouring a light brick colour. Then mould it to resemble a roof and put it on the top of the cake, filling in the gaps at the sides with almond paste. Make a small chimney of almond paste and stick it on to the roof.

Roll out the rest of the almond paste, and cut a strip for the path. Then colour the remainder green and put half on each side of the path. Finish it off with a little fence made of matches with cotton twined round the matches to resemble the bars of a fence. Stand some little figures in the garden.

If liked, flower beds can be made up against the house by sprinkling a little chocolate powder over the almond paste, and flowers can be made by using a small piece of angelica and putting a tiny blob of almond paste coloured pink at the top.

Animal biscuits are popular at any party. These are made in pairs, with a layer of jam or lemon curd inside and icing on top

These alluring "flower baskets" are decorated with coffee icing and crystallised petals, and topped with angelica handles

White Méringue Icing

1 tablespoonful warm water.
1 tablespoonful white of egg.
Icing sugar (sieved).

BEAT icing sugar into the warm water, add the slightly beaten white of egg, and continue

adding icing sugar until the mixture is creamy, beating well all the time.

Chocolate Butter Icing

BEAT together 1 oz. of butter and 1½ oz. sieved icing sugar until thick and creamy, then add a little grated chocolate dissolved over warm water.

Almond Paste

6 ozs. ground almonds.
7½ ozs. (half icing, half castor) sugar.
6 drops almond essence.
Egg to mix (about ¾).
Small ½ teaspoonful each—vanilla essence, rum, sherry, lemon juice.

STIR the ingredients together, then knead until they form a dough. Roll out on a board over sieved icing sugar.

Hedgehog Cakes

4 ozs. butter.
4 ozs. castor sugar.
2 eggs.
4½ ozs. flour.
¼ teaspoonful baking-powder.
½ oz. ground rice.

BEAT the butter and sugar to a cream. Add the beaten eggs gradually, and beat well. Then add the flour, ground rice and baking-powder, and mix thoroughly. Bake in bun tins in a fairly quick oven. When cold, ice with chocolate glacé icing made as follows :—

Put four tablespoonfuls of warm water into a basin and beat in sieved icing sugar until creamy. Melt some grated chocolate over hot water (do not let the chocolate get more than lukewarm) and add it. Continue beating until well mixed, then spread smoothly over the cakes.

Cut some blanched almonds into little quills, and stick them into the icing to resemble the back of a hedgehog.

Flower Baskets

4 eggs.
4 ozs. castor sugar.
2 ozs. melted butter.
3 ozs. flour.
Pinch of baking-powder.

BEAT the eggs and sugar with a whisk over hot water till creamy. Whisk till cold. Add flour and baking-powder, then the melted butter. Bake in bun tins in a hot oven. When cold, ice with coffee butter icing made as follows :—

Beat together 6 ozs. butter and 9 ozs. sieved icing sugar until the mixture is thick and creamy. Then add coffee essence to taste. Spread some of the icing smoothly over the tops of the buns. Put the rest of the icing into a forcing bag with an eight-star icing pipe and decorate round the edges of the buns, leaving the middle bare. Then fill in the centres with crystallised petals (violet, rose, mimosa, etc.), and finish each basket off with a handle of angelica.

Iced Biscuits

THE recipe for these delicious biscuits, held over owing to lack of space, can be obtained from Lilian Mattingly, c/o MODERN HOME, 18, Henrietta Street, London, W.C. 2. Send her all your cookery problems, enclosing a stamped envelope for reply.

A CHILDREN'S GAME

HERE is a game for children. A strip of "enchanted ground," about a yard wide, is made down the middle of the room. A length of stair-carpet will serve for it, or two chalked lines.

One person stands within the strip, and it is her aim to prevent any others crossing. The rest of those taking part are constantly jumping backwards and forwards across the strip, and the one in the middle darts up and down trying to touch them as they pass over. Anyone so touched becomes "enchanted," and has to stay in the middle and help with the capture of the others.

The winner of the game is the one who longest evades capture.

By JOAN WOOLLCOMBE

Raine McCorquodale, daughter of Barbara Cartland, the novelist, in the nursery with her Nannie

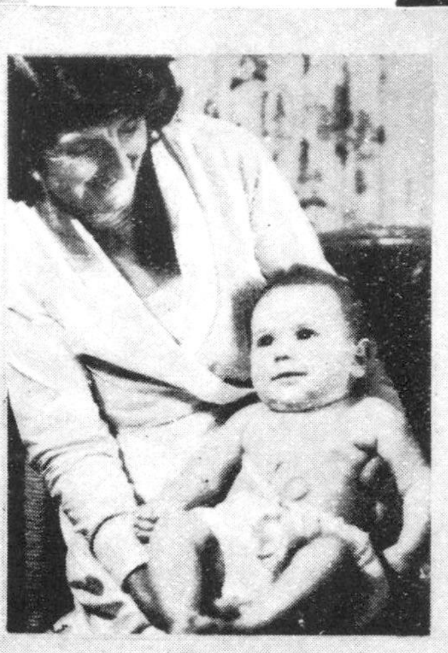

Edward Hardwicke, the little son of Sir Cedric and Lady Hardwicke, has old-fashioned London nurseries

Nannie Sculpher, nurse to the children of the late Sir Nigel and of Lady Playfair, is now their trusted maid

Courtesy of Lady Playfair

The nursery-trained "Nannie" or the college-trained "Nurse"? Which do you prefer?

INCREASINGLY often do we see—and sigh to see—a certain type of obituary notice. It shows one generation making way for another, but it is an obituary that instantly evokes a picture that makes us home-sick for the best part of childhood. Actually, it runs something like this:

"Smith.—On January 5th, 1934, after a short illness, at X—— Manor, Ellen Emma Smith, aged 80, for 65 years the most beloved Nannie and faithful friend of Lady X, her children and grandchildren."

In that short notice is the epitome of the English nursery system, with its tremendously powerful and much-loved "non-commissioned officer" factor—*Nannie*. Nannie who, in about the year 1870, graduated from below-stairs to try her hand in the nursery; to nursery work of a fetch-and-carry sort under a sharp-tongued tyrant who was her predecessor even as she, now, is the predecessor of the Nannie of to-day.

This young "Ellen Emma Smith" had, in all probability, gone into service long before the now respectably fixed school age: there were too many in the crowded cottage home at the gates of the Manor of X. But early enough, Ellen Emma showed she had a "way" with children and so was soon promoted to the nurseries to be the ally and always respectful playmate of the elder child directly the second baby arrived. Her wages were small enough: for in the 1870's even the housemaid was content with some £12 a year and one day off every six weeks: but, curiously, and in spite of the really tremendous power she later wielded, Ellen Emma remained remarkably humble to the last day of her life. Not that she did not have her difficult moments, this perpetual spinster who emptied her affections upon another woman and her children: but never so difficult that she was not amenable to her "dear mistress"—with whom she had, in fact, grown up into womanhood.

But she and her colleagues saw "life" at its best, and those that remain, remain as a curiously stable factor in a world apparently increasingly distracted. Nursery tea remains a rite long after late dinner has become a post-cocktail snack. . .

Before, for strictly practical purposes, we explore the possibilities (and cost!) of the Nannie as she is to-day, the famous product of Britain, and until recently, one of our most sought-after exports, it is worth while remembering her at the height of her achievement and power. Remembering her in the persons of some extremely famous Nannies, who—did we but know it—were as much beneficent despots to our

NANNIES
—old style and new

Miss Emma Squires, nurse to Lord Reading's family, who was in their service for more than forty years

Courtesy of Lady Reading

parents as to our grandparents; pausing only to gaze with some satisfaction on the pleasant sight of a carriage as it drives around the Royal Parks, to-day. Sitting sedately inside are two small girls, usually bareheaded—the younger on the lap of a quiet, dignified woman, dressed generally in grey tailor-made, the most famous of all contemporary Nannies, described, by one who knows her, as an extremely fine as well as an able woman whom both her small charges obey without hesitation—the Nurse to T.R.H. the Princess Elizabeth and the Princess Margaret Rose and the paramount Nannie of Mayfair!

This Nannie had charge of Lady Caroline Blackwood, elder daughter of the Marchioness of Dufferin and Ava

Keystone

These famous Nannies have their compensations for lifetimes of devotion. Perhaps the most delightful account of all is the account given by Lady Horner of the nurse to her own family of four children. "Nannie Day," says Lady Horner, writing of her, "was a very good playmate nurse. She was quite as keen about bird-nesting or flower-hunting or picnics as any of the children, and they were always happy with her. Looking back on those days, I can't remember any nursery punishments. Even going to bed was fun and the ritual of the bath was never docked of one of its delightful features. She stayed with me till Mark was five or six, gay, energetic, religious and sensible, creating a pleasant nursery world around her. The children adored her, as all properly-minded children do adore their nurses: and I never saw anything but good and happy faces."

How much, too, of the unshakable integrity as well as the fine imagination and intellectual equipment of the most (*Continued on page* **140**)

NANNIES—OLD STYLE AND NEW

famous of all recent English editors, do we owe, quite definitely to that remarkable woman who was his nurse? St. Leo Strachey, of the *Spectator*, writes (as does Lady Horner in her book) of his own nurse. Mrs. Leaker, who had married title by the usual brevet rank accorded such notables, played many parts in the household of his childhood and youth—nurse, cook and housekeeper. Of her, Mr. Strachey says: "She was one of the most remarkable women, whether for character or intellect, that I have ever come across . . ." and adds that she was "an example of Sir Thomas Browne's dictum that we live by an invisible flame within us."

Children were then reared on lusty mental food; for Mrs. Leaker read the future Editor of the *Spectator* to sleep with the witches' scene in *Macbeth* and the death scene in *Othello*. Mrs. Leaker speaks for all the legions of faithful servants when she writes, much later: "*I have not had an unpleasant life, although I was an old maid and was a servant for fifty years. I was a nurse, and no mother could have loved her children more than I loved those I nursed. . . .*"

The death of Emma Squires a year or two ago reminds us that the "faithful servant" is essentially part of the family to whom she devotes her life. Squires came to Lord Reading's family in 1889 and remained as nurse to the little son of a young barrister, Rufus Isaacs. She stayed on after the future Lord Erleigh grew up as maid to Lady Reading, travelled to the States during the War and went to India during her master's Viceroyalty. Over forty years she remained with the family whose friend she was.

With Miss Helen Sculpher we bring the tradition up to the present: she has been more than twenty-three years in the service of the late Sir Nigel and of Lady Playfair; first as cook and then (in her true *métier*) as friend and nurse of the three sons, Giles, Lyon and Andrew. She remembers back, already: remembers that she has never believed in any form of corporal punishment and that (a word for mothers!) the best of all is the mother who "does not interfere."

It is the best Nannies, whether retired or active, who pay tributes to their "dear mistresses"—as does Miss Sculpher. She talks, with salutary firmness, about the high-falutin' ideas that afflict those who cannot put themselves out to do jobs that are not, strictly speaking, their own.

In passing, it is worth remarking that the English Nannie is not a sentimental figure at all: but a shrewd person, capable of the most astringent common sense as well as the most amazing self-sacrifice.

Remarkable and almost unbelievable stories of Nannies' self-sacrifice occasionally come to light: such as that told me by Mrs. Tew of Folkestone whose family Nannie, Fanny Smith, died only last year. With her death the family discovered that this old lady had, under a vow of secrecy, *returned* the small pension granted her by the family to their solicitor—recognising that the needs of a growing family would probably be greater than hers. Mrs. Tew, in describing her, stresses that fast vanishing custom of the "going-down-to-the-drawing-room-after-tea," that hour's play which was so often all Nannie's charges saw of mother! The result of this, says Mrs. Tew, of Fanny Smith, was that "we all loved her more than my mother. I could tell you several instances of my childhood in which she figured, and I can see her in many phases: singing *Safe in the arms of Jesus* to my little dying brother *and* pursuing me with a hair-brush after I had given her what she called 'sauce.'"

"Nannie" is still one of the most honourable titles it is within the power of a family to bestow.

To the younger moderns comes the problem: how to find Nannie (when things are so much more difficult, means more straitened and ideas modernised), how to keep her, what to pay her—and the pros and cons of the selection of a "nursery-trained" as against a "college-trained" woman.

The younger married woman has, before she "hires" the woman who, next to herself, is the most important unit in her household, to decide which of the two categories she will approach. As one veteran Nannie put it to me, "There's Institution-trained and college-trained nurses and—*there's Nannies, nursery trained.*"

But, in spite of the understandable bitterness in the veteran's tone, both types have their definite advantages under certain conditions: but the details of the finding, engaging and retaining of the regular college-trained children's nurse are so much more cut-and-dried: for instance, the Norland Institute have rightly drawn up rules and conditions that safeguard both their trainees and those who engage them.

The engagement of a real old-style Nannie is a different matter: so much is done by personal recommendation and so much more by the flair of certain agency heads for selecting "*just the Nannie that will suit you.*" Here the genius for personal interview is of the utmost importance: first in the agency interviewer, and then in the young mother who endeavours, in a talk, to find out not only whether Nannie will help with her nursery dusting, but whether she is exactly the sort of woman fitted by intuition and experience, to take the most important post in her power to give.

The question of salaries arises. A really first-rate, educated lady-nurse appears to command from £90 to £120 per annum: a younger Nannie from £50 to the figure that mellow Nannies demand—and get!

The young woman, determined to secure a "real old-fashioned Nannie" may either engage a contemporary, graduating from under-nurse with whom she will actually do a great deal of work herself; or she may obtain a Nannie from one or other of the sources open to her—personal recommendation or a good agency.

For the latter, I have two admirable and famous Bureaux in mind: neither is formidable to enter, even for the youngest modern of us all, and both are run by clever and shrewd women. First, there is the well-known "Mrs. Boucher's"—perhaps the most famous of its kind in the world: from here Nannies and lady-nurses of all types go to every corner of the globe and to almost every pre- and post-War family of note. Mrs. Boucher herself popularised the "lady-nurse," who is in some cases the able successor of the old-fashioned Nannie, when she can often combine the work of the nurse and the nursery-governess. Mrs. Boucher's, also, has a temporary staff—composed of nurses whom they have known and placed for a great number of years, and this side of the organisation is run on the lines of a hospital—for nurses are sent out actually on receipt of a wire or telephone by the hour, day, week or month!

Again, "Mrs. Boucher's" will select her nurse for the mother living abroad: do the interviewing and arrange her journey for a reasonable special fee.

There is also the more recently famous "Cow and Gate" Bureau, run under the supervision of Mrs. Yellen, whose success is based entirely upon her insistence upon the value of the personal interview, both with client and Nannie. At this Bureau carefully chosen Nannies are introduced to equally carefully selected "Mummies."

It is difficult, in sober terms, to assess the value of just such agencies: the paramount importance of the right Nannie for the right household cannot be over-estimated. It is the expert at the agency who will advise whether or not Nannie will do her nurseries, wash, make and mend: will meal with the servants, or will not . . . and so on. It is, so often, the expert who advises the old-style Nannies to unbend a little, undertake a little more for the less-moneyed parents—and finds a real treasured friend for the inexperienced modern mother with her first baby!

A DUCK *for* BABY'S BATH

It is Filled With Sponge and Floats

The duck is made of white towelling which makes him look fluffy.

A TOY that is useful as well as amusing will please the little one, and his " Mummie " even more.

This duck takes the place of a sponge, being made of towelling and stuffed with sponge. He floats upright, being properly weighted like the keel of a boat.

He is amusing, too, to make.

MATERIALS REQUIRED :

¼ yard Turkish towelling.

2-inch square yellow sateen or linen.

An old bath sponge.

1 flat pebble. 2 black beads.

The Duck Transfer No. 880.

The transfer is used as a pattern. Lay it on the towelling, and cut out the various pieces. Turnings are allowed for, and the dotted lines show where the stitching comes.

Sew the two body pieces together on the wrong side, leaving a two-inch opening underneath the duck.

Turn it inside out. Cut the sponge into small pieces, and stuff the duck with these, remembering to leave room for the sponge to swell in the water.

Cover a flat pebble with the pieces of towelling and stitch this into the two-inch opening at the base in order to balance the duck when in the water.

Having stitched the two pieces for the beak together, on the wrong side, turn it inside out and pad it with a very small quantity of vegetable down. Neatly sew the beak to the head, turning in the raw edges. The wings are made double. Sew the pieces neatly together, turning in the raw edges and stitch them in place on the duck.

Finally stitch on two black beads to make the eyes, and the duck is ready to be used as a toy for the bath or as a child's sponge.

A Fleet of Little Ducklings

IT would be an easy matter to make smaller ducks from the same transfer, by making smaller shapes.

Place a piece of tracing paper over the transfer and pencil the shape of the duck and its pieces one inch or so smaller inside the outlines. Cut round the pencil lines and use the pieces as patterns for the ducklings.

It would be a good idea to use pale yellow towelling for this, to make them more like real little ducklings.

In the same way you could make a large Grandfather duck by pencilling outside the shapes.

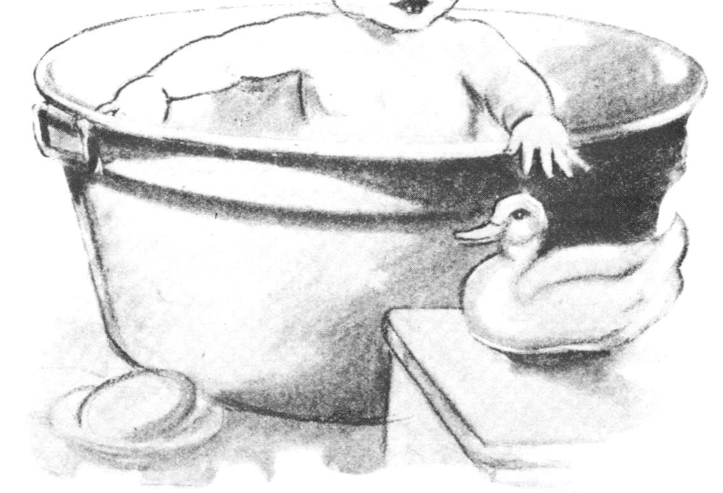

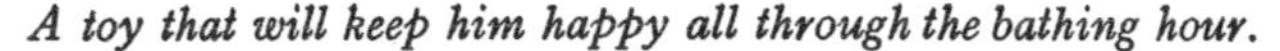

A toy that will keep him happy all through the bathing hour.

MADE OF PAPER

A Simple Way of Amusing and Interesting the Children

When people still used penknives to cut quill-pens and kept them very sharp, they used to cut out wonderful little pictures in paper. Some they tucked inside their watch-cases just for fun; some they mounted; and some they hid away in a safe place and showed to their children as the greatest of treats, and with many a "Now, don't touch them, or they'll get torn."

I can't do anything as lovely; but I have a very humble accomplishment which has often stood me in good service with the help of a pair of scissors, and odds-and-ends of paper—especially in starting a friendship with a shy child, in amusing a party of children who need to be "cooled down" after a romp, or in keeping a little invalid contented in bed.

Parents are often so tactless; they drag a luckless infant up to the lion's mouth of an unknown stranger, and expect it to make polite conversation. All the best children hate it as much as I do. I shake hands and leave them alone. But when I borrow mummie's scissors and begin cutting up an old envelope I find in my bag, they steal nearer to watch.

Fans into Paper Dolls

You know how you can fold a piece of paper to and fro and crease it carefully into a make-shift fan? The child smiles; perhaps it says, "Let me!" but, taking no notice, I begin at one set of folds, tracing, with my scissors, half the outline of a little figure; half a tall hat, a head rounding back into a slender neck, widening for shoulders and a bent elbow, the arm reaching to the second set of folds which must be left uncut if linked figures are desired.

Cut, therefore, to the folded edges, and starting again the width of the arms below, cut up the under-sleeve, outline the side and bottom of a lounge coat, before embarking upon the trousers (which should end heeled shoes); when the blades work upwards again with the fork of the legs terminating at the folds' edges.

I drop the little man into my lap unnoticed, and open out the fan, with its regular tracing of open-work serving as decoration and accepted by the child with a shy smile. But when the little men are unwrapped before its eyes there are delighted chuckles and all shyness has fled.

A larger sheet of paper is found, a longer fan is made of many more folds. Imagination and the scissors are at work on little girls with fluttering pinafores, flapping sunbonnets, towsled hair, skipping-ropes—anything, indeed, the cutter can mesmerise the child into suggesting that is within the measure of possibilities.

"A Boat! A Boat!"

What next? Why, a boat to go sailing in the bath at bedtime (now all too near for eyes full of sleepy-dust).

The completed paper objects. From left to right—top row: ball or bomb, fan, box; below: boat with central pyramid, barge

Take a sheet of paper the size and shape of a page of the *Farmer & Stock-Breeder*, fold the top A down to the bottom B, and crease along the line C—D (Fig. 1). Take the ends of the fold C—D down to meet each other at E (the middle of the page, Fig. 2).

There will be two single flaps beyond the base of the triangle. Fold these up on to the triangle, first one side and then the other (Fig. 3). Slip your hand up the centre of the triangle, flatten it out into a square (Fig. 4), arranging the flaps neatly under each other on each side. Take the corner J and fold the square into a triangle by meeting J with K; turn over and repeat on the other side.

Slip the fingers again up this second triangle (Fig. 5) and form a second square (Fig. 6) by flattening it out the opposite way. Take the folds J and K lightly between thumbs and first fingers, and pull gently apart into a boat with a central pyramid (Fig. 6). The whole process is that of making alternate triangles and squares of decreasing size, but with added firmness. By repeating the processes of Figs. 5 and 6, a more seaworthy vessel will result, though relatively smaller.

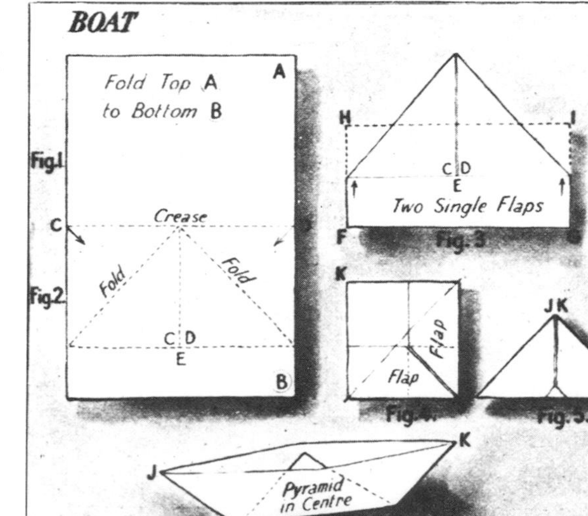

Diagram showing how to make the boat

Box First, Then Barge

The boat is most widely known, and stands more squarely on dry land; the lidless box I will now explain is useful for small collections of samples; and the barge trims better than the boat when afloat in the bath.

Begin with a perfect square of paper; fold each corner into the middle and mark each with an X (this lettering will make it easier to follow my directions correctly—see Fig. 1).

Fold A and B back on C and D (after having lettered these corners) so that the X's are uppermost; repeat process on opposite side. Raise A and B to the fold, thus covering the X; turn and repeat on opposite side (Figs. 2 and 3).

Open the paper at Fig. 3 so that the lines A—B and C—D meet in the middle of a long parallelogram; double this back into a square (Fig. 4). Lift the corners C and A and make the lines C—E and A—E coincide with F—G as far as they will, the ends C and A projecting beyond in the outline of a boat; turn and repeat on other side (Figs. 4 and 5).

The paper has now the appearance of twin boats. Holding at the centre E, pull up the X corner (inside the C—A boat) into the shape seen in Fig. 6; flatten on the table, and turn the corners C, X and A to meet each other at O in the middle, thus forming a square again (Fig. 6). Double this I J down on to the line (Fig. 6) marked "bottom of box"; repeat process with second boat.

The box is now completed and can be opened into a lidless affair like a carpenter's cap with two flapped sides and two plain. The transformation to a barge is made easier by creasing along the middle of the two plain sides so that top and bottom of the box meet (on the plain sides only).

Next, flatten the flap-sides back against the outside of the bottom of the box, flaps uppermost. Turn the whole thing over and you see (Fig. 7) two of the X corners meeting each other. Fold in half, with the two X's outside, along the line P—Q; and with both thumbs and first-fingers pinching P and Q, draw them gently apart. With a little further emphasising of the creases for firmness, you have a barge with a deep hold in the middle and a high deck fore and aft.

A Paper Bomb

The paper bomb is a cunning contrivance, but should not be taught to naughty boys! It was shown me by an old lawyer who (born in 1802) had seen Lady Hamilton; he told me to fill it with water and throw it at my teacher, but, of course, I never did! Dropped from a height (when it has been filled with water by a pen-filler at its single minute entrance) it squelches and bursts in a most engaging fashion.

Begin by folding a perfect square in half so that the opposite sides meet, and crease the fold along with the first finger and the thumbnail. Open out the square and crease in the same manner, but at right angles. Open out on the reverse side of the paper and similarly, in two separate operations, crease two diagonals.

Notice that the raised ribs of the two diagonals meet the two sunken valleys of the first straight creases, and that this facilitates the folding of the square into two flat triangles with folded triangles between. Mark the bases of the two flat triangles A—B and C—D.

With the bases towards you, lift A and B to the peak of the triangle on one side, and C and D on the opposite side, thus forming a square. Mark the four new corners now made midway between the apex and base of the first triangles, E and F, and G and H. On one side fold over E and F to meet each other on the line made when C and D were turned up to the peak; on the other turn G and H to the line made by B and A when turned upwards.

The sides of the bomb are now closed by tucking B and A back from the apex into the double pocket of G and H; and (on the opposite side) D and C into the pocket of E and F. This looks dull and complicated to read; but if you have carried out the processes in order, as directed, lettering each, your fingers will make all plain to you. It now only remains to apply your lips to the minute entrance at the bottom of the bomb and plump it out with a vigorous breath. (See photographic group of paper toys.)

For Grown-Ups and Children

I should advise the grown-ups in the family to try a preliminary canter (if the young folk are still of nursery or schoolroom age) and then, each with a sheet or square of paper (each, if you please, with a cracker-cap on the head from the Christmas dessert), set about copying a right-hand neighbour's manipulations until the circle round the table is completed.

Should some of the toys be known to some of you before, the ignorant will learn all the quicker; and I hope if they are new to the youngsters, twenty-years-on they will be teaching to *their* youngsters the simple parlour tricks "Countrywoman" has so often found invaluable.

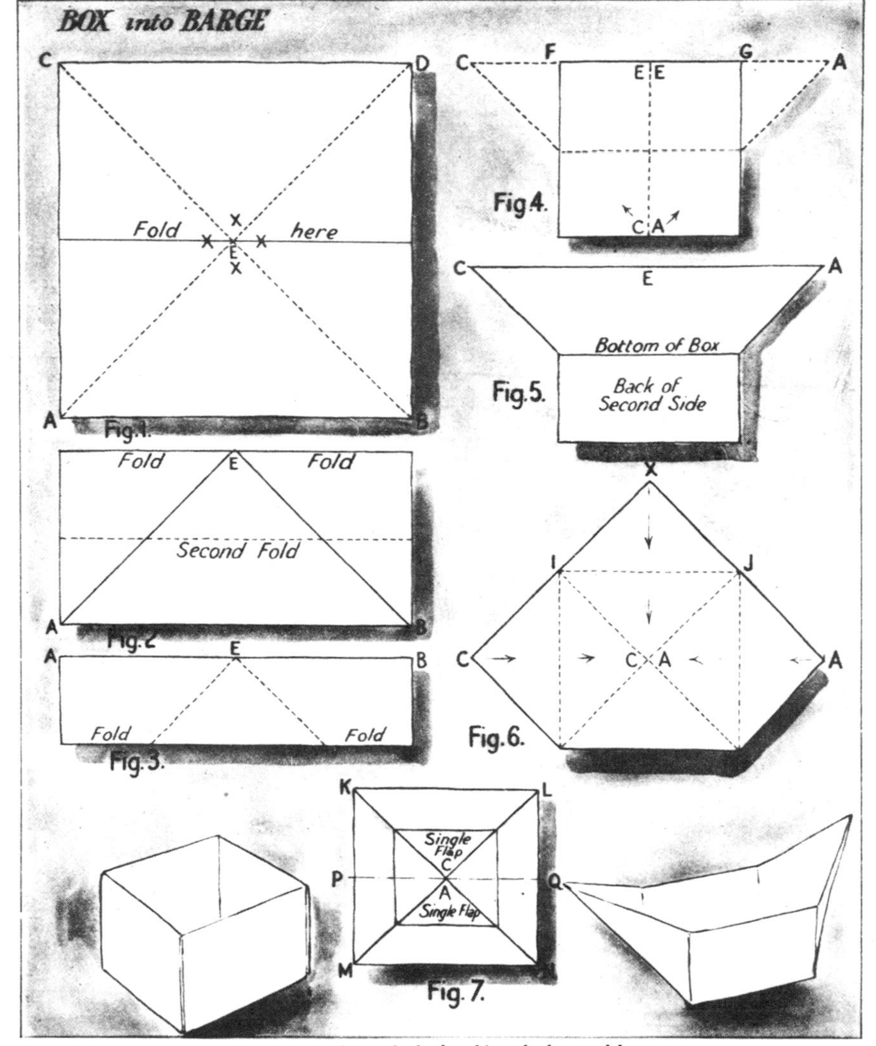

Here is seen the method of making the box and barge

By COUNTRYWOMAN

Ensuring the Happin

Illustration by Clara Elsene Peck

by Margaret Marriner, M.B., Ch.B.

(Author of "First Aid to Marriage")

who shows parents the way to right understanding of the child mind, so as to prevent disharmony at home and warping of personality

"A few strong instincts and a few simple rules suffice us."—EMERSON.

"CAN'T you give me some kind of an A.B.C. to understand my young folks?" asked a mother of several children, ranging in ages from five to eighteen. "I'm so busy; I cannot possibly read all the books on Psychology—and still, I feel I want to profit by what doctors and others have discovered about the human mind." I sat down and worked it out in as simple a language as possible.

I find it very helpful—and it is also scientific—to look at the mind as an instrument—an instrument with ten strings when it is fully grown, and fewer when it is younger. These strings are the instincts. All approach to the personality is done through these instincts, and if they are properly handled we get harmony and beautiful music; if they are mishandled or neglected, we get jarring tones and unhappiness. The ten instincts are listed on the opposite page, and to understand our children we must memorise them all.

Topping and permeating all tendencies of childhood, is the instinct of *Self-Preservation.* This instinct is the first to attach itself to the human being, and the last to leave it. As the years go by we may learn to love our neighbours as ourselves, but in infancy and early childhood self-love reigns supreme. If this self-love persists in adult life and does not learn to project itself towards others, psychologists call it Narcissism, after the Greek youth Narcissus, who beheld the reflection of his young beauty in a bathing-pool, and ever after loved himself.

"Don't be selfish," we do and must admonish our children, but the wise father and mother realise that because the child is so weak and not, so to

ess of our Children

These are the ten instincts all parents should recognise in their children:

Self-Preservation—Self-Assertion—Submission—Curiosity—Sociability—Acquisition—Sex—Protection—Beauty—Enjoyment

speak, fully established, Mother Nature tells it to look very well after itself. She wants it to live and flourish because she is far more concerned with the young than with the old. Life *must* continue, is the law underlying this instinct of Self-Preservation.

If a child says, "I wish I were dead," we get duly frightened. We know it has been deeply hurt, for the love and zest of life is Nature's great gift to every child. This instinct of Self-Preservation makes the child skip and hop and for ever be on the move. "Oh, do be quiet," we say, but we forget that life is movement. Growth can only take place if every muscle, nerve, bone and organ is duly exercised, for if they are used they are nourished.

In childhood we are small; we are feeble; we are surrounded by dangers. We are entirely dependent on those terrible grown-ups, who can do what they like. *They* can sit up for dinner, go and come as it pleases them, wash or not wash. How happy they must be! Against this feeling of dependency, Nature, in a wonderful way, gives children the instinct of *Self-Assertion* very early. If a child has not been bullied and made miserable by grown-ups or bigger children, it is wonderfully sure of its own importance; and, when we examine the situation closely, what a good thing it is!

So far the child has achieved nothing; but never mind, it has every right to the good things of life. Even a tiny baby wants to be noticed. Look how it sits up in its cot and tries to look important when a stranger enters the room; it wants to assert itself; it doesn't want to be left in obscurity. If a child cannot assert itself it is miserable; nothing hurts a child so much as living with a bully. The deepest troubles of later life rise from lack of opportunity to assert and (*Continued on page* **146**) make oneself some kind of success in childhood.

Doctors find that people who can do *one* thing at least really well, usually enjoy life and are not subject to neurasthenia. It is most important that we realise this deep-seated instinct in our children to *assert* themselves. Sometimes it needs curbing and sometimes it needs encouraging.

A new school of teaching has sprung up. It preaches self-development for children, but it does not reckon with the instinct of *Submission*. A happy child does not object to obedience, in fact it likes it. It is not in the least "against nature" to obey; we are, in fact, never happier than when we submit to somebody who is wiser and better than ourselves. It is only when the child is unjustly treated that it revolts against rules and laws. . . . "Honour thy father and thy mother," is a good law.

My own little girl said one day to me, quite of her own accord, "I should hate it, if nobody told me how to behave." She had lately returned from a visit to some little friends who were allowed to do as they liked.

A child has very little reasoning power. It is too great a burden for it to pick and choose for itself in this complicated life; it is real peace for it to trust implicitly in somebody else. Lucky is the child whose horizon is bounded by loving, sensible parents! "Don't forget to come and kiss me good-night," says the happy child, going early to bed. In these words it shows the confidence and submission to all-powerful, kind parents. Imagine the confusion if every child could argue what time it was good for it to go to bed! If we are wise parents and understand this instinct of submission we need not be frightened of being firm with our children.

Some people are even so happy in this submission that they do not want to grow up. Doctors who try to heal the mind are always coming across this deep longing in the human heart for somebody to submit to in love. Unfortunately civilised life with its strain and stress has not much use for grown-up children; childhood alone has the privilege of submissive adoration.

A certain amount of curiosity should be encouraged in young children; we expect them to be curious and we know there is something lacking when a child is not interested in its surroundings—yet the tired mother quite often shuts up the children. I know it is a trial when your little son asks in a loud voice in a crowded bus, "Mummy, why has that man got such a red nose?" but don't forget that it is at bottom not only curiosity but friendliness and interest in his fellow human beings that prompts the child.

As we get older we get less curious, but an intelligent child has got the instinct of *Curiosity* well developed. It is a big thing to have been born into this world; the least we can do is to find out all about it. Perhaps it would be a good thing if we, as parents, woke up and started with our children to discover all the marvellous and beautiful things by which we are surrounded.

I love the story about the old man of eighty, setting out to see Italy.

"You are rather old to go to Italy," said a friend.

"*Old*, yes, that's why I'm going," he returned. "It would not do for me to die and for God to ask me, 'What do you think of my beautiful Italy?' and for me to say that I had never been there!"

We hear a good deal of introverts and extroverts these days: by telling your child not to ask questions, you curb his zeal for knowledge and insight, and make him close up. Later in life you will be glad if he tells you all his troubles and is more of an extrovert than an introvert. The introvert with his self-consciousness has a much harder time in this modern world than the extrovert with his enquiring and mentally alert mind. The latter is a much better mixer.

When a child is quite young it can often play happily by itself, but when it gets a little older it needs the company of other children as we all know. It is its *Social*, or *Herd Instinct* that is showing itself. Primitive man probably kept to himself with his mate in the beginning of Time, but then he found that he could better defend himself against animals and inclement weather when he kept close to others. Deep in us, therefore, goes on the fight between the wish to stand alone and the necessity for others. As the child is getting older, parents are often bewildered by its different moods. One day the young boy or girl will shut himself up in a room all alone; and the next day no society is numerous or gay enough.

In these days of small families, it is often difficult to satisfy the Herd Instinct in our children: father and mother must be the playfellows, instead of brothers and sisters. Even school does not satisfy in the same way as the crowded nursery of our own days. It seems to me one of the saddest things in life that our children are missing all the fun we used to have with our numerous brothers, sisters and cousins. What games we had! And how much we learnt in childhood of the rough and tumble of life. Parents must realise what a healthy thing in their children is this longing for company, and do all they can to bring little friends to the house.

When our children begin to "collect things" it is a sign of the instinct of *Acquisition* awakening. They are not any longer satisfied in just being themselves; they must surround themselves with *things*: it becomes embarrassing when the boy's room is littered with marbles, butterflies, bits of stone; the girl's with boxes, beads, ribbons, all kinds of untidy things. And if you destroy any of these objects that seem so valueless to you, they are broken-hearted. I remember how I dreaded my mother tidying my room. Some treasure was sure to be missing after she had been trying to make order out of chaos. The growing child is losing its childish confidence and self-assertion when it begins to "collect." Up to now it has been so happy, but now it suddenly discovers that it is small and unimportant and has a long way to go before it has any real assets.

The world instead of being friendly, begins to appear inimical; others possess this and that but a child has nothing. Father, for instance—how much he has compared with his children! Nearly every boy, if his father is not very wise, goes through a period of envying his father. The instinct of *Acquisition* is evolved out of this conflict.

The small child is curious about the outside world; but older children, about ten and eleven or later, begin to get curious about themselves. Up to now they have looked with wonder at the pear and apple tree, laden with blossom in the spring, and heavy with fruit in the autumn, but now they begin to guess that they themselves will one day be able to take part in Nature's great scheme: for are not babies being born? This is indeed a wonderful thing, and they begin to ask questions. A lot has been written about sex information; all we can do is to answer questions frankly as they arise, and telling the children to come to us for any information they want.

Children vary a great deal in this respect. Some are much more curious than others. I do not see any advantage in telling them things too early. It is very embarrassing to give them information they do not want; probably they won't understand it at all. I remember trying to explain the facts of life to my daughter of fourteen, as I thought it was time she knew everything. Haltingly I did my best and hoped she had understood. I was astonished to the extreme, therefore, when she came some weeks afterwards and asked me whether I thought she was having a baby as she had been kissed.

The *Sex* instinct is in growing children only an impulse, a matter of curiosity; but it has to be watched carefully and each child must be treated individually. Years pass before, in Western man and woman, it finally takes shape, drawing him or her to an individual with so much strength that marriage can be contemplated. But it is struggling all through adolescence.

There is the danger of the young adult attaching himself or herself with quite uncontrolled devotion to some person long before they are ready for marriage. Sometimes it is daughter to father, or son to mother—at times it is some quite unworthy person of the same sex as themselves. In *Dusty Answer*, by Rosamond Lehmann, we see Judith, the lonely girl, violently attracted to Jennifer, who is quite unworthy of her affection. . . . "Always Jennifer. It was impossible to drink up enough of her, and a day without her was a day with the light gone."

Parents should guard against these uncontrolled attachments of adolescence. The great thing is to fill the children's life with plenty of wholesome pleasures.

Close to the Sex instinct stirs the instinct of *Protection*. The young boy or girl will suddenly show a tenderness and kindness to things weaker than themselves. They will handle a kitten or a puppy in a new way; the raw boy will astonish us by sometimes offering to nurse the refractory baby. In the old days little brothers and sisters found a good friend in the older brother. Nowadays, as there is so often no small brother or sister to protect, this instinct finds its outlet in the relationship to animals or sometimes to a mother if she is weak or an invalid.

Sometimes we think that we are perhaps trying too hard to make our children happy. Would it be better for them to have a little hardship—know what it is to be miserable?

But—no! We are doing right, trying, according to our means, to give them a carefree and joyous time to look back upon, for childhood shouldn't only be a preparation for life but in itself a happy background for all that is to come. If we have had a happy childhood, we have ballast in our ship of life. Whatever happens to us later we can always say: we were at least happy as children. Parents are on safe ground when they let the instincts of *Enjoyment* and *Beauty* rule their children.

The child feels things so deeply; its immature mind is quite unable to see the silver lining—a cloud is a cloud, and darkness is darkness. But on the other side of the picture—how it can laugh!—and how it loves beautiful things!

A child plays because in its play it is learning the more serious business of life. We know that there is something wrong with a child who sits about listless. Very often the first thing a mother tells a doctor is, "Tommy is so quiet, he does not laugh and play. What can be wrong with him?

Do you think he is ill?"

To kill the laughter in a child's heart is wicked. Charles Dickens could never forgive his father for not preventing his suffering in the shoeblack factory. Years after he wrote, "It is wonderful to me that even after my descent into the poor little drudge I had been ever since we came to London, no one had compassion enough on me—a child of singular abilities, quick, eager, delicate, and soon hurt, bodily and mentally, to suggest that something might have been spared—as certainly it might have been—to place me in a common school."

Much unhappiness in childhood is now averted by the work of such organisations as the National Baby Week Council, whose week this year from July 1st to 7th, is directed mainly towards the care of the pre-school child; and those who have studied the question know that the joys of childhood, as the sorrows of childhood, reach right into manhood and womanhood. A man of thirty said to me the other day, "They all told my father and mother that they spoiled me, but do you know, in spite of having such a lot as a child—riding, lovely holidays, good theatres, I can enjoy, even now, the simplest things. I feel so grateful to them for having taught me to appreciate all the good and beautiful things of life."

If parents recognise these ten instincts in their children and see that they are well balanced, they will one day have the satisfaction of having produced harmonious personalities. They have used the psychological knowledge we, in our generation, have been so fortunate in gaining. *Their* children will not be subject to neurasthenia. They will have a happier and fuller life than we ever had, for the strings of their mind will be in tune and they will not know fear, the danger signal that all is not well with us.

knitting a sunsuit

The sun suit illustrated will fit a child of from one to two years. The set includes a cap and separate collar, which serve to protect the child's skull and back of the neck from over-exposure

Materials required : 3 oz. Bairnswear 3-ply Lambswool in bright colour ; 1 oz. ditto in white ; 1 pair No. 10 knitting needles ; 1 crochet hook No. 14 ; 2 buttons. **Measurements :** Width of trousers, 10 in. ; length of trousers at centre front, 8½ in. **Tension :** 8 stitches to the inch. **Abbreviations :** k., knit ; p., purl ; tog., together ; rep., repeat ; st., stitch or stitches ; m., make ; d.c., double crochet ; ch., chain ; rem., remain.

The Front.—Cast on 35 sts. in white wool. Work 8 rows in moss st. Break off white wool and join on coloured wool. **Next Row :** Purl. Break off wool. Place these sts. on a stitch holder. For the other leg cast on 35 sts in white. Work 8 rows in moss st. Break off white wool, join on colour. **Next Row :** Purl. Cast on 14 sts., then put sts. from stitch holder on to empty needle, seeing that both legs are on purl side of work. Now p. 2 sts. from right leg,turn. **Next Row:** K.18, turn. **Next Row:** P. 20, turn. Rep. these last two rows, working over 2 sts. more on each row until all sts. have been worked. Work over 3 sts at each end of last 2 rows, then work 1 row purl. Now proceed : **Row 1 :** Knit plain. **Row 2, and Alternate Rows :** Purl. **Row 3 :** K 35, k. 2 tog. through back of loops, k. 10, k. 2 tog., k. 35. **Row 5 :** K. plain. **Row 7 :** K. 36, k. 2 tog. through back of loops, k. 6, k. 2 tog., k. 36. **Row 9 :** K. plain. **Row 11 :** K. 37, k. 2 tog. through back of loops, k. 2, k. 2 tog., k. 37. **Row 12 :** Continue in stocking st. until the work measures 7 in. down centre front ending with a plain row. Cut wool, join white. **Row 1 :** Purl. Work 8 rows in moss st. Cut white wool and join colour. Work 6 rows in stocking st. Cut wool, join white. **Next Row :** Purl. Work 8 rows in moss st. Cast off.

The Back.—Work exactly the same as for the front. Sew together between legs.

The Straps.—Cast on 8 sts. in white and work in moss st. for 15 in. **Next Row :** P 1, k. 1, p. 1, k. 1, m. 1, p. 2 tog., p. 1, k. 1. **Next Row :** * K. 1, p. 1, rep. from * to end of row. Now decrease 1 st. at each end of needle on every alternate row till all sts. are used up. Work the other strap the same. Work a row of d.c. all round edges of both straps.

The Collar.—Cast on 144 sts. in white. Work 8 rows in moss st. **Row 9 :** * K. 1, p. 1, rep. from * twice, then join on colour ; k. in colour till 6 sts. rem., then join on another ball of white. In white * k. 1, p. 1, rep. from * to end of row. **Row 10 :** * P. 1, k. 1 in white, rep. from * twice, change to colour, p. to last 6 sts., change to white, p. 1, k. 1 to end of row. **Row 11 :** * K. 1, p. 1, in white, rep. from * twice, change to colour, ** k. 2 tog., k. 6, rep. from ** till 2 colour sts. rem., k. 2, change to white, k. 1, p. 1 to end of row. **Row 12 :** Same as **row 10. Row 13 :** * K. 1, p. 1 in white, rep. from * twice, change to colour, k. 2 tog., k. till 8 sts. rem., k. 2 tog., change to white, k. 1, p. 1 to end of row. **Row 14 :** Same as **row 10.** Rep. last 2 rows four times. **Row 23 :** * K. 1, p. 1 in white, rep. from * twice, change to colour, ** k. 2 tog., k. 6, rep. from ** till there are 7 colour sts. left, k. 5, k. 2 tog., change to white, p. 1, k. 1, to end of row. **Row 24 :** Same as **row 10.** Now rep. **rows 13 and 14** three times. **Row 31 :** * K. 1, p. 1 in white, rep. from * twice, change to colour, ** k. 2 tog., k. 6, rep. from ** till 9 sts. rem. in colour, k. 6, k. 2 tog., k. 1, change to white, k. 1, p. 1 to end of row. **Row 32 :** Same as **row 10. Row 33 :** Same as **row 13. Row 34 :** Same as **row 10. Row 35 :** * K. 1, p. 1 in white, rep. from * twice, change to colour, ** k. 2 tog., k. 6, rep. from ** till 6 colour sts. rem., k. 2 tog., k. 4, change to white, k. 1, p. 1, to end of row. Cast off.

The Cap.—Cast on 108 sts. in white wool. Work 8 rows in moss st. Change to colour. Work 6 rows in stocking st. Change to white. **Row 1 :** Purl. **Row 2 :** * K. 1, p. 1, rep. from * to end of row. **Row 3 :** * P. 1, k. 1, rep. from * to end of row. Rep. **row 2.** Cut white wool and join on colour. Work in stocking st. for 1 in. Now shape for the crown. **Row 1 :** * K. 10, k. 2 tog., rep. from * to end of row. **Row 2 :** Purl. **Row 3 :** * K. 9, k. 2 tog., rep. from * to end of row. Continue working 1 st. less between decreasings until 12 sts. rem. Break wool, run it through the sts. on needle and pull tog.

To Make Up.—Press all pieces under a damp cloth with a hot iron. Sew up side seams of trousers and cap, and sew buttons 2 in. from side seams of front of trousers. Cross straps in front and sew on to back of trousers to correspond with buttons in front. Sew little woolly animal motif to one leg. Make round tassel and fasten to top of cap. Join white wool to top edge of white border of collar. Work 8 ch. and fasten this along edge as a loop. Work another on opposite side of collar. Work a chain 20 in. long with 2 strands of white wool, thread through the collar loops, and tie in bow.

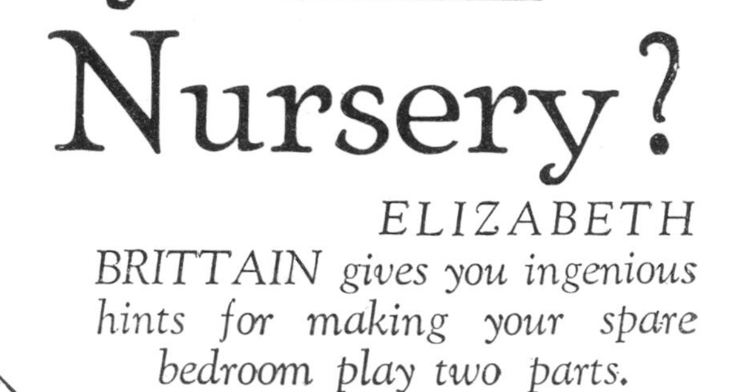

Why Not A Nursery?

ELIZABETH BRITTAIN gives you ingenious hints for making your spare bedroom play two parts.

A handy washing corner can be made in a recess.

A toy cupboard is easily contrived

—and so is a brick-box, which makes an extra seat as well.

"If only I had a nursery!" many a mother sighs, especially when her small treasure has reached the toddler stage. He is all over the house, here, there and everywhere, with his feet and fingers into everything. The toys adoring relatives and kind friends have showered upon him strew the sitting-room; polished furniture and light wallpaper bear the pattern of sticky baby fingers; if anyone should drop in unexpectedly, the place is not fit to be seen. But the little chap must play somewhere, and his bedroom is probably too small; in any case, it is not healthy for a child to spend much of the day in the room he has slept in all night.

Well, why *not* a nursery? Very few small houses have a third sitting-room, but most of them have at least one spare bedroom, which is only used on the more or less rare occasions when someone comes to stay with you. Why not turn that into a nursery; a place where baby can play safely and happily without getting under your feet, and spoiling your furniture, and making the house in a pickle? And if you start your nursery while he is still *quite* a baby, you may be able to do all the bathing, feeding and changing there.

The room will need a certain amount of preparation to do double duty, but this need not be an expensive matter. First of all, take down the bed and stow it away—that cupboard under the stairs may hold it, or the loft, if you oil the wire portion to prevent rust. The mattress, tightly rolled and wrapped in newspaper and sacking, will not be an impossible bundle to store.

Now you will need to do a certain amount of re-decorating. The wallpaper will be ruined by baby fingermarks, if something is not done to protect it. Paper the walls, to about four feet up from the wainscot, with a plain varnished paper to tone with the wallpaper.

Three rolls will do a fair-sized room, but you can easily calculate your needs, as practically all wallpapers are twenty-one inches wide, and a roll is eleven and a half yards long. With soap and water varnished paper can be kept clean for years. If you cannot get it quite plain, there are many quiet and effective patterns. Narrow borders can be had to match at a few pence a yard, but a threepenny or sixpenny roll of "passe-partout" in a colour to tone would look equally well.

THE FLOOR. AND THE FIRE—

If the floor has not a covering already, you will need something, for there is always a danger of splinters from stained boards. Linoleum is best, as it can be kept clean so easily, and it should cover the whole surface, right up to the walls. A plain linoleum is better than a patterned one from baby's point of view, as it will in time have to represent the sea, fields, the background of a railway line, or some other setting that childish imagination will suggest. One or two rugs—they need not be expensive—will be cosy for the little fellow to sit on in the colder weather.

In the winter, some kind of artificial heating will be necessary—though not every day, except in a really cold spell. To keep a coal fire going means a good deal of work; a gas or electric fire, although it can be hired, or bought by instalments, for a small weekly amount, is expensive to run continuously, unless you are in a district where gas or electricity is *very* cheap; but a good oil heating stove, placed in the hearth, will give all the warmth a small room needs, except on very bitter days. It is the cheapest of all to run, and will be quite healthy and free from smell if kept clean.

Whatever kind of heating you use, you must have a fireguard, preferably a folding one with a safety catch, firmly attached, so that baby cannot possibly knock it over.

You will need bars at the window, too; ordinary brass curtain rods, cut to measure, do excellently, but *do* fix them vertically; no child can resist climbing horizontal ones, as soon as he is big enough to reach them!

—AND THE FURNITURE

Now for the furniture. You do not want to use the wardrobe and dressing chest as toy cupboards, or you will find yourself in a quandary, when visitors come to stay and need accommodation for their clothes. And the washstand is no use to sonny. So range these pieces of furniture along an end wall. (They will not look well there, but you are not arranging the room for effect. You might, if you like, hang a curtain to conceal them.) Now, even in a small room, you will find that the little chap has quite an area of floor space to play in.

The actual nursery furniture need not take up much of this space, nor need it be expensive. Much of it can be contrived at home. You need a low table, a good sturdy one; an old kitchen table with the legs cut short will answer splendidly. (Daddy can do this, but it needs care, for it is not so easy as it looks to get the legs all exactly the same length, and a table that wobbles is an exasperation to a child.) You need a low chair, too, at which sonny can sit comfortably at his table. Here, again, a kitchen chair could be cut down for him.

A toy cupboard there must be, of course. You may already have, or be able to pick up second-hand, a low cupboard that a coat of cream, brown or blue paint will make attractive; if not, you will find that orange boxes, covered and curtained with material matching the window curtains, will be satisfactory. The boxes cost only sixpence each and are exceedingly strong. Be sure that you get the boxes all the same size, as they vary considerably. Two, side by side, standing on end, will probably be enough to start with, though three or four may just fill a fireside recess neatly, and will provide

An attractive frieze for the walls of the washing corner would be quite simple to make, if you followed these sketches.

BINDING BEAUTY

cupboard room for years. Tack a piece of the material over the tops and sides, and fix the curtain on two expanding wire rods, price twopence or threepence each, according to the number of boxes used.

A long padded seat under the window, both useful and decorative, could be made in the same way, with a long box, or several fastened together.

Sooner or later you will need a bookshelf, and this can easily be made at home, as shown in the illustration. You can buy the pieces of wood ready planed and cut to your own measurements at about sixpence a foot, and fixing them together by long screws is a simple matter. They can be added to as the books increase and, if made two feet high with the top a foot wide, will prove invaluable.

One more suggestion, and your nursery will be really well equipped. This is a brick box. A fourpenny sugar box is just the thing. Fix four silencers underneath (at the cost of twopence). If you have not been able to get the lid of the original box, make a lid from another one, and attach it with two hinges (costing threepence a pair). Pad this seat with old stockings and socks, tack a piece of your curtain material over it, and add a pleated frill round the box. You now have a comfortable seat, and a box ready to hold as many bricks as you can buy.

A WASHING CORNER

From the grocer you can buy a smooth, well-made sugar box for fourpence. Sandpaper this and give it a coat of white enamel or cellulose paint. On it place a small white enamel bowl and a soap-dish, and fix a little hook on the right-hand side for a looped face flannel. A small enamel jug and a pail stand on either side.

On the inside of the door fix a small mirror and beneath it a white enamelled cigar box to hold a brush and comb. Another hook will hold a small looped towel.

An attractive frieze for the walls could consist of a very simple pond with a white duck followed by a stream of yellow ducklings going for a swim. From the sketches on page 60 you will see how very easy they are to do. This corner is, of course, only intended for casual washings before and after meals, or as occasion demands, not for the real business washings of the day, but it will be found a help in encouraging clean habits. Failing a cupboard, a curtained recess will do nearly as well.

And there is a nursery in which sonny will play happily for hours, while you go about your housework. But you will not want to shut him away out of earshot. In warm weather, a good idea is to get daddy to make a little low gate to fasten across the doorway. It could be fixed by means of small bolts that shoot into sockets screwed to the door frame; fitted in this way it can be detached in a few seconds.

The door of the room can be fastened back, or better still, taken off its hinges altogether for the summer months, if you have room to store it. In winter you can set the door a little way open, keeping it in place by means of doorstops—or flatirons!—and mask the opening with a screen, to prevent draughts. Then you can always hear sonny when he calls.

When people come to stay with you, it will not be a serious task to put up the spare bed in the nursery, and rearrange the furniture.

Of course, sonny will have to give up his nursery for the time being, but that cannot be helped: he will, at any rate, have a playroom of his own most of the year.

MATERIALS

Six yards casement cloth, 5 cards dark green Coats' bias binding, 1 card each of red, brown, white, and light green, rail and curtain fittings, Clark's "Anchor" stranded cotton to match bias binding.

The curtains and cushion should be made to measure as required. Cut to the right size, leaving inch turns all round. Turn the hems over on the right side and mitre the corners. Lay the bias over the edges and tack.

Draw out the simple design, as shown in the diagram, and tack the coloured bias over the drawing, using it like braid. Where the bias goes round a steep curve, the inner edge should be whipped and slightly drawn up.

When the bias is all tacked and the edges neatly tucked under the border or another section of the design, catch it all in position with a wide, quick buttonhole-stitch, using three strands of matching cotton, or with ordinary machining.

The effect in the original was gained by using brown for the hill and tree trunk, red for the house roof, and white for the walls. The tree top and window shutters are light green, and the curtain border dark green.

The curtains can be used to cover an old chest of drawers. Cut a ply-wood top to fit the chest and leave a two-inch margin at the sides and along the front. Purchase the necessary length of bendable curtain rail.

In fixing the rail, be sure that the top drawer opens.

THE TOY CORNER

As the illustration shows, the idea is suggested to make a corner for the children's toys. An ordinary box fitted with shelves will do excellently.

Make and fit the curtains as window curtains, then make the cover for the top to come neatly over the rail and curtain top.

It would give a better finish to the set of shelves if a ply-wood top were cut to fit, leaving a two-inch margin at the sides and along the front. The length of bendable curtain rail can be purchased from the sixpenny stores.

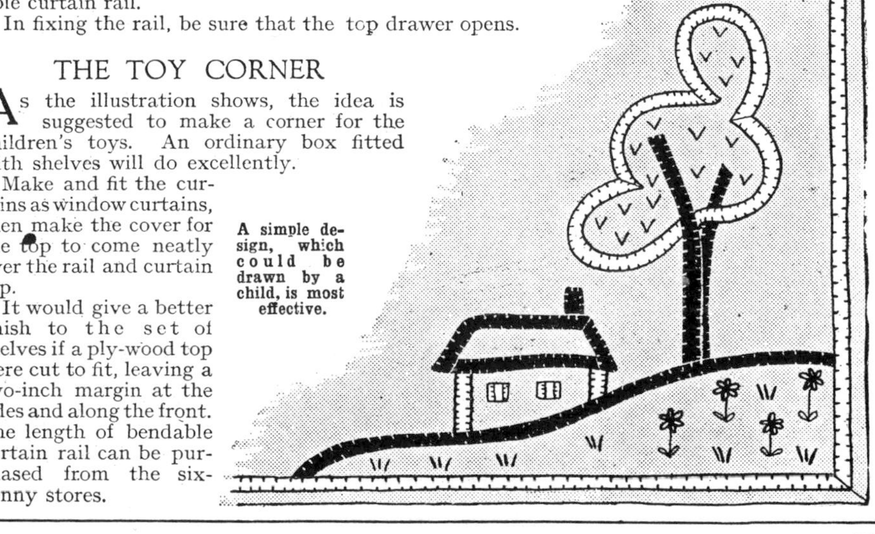

A simple design, which could be drawn by a child, is most effective.

Old Scottish Rhymes

(*Left, above*)

KILTY, Kilty cauld knees
couldna play a drum,
His father took the bellises[1]
and blew him up the lum.[2]

(*Centre, below*)

CAM ye by the kirk,
Cam ye by the steeple,
Saw ye oor gudeman
Riding on a ladle?
Hoot fye, the bodie!

[1] *bellises—bellows.*
[2] *lum—chimney.*

(*Right, above*)

THERE was an auld man
stood on a stane,
Awa' in the croft his leefu'
lane,
And cried on his pretty sleek
kye to come hame.
Kitty my maily, and Kitty
her mither,
Kitty my doo, and Kitty
Billswither,
Ranglety, Spanglety, Crook,
and Cowdry,
And these were the names
of the auld man's kye.

Illustrations by
Mildred R. Lamb

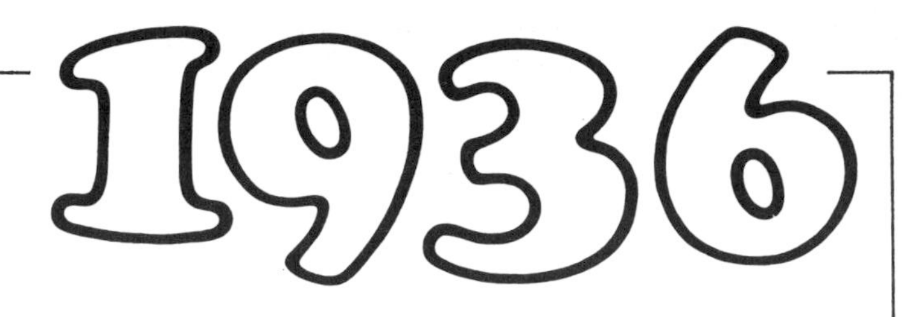

How
To Make
TOY ANIMALS

THE CAMEL

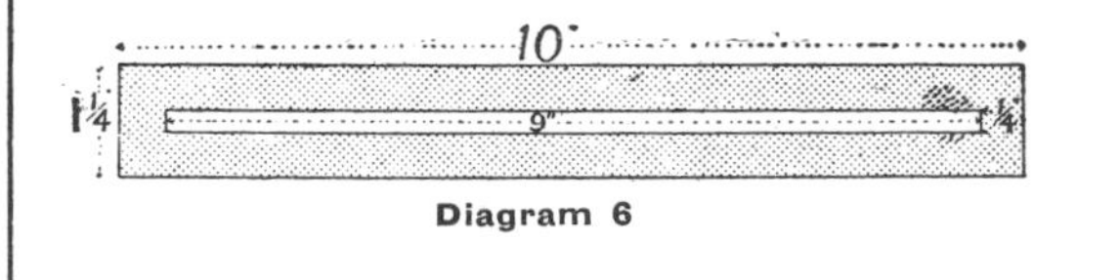

Diagram 6

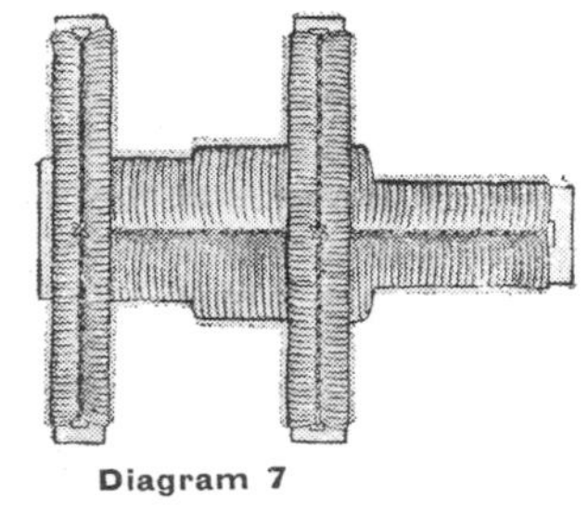
Diagram 7

MATERIALS: *Two packets (2 oz. each) of Beehive Camelaine wool, 2 black beads for eyes, a scrap of brown wool for the nose, ears and tail. Wire and cardboard.*

Cut out a cardboard shape similar to Diagram 5, and proceed as for the Teddy Bear. For the legs take a piece of cardboard ten inches by a quarter of an inch, with a slit nine inches by a quarter down centre. (See Diagram 6.)

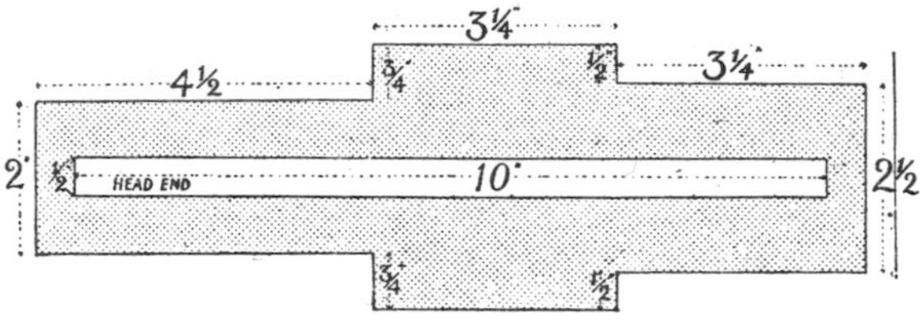

Diagram 5

Make the legs in the same way as the Teddy Bear's. Attach them where shown in Diagram 7.

Cut the wool along each outer edge as for the Teddy Bear, and slip out the cards. Bend into shape, aiming at a finished shape similar to Diagram 8.

Clip the wool where necessary to improve the appearance

Make ears as for the Teddy Bear, and sew them into position.

Sew in the eyes. See Diagram 9 for the shape of the nose, to be stitched with brown wool.

For the tail, wind some wool over the fingers, making four loops about four inches long. Bind three inches of this with wool (see Diagram 10), cutting the loops at one end to form a tuft, and sewing the other end in position.

The ears and nose can be made of scraps of felt, if preferred.

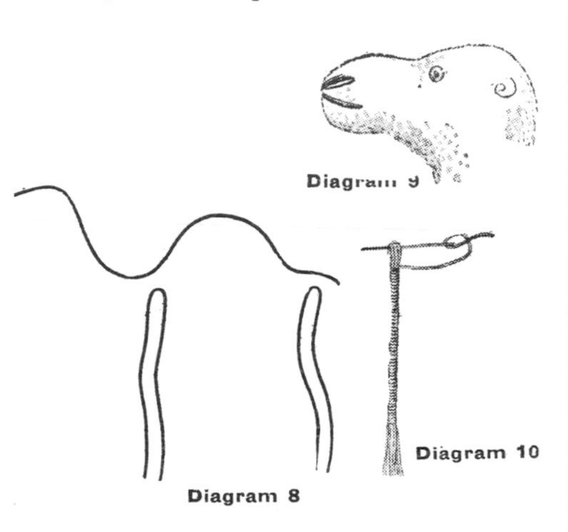
Diagram 9

Diagram 8

Diagram 10

THE TEDDY BEAR

MATERIALS REQUIRED: *1 oz. of medium quality 3-ply fingering wool, a No. 11 "Aero" crochet hook, 2 small black beads for eyes, and a piece of ribbon for the neck. Wire and cardboard.*

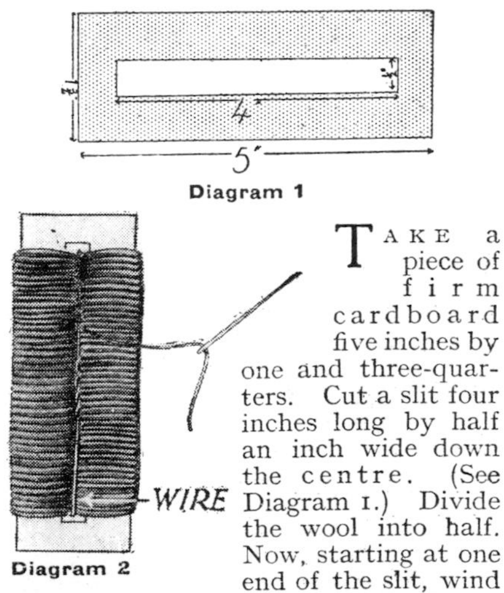

Diagram 1

Diagram 2

Take a piece of firm cardboard five inches by one and three-quarters. Cut a slit four inches long by half an inch wide down the centre. (See Diagram 1.) Divide the wool into half. Now, starting at one end of the slit, wind the wool completely round the shape, the whole length of the slit. (See Diagram 2.)

Bind the wool firmly by passing the wire through each end of the slit and fastening it in the middle of the shape over the wool. (See Diagram 2.) Then stitch the wool and the wire firmly through the slit with small, strong stitches. Use strong thread for this. (See Diagram 2.)

Now for one pair of legs, take a piece of cardboard seven inches by one inch, with a slit down the centre six inches by a quarter of an inch (Diagram 3). Divide the remaining wool into half,

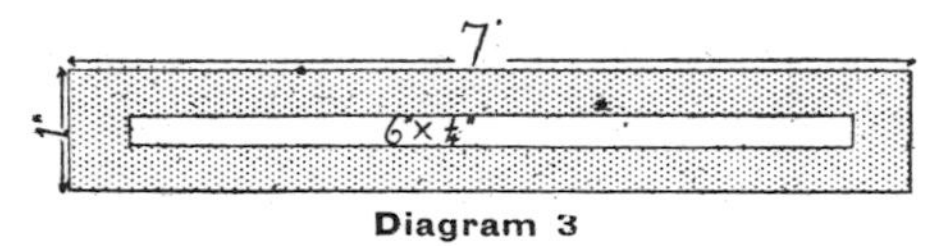

Diagram 3

leaving just sufficient to crochet the ears. Repeat the process for the pair of arms.

Sew the centre of the arms to the first shape made, one and a half inches down the centre wire, fastening right through very firmly. (See Diagram 4.) Sew the centre of the legs to the other end of the wire—right at the end of the slit. (See Diagram 4.)

Cut the wool along each outer edge of the cards, as shown by the dotted lines in Diagram 4, and slip out the cards. The section above the arms forms the head, and this should be bent forward so that the end of the wire comes in place for the nose.

Bend the arms and legs into shape as you see in the photograph in the photogravure section, turning up one inch at the end of the legs to form the feet.

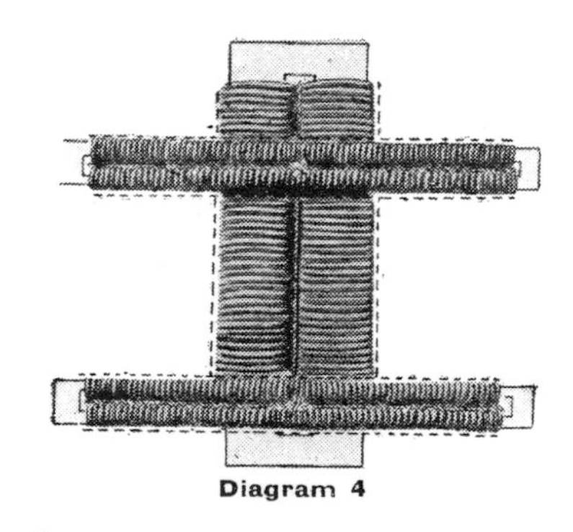
Diagram 4

Clip the wool where necessary to improve the shape. Sew in the eyes.

A few black wool stitches will form the nose and mouth.

To make the ears, crochet five chain and slip-stitch to first st. to form a ring. Work 5 double crochet into this ring and work 1 ch. to turn. Work 3 rows more, increasing one stitch at the end of each row, thus forming a semi-circle. Sew the ears in place, catching them on to the wire for firmness.

Tie the ribbon round the neck.

A MOST *cuddlesome pair are the Penguin and his Teddy Bear friend. Little people will welcome them with open arms on Christmas morning. They are made on cardboard, after the style of old-fashioned woolly balls.*

THE PENGUIN

MATERIALS REQUIRED: 1 *oz. of black and* 1 *oz. of white wool, a small piece of bright yellow felt for the beak and feet,* 2 *brown animal eyes,* 1 *pair of No.* 9 *knitting needles. Wire and cardboard.*

TAKE 2 pieces of cardboard six inches by two and a half inches, with a slit down the centre five inches by half an inch (Diagram 11). On one piece is wound the black wool (leaving enough wool to knit the flippers) and on the other the white wool, in the manner described for the Teddy Bear.

Place one on top of the other (see Diagram 12), and bind the two together with the wire, passing it through the ends of the slits of each card, and fixing it with stitching as already explained. See Diagram 12.

Cut the wool along each outer edge, and slip out the cards.

Bend one end a little in one direction and the other a little in the opposite direction, forming a slight S, as the side view of the penguin shows. Clip rather closely.

To make the beak, take half a semi-circle of felt with sides each one and a half inches (see Diagram 13). Roll this up and sew it neatly (see Diagram 14). Fix this to the end of the wire for the beak.

Sew in the eyes.

To make the feet, take two pieces of wire four inches long. Form them into circles, twisting the ends together. Then bend into shape (see Diagram 15). Now cut out four pieces of felt the exact shape of the wire. Use two pieces for each foot, sewing one above and one below the wire. See dotted lines in the diagram. Fix on to the penguin half an inch from the end of the centre wire.

THE PENGUIN

To make the flippers, cast on twelve stitches. Knit one inch of stocking-stitch, then decrease one stitch at the beginning of every row until 1 st. remains. Fasten off. Fold the flipper in half (see Diagram 16), and sew the outer edges together. Repeat for the second flipper. Attach the flippers to the penguin just below the shoulders, as in the sketch.

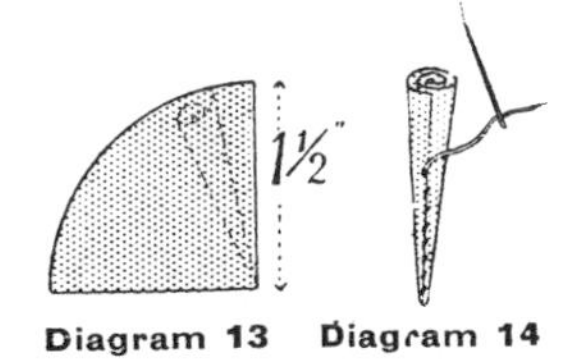

Diagram 13 Diagram 14

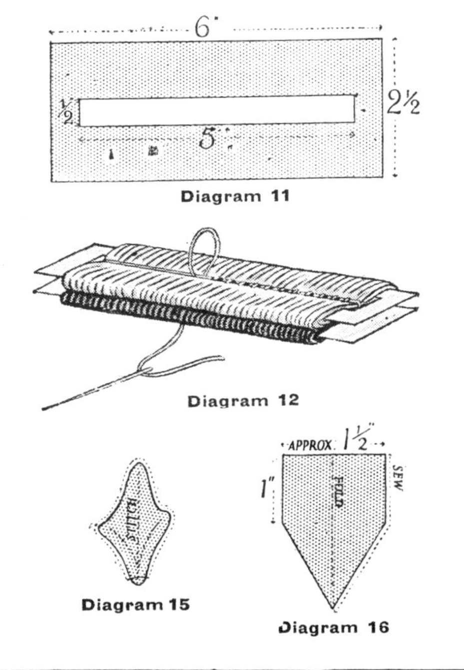

Diagram 11

Diagram 12

Diagram 15

Diagram 16

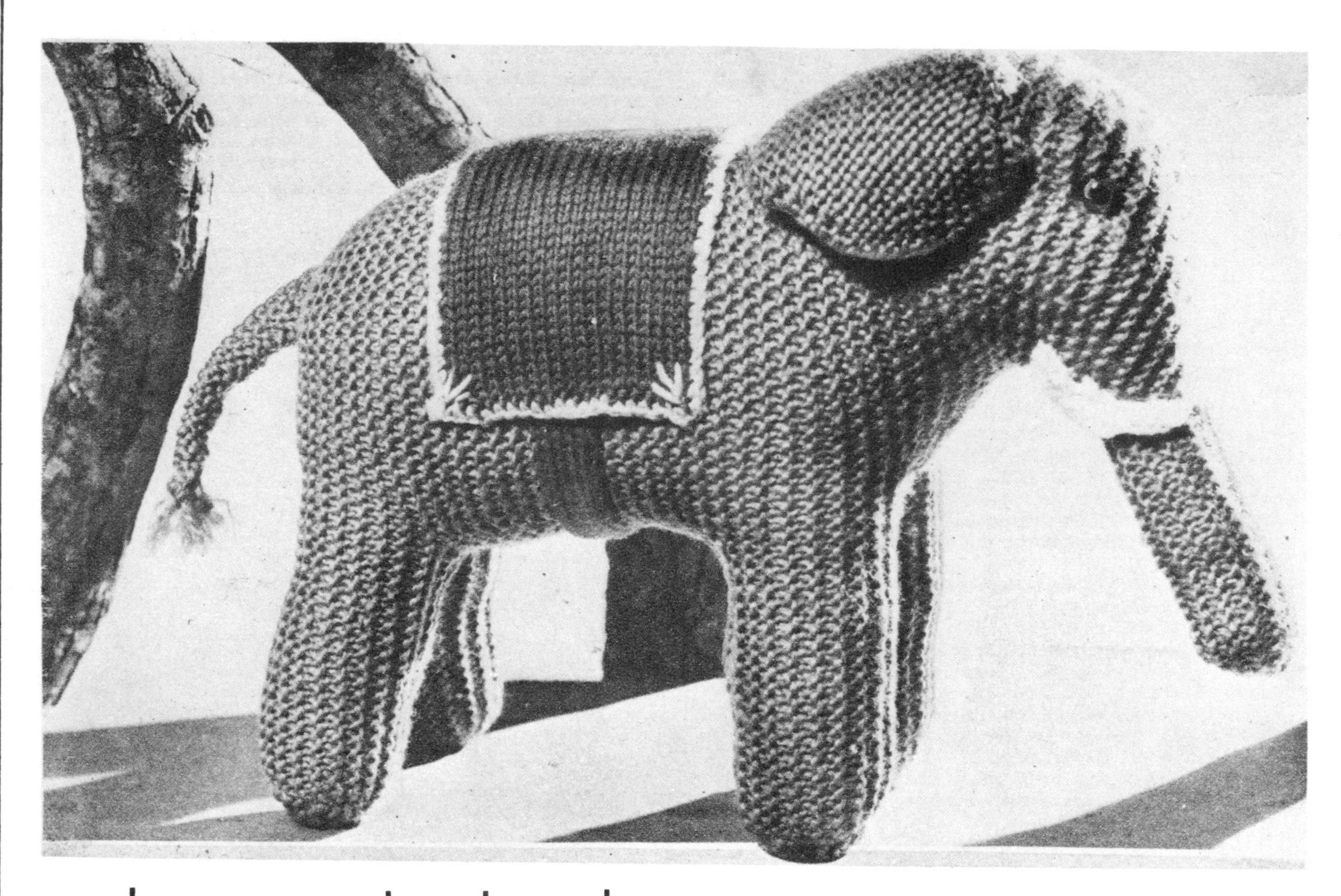

a knitted elephant

MATERIALS: *Three ounces of "Beehive" Double Knitting wool 4-ply, in elephant grey; ½ an ounce of the same wool in jade green for the saddle cloth, and a few yards in yellow to edge the saddle cloth; a pair of "Aero" knitting pins No. 11, and an "Aero" crochet hook No. 11; 2 black shoe buttons for eyes and kapok for stuffing.*

ABBREVIATIONS: *K., knit plain; p., purl; st., stitch; tog., together; inc., increase (by knitting in the front and back of the same st.); s.s., stocking st. (k. on the right side and p. back); ch., chain; d.c., double crochet.*

THE work is carried out in plain knitting (except for trimmings), so on those rows where shaping only is given, it will be understood that the rest of the row is knitted plain.

To Work

BEGIN at the back of the body and cast on 16 sts.

K. 2 rows plain, working into the back of the sts. on the first row.

3rd row: Inc. in the first st. and k. to the end of the row.

4th row: Cast on 21 sts. for the hind leg and k. across 38 sts.

5th row: Inc. in the first st.

6th row: K. plain.

Repeat these 2 rows 5 times more (44 sts.).

K. 5 rows.

22nd row: Cast off 19 sts. and k. 25 including the one on the pin after casting off.

23rd row: K. plain.

24th row: K. the first 2 sts. tog. (24 sts.).

K. 26 rows.

51st row: Inc. in the last st.

52nd row: K. plain.

53rd row: Inc. in the first st. for neck.

54th row: Cast on 19 sts. for the foreleg and k. 45.

55th row: Inc. in the first st.

56th row: K. plain.

Repeat these 2 rows 7 times more (53 sts.).

71st row: Inc. in the first st.

72nd row: Cast off 24 sts. and k. to end (30 sts.).

73rd row: K. the last 2 sts. tog. (29 sts.).

74th row: K. plain.

Repeat these 2 rows twice more (27 sts.).

79th row: K. the last 2 sts. tog.

80th row: K. the first 2 sts. tog.

Repeat these 2 rows once (23 sts.).

K 4 rows plain.

87th row: K. the first 2 sts. tog., inc. in the last st.

88th row: K. plain.

Repeat these 2 rows twice more (23 sts.).

93rd row: K. the first 2 sts. tog.

94th row: Cast on 20 sts. K. across the row taking the last 2 sts. tog. (41 sts.).

95th row: K. 2 sts. tog. twice at the beginning of the row (39 sts.).

96th row: K. 2 sts. tog. twice at the end of the row.

Repeat these 2 rows 4 times more when 21 sts. will remain. Cast off.

K. another piece exactly the same.

Underbody and Inside of Legs

1st row: Cast on 3 sts. and k. one row into the back of these sts.

2nd row: Inc. in the first and last st.

3rd row: K. plain.

Repeat these 2 rows twice more (9 sts.).

8th row: Cast on 21 sts. for the hind leg, k. 30.

Repeat this row once, knitting 51 sts.

K. 16 rows.

26th row: Cast off 19 sts. and k. to end of row (32 sts.).

Repeat this row once, knitting 13 sts.

28th row: K. the first and last st. tog.

K. 25 rows on 11 sts.

54th row: Inc. in the first and last st.

55th row: K. plain.

56th row: Cast on 19 sts. for the foreleg, k. 32 sts. to the end.

Repeat this row once, knitting 51 sts.

K. 16 rows.

74th row: Cast off 24 sts., k. 27.

Repeat this row once when 3 sts. will remain.

76th row: Inc. in the first and last st.

K. 5 rows on 5 sts.

82nd row: K. 2 sts. tog. at each end of the row and cast off.

The Foot-Pads

Cast on 4 sts.
1st row: K. plain.
2nd row: Inc. in the first and last st.
3rd row: K. plain.
Repeat these 2 rows once.
K. 4 rows plain.
10th row: K. the first and last 2 sts. tog.
11th row: K. plain.
Repeat the last 2 rows once when 4 sts. will remain. Cast off.
K. 3 pieces more exactly the same.

The Ears

Cast on 4 sts.
1st row: K. plain.
2nd row: Inc. in the first and last st.
K. 3 rows plain.
Repeat these 4 rows once. (8 sts.)
10th row: Inc. in the first and last st.
11th row: K. plain.
Repeat these 2 rows 4 times. (18 sts.)
K. 14 rows plain.
34th row: K. the first and last 2 sts. tog.
35th row: K. plain.
Repeat these 2 rows twice more.
40th row: K. 2 sts. tog. in the middle of the row.
41st row: K. plain.
Repeat these 2 rows once more (10 sts.) Cast off.
K. another ear exactly the same.

The Tail

Cast on 3 sts.
1st row: K. plain.
2nd row: Inc. in the first and last st.
3rd row: K. plain.
Repeat these 2 rows twice more.
K. 6 rows on 9 sts.
14th row: K. the first and last 2 sts. tog.
K. 7 rows on 7 sts.
Repeat these 8 rows once.
K. 8 rows and cast off.

The Saddle-Cloth

With green wool cast on 20 sts. and work 60 rows in s.s. On the next row cast off 7 sts. and k. 13.

Repeat the last row once, knitting 6 sts. Work 40 rows on these 6 sts., or enough to go round the body, and join to the opposite side of the saddle-cloth, then cast off.

With yellow wool work d.c. all round the edge of the saddle-cloth, putting 3 d.c. in each corner st. and missing a st. on the edge here and there to keep the crochet edge flat.

The Tusks

With white wool make 11 ch. Miss the first ch. and work 1 d.c. in each of the next 5 ch., then slipstitch along the remaining 5 ch. Fasten off.

Work another tusk exactly the same.

To Make Up the Elephant

Sew the two body pieces together from neck to end of back, then press this seam, and the rest of the knitting, putting a damp cloth over the wrong side. Sew from the throat along the trunk over the head to the neck. Sew in the underbody and add the foot-pads. Turn the work and stuff well with kapok, using a blunt instrument to press the stuffing well into the legs, head and trunk, to make a good shape. Sew up the opening at the back. Sew up the long seam of the tail, stuff lightly and secure at the rear. Sew the ears in position, and the shoe buttons in place for the eyes. Sew on the tusks, placing the broad part to the face, and stitch the narrow end to the trunk (see position on the illustration). Finally, sew on the saddle-cloth.

Egg-Shell Candle-Shades

By S. Leonard Bastin

Some very attractive candle-shades can be made from egg-shells. Make holes at both ends of the eggs, then remove the contents by blowing out the white and yolk. Now, at the thick end of the shells, carefully cut, with scissors, a round opening which will allow the heat to escape from the candle.

At the other end cut a somewhat smaller opening and snip the edge in the form of V-shapes as shown in the sketch. These openings allow the admission of air when the egg-shell is resting on the top of the candle.

Plain egg-shells are quite pretty for the candle-shades, but much more attractive ones can be secured by decorating the shells. These can be coloured with dyes, or designs, or simple pictures, etc., may either be pasted or painted on them.

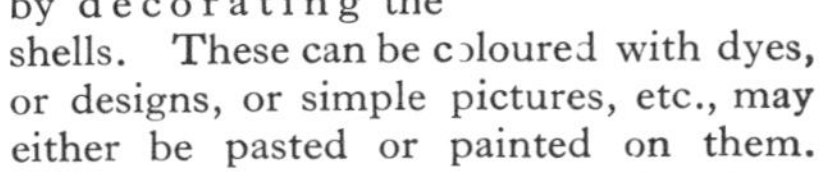

The best form of picture is the silhouette, such as a sailing boat painted in solid black, the sea being more faintly indicated. Naturally, as the candle burns, the egg-shell lowers with it, so that it always remains just in the right position.

HERE are the embroidery stitches—actual size—used for the gay "fairy tree" motifs.

The Magyar Play Frock

For the Very Junior Miss—in Softest Blue Scattered with Embroidered "Fairy Tree" Motifs

MATERIALS.—5 ozs. Bairns-Wear 3-ply Lambs Wool, pale blue, ½ oz. each of navy blue, orange and lemon yellow; one pair No. 9 "Stratnoid" knitting pins; one No. 11 "Stratnoid" crochet hook.

Measurements.—From back of neck to lower edge, 17¼ inches; from front neck to lower edge, 16 inches; width all round under arms, 27 inches; sleeve seam, 2½ inches.

Abbreviations.—K., knit; p., purl; st., stitch; st.-st., stocking-stitch; rem., remain (ing); dec., decrease (ing); inc., increasing; beg., beginning; d.c., double crochet.

Tension.—7 sts. to one inch in width. Always work into the back of cast-on sts. to produce a firm edge.

The Front

Beg. at lower edge, using pale blue wool. Cast on 96 sts. and work 6 rows in st.-st. Continue in st.-st., dec. 1 st. at each end of next and every 10th row following, until 82 sts. rem. Work without alteration for 25 more rows, ending after a purl row. Work now measures 10 inches from beg.

Make slots for waist-cord as follows: K. 6, turn, p. 6. Work backwards and forwards on these 6 sts. for 11 rows, ending with a k. row. Break wool. * Work backwards and forwards for 11 rows on the next 14 sts., ending with a k. row. * Rep. from * to * 4 times, then work 11 rows over rem. 6 sts. *Next row.*—P. across the 82 sts. (6 slots in all). Work 6 more rows in st.-st., then—

Shape for armholes (mark here with a coloured thread). Still in st.-st., dec. 1 st. at beg. of every row, until 52 sts. rem. Work eyelet holes for neck-cord as follows: K. 2 tog., k. 9, * k. 2 tog., make 2 sts. by twisting wool twice round right-hand needle, k. 2 tog., k. 5. Rep. from * twice more, then k. 2 tog., wool twice round needle, k. 2 tog., k. 10. *Next row.*—P. 2 tog., p. along row, working a k. and a p. st. into the double twists. (50 sts. on needle.) Work 4 more rows in st.-st., dec. 1 st. at beg. of each row.

Neck Shaping.—K. 2 tog., k. 12, cast off 19, k. 13. *Next row.*—P. 2 tog., p. 11. Place the other 13 sts. on st. holder for time being. *Next row.*—P. 2 tog., k. 11. *Next row.*—K. 3, k. 2 tog., wool twice round needle, k. 2 tog., k. 5. *Next row.*—P. 2 tog., p. 4, k. 1, p. 3, p. 2 tog. *Next 4 rows.*—Work in st.-st., dec. 1 st. at both ends of each row. Cast off. Now transfer sts. from st. holder to needle. P. 13. *Next row.*—K. 2 tog., k. 2, k. 2 tog., wool twice round needle, k. 2 tog., k. 5. *Next row.*—P. 2 tog., p. 4, k. 1, p. 3, p. 2 tog. *Next 4 rows.*—Work in st.-st., dec. 1 st. at both ends of each row. Cast off.

The Back

Work exactly as for front, including slots, until armhole shaping is reached.

Shape for armhole (mark with coloured thread).—Continue in st.-st., dec. 1 st. at beg. of every row, until 40 sts. rem. Work eyelet holes as follows: K. 2 tog., k. 3, * k. 2 tog., wool twice round needle, k. 2 tog., k. 5, rep. from * twice more, then k. 2 tog., wool twice round needle, k. 2 tog., k. 4. *Next row.*—P. 2 tog., purl along row, working a k. and a p. st. into the double twists. Work 4 more rows in st.-st., dec. 1 st. at beg. of each row. Cast off.

The Sleeves (two alike)

Beg. at lower edge. Cast on 58 sts., and work 22 rows in st.-st. Now shape for top. Still in st.-st., dec. 1 st. at beg. of every row, until 22 sts. rem. Work 4 more rows, then make eyelet holes as follows: * K. 2 tog., wool twice round needle, k. 2 tog., k. 5, rep. from * once more, then k. 2 tog., wool twice round needle, k. 2 tog. Work 5 more rows in st.-st. Cast off.

Neck and Waist-cords.—Take 9 strands of pale blue wool, each 2¼ yards long, and twist tightly. When the cord is well twisted, slide the loop of a large key or similar weight over one set of ends and, keeping the cord taut, bring to the centre, then bring the two sets of ends together and suspend the weight, allowing the two halves of the cord to twirl around each other. When it has ceased to twirl, cut off the weight and secure the ends by knotting, leaving a fringe of about two inches. For the waist-cord, take 12 strands of pale blue wool, each 3 yards long, and twist in exactly the same way. A fringe of 3 inches should be left on both ends.

Make-up and Finish.—Sew sleeves into armholes, then work a row of d.c. round neck, sleeves and foot of dress, and round each slot, using matching wool. Press garment flat, using a warm iron over a damp cloth. Join side and sleeve seams in one operation. Now, using navy blue wool, work a row of open blanket-stitch round lower edges of sleeves and dress. The sts. should be about ½ inch apart and ⅓ inch deep.

The diagram above shows you how to embroider the "fairy-tree" motifs. Beg. at lower front and work four motifs in a row, about 2 inches above hem-line. Use navy wool for the base and "trunk," orange for the "boughs." Complete motif with a lazy-daisy stitch in lemon yellow, above the "boughs."

At a distance of about 4 rows of knitting above first row of motifs, work another row—3 motifs this time, each one being placed between two in the previous row. Now 4 again, and then 3, allowing about 4 rows of knitting between each line of motifs. The waistline has now been reached. Work two more motifs in a row above the slots, then 3 more above these.

Embroider the back and sleeves in the same way. The sleeves have two motifs in the first row, then one placed above and between these two; then two; then one.

Lightly press the seams and embroidery. Insert waist and neck cords.

IN FOXGLOVE STITCH

A Dainty Knitted Frock For the Small Girl

This unusual little knitted frock, with its rows of foxglove patterning, would look delightful made up in a soft shade of pink or a forget-me-not blue for a fair-haired little girl, or in daffodil or lavender-blue colouring for her dark-eyed and dark-haired sister.

The directions given below are simple to follow.

Materials Required

6 ozs. Lister's "Lavenda," 3-ply, 1 pair needles No. 8, 1 pair needles No. 10, 2 small buttons.

Abbreviations.—K, knit; P., purl; tog., together; sts., stitches; ins., inches.

Measurements.—Length, 17 ins. All round under-arm, 20 ins. Sleeve seam, 3 ins.

Tension.—5½ sts., 1 in. on No. 8 needles. 1 pattern (14 rows), 1½ ins. deep.

FRONT

With No. 8 needles, cast on 263 sts.

1st row.—P. 3, *, K. 10, P. 3. Repeat from * to end of row. *2nd row.*—K. 3, *, P. 10, K. 3. Repeat from * to end of row. *3rd row.*—P. 3, *, K. 2 tog., K. 6, K. 2 tog., P. 3. Repeat from * to end of row. *4th row.*—K. 3, *, P. 8, K. 3. Repeat from * to end of row. *5th row.*—P. 3, *, K. 2 tog., K. 4, K. 2 tog., P. 3. Repeat from * to end of row. *6th row.*—K. 3, *, P. 6, K. 3. Repeat from * to end of row. *7th row.*—P. 3, *, K. 2 tog., K. 2, K. 2 tog., P. 3. Repeat from * to end of row. *8th row.*—K. 3, *, P. 4, K. 3. Repeat from * to end of row. *9th row.*—P. 3, *, K. 2 tog., K. 2 tog., P. 3. Repeat from * to end of row. *10th row.*—K. 3, *, P. 2, K. 3. Repeat from * to end of row. *11th row.*—P. 3, *, K. 2 tog., P. 3. Repeat from * to end of row. *12th row.*—K. 3, *, P. 1, K. 3. Repeat from * to end of row. *13th row.*—*, P. 2, P. 2 tog. Repeat from * to within 3 sts. of end of row, P. 3. *14th row.*—Knit.

One line of foxgloves is completed.

15th row.—K. 3, *, cast on 10, K. 3. Repeat from * to end of row.

Repeat 2nd to 14th rows.

A second line of foxgloves is completed.

Continue thus, repeating 15th row, then 2nd to 14th rows, until 8 lines of foxgloves have been worked (an extra line of foxgloves may be worked if extra length is desired).

Change to No. 10 needles. 63 sts. remain. Work in stocking stitch for 8 rows. Shape for armholes by casting off 2 at beginning of next 6 rows. Continue without shaping until work measures 2 ins. from where armhole shaping begins.

Shape for neck as follows :—

Next row.—K. 21, cast off 9, K. 21.

Continue on these 21 sts., knitting 2 tog. at neck edge for next 2 rows. Continue without shaping until work measures 3½ ins. from where armhole shaping begins. Cast off. Return to other 21 sts. and work in same manner.

BACK

Work exactly as for front until armhole is completed. With wrong side of work facing.

Next row.—P. 26, cast on 4, turn. *Next row.*—Knit. *Next row.*—Purl to within 5 sts., knit 5.

Repeat last 2 rows until armhole is 3 ins. deep.

Starting at garter stitch border, shape for neck as follows :—*Next row.*—Cast off 9, knit to end. *Next row.*—Purl. *Next row.*—K. 2 tog., knit to end of row. *Next row.*—Purl to within 2, purl last 2 tog.

Next row. — Continue without shaping until armhole measures same as front.

Cast off. Return to other 25 sts.

Starting at centre back. *Next row.*—K. 4, purl to end of row. *Next row.*—Knit. Repeat these 2 rows three times.

Next row.—K. 3, cast off 2 to make buttonholes, purl to end of row. *Next row.*—Knit to within 3 sts. of end, cast on 2 to replace cast off 2, K. 3.

Continue in stocking stitch with garter stitch border as before until armhole is 2½ ins. deep. Make another buttonhole. Continue until armhole is 3 ins. deep.

Starting at garter st. border, shape for neck as follows :—*Next row.*—Cast off 4, purl to end of row. *Next row.* — Knit. *Next row.*—K. 2 tog., purl to end of row. *Next row.*—Knit to within 2, knit last 2 tog. *Next row.*—Continue without shaping until armhole measures same as Front. Cast off.

SLEEVES

With No. 10 needles, cast on 39 sts. and knit in K. 1, P. 1 rib for 10 rows.

Change to No. 8 needles and work 15th row of foxglove pattern.

Complete one line of foxgloves (2nd to 14th row of foxglove pattern). Cast off loosely.

COLLAR

Cast on 185 sts. on No. 8 needles and repeat first 14 rows of foxglove pattern (as Front, 1st and 14th rows), but work 3 sts. at each end of needle in garter stitch. Cast off loosely.

To Make Up

Press lightly under damp cloth the stocking stitch yoke only. Sew up shoulder seams. Sew collar into position round neck, easing to fit, and sleeves into armholes. Sew up side and sleeve seams. Sew buttons in place at back to correspond with buttonholes.

Some things for the children

Photos: H. Armstrong Roberts.

It is the *light* of the sun, not its heat, that makes sun-bathing so good for the kiddies, so do not give them their sun-baths in the hottest part of the day, but about eleven in the morning and four in the afternoon—and, of course, protect their little heads with shady hats.
Photo: Dr. Weller—Berlin.

1936

Our Parents' Pages

Conducted by DOCTOR HELEN

Photo: Dorien Leigh

Even a holiday has its dull moments. Here are some jolly games which will appeal to children and grown-ups alike and can be played equally well on the sands or in the park or garden at home.

THE grown-up—or child—who knows lots of nice games to play is sure to be popular on holiday, and when you and your family meet other parents and their families day by day on the same stretch of beach, it is a great chance to break the ice and be really jolly together if you can suggest a game to be played with simple rules and apparatus.

Even if you have to be content with an "outing" here and there these holidays, the games I am going to describe to you add to the fun of a day spent in a park or on a common. Incidentally, they are equally suitable for the back garden at home.

"HOLE-BALL" is best played on the sands, though it can be adapted for quite a small garden or a park. The older boys and girls will enjoy preparing the "course." A level piece of dry sand should be chosen, and on it three circles marked one inside the other, as the diagram shows. These are most easily drawn by using a piece of string about seven feet long. One child stands at the thrower's base, holding one end of the string firmly, and just turning on his heels, while a second takes the other end of the string and, stretching it tightly, walks round him, tracing a circle with his toe as he goes. Then twelve holes large enough to take the chosen ball must be dug just outside the biggest circle. The younger children will be able to dig these, if they are shown where to make each one. They will be evenly spaced if they are dug at a distance of half the length of the string apart. The diagram shows what the "course" should look like when ready.

The game can be played by any number of people, who should divide into two sides. If the numbers are unequal one player can have two turns. The object of the game is to throw the ball into as many holes as possible without a miss. Directly a hole is missed, the next member of the side takes his turn, attempting to put the ball into the hole that the previous player missed, and so on round the clock face, till one side is out. Then the other side goes in. The side wins which scores the most holes in one innings.

Grown-ups and boys and girls over ten, or whatever age is decided upon, stand in the centre to throw; the "ten-year-olds" stand anywhere behind the next circle.

It is a good plan to number the holes from one to twelve, always starting a game at 1, and going round in order, for owing to wind or the shape of the hole, it will be found much easier to "hole" the ball in some than in others.

A SIMPLE form of "KING TENNIS" is easy to rig up, and provides the energetic with exhilarating exercise and much excitement. Two sticks a little over five feet long and a wide piece of white tape make quite a

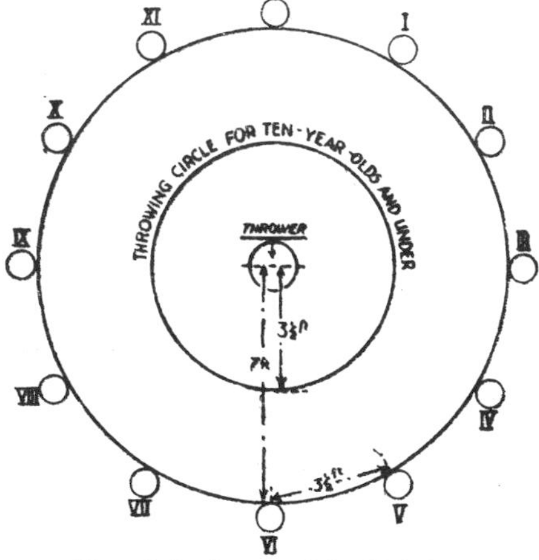

Plan of the "course" for Hole-Ball.

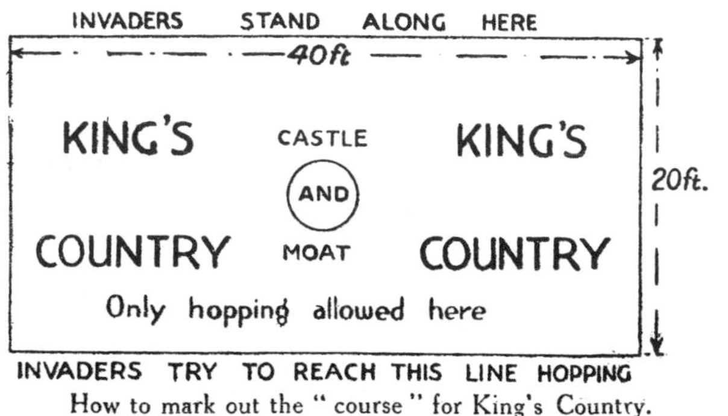

How to mark out the "course" for King's Country.

Our Parents' Pages

[continued from previous page]

satisfactory "net." It should be five feet from the ground. A rubber quoit or ring can be obtained at a sports dealer's for one-and-threepence, and sometimes at the sixpenny stores. Rope quoits or rings can be used, but they are not nearly so pleasant to play with, for they hurt one's fingers badly if one fails to catch them cleanly; and also they are dangerous for young children, who may get a nasty knock if they are not giving their full attention to the game.

The "court" should be thirteen paces by six, or more exactly forty feet by eighteen feet, and the line for receiving service should be five feet from the "net," but one can have a very good game without marking out an accurate court, and, indeed, just throwing and catching quoits is great fun, and with practice great skill can be developed. Ordinary tennis scoring, or any system of scoring points preferred, may be used.

The rules are based on those of lawn tennis, but it is usual to make a rule that the quoit must not be thrown overhand; it must be caught with one hand, and if a player "muffs" the catch he loses the point.

In even a tiny garden a ring-tennis arrangement can be rigged up. The court can be marked with whitening, making a brush of a piece of newspaper rolled up, and using a tightly stretched string to keep the lines straight. Perhaps the tape used for a net can be fastened to a tree or palings, or to a clothes-prop. There are many ways of contriving "nets," and of fixing them up. If by chance there are more boys and girls than can play at once, the "net" can be held by those waiting to play. Even in a park, if children have a rubber quoit, they will find some way of managing to get a good game.

"King's Country" is an exciting game to play on the sands. A castle is built and surrounded by a moat about four feet away from it, and the King's Country is marked off so that the castle is in the centre of the country, which should be made about forty feet by twenty feet. The players divide into two sides, and the side that wins the toss are the King's Men, and the other side the Invaders. The Invaders stand anywhere they like on the long sides of the King's Country. In the King's Country outside the castle moat, both the King's Men and the Invaders may only hop. If the Invaders are seen to use two feet, they are claimed by the King, and must go across and defend the castle. If the King's Men use two feet, they fall out of the game. The Invaders try to hop across the King's Country without being touched by the King's Men or forced to put their second foot down. If more than half the Invaders get across without being captured, the Invaders have won; if the King captures more than half, he has won. After one game, Invaders and King's Men change places.

Towards the end of the holidays it would be jolly to arrange a Treasure Hunt either for the family party or for a larger group, asking other children and older people to join in. Here is an entirely new sort of Treasure Hunt, and a novel way of laying the trail. It has been tested several times and found to work splendidly for large or small parties, either on the sands or in a garden or park.

It does not matter how simple the treasure is—chocolate, oranges, pencils, or some toy or useful article from the sixpenny stores will serve. The main point is not the treasure; people will almost forget about that in the excitement of the hunt. It is the thrill of searching for the clues and finding them, and trying to be quicker than other "huntsmen" that is so absorbing.

First of all some short rhyme or ordinary sentence must be made up which states plainly where the treasure is hidden.

1. "Treasure's buried under eight,
Hurry, or you'll be too late."

2. "I'm in a bag upon a chair."

No. 1 will make a moderately long Treasure Hunt; No. 2 would make a short one. If No. 1 is chosen, forty-eight cards or flat stones will be needed, one for each letter (and apostrophe) of the message. Halves of postcards serve very well, though in some ways flat stones are better for an outdoor Treasure Hunt, but they make rather a heavy load for the setters of the trail to carry round with them.

With a paint brush and black or coloured ink the cards or stones are numbered from 1 to 48 in the corners. Then the letter belonging to the number, as shown in diagram (c), is painted on. These 48 cards or stones are then placed anywhere within the limits of the area selected for the Hunt. Consecutive numbers should not be hidden near to each other, and the key letters of "key" words, such as "underneath" and "eight" should be well hidden. It is better not to "hide" them in the real sense of the word, but to place them so that they can be seen without anything being moved. This saves them getting misplaced by the first "huntsmen" who find them. If cards are used they will need weighting down with stones, or fixing to the ground with hair-pins, or attaching with string to bushes or palings, lest they be blown away or moved. Should someone not joining in the hunt take one or two away, it will not matter, for there will be enough to enable the "huntsmen" to guess the rhyme.

1 T	2 R	3 E	4 A	5 S	6 U
7 R	8 E	9 ,	10 S	11 B	12 U
13 R	14 I	15 E	16 D	17 U	18 N
19 D	20 E	21 R	22 E	23 I	24 G
25 H	26 T	27 H	28 U	29 R	30 R
31 Y	32 O	33 R	34 Y	35 O	36 U
37 ,	38 L	39 L	40 B	41 E	42 T
43 O	44 O	45 L	46 A	47 T	48 E

(a)

1 I	2 ,	3 M	4 I
5 N	6 A	7 B	8 A
9 G	10 U	11 P	12 O
13 N	14 A	15 C	16 H
17 A	18 I	19 R	

(b)

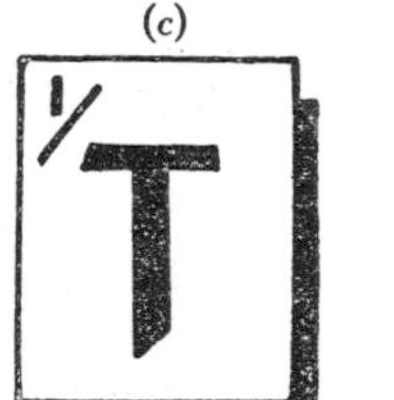

(c)

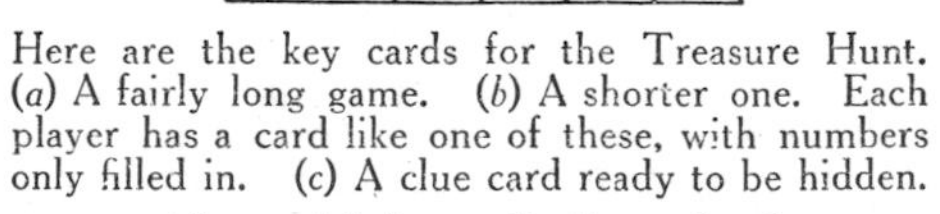

Here are the key cards for the Treasure Hunt. (a) A fairly long game. (b) A shorter one. Each player has a card like one of these, with numbers only filled in. (c) A clue card ready to be hidden.

Beside preparing the 48 cards to be used as clues, a card must be drawn out for each "huntsman," or better still, for each pair of partners. It will be found that the Hunt goes better if players work in twos. These partnerships can either be arranged beforehand by the organisers, or chosen at the time. Postcards do very well for the numbered card to be given to each person. They should look like diagram (a) or (b), except that the numbers only will be written on them, one in each square, leaving room for the "huntsmen" to write in the letters as they find them. For instance, when they find the card with "19 D" written on it, they will write in "D" in the square labelled 19, and so on, till they have found out enough to make sure where the treasure is. Then they will hurry off and secure it.

Two people will be needed to arrange the Hunt and to lay the trail. It is a pity for more to be in the know, and thus be unable to compete. Those two need not rule out and number the cards. Anyone can do this without finding out anything about the Hunt. They can also number the cards to be used for laying the trail, leaving the organisers to write in the letters. Of course, these preparations can be made before the holidays, or on some wet day. One can indeed keep a Treasure Hunt in stock.

It is important to choose the right place for the "Meet," and to start the "huntsmen" off in such a way that they are likely to find at least one or two clues in the first few minutes, for this works up the excitement.

One other duty falls to the organisers, and that is to collect up again the clue cards and so prevent the scattering of litter against which all decent-minded people are fighting.

(Doctor Helen will provide further interesting and helpful reading for mothers and fathers in Our Parents' Pages next month.)

A charming picture of Shirley Temple in her latest film, "Dimples."

Shirley cutting her seventh birthday cake last year. She will be eight on April 24th. (Fox Films Photos.)

SHIRLEY TEMPLE, whose photo appears at the top of the page, will be eight years old on April 24th, and she has sent us this special message for our Birthday Cake Supplement: "Mummy makes lovely birthday cakes. I have lovely birthday parties, too. I wish you could come to the next one I have!"

Since it is impossible, we are giving you the recipe Mrs. Temple is going to use for Shirley's next birthday. It appears on this page as the Eight-Year-Old's Birthday Cake.

EIGHT-YEAR-OLD'S BIRTHDAY CAKE

INGREDIENTS:

¾ lb. of plain flour. *1 breakfastcupful of castor sugar.* *1 teacupful of milk.*
5 oz. of butter or margarine. *4 eggs.* *2 teaspoonfuls of baking powder.*

For the FILLING AND DECORATION:

Lemon curd for two layers. *Apple jelly for one layer.* *Mimosa balls (crystallised).*
5 oz. of icing sugar mixed with 1 tablespoonful of lemon juice.

GREASE and line a tin measuring 8 inches across. Cream the butter and sugar, add the yolks of the eggs and beat well. Sift the flour and baking powder. Add half the milk to the cake mixture, then half the flour, and when it is stirred in add the rest of the milk followed by the flour. Lastly, fold in the stiffly beaten egg whites with a metal spoon. Do not beat the cake any more. Place in the tin and bake in the centre of a steady and fairly hot oven for 1 hour, or until the centre is elastic on being pressed.

Photo: Fox Films

DECORATING THE CAKE

Split the cake into four rounds, putting apple jelly filling between the two centre slices, and lemon curd in the top and bottom, then fit the pieces very neatly together and spread water icing over the top but not over the sides of the cake. To make the icing just mix the lemon juice and sugar in a small saucepan and when it is liquid enough to coat the back of the spoon easily, pour it quickly into the centre of the top of the cake. Before the icing sets put a row of crystallised mimosa all round the edge. Put the birthday candles on the cake, and if you like put a doll in the middle, or, if you have no doll, use a slice of crystallised pineapple. The lemon curd and the apple jelly can be bought or made at home, just as you like.

BIRTHDAY TREAT SANDWICH

INGREDIENTS:

3 oz. of margarine. *3 oz. of castor sugar.*
2 eggs.
¼ lb. of self-raising flour.

For the FILLING AND DECORATION:

Apricot jam.
3 small bananas.
A small carton of whipped cream.
¾ oz. of plain chocolate.

GREASE a deep sandwich tin measuring 7 inches in diameter. Beat the margarine and sugar to a soft white cream, then add the yolks of the eggs and beat again. Stir in 2 tablespoonfuls of water and then the flour. Add the stiffly beaten whites as lightly as you can, then place the mixture in the tin and bake for about 20 minutes in a fairly hot oven at a temperature of 370° Fah.

DECORATING THIS PRETTY CAKE

When the cake is cold, split it in half and spread with apricot jam. Put the two halves together. Put the cream in a basin and whip it with a fork until it is stiff, then stir in a spoonful of castor sugar. Cut the small knobby ends off the bananas and cut the bananas themselves into as many long strips as will represent the age of the child for whom the cake is made. If he or she happens to be a six-year-old just split the three bananas in halves. If the pieces are too long, cut them to the length required or halve them. Spread the top of the cake with a little jam, then with a layer of whipped and sweetened cream. In the centre put the ends of the bananas you cut off, putting them quite close together to form the centre of what is going to be a flower. Just before you want to put the cake on the tea-table cover the cream and the banana centre with a fairly thick layer of grated chocolate, and last of all arrange the pieces of banana to form the petals of a kind of sunflower or large daisy.

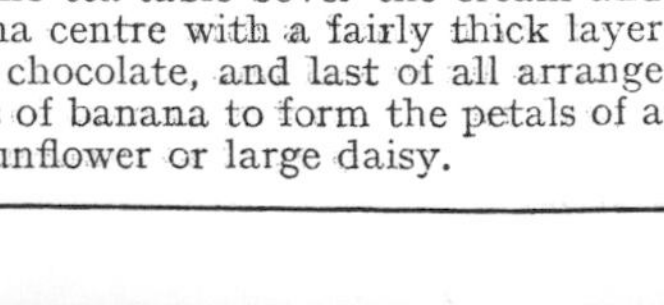

PRINCESS ELIZABETH, who has become a more important little lady than ever, will be eleven on April 21st, so we print a special birthday cake in her honour. The recipe is on this page.

Photo: Marcus Adams

THE PRINCESS ELIZABETH BIRTHDAY CAKE

INGREDIENTS:

½ lb. of self-raising flour. *6 oz. of butter or margarine.* *6 oz. of castor sugar.*
4 eggs. *2 tablespoonfuls of fine desiccated coconut.* *¼ gill of milk or water.*

For the ICING AND FILLING:

A 3-oz. cake of chocolate. *6 oz. of butter.* *10 oz. of soft icing sugar.*

For DECORATING:

Almond paste (see 21st Birthday Cake, page 83). *A little green coloured coconut.*
11 small tufts of fresh primroses.

To make this dainty and original cake, grease and line a tin measuring 7 inches across, or, if you want a really large cake, take half as much again of the cake ingredients and use an 8-inch tin. Cream the butter and sugar till soft and light, then add the egg yolks and beat well. Add the flour, sieved with the coconut, and milk by degrees without beating too much, and lastly add the stiffly beaten egg whites as gently as possible. Place in the tin and bake in a steady and moderate oven for about 1 hour or until the centre feels elastic on being pressed.

ICING AND DECORATING

Put the chocolate in a saucer and stand it in a warm place. While it is getting soft beat the butter to a cream. Stir in the icing sugar and chocolate, beating it all well together. If you like, add a few drops of vanilla essence.

Split the cake in half and put a layer of chocolate butter icing in the middle and a very thin layer on top. The rest of the icing is spread round the sides of the cake rather thickly, and is then marked round in one direction with a fork to make it look like a basket.

Put some almond paste on top, only make it rough instead of smooth, and let it be a trifle softer than usual. A rim of almond paste can go round the edge to make it look like the top of the basket, not forgetting two small raised up parts for handles. This can be spread with the remains of the chocolate butter icing. Make eleven little holes in the paste to receive the primroses.

The cake can be done so far and left till next day for the final decoration. For this you will want some freshly gathered or bought primroses, out of which you can make tiny buttonholes. Do eleven of these, putting about three primroses and a bud in each, and if the stalks are strong do not let them be *too* short. Round the end of the stalks tie a piece of damp greaseproof paper, and stick each little bunch in the hole you have made in the almond paste. Round each little bunch sprinkle some green coconut, to give the effect of grass, until the top of the cake is covered in this way.

To make an extra special finish and give a pretty frilly effect, you can make two bows of baby ribbon to ornament the handles of the basket. Three pale colours look well together, and you could have 1½ yards each of narrow white, pale yellow and pale green ribbon. This is enough for two good bows or rosettes, so you cut the ribbons in half. To make each bow, fold the ribbons in half and tie an ordinary bow, then separate all the little bows and arrange them nicely to make a rosette. A small piece of wire can be used for fixing the bow in place.

"SHOW" CHILDREN

We are all rightly proud of our children, but sometimes we let the youngsters see it a little too clearly. We put them " on show " to the world, and then wonder that they become precocious and fond of " showing off." Here is an article which shows how easily this may happen nowadays

"WHAT that child of Mrs. Blank's needs is a jolly good spanking!"

Most of us have heard, and not a few of us have uttered, remarks of this kind—not altogether without reason, either, as we have been unwilling witnesses while a precocious small maiden, or, more rarely, a small boy, has been " showing off " for our benefit.

The precocious child is a product of our times. In the not-so-far-away days when children were " seen and not heard," all tendencies to precocity were quickly frowned upon and nipped in the bud. Moreover those were the days of large families, where the wholesome influence of numerous brothers and sisters could be relied upon promptly to discourage any attempts of this kind, and where every member of the family quickly found his or her proper level, and remained there.

One of the greatest changes that have come about in recent times is the attitude of the world in general and of parents in particular towards tiny children. The pendulum has swung completely the other way, and often enough we find the children transferred from the background to the very forefront and centre of family life, and acquiring in consequence a mistaken but very natural impression of their own supreme importance.

" You simply must see Betty tap-dancing ! " exclaims the proud mother, as she draws the little four-year-old to her side. " She's picked it up all by herself, and everyone says she is really wonderful. Come along, darling, and show this auntie what a clever little girl you are."

And she does not realise that she is making the child believe that she is exceptionally talented and superior to other children—and even to grown-ups—who cannot tap-dance.

Children to-day are extremely quick-witted, and the small boy or girl with a clever gift for repartee, who is allowed to interrupt every conversation with pert remarks, soon becomes unbearable.

It is, of course, only natural that every parent shall be thrilled and delighted as baby learns to walk and talk, and begins to display all those endearing little characteristics of early childhood. It is only right, too, that the toddler shall be encouraged to further efforts of physical and mental development by praise and admiration ; but later, when baby thoroughly understands all that is being said (and few parents realise how quickly this stage is reached !) praise must be seasoned with a good deal of prudence.

" Isn't Mary growing pretty ? Her hair is such a lovely shade, and it's more curly than ever," remarks Mary's mother in her hearing, as she twists the admittedly charming ringlets round her finger. " I always hoped she would have blue eyes, and a clear complexion, but I never thought she would turn out such a little picture." And her words are not lost upon Mary.

Photo : Lisa

Daddy should beware, also, how he boasts what a sturdy little fellow his son is, and how useful with his fists. Master Jack may easily get the idea that Might is Right and that a bullying manner is going to win him whatever he wants in this world.

Wise parents never discuss their children in their presence, either to praise or blame them, and it is a good rule to remember that children should invariably be talked " to," and not " at " or " about." There is nothing that makes for greater self-consciousness than the knowledge that grown-ups find their virtues, or even their sins, a worthy topic of conversation. There is an art in knowing when to praise and when to remain unimpressed, and this is perhaps one of the most difficult lessons which everyone who has the control of children must learn, for these small people vary so tremendously in the kind of treatment they require. While the diffident child needs consistent encouragement and admiration, the precocious child is all the better for a very matter-of-fact attitude to his achievements.

So far we have only considered the precocious child who is the victim of the over-attention of his adoring parents. There is, however, another, far less simple type whose precocity is defensive, and is actually the result of a deeply embedded inferiority complex—to use a favourite expression of to-day. Such a child is perhaps the youngest of the family, or the hitherto only child who feels his place is usurped by the new baby, or possibly he suffers from some slight physical disability or peculiarity, so that it seems to him that he is " out of the picture " and rather despised and neglected. As a result he endeavours to bolster up his self-esteem by showing off, by " throwing his weight about," or even by being deliberately naughty—anything to draw attention to himself.

At first sight such a child appears merely difficult and tiresome, and the impatient parents probably decide that he needs a firm hand, so that he receives those checks of which the more usual type of precocious child stands in such sore need. But actually his is a case for sympathetic understanding. Every effort should be made by means of a little extra attention and affection to find out what is going on at the back of that little mind, and to set things to rights, so that he feels he has a real and accepted position in the scheme of things that make up his little world.

If Jack or Jill has not been cured of showing off by the time schooldays dawn, he or she will receive a rude jolt upon entering the rough and tumble of life among equals.

Jack may have tyrannised over smaller playmates at home, but at school he will find his own level.

Jill will discover that children of her own age are not impressed by her singular beauty or cleverness.

School life is a great leveller, but it is kinder to children not to let them climb so high that they are let in for so bumpy a fall !

(If these Parents' Pages have interested you, talk them over with your husband or your friends, and, if you like, write and tell us your views or seek advice on your particular problems connected with the management of your kiddies. Letters should be addressed to the Editress at the address given on page 89 and a stamped, addressed envelope enclosed for a reply. Watch for further interesting articles next month. They will give you something to think about, something to discuss, and perhaps throw light on the very point that is worrying you at the moment.)

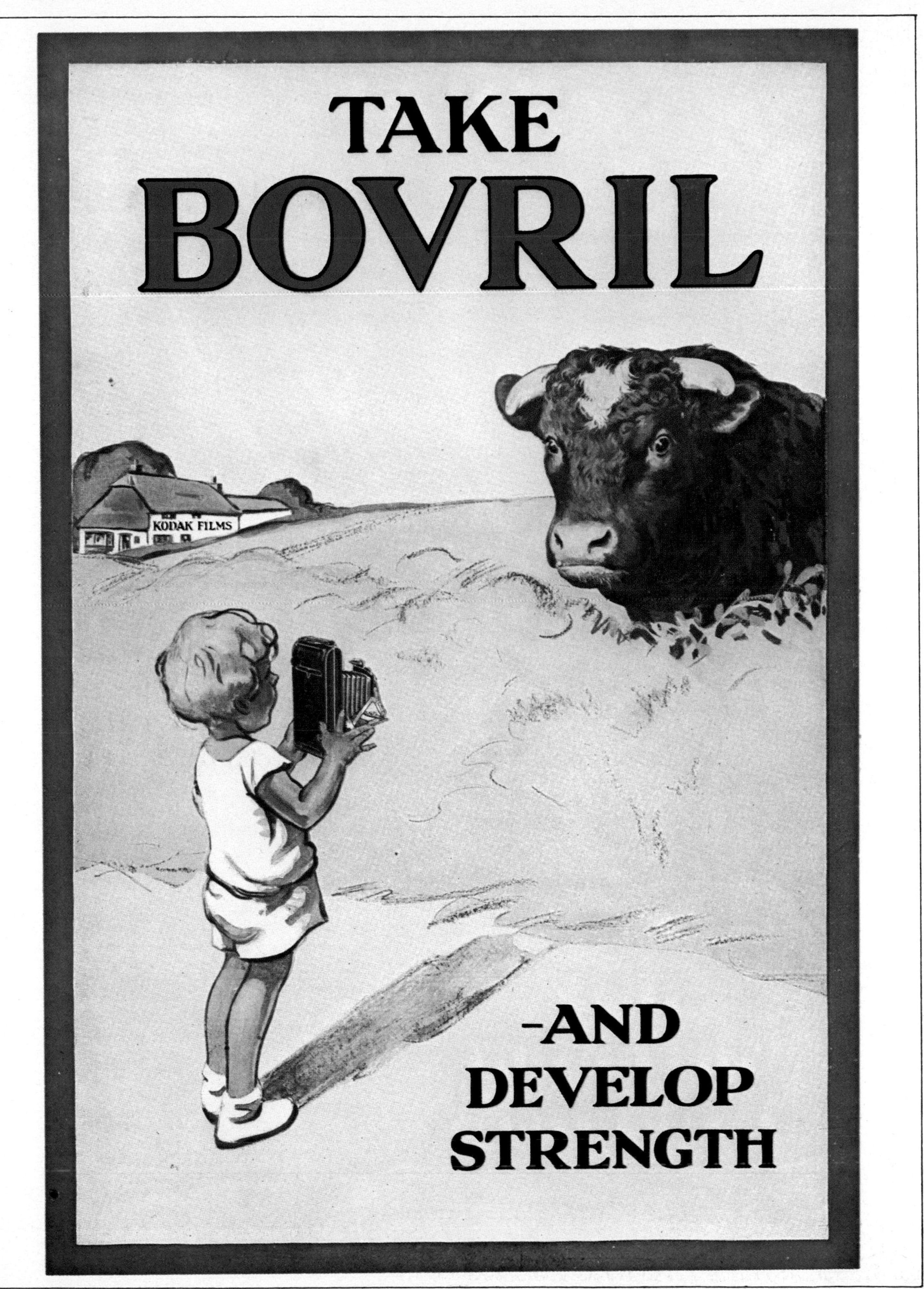
TAKE
BOVRIL
KODAK FILMS
-AND
DEVELOP
STRENGTH

Telegraph Boy.—He arrives with a Greetings telegram for his hostess, a happy thought of mummy's, but written in his own round and rather wobbly hand. His suit of navy blue Viyella is boldly edged with scarlet tape, and no one will ever guess that the peak of his cap was once an eye-shade!

Pirate.—Bold, bad and devil-may-care is this young man with his eye in a sling and a fearsome-looking (wooden!) knife in his sash. He wears his white summer pants with a short blue cotton jacket, and a couple of curtain rings, two red hankies and his Wellington boots complete the outfit.

Crinoline.—Her gingham skirt with its frame of stiff book muslin beneath, will cause a lot of fun when she sits down, so will those lace-edged pantalettes. She'll love her tiny red velvet jacket, and the pill-box, too, but if the party is anything like a party, her chignon won't last long!

Shepherd.—Send your small son to the party in brown corduroy leggings, cross-laced with green braid, a white woolly lamb-skin across his shoulder (teddy bear cloth in disguise) and a bright little feather in his pointed felt hat.

Shepherdess.—His diminutive partner wears a frock with a full printed cotton skirt, and a lavender sateen top trimmed with green velvet ribbons to match that enormous hat.

THE ROSE.—A shy little bundle this, completely overawed by her very first party, and the layers and layers of pink crêpe paper petals that make her skirt. The bunchy green sleeves are paper, too, but not so her saucy little cap—that is green velvet.

THE GARDENER.—It shouldn't be difficult to find an ancient straw sun hat, and the rake can be improvised in wood. Dye a pair of old grey flannels brown, and then sacrifice the green baize knife cloth (perhaps !) to make that workmanlike apron.

CHINESE.—That plaited woollen pig-tail will be a great temptation to his frolicsome fellow guests—better stitch it to his cap. His blue cotton tunic has the most realistic Chinese symbols appliquéd in red, to match his trousers.

SUNFLOWER.—It takes no time to turn Pam into a sunflower ! Around the waist of her yellow frock nanny sews layers of yellow crêpe paper petals. The neck-frill is green paper, the cap green sateen.

THE BRIDE.—Clutching a posy of white paper flowers, this youthful bride makes a surprising entry in a stiff white calico gown. Whether she comes home with that veil intact remains to be seen !

THE BRIDEGROOM.—The pride of his young life is the grey beaver "topper." His trousers were made from a pair of daddy's flannels, his coat is an old one, dyed.

NOW It Is TIME for TEA!

An Amusing and Original Clock Cake With a Foundation of Coconut Sponge

THIS novelty cake is coated with white icing, with chocolate icing for the clock design.

INGREDIENTS:
- 2 *eggs.*
- 4 *ozs. butter or margarine.*
- 5 *ozs. castor sugar.*
- 2 *ozs. desiccated coconut.*
- 6 *ozs. self-raising flour.*
- $\frac{3}{4}$ *to* 1 *gill milk.*
- $1\frac{1}{2}$ *teaspoonfuls rose water.*

FOR THE COATING ICING:
- $\frac{3}{4}$ *lb icing sugar.*
- $1\frac{1}{2}$ *teaspoonfuls rose water.*
- *About* $2\frac{1}{2}$ *tablespoonfuls water.*

FOR THE CHOCOLATE ICING:
- 2 *ozs. icing sugar.*
- $\frac{1}{2}$ *oz. chocolate.*
- 1 *dessertspoonful water.*

FOR this cake, use a cake-tin about 6 to $6\frac{1}{2}$ inches in diameter.

Beat the sugar and fat to a soft cream. Add one egg and stir the mixture quickly for a few moments until it is smooth. Then add the second egg. When both eggs are well beaten in, sift the flour and stir it in gradually. Add the coconut, and some milk to moisten the mixture, as may be required.

Add the rose water, and turn the mixture into the greased cake-tin. Bake the cake in a moderate oven—one hour should be sufficient time to allow.

Test the cake with a skewer to find if it is ready before taking it out, and when it is ready, turn it on to a cake rack and leave it to get cold.

The outline of the clock face, the numbers and the hands are made of chocolate icing.

Note: When the mixture is put into the tin to bake, slightly hollow out the centre of the cake by spreading the mixture towards the sides of the tin.

If the flavour of rose water is not liked, substitute a few drops of vanilla or any other suitable flavouring essence.

To Make the Coating Icing: Rub the icing sugar through a hair sieve and mix it to a smooth coating consistency with moderately hot water, adding also the rose water to flavour, if liked.

To Ice the Cake: Cut off a slice from one side of the cake as shown and stand it upright with the cut side on the cake rack.

Place a dish under the rack, and pour the prepared white icing over the cake, coating it evenly. Leave the cake until the icing has set.

To Make the Chocolate Icing: Grate the chocolate and dissolve it in the water, then let it get cool.

Sift the sugar and mix it with the cooled, dissolved chocolate to a soft, smooth consistency, adding a little more water, as required.

[CONTINUED ON OPPOSITE PAGE]

A slice is cut from the cake so that it has a flat base to stand on.

IN THE SWIM

CHILD'S SWIM SUIT

(Age 4–6 years.)

THE *Back.*—With white wool cast on 40 sts. and work in moss-st. for 8 rows. Change to blue wool and work 8 rows in st.-st.

Change to white wool and work 2 rows in garter-st. These 10 rows form the pattern and are repeated throughout. Work 18 more rows.

Leave these sts. and work another piece in the same way.

Next row : K. 40, then k. the 40 sts. for the other leg on to the same pin (80 sts.). Continue in pattern for 23 rows, then on the next and every following 8th row, dec. at both ends of the pin until 72 sts. remain.

Work 7 more rows, then dec. at both ends of next and every alternate row until 52 sts. remain. Work 1 more row.

Now inc. at both ends of next and every alternate row until there are 68 sts. on the pin. Work 13 more rows.

Now dec. at both ends of every row until 44 sts. remain.

Next row : Work 22, turn.

Continue on these 22 sts. for 3 more rows. Now dec. at neck edge of the next and every alternate row until 8 sts. remain. Work 9 more rows. Cast off.

Join the wool to the other 22 sts. and work to correspond.

The Front.—Work exactly as for the back.

The Gusset.—With blue wool, cast on 2 sts. Work 2 rows, then working in pattern, inc. at both ends of the next and every alternate row until 24 sts. are on the pin. Work 5 more rows.

Now dec. at both ends of the next and every alternate row until 2 sts. remain. Work 1 more row. Cast off.

TO MAKE UP

Press the work under a damp cloth with a hot iron. Sew up side seams and the piece below armholes, also right shoulder. Sew up the moss-st. leg seams and then sew in gusset. With white wool work a row of d.c. round neck and armholes, making a buttonhole loop on left front shoulder. Work d.c. round the diamond side openings. Sew buttons on to shoulder.

MATERIALS

Three ounces of "Wendy" Beach wool in blue, and one ounce of the same wool in white; a pair of No. 10 "Aero" knitting pins; a small crochet hook; 1 button.

MEASUREMENTS

From shoulder to lower edge, 19 ins.; round chest, stretching to 24 ins.

GIRLIE will feel very proud and gay in this smart little striped bathing costume which Finella has designed for her.

THE CLOCK CAKE

To Decorate the Cake : **Mark an inner circle on the face of the cake, using a pastry cutter.**

Put the chocolate icing into an icing pump with a piping tube affixed, and pipe the numbers on the cake, spacing them evenly. Next pipe the hands of the clock.

Now mark an outer circle and pipe round it, using a small fancy patterned icing tube. The Clock Cake is then finished and ready to be placed on a cake board.

"Finella" Designs for your Kiddies

Illustrated on facing page

MARGARET ROSE JUMPER

(6–7 Years)

MATERIALS

Five ounces of Patons' Real Shetland wool, 2-ply; a pair each of Nos. 10 and 13 Stratnoid knitting pins.

MEASUREMENTS

Length, 16½ ins.; round chest, 26 ins.; sleeve seam, 16½ ins. (including cuff).

TENSION

Six stitches and 9 rows to 1 in.

THE *Back.*—Using No. 13 pins, cast on 78 sts. and work in k. 1, p. 1 rib for 3 ins. Change to No. 10 pins and work in st.-st. until work measures 11 ins. from the beginning, then shape armholes by casting off 5 sts. at the beginning of the next 2 rows and dec. at both ends of the next 4 rows (60 sts.).

Continue without further shaping until work measures 15½ ins. from the beginning, then work across 22 sts., cast off 16 sts., work to end. Continue on last set of 22 sts. and dec. at neck edge on the next 2 rows.

Shape shoulders by casting off 5 sts. at the beginning of the next 4 rows which start at the armhole edge.

Join the wool to the remaining sts. and work the second shoulder to match.

The Front.—Work as for back until work measures 12½ ins. from the beginning, then work across 22 sts., cast off 16 sts., work to end. Continue on last set of 22 sts., and dec. at the neck edge on the next 2 rows.

Continue without further shaping until work measures 16 ins. from the beginning, then shape shoulders by casting off 5 sts. at the beginning of the next 4 rows which start at the armhole edge. Join wool to remaining sts. and work other side to match.

The Neck Borders.—Join one shoulder seam only. Now holding the right side of work towards you and using No. 13 pins, pick up 100 sts. round neck and work in k. 1, p. 1 rib for 1½ ins. Cast off loosely in k. 1, p. 1 rib, using a No. 10 pin.

The Sleeves.—Using No. 10 pins, cast on 20 sts. and work in st.-st., casting on 2 sts. at the beginning of every row until there are 60 sts. on the pin.

Continue in st.-st., dec. at each end of every 8th row until 34 sts. remain. Continue straight until work measures 16 ins. Change to No. 13 pins and work in k. 1, p. 1 rib for 2 ins. Cast off in k. 1, p. 1 rib, using a No. 10 pin.

Work another sleeve to match.

TO MAKE UP

Press all parts except ribbing with a warm iron over a damp cloth. Sew sleeves into armholes. Join side and sleeve seams and press all seams. Join the second shoulder seam.

ELIZABETH JUMPER

(10–12 Years)

MATERIALS

Five ounces of Patons' Real Shetland wool, 2-ply; a pair each of Nos. 10 and 13 Stratnoid knitting pins.

MEASUREMENTS

Length, 18 ins.; round chest, 31 ins.; sleeve seam, 18 ins. (including cuff).

TENSION

Six stitches and 9 rows to 1 in.

ABBREVIATIONS

St., stitch; k., knit; p., purl; tog., together; inc., increase by knitting twice into same st.; dec., decrease; s., slip; p.s.s.o., pass the slipped st. over; st.-st., stocking-stitch (k. 1 row, p. 1 row alternately). Moss-st. is k. 1, p. 1 alternately; when working on an even number of sts., begin alternate rows with p. 1. Garter-st. is every row k.

THE *Back.*—Using No. 13 pins, cast on 92 sts. and work in k. 1, p. 1 rib for 3 ins. Change to No. 10 pins and continue in st.-st. until work measures 12 ins. from the cast-on edge, then shape armholes by casting off 5 sts. at the beginning of the next 2 rows and dec. at both ends of the next 5 rows (72 sts.).

Continue without further shaping until work measures 17 ins. from the beginning. Now shape the neck: Work across 27 sts., cast off 18 sts., work to end. Continue on last set of 27 sts., and dec. at neck edge on the next 3 rows.

Now shape shoulders by casting off 6 sts. at the beginning of the next 4 rows starting at armhole edge.

Join wool to the remaining sts. and work other side to match.

The Front.—Work as for back until work measures 13½ ins. from the cast-on edge, then shape neck: Work across 27 sts., cast off 18 sts., work to end. Continue on last set of 27 sts. and dec. at the neck edge on the next 3 rows.

Continue without further shaping until work measures 17½ ins. from the cast-on edge, then shape shoulders by casting off 6 sts. at the beginning of the next 4 rows, starting at armhole edge. Rejoin wool to remaining sts., and work other side to match.

The Neck Borders.—Join one shoulder seam only. Now, holding the right side of work towards you, and using No. 13 pins, pick up 118 sts. round neck and work in k. 1, p. 1 rib for 1½ ins. Cast off loosely in k. 1, p. 1 rib, using a No. 10 pin.

The Sleeves.—Using No. 10 pins cast on 24 sts. and work in st.-st., casting on 2 sts. at the beginning of every row until there are 72 sts. on pin. Continue in st.-st., and dec. at each end of every 8th row until 52 sts. remain. Continue straight until work measures 20 ins.

Change to No. 13 pins, and work in k. 1, p. 1 rib for 2 ins. Cast off in k. 1, p. 1 rib, using a No. 10 pin.

Work another sleeve to match.

TO MAKE UP

Press all parts except the ribbing carefully with a warm iron over a damp cloth. Join the second shoulder seam. Sew the sleeves into the armholes. Join the side and sleeve seams. Press all seams.

MARGARET ROSE COAT

MATERIALS

Eleven ounces of Wendy Homespun Wool, 4-ply; a pair of No. 10 Stratnoid knitting pins; 4 buttons; a medium crochet hook.

MEASUREMENTS

Length, 25 ins.; chest, 26 ins.; sleeve seam, 15 ins.

TENSION

Six stitches and 9 rows to 1 in.

THE *Back.*—Cast on 156 sts. and work in moss-st. for 8 rows, working into the backs of the sts. on the first row.

Now work in st.-st. and dec. as follows:

9th row: K. 26, s. 1, k. 1, p.s.s.o., k. 36, k. 2 tog., k. 24, s. 1, k. 1, p.s.s.o., k. 36, k. 2 tog., k. 26. Work 5 rows in st.-st. without shaping.

15th row: K. 26, s. 1, k. 1, p.s.s.o., k. 34, k. 2 tog., k. 24, s. 1, k. 1, p.s.s.o., k. 34, k. 2 tog., k. 26. Work 5 rows without shaping.

Photo: Fall

If you can't give your kiddie a real Welsh Corgi, like the three jolly little fellows above, you can make him a very lifelike toy one from the instructions on page 172. See also the photograph on the opposite page.

ROYAL FAVOURITES

Mothers are looking to our young Princesses to set the fashion in children's wear this season, and they will heartily approve the simple styles chosen by the Queen for her little daughters. This month we give instructions for knitting the practical holiday jerseys shown on the left, and the typical tailored coat with double-breasted fronts and wide revers illustrated below.

Here is our knitted model of Dookie, the Corgi dog who is the beloved playmate of Princess Elizabeth and her little sister.

Designs For Your Kiddies
[continued]

21st row: K. 26, s. 1, k. 1, p.s.s.o., k. 32, k. 2 tog., k. 24, s. 1, k. 1, p.s.s.o., k. 32, k. 2 tog., k. 26.

Continue in this way, dec. on every 6th row above the previous decs. until 19 such dec. rows have been worked (80 sts. remain).

Continue straight in st.-st. until work measures 19 ins. from the beginning, then shape the armholes by casting off 4 sts. at the beginning of the next 2 rows and then dec. at both ends of the following 4 alternate rows.

Continue without further shaping till work measures 24½ ins. from the beginning. Shape the shoulders by casting off 7 sts. at the beginning of the next 6 rows. Cast off.

The Right Front.—Cast on 90 sts. and work in moss-st. for 8 rows, working into the backs of the sts. on the first row. Now work in st.-st. and dec. as follows:

9th row: K. 24, s. 1, k. 1, p.s.s.o., k. 36, k. 2 tog., k. 26. Work 5 rows in st.-st. without shaping.

15th row: K. 24, s. 1, k. 1, p.s.s.o., k. 34 k. 2 tog., k. 26.

Continue in this way, dec. above the previous dec. on every 6th row until 19 such dec. rows have been worked (52 sts. remain). Continue straight in st.-st. until work measures 14 ins. from the beginning (ending with a p. row), then work a pair of buttonholes as follows:

Next row: K. 4. cast off 5, k. 12, cast off 5, k. to end. On the following row cast on 2 sets of 5 sts. to take the place of those cast off. Continue straight in st.-st., and when work measures 4 ins. from the last set of buttonholes, work another set as before.

Then continue without shaping till work measures 19 ins. from the beginning.

Now shape the armholes by casting off 4 sts. at the beginning of the next p. row and then dec. at the same edge of the following 4 p. rows, but at the same time start to inc. for the revers at the end of the first and every alternate p. row (i.e. every 4th row) until there are 56 sts. on the needle.

Cast off 35 sts. at the beginning of the next k. row and continue straight till the work measures 24½ ins. from the beginning. Shape the shoulders by casting off 7 sts. at the beginning of the following 3 p. rows.

The Left Front.—Work as for the right front, omitting the buttonholes and with all shapings reversed.

The Right Front Facing.—Cast on 16 sts. and work into the backs of the sts. all across. Work straight in st.-st. till work measures 14 ins. from the beginning, ending on a k. row.

Next row: P. 4, cast off 5, p. 7. On the following row cast on 5 sts. to take the place of those cast off. When work measures 4 ins. from the last buttonhole, work another as before, then continue straight till work measures 19 ins. from the beginning.

Now work in moss-st. and inc. at both ends of the first and every following 4th row until there are 40 sts. on the needle. Cast off 35 sts. at the beginning of the next row which commences on the wrong side of work (p. side) and continue in st.-st. on remaining sts. until facing is as long as the front to the shoulder. Cast off.

The Left Front Facing.—Work as for the right front facing with all shapings reversed, and without the buttonholes.

The Sleeves.—Cast on 48 sts. and work in moss-st. for 8 rows, working into the backs of the sts. on the first row.

Now work in st.-st. and inc. at both ends of every 10th row until there are 72 sts. on the needle.

Continue straight till work measures 15 ins. from the beginning, then shape the top of the sleeve by casting off 4 sts. at the beginning of the next 2 rows and then dec. at both ends of every row until 16 sts. remain. Cast off.

Work another sleeve to match.

The Collar.—Join the shoulder seams and pick up 38 sts. round the neck from the casting off of the revers round to the same point on the opposite side. Work in moss-st. for 3½ ins. Cast off.

To Make Up

Press the work carefully on the wrong side with a hot iron over a damp cloth. Sew the sleeves into the armholes and join the side and sleeve seams. Double over the collar and sew in place. Place the front facings in position and work d.c. through the two edges from the bottom to the collar. Invisibly catch-stitch the inner edge in place, over-sewing the buttonholes. Fold over the revers and press flat. Press all seams and sew buttons in position.

'DOOKIE' THE WELSH CORGI

Materials

Two ounces of T. H. Lily Scotch Fingering, 3-ply, in beige; small quantities of dark brown and red wool; a pair of No. 12 Stratnoid knitting pins; 2 dark brown buttons and kapok for stuffing.

Size

The toy measures about 14 ins. from nose to tip of tail.

The dog is knitted in 9 pieces, all in garter-st., namely 2 sides, 1 under-part, inside of mouth, tongue, 4 pieces for ears.

The Side Pieces.—Cast on 2 sts. and k. 1 row. *2nd row:* Inc. in both sts. *3rd row:* K. *4th row:* Inc. in first and last sts. *5th row:* K. Repeat these 2 rows twice.

10th row: Inc. in first st., k. last 2 sts. tog. *11th row:* K. Repeat the last 2 rows 7 times.

26th row: Cast on 6 sts. and k. to end. *27th row:* K. *28th row:* Inc. in first st. *29th row:* K. Repeat the last 2 rows once. *32nd row:* Inc. in first st. *33rd row:* Inc. in last st. Repeat the last 2 rows once.

36th row: Cast on 18 sts., k. to end. *37th row:* K. *38th row:* K. 5, turn. *39th row:* S. 1, k. 4. *40th and 41st rows:* K. Repeat the last 4 rows 3 times.

54th row: Cast off 9 sts., k. to end. *55th row:* K. last 2 tog. *56th row:* K. Repeat the last 2 rows 4 times. *65th to 67th rows:* K. *68th row:* Inc. in first st., k. to end. *69th to 78th rows:* K.

79th row: K. first 2 sts. tog. *80th to 90th rows:* K. *91st row:* K. first 2 sts. tog. *92nd row:* Inc. in first st. *93rd to 112th rows:* K.

113th row: Inc. in first st. *114th to 117th rows:* K. *118th row:* Inc. in first st. *119th row:* K. *120th row:* Inc. in first st. Repeat the last row 3 times.

124th row: Cast on 8 sts. K to end. *125th row:* Inc. in first st. *126th row:* K. 5, turn. *127th row:* S. 1, k. 4. *128th row:* K. *129th row:* Inc. in first st. Repeat the last 4 rows 3 times.

142nd row: Cast off 10, k. to end. *143rd row:* K. last 2 sts. tog. *144th row:* K. first 2 sts. tog. Repeat the last 2 rows once.

147th row: Inc. in first st., k. last 2 sts. tog. *148th row:* K. first 2 sts. tog. *149th row:* K. last 2 sts. tog. *150th row:* K. first 2 sts. tog. *151st row:* Inc. in first st., k. last 2 sts. tog. *152nd row:* K. first 2 sts. tog. *153rd row:* K. last 2 sts. tog. *154th to 157th rows:* K.

158th row: Inc. in first st. *159th row:* K. Repeat the last 2 rows once. *162nd row:* K. 7, turn.

On these 7 sts. proceed as follows: K. 10 rows, then dec. at the beginning of the next and following 2 alternate rows.

Next row: K. 2, k. 2 tog. *Next row:* K. 2 tog., k. 1. *Next row:* K. 2 tog. Finish off.

Now return to remaining sts., join on wool, and finish the 162nd row.

163rd row: K. first 2 sts. tog. *164th row:* K. *165th row:* K. first 2 sts. tog. *166th row:* Inc. in first st. Repeat the last 2 rows twice.

171st row: Cast off 8, k. to end. *172nd row:* Inc. in first st. *173rd row:* K. first 2 sts. tog. Repeat the last 2 rows 4 times. *182nd row:* K. *183rd row:* K. first 2 sts. tog. *184th row:* K.

185th to 187th rows: K. first 2 sts. tog. *188th row:* K. 2 tog. at both ends. *189th and 190th rows:* K. first 2 sts. tog. *191st row:* K. 2 tog. twice. *192nd row:* K. 2 tog. Finish off.

Work another piece in the same way.

The Underpart.—Cast on 2 sts. *1st row:* Inc. in both sts. *2nd to 4th rows:* K. *5th row:* Inc. in first and last sts. *6th to 8th rows:* K. Repeat the last 4 rows once.

13th and 14th rows: Cast on 20 sts. and k. to end. *15th row:* K. 5, turn. *16th row:* S. 1, k. 4.

17th row: K. 20, k. 2 tog., k. 4, k. 2 tog., k. 20. *18th row:* K. 5, turn. *19th row:* S. 1, k. 4.

20th row: K. 19, k. 2 tog. 4 times, k. 19. *21st row:* K. 5, turn. *22nd row:* S. 1, k. 4.

23rd row: K. 17, k. 2 tog. 4 times, k. 17. *24th row:* K. 5, turn. *25th row:* S. 1, k. 4.

26th row: K. 17, k. 2 tog. twice, k. 17. *27th row:* K. 5, turn. *28th row:* S. 1, k. 4.

29th row: K. 16, k. 2 tog. twice, k. 16. *30th row:* K. 5, turn. *31st row:* S. 1, k. 4. *32nd row:* K. Repeat the last 3 rows twice.

39th and 40th rows: Cast off 9, k. to end. *41st to 50th rows:* K. first 2 sts. tog. *51st to 70th rows:* K.

71st row: Inc. in first and last sts. *72nd to 85th rows:* K. *86th row:* Inc. in first and last sts. *87th to 100th rows:* K.

101st row: Inc. in first and last sts.

"DOOKIE," THE WELSH CORGI

102nd row : K. Repeat the last 2 rows twice. *107th and 108th rows :* Cast on 8 sts. and k. to end. *109th row :* K. 5, turn. *110th row :* S. 1, k. 4. *111th row :* K. Repeat the last 3 rows 7 times.

133rd and 134th rows : Cast off 10 sts., k. to end. *135th row :* K. *136th row :* K. 2 tog. at both ends. *137th and 138th rows :* K. *139th row :* K. 2 tog. at both ends. *140th to 142nd rows :* K.

143rd row : K. 2 tog. at both ends. *144th and 145th rows :* K. *146th row :* K. 2 tog. at both ends. *147th row :* K. *148th row :* K. 2 tog. twice. *149th row :* K. 2 tog. Finish off.

The Ears.—Work 4 pieces all alike, 2 in beige wool and 2 in dark brown, as follows :

Cast on 12 sts. and k. 12 rows. *13th row :* K. 2 tog. at both ends. *14th to 20th rows :* K. Repeat the last 8 rows once.

29th row : K. 2 tog. at both ends. *30th to 32nd rows :* K. *33rd row :* K. 2 tog. at both ends. *34th row :* K. 2 tog. twice. *35th row :* K. 2 tog. Finish off.

The Mouth.—With dark brown wool, cast on 2 sts.

1st row : Inc. in both. *2nd to 6th rows :* K. *7th row :* Inc. in first and last sts. *8th to 12th rows :* K. *13th row :* Inc. in first and last sts. *14th to 30th rows :* K.

31st row : K. 2 tog. at both ends. *32nd to 43rd rows :* K. *44th row :* K. 2 tog. at both ends. *45th and 46th rows :* K. *47th row :* K. 2 tog. twice. *48th row :* K. 2 tog. Finish off.

The Tongue.—With red wool, cast on 6 sts. and k. 12 rows. *13th row :* K. 2 tog., k. 2, k. 2 tog. *14th row :* K. 2 tog. twice. *15th row :* K. 2 tog. Finish off.

To Make Up

Sew together the two side pieces from a point just below the tail, right along the back, over the head, and finish at the point of the upper jaw where the mouth commences. Leave open a part of this seam, along the back, for stuffing. Sew the two side pieces together also from the point of the lower jaw to about one inch above the front legs. Now fit in and sew the underpart, fitting legs to legs, the place where the underpart was commenced going to the back of the animal.

Next take the dark brown mouth-piece and fold it in two, but making one end a little longer than the other, place the square end of the tongue inside, and stitch firmly. Stitch the brown piece to the mouth opening, the longer end to the upper jaw, and leave the pointed end of the tongue hanging loose. Stuff firmly with kapok, pressing down well into the paws and legs, sew up the back seam, and pat the animal into a good shape.

Now sew the ear pieces in pairs, one beige and one brown piece going to make one ear. Fold and stitch at the square ends, the brown inside the fold, and stitch in position near the top of the head, with the points straight up. Sew on the buttons for eyes. A strip of red knitting (5 stitches) is fixed round the neck for a collar. With a needleful of the brown wool, make several long stitches to form a patch on the point of the nose.

For Baby's Bath Time

HERE is a practical and pretty screen for Baby's bath-time, and one that you can quite easily make yourself.

First, buy a three-fold towel-horse, then take the measurements of the centre frame. Any joiner will cut a piece of plywood to fit these measurements if your husband cannot do the job for you. Then nail the plywood with light tacks to the framework of the towel-horse. Now paint the whole affair with white enamel paint—or any light colour which suits your nursery scheme.

Cut out a piece of gay cretonne to fit the centre panel, then cut out the useful patch pockets, making them the sizes you think you will need. It is a good plan to line one of the pockets with waterproof, to take the wet sponge. Sew the pockets to the cretonne, taking care to sew a piece of waterproof over the part of the cretonne which is to be covered by the sponge pocket.

Tack the completed cretonne holder on to the plywood—using drawing pins, so that it can be taken off and washed when necessary. And there you have a splendid means of keeping all Baby's things conveniently to hand during his tub-time. Once Baby is comfortably settled with his bottle the screen can be folded neatly away.

For Snowy Days

Designed by Judy Jardine

MATERIALS REQUIRED: For complete set: 1 pound of Sirdar "Kasha" wool 6-ply, colour No. 427 (quantities for each garment stated against garment); 1¼ ounces of white Angora wool; 2 white buttons; ¼ yard of ½-inch elastic for insteps; 1¼ yards of elastic for waist and muff; 18-inch zipp fastener (white); ¼ yard of white Jap silk; 9 inches by 15 inches of wadding or cotton-wool; 1 pair of No. 9 Stratnoid needles.

MEASUREMENTS: COAT: Length from shoulder, 22½ inches; chest, 26 inches; inside sleeve seam (with cuff), 15½ inches.

LEGGINGS: Waist to heel, 28 inches; waist, 24 inches; front seam, 12½ inches; back seam, 14 inches.

CAP: Round head, 21 inches.

MUFF: 15 inches by 9 inches.

TENSION: 6 sts. or 9 rows = 1 inch.

ABBREVIATIONS: st. = stitches; k. = knit; p. = purl; beg. = beginning; inc. = increase by knitting twice into same st.; dec. = decrease by knitting 2 sts. together; tog. = together.

The Coat

(FOR GIRL)

(8 ounces of "Kasha" wool and ½ ounce of Angora)

The Back

(Skirt is omitted for BOY. Instead, cast on 79 sts. and work 2½ inches of ribbing (k. 1, p. 1), after which work 5 inches in pattern, and proceed to armhole shaping.)

Most becoming to any little girl, and ideal for cold days. (Age 7-8 years)

For GIRL, cast on 119 sts. with "Kasha" wool, and knit into back of every st. Slip first st. of every row throughout. Next 7 rows, knit. Change to Angora wool.

1st row.—Knit.

2nd and 4th rows.—k. 7, p. 7 alternately.

3rd row.—p. 7, k. 7 alternately.

Return to "Kasha" wool. Next 8 rows, knit.

The pattern is now begun, and consists of one row only, repeated over and over, herring-bone effect being entirely dependent on number of stitches used.

Pattern row.—k. 2, p. 2 to within 3 sts. of end, k. 3.

Work in pattern for 11½ inches from beg. of work.

Next row.—k. 2 tog., k. 1 to end of row., k. 2 tog. at end (79 sts.).

Next 11 rows, knit.

Return to pattern and continue for 5 inches more.

Armhole shaping is now begun. Keeping carefully to continuity of pattern, cast off 3 sts. at beg. of next 2 rows, then dec. once at both ends of needle in next and every alternate row until 63 sts. remain. Continue until armhole measures 5 inches on the straight, then cast off 5 sts. at beg. of next 6 rows, leaving 33 sts. on spare needle for back of neck.

For front, cast on 126 sts. and work 18 rows of border as for

For Snowy Days

back. In next 2 border rows, dec. once at each end of needle (122 sts.). The front is now divided.

Left Side.—(For Boy, this will be *Right* side—cast on 31 sts. and work ribbing, etc., as in note for Back.)

For Girl, work in pattern for 47 sts. only, leaving remaining 75 on spare needle. Continue as for back until armhole shaping is reached, finishing at armhole edge. Shape as follows: Cast off 2 sts. at armhole edge of next row, and knit back in pattern. Repeat these 2 rows once. Now dec. at armhole edge in next and every alternate row until sts. are reduced to 23. Continue in pattern until armhole measures 4 inches on the straight, finishing at armhole edge. Keeping armhole edge straight, k. 2 tog. at neck edge in every row until 15 sts. remain, finishing at armhole edge. Cast off 5 sts. at beg. of next and alternate rows until all are cast off.

Right Side.—(For Boy this will be *Left* side—cast on 47 sts., and proceed as before.)

For girl, return to sts. left on spare needle. Join in wool and cast off 4 sts. (this is to allow for zipp) and work on remaining 71 sts. only, as for left side, until 4 inches of armhole are worked, finishing at armhole edge. (There should be 39 sts. on needle.) From now on work on 23 sts. only, leaving 16 sts. on needle for collar. Continue as for other side, until sts. number 15, and cast off as before.

The Collar

With right side facing and using "Kasha" wool, k. 16 along right front, then pick up 11 sts. to shoulder, k. 33 across back of neck piece (left on needle), pick up 10 sts. along left front (70 sts).

(For Boy, reverse these directions.)

Knit 20 rows of border as before. Cast off loosely.

The Front Border

Hold work with right side facing, and use "Kasha" wool. Beginning at lower border pick up 94 sts. all along front (for Boy, 108 sts.) and 11 sts. along side of collar. Repeat 20 rows of border. Cast off.

The Sleeves. (Both alike)

With "Kasha" wool cast on 42 sts. and work 20 rows of border as before.

21st row.—p. 2 tog., p. 38, p. 2 tog.

Work 8 rows in ribbing (k. 1, p. 1), decreasing once at end of last row, to leave 39 sts. Continue in pattern on these 39 sts., and inc. once at both ends of every 8th row until sts. number 63. Continue until work measures 15½ inches.

Cast off 3 sts. at beg. of next 2 rows, then dec. at both ends of next and alternate rows until 23 sts. remain. Cast off.

To Make Up

Pin out pieces to required measurements, and press on wrong side with warm iron over damp cloth.

Join side and shoulder seams. Sew up sleeve seams and stitch sleeves into position, keeping seams in line with side seams. Turn up cuff. Very carefully stitch zipp fastener into position, beginning at cast-off portion at border and continuing to edge of collar. (For Boy, begin at edge of ribbing.) (*Note.*—Border edging coat lengthwise should fall over zipp, hiding it completely.) Work crochet loop at side of collar-flap, and sew on button to correspond. Press all seams.

The Leggings

(Boy or Girl—5½ ounces of "Kasha" wool)

Right Leg

With "Kasha" wool cast on 72 sts. Knit in ribbing (k. 1, p. 1) for 6 rows.

7th row.—* k. 2, wool forward, k. 2 tog. *; repeat from * to * to end.

Next 7 rows.—Ribbing, inc. once at end of last row to make 73 sts.

Now work as follows:

15th row.—k. 2, p. 2, k. 2, p. 1, turn.

16th row.—k. 2, p. 2, k. 3.

17th row.—(k. 2, p. 2) three times, k. 2, turn.

18th row.—k. 1 (p. 2, k. 2) twice, p. 2, k. 3.

19th row.—(k. 2, p. 2) five times, k. 1, turn.

20th row.—(p. 2, k. 2) four times, p. 2, k. 3.

21st row.—(k. 2, p. 2) seven times, turn.

22nd row.—p. 1 (k. 2, p. 2) six times, k. 3.

23rd row.—(k. 2, p. 2) eight times, k. 2, p. 1, turn.

24th row.—(k. 2, p. 2) eight times, k. 3.

25th row.—(k. 2, p. 2) ten times, k. 2, turn.

26th row.—k. 1 (p. 2, k. 2) nine times, p. 2, k. 3.

27th row.—(Right across) k. 2, p. 2 to within 3 sts. of end, p. 3.

28th row.—p. 2, k. 2 to within 5 sts. of end, p. 2, k. 3.

29th row.—Knit twice into 1st st., k. 1, then p. 2, k. 2 to within 3 sts. of end, p. 2, then knit twice into last st.

30th row.—k. 1, then p. 2, k. 2 to end. Finish with p. 2.

31st row.—p. 1, then k. 2, p. 2 to end. Finish with k. 2.

32nd row.—As 30th.

33rd row.—Purl twice into 1st st., then k. 2, p. 2 to within 2 sts. of end, k. 1, knit twice into last st.

Keeping carefully to pattern as now set, continue and inc. once at both ends of needle in every 4th row until sts. number 111. Continue until work measures 14 inches along longer side.

Dec. at both ends of next and every alternate row until sts. are reduced to 63, then at both ends of every 4th row until 55 sts. remain. Continue until work measures 28 inches on longer side, making sure to finish at long edge.

Next row.—Cast off 32 sts., knit in pattern 23 sts. Work in pattern for 2 inches. In next and every alternate row, dec. at both ends of needle until 15 sts. remain. Cast off.

For Snowy Days

Left Leg

As for right, but make row of holes in 6th row, so as to keep smooth side of holes same for both legs. Fold in opposite direction to right leg when sewing up.

To Make Up

Press as for coat. Sew up leg seams, and front and back seams. Work an even row of double crochet all round each foot, and sew wide elastic to insteps. Thread narrow elastic through waist.

The Cap

(Boy or Girl—1 ounce of "Kasha" wool, ¼ ounce of Angora wool)

With "Kasha" wool cast on 31 sts. and work in pattern; inc. at both ends of needle in every alternate row until sts. number 63. Work 18 rows in pattern on these 63 sts. Leave on a spare needle.

Work another similar piece.

Border

With "Kasha" wool knit along 126 sts. on the two needles. *Next row*—k. 4, k. 2 tog., and repeat to end, when k. 4. Change to Angora and work border as before, but use Angora for garter-st. and "Kasha" wool for 4 rows between. Cast off very loosely.

Press carefully on wrong side. Fold cap in half, and sew up seams. Join border seam and turn up. Sew button at centre-front. This cap is worn with seams to front and back.

The Muff

(Omit for Boy—1½ ounces of "Kasha" wool, ½ ounce of Angora wool)

With Angora wool cast on 91 sts. Work border as for Cap, then change to "Kasha" wool, and knit 2 rows, and inc. once at both ends of each row (95 sts.). Make row of holes as for Leggings, and then work 1 row plain. Work in pattern for 9 inches, and finish as for other end, decreasing to 91 sts. Cast off.

To Make Up

Press knitting to size. Fold silk lengthwise, lay on wadding, and cut to size of pattern-piece of knitting, omitting borders. Allow a little silk for turnings. Sew up silk on three sides, place wadding between, and join edge. Sew to knitting, and join the whole into muff-shape, keeping seam to back. Gather border by means of elastic through holes, allowing space for the hands. Crochet three lengths of chain, using wool double, each piece 1 yard long. Plait into thick cord and attach to muff, so as to hang round neck.

A PAIR OF CHILD'S SLIPPERS

made from an old felt hat

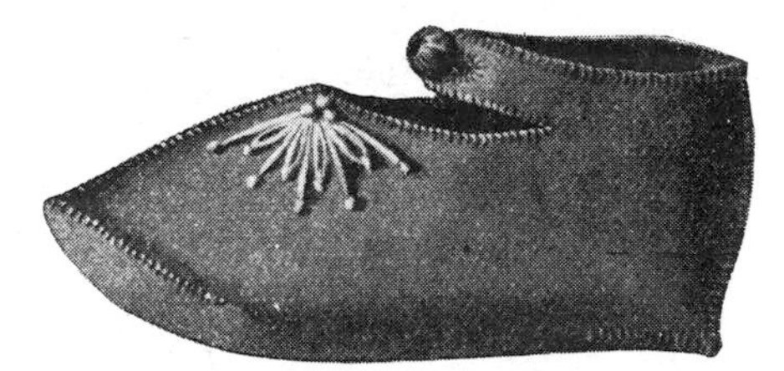

LITTLE Puck indoor slippers for children may be made from discarded felt hats, providing they are reasonably soft and have a small brim. The slippers are easily and quickly made, as the soles and uppers are cut in one piece. A small diagram of the pattern is given here. Enlarge this to the required size so that the centre portion is a little larger than the child's foot, and place it on the hat in the way that will cut the felt to the best advantage, making provision for a similar piece for second slipper. Generally the best method is to have the toe pointing to centre crown, and the back part of slipper coming from the brim.

Pin the pattern into position and carefully cut out.

If the hat has faded portions, it may be better to work up the inside for the right side of slipper.

Buttonhole together the edges down the back of slipper, and then round the half-circular piece for heel. In the same manner stitch together the two front pieces to point, to form the upper, and finish the seaming by joining each side of foot to point.

Buttonhole all raw edges and make a small buttonhole in one tab, on the other sew a small round bead or button. Finally, a little embroidery worked either side of the centre join on upper completes an attractive and most useful pair of slippers.

E. M. T.

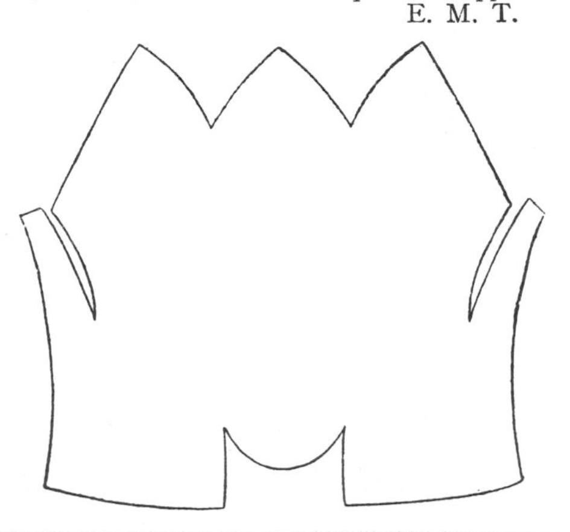

Cosy Pyjamas ❖ By D. M. Beckett

MATERIALS REQUIRED: 8 1-oz. balls of Templeton's Baby Wool; 1 pair of Stratnoid knitting needles, size 10; 3 small buttons for fastening; ¾ yard of white elastic for the waist; a little wool for embroidery in any colours preferred.

ABBREVIATIONS: k. = knit; p. = purl; sl. = slip; st. = stitch; tog. = together; st.-st. = stocking-stitch; rep. = repeat; beg. = beginning; rib = k. 1, p. 1; inc. = increase; dec. = decrease.

TENSION: 13 sts. = 2 inches in width, and 17 rows = 2 inches in depth.

MEASUREMENTS: JUMPER—Width around under arms = 26 inches; length = 16 inches; sleeve seam = 13½ inches. TROUSERS = 18 inches down inside leg-seam.

To fit ages 5 to 7 years.

The Jumper

The Back

Commencing at bottom of back, cast on 80 sts. and rib for 2 inches, then change to st.-st., and continue until 12 inches deep. Shape for armholes by dec. at each end of every row until 62 sts. remain. Continue on these sts. until armhole measures 4 inches deep, then shape for neck and shoulders by working to centre 15 sts., cast them off, work to end. Cast off 7 sts. at beg. of next 3 rows, starting from armhole end, and dec. at neck end on each row.

Work other shoulder to correspond.

The Front

Working as for back, cast on 84 sts. and continue until work measures 8½ inches deep. Commence front opening: With right side facing, work to centre 10 sts., then turn and cast on 10 sts. to beg. of this needle; rib these sts. throughout, leaving centre 10 sts. on left-hand needle, or right side in wear, for buttonhole side, which is continued right up. Continue, keeping 10 sts. in rib and remainder in st.-st. throughout until seam measures 12 inches, as back to armhole shaping. Then shape for the armhole by casting off 3 sts. at beg. of next row starting from seam end, and continue, dec. at armhole end on next 7 rows. This leaves 27 sts. and 10 rib sts. Continue on these sts. until armhole measures 3½ inches in depth, and shape for neck by casting off 10 sts.

[CONTINUED]

Cosy Pyjamas (Continued)

at beg. of next row starting from neck end, and continue dec. at neck edge on next 6 rows, starting from neck end. Shape shoulder as in back.

Work other front to pair, without casting on 10 sts. as they are allowed for, and make buttonholes as follows: On 12th row of ribbing, rib 4, cast off 2, rib 4, knit to end. Then on return row cast on 2 sts. over 2 cast-off sts. in previous row. Continue until 20th row from buttonhole is reached; on 20th row work second buttonhole as first, and third buttonhole on 20th row from 2nd. Third and last buttonhole comes 4 rows from neck shaping.

The Sleeves

Cast on 49 sts. and rib for 2 inches, then change to st.-st. and continue, inc. at each end of every 5th row until 77 sts. are on needle and seam measures 14½ inches from start. Shape for top by casting off 3 sts. at beg. of next row when right side facing, then dec. at each end of every row until 13 sts. remain. Cast off.

Work another sleeve to pair by shaping for top as follows: Cast off 3 sts. at beg. of next row when wrong side facing, then continue as in first sleeve to end.

The Collar

Cast on 97 sts. and rib, inc. at each end of every other row until 2½ inches are completed. Cast off loosely and in pattern.

The Pocket

Cast on 31 sts. and rib for 8 rows, then change to st.-st. and work for 3 inches. Cast off.

The Trousers

Cast on 114 sts. and rib for 8 rows, than change to st.-st. and dec. at each end of 7th, then every 6th row, until 92 sts. are on needle. Continue, and inc. at each end of every 4th row until 126 sts. are on needle. When seam measures 18 inches, shape for top by dec. at each end of next row, then st.-st. 7 rows, then dec. at each end of 8th, and every 8th row until 105 sts. remain. Work for extra depth at back of trousers as follows: With right side facing, knit to 10 sts. from end, turn and work back to end, then work to 20 sts. from the end, and back, and continue likewise, knitting 10 sts. less from end each time until 60 sts. from end are shaped. Work right to end. Change to rib on next row and work 3 rows in k. 1, p. 1 rib, then on next row work for holes as follows: Rib 2, wool forward, k. 2 tog., then * rib 8, wool forward, k. 2 tog., ten times, * then rib remaining 3 sts. Rib for 5 more rows, then cast off in pattern and loosely.

Make another leg to pair, by following instructions and calling right side wrong, and wrong side right throughout.

To Make Up

Pin all parts to size and shape, and press well, using damp cloth and warm iron. Sew up all seams, and put in sleeves. Sew on collar, and work buttonholes. Work design to choice on pocket in neat oversewing stitch. Press on wrong side when finished, and sew on pocket to jumper where required. Give all good press on right side, then run elastic through trousers and fasten, and sew on buttons to front opening.

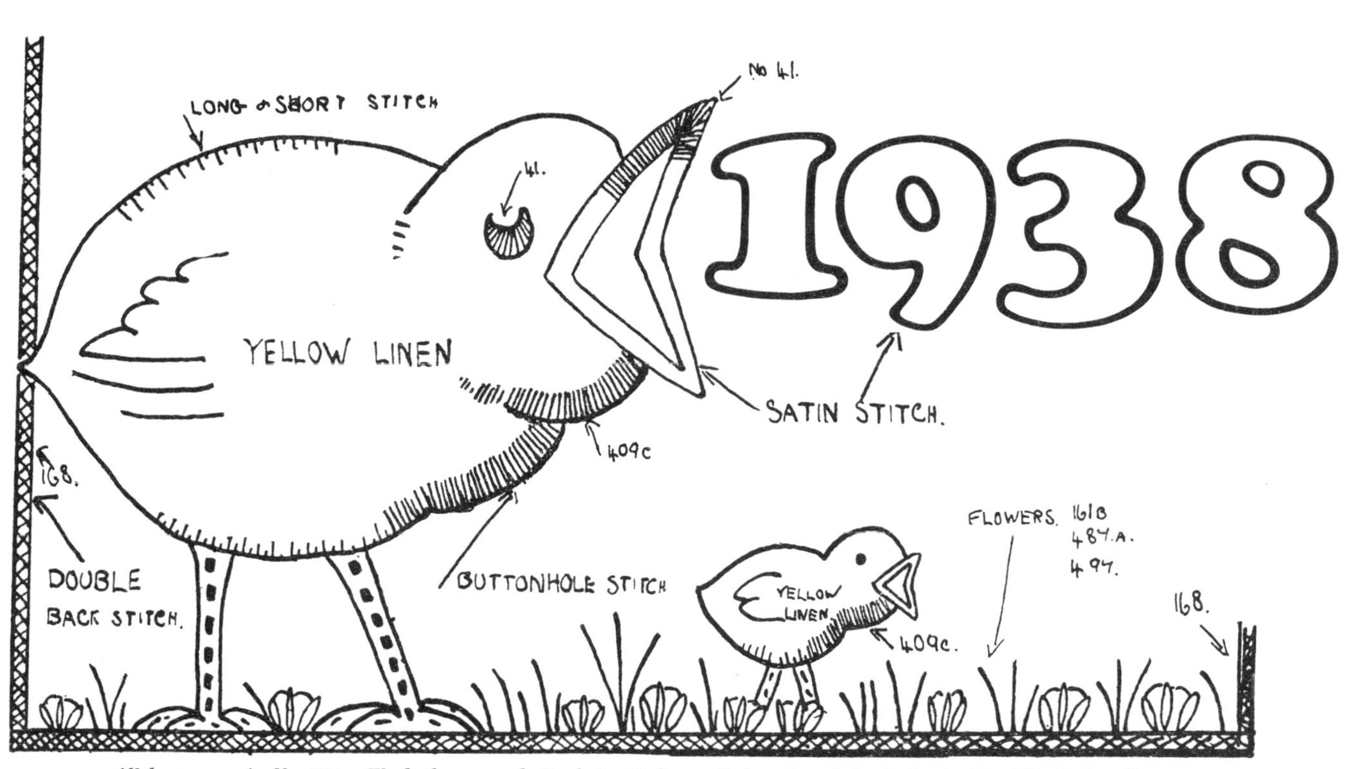

All leaves are in No. 168. Work the group buttonhole-stitch round the edge of the feeder in No. 155, dark yellow

Dainty Feeders

Designed by Elizabeth C. Mitchell

THE time of thick, ugly feeders has passed, and we hope for good. Modern feeders are charming and original.

The following instructions tell you how to make these attractive feeders. Note the very practical shape of the new tie-round style. With this it is impossible for the ends to fall into the child's food, as so often was the case with the old-fashioned shape.

How To Make

Use Peri-Lusta Stranded Mercerised Cotton (boil-fast) for all the embroidery. Choose a fine white "Old Bleach" linen for the feeders. These are both excellent for washing. Cut out to the size given, and do not forget to allow for turnings. Tack the hem on the right side of each feeder, and hem with a small stitch. Finish the hem with group buttonhole-stitch all the way round. Place the embroidery design a little from the bottom (see photograph for exact position), and work as in the detailed instructions. Sew the tapes into position, and press the feeders when finished.

The Rabbit and Chicken Feeders

Trace the designs on to tracing paper, and prick with a fine needle all round the edges of each design. Place into position on the feeder, and rub a little powdered charcoal over the needle holes. Lift the tracing-paper carefully, and you will find a clear impression left of the design. With a fine paint-brush, using light-coloured paint, go round the design. This is quite as good as a transfer, if carried out carefully.

The rabbit and the chicken are in appliqué work; they are cut out of coloured pieces of linen, placed into position on the feeders, and tacked down lightly.

Fix the shapes firmly into position with a long and short stitch all round, and then buttonhole neatly.

Work the flowers and leaves to the colour chart. Do not apply white for the rabbit's tail, but cut away the brown linen, leaving the white linen of the feeder to show as the bunny's little "scut."

The Feeder Holder

Cut the linen to the size given, remembering to allow for turnings. Tack the hem on the right side and hem, finishing with group buttonhole-stitch in the same colour as the edge of the feeders.

Sew a button and loop into position, and work the initial of each child in the middle of the ring (see the photograph).

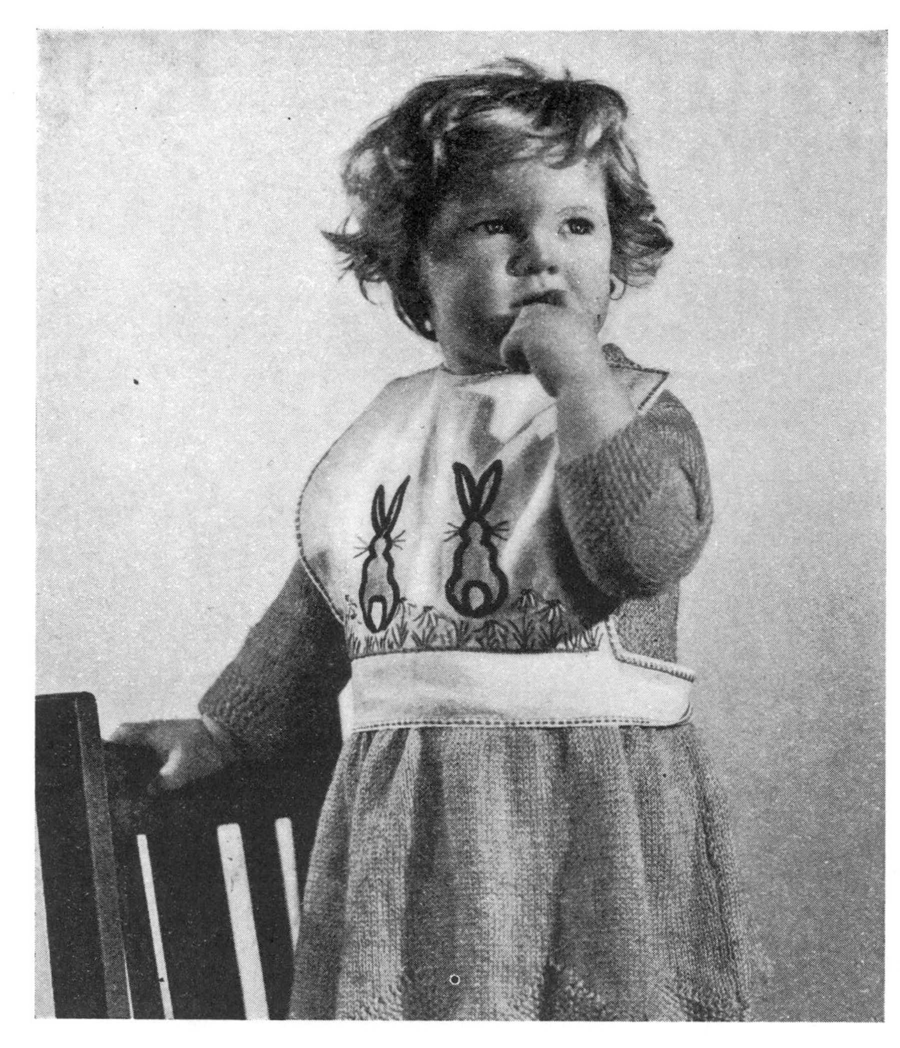

(Left) *The Rabbit feeder is both attractive and practical*

(Below) *The simple ring keeps the feeder unsoiled when not in use*

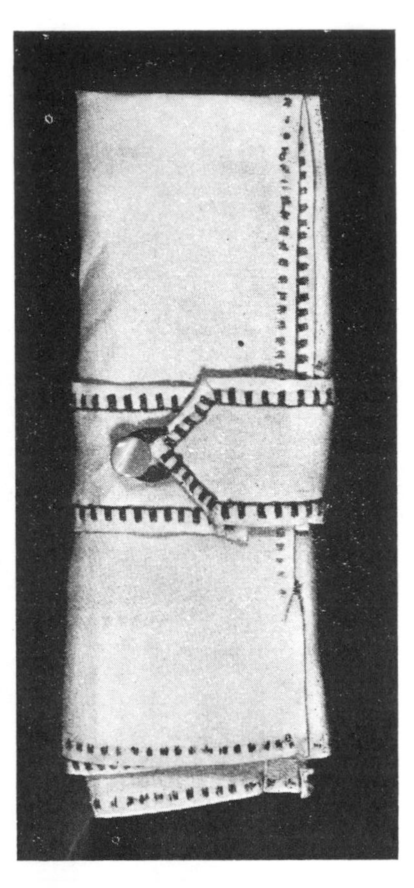

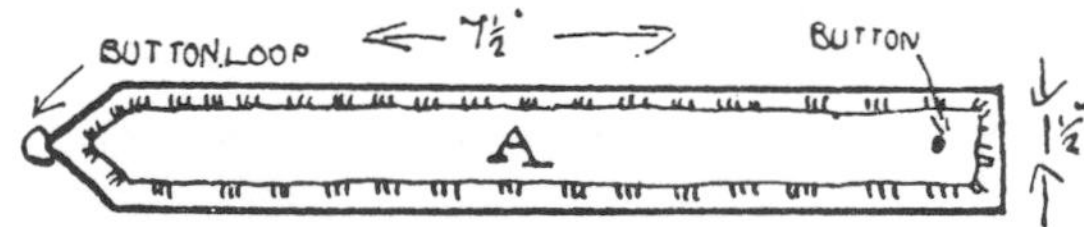

How to make the dainty little ring to hold the feeder when not in use. Use a colour to match the edge of the feeder

Note the practical shape of these feeders

Dainty Feeders

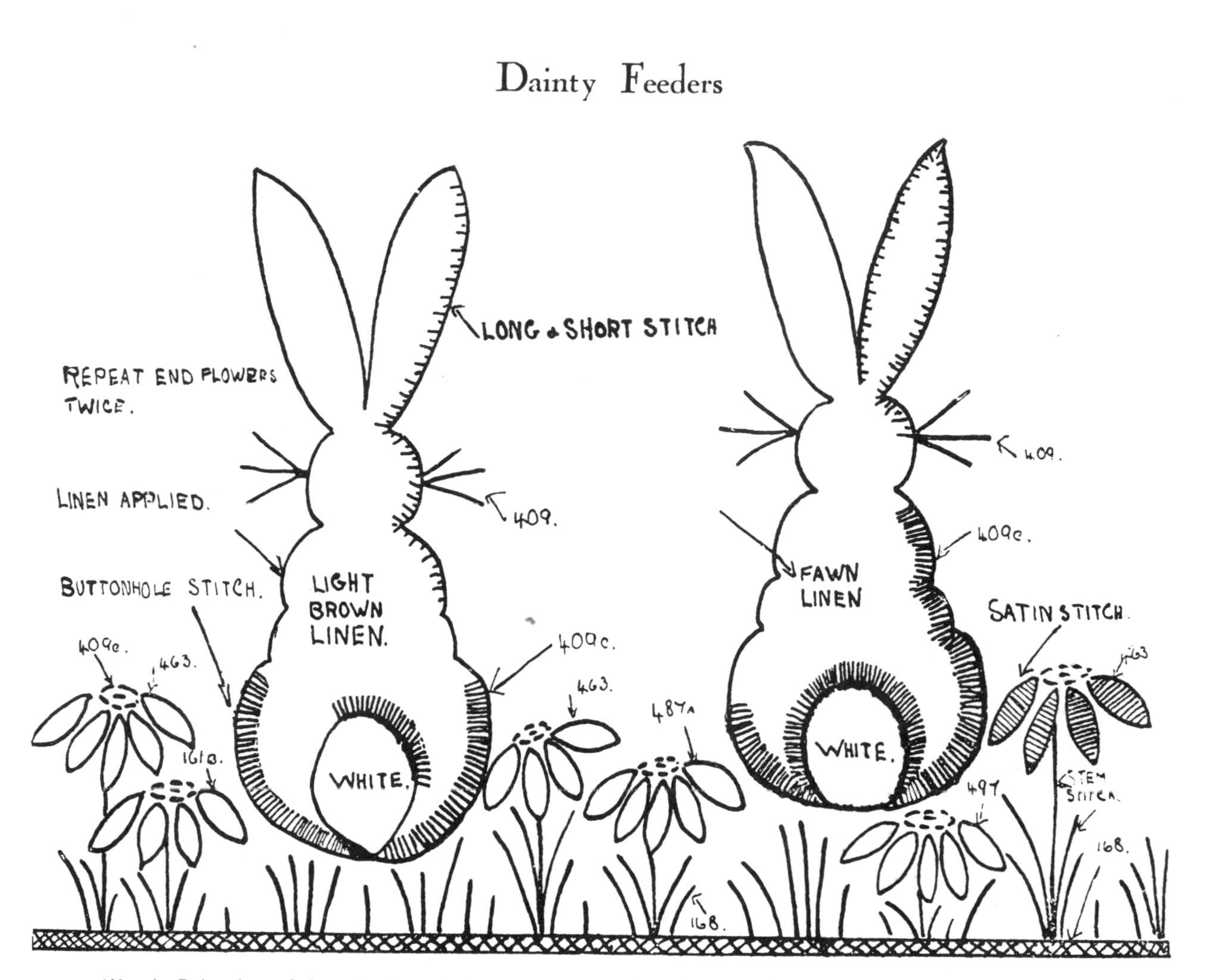

(Above). *Before buttonholing, fix the animals on to the feeder with a long and short stitch all round. Work the group buttonhole-stitch in No. 497 (pale mauve)*

(Below) *When cutting out allow ½-inch for turnings. Turn the hem on the right side with a small stitch*

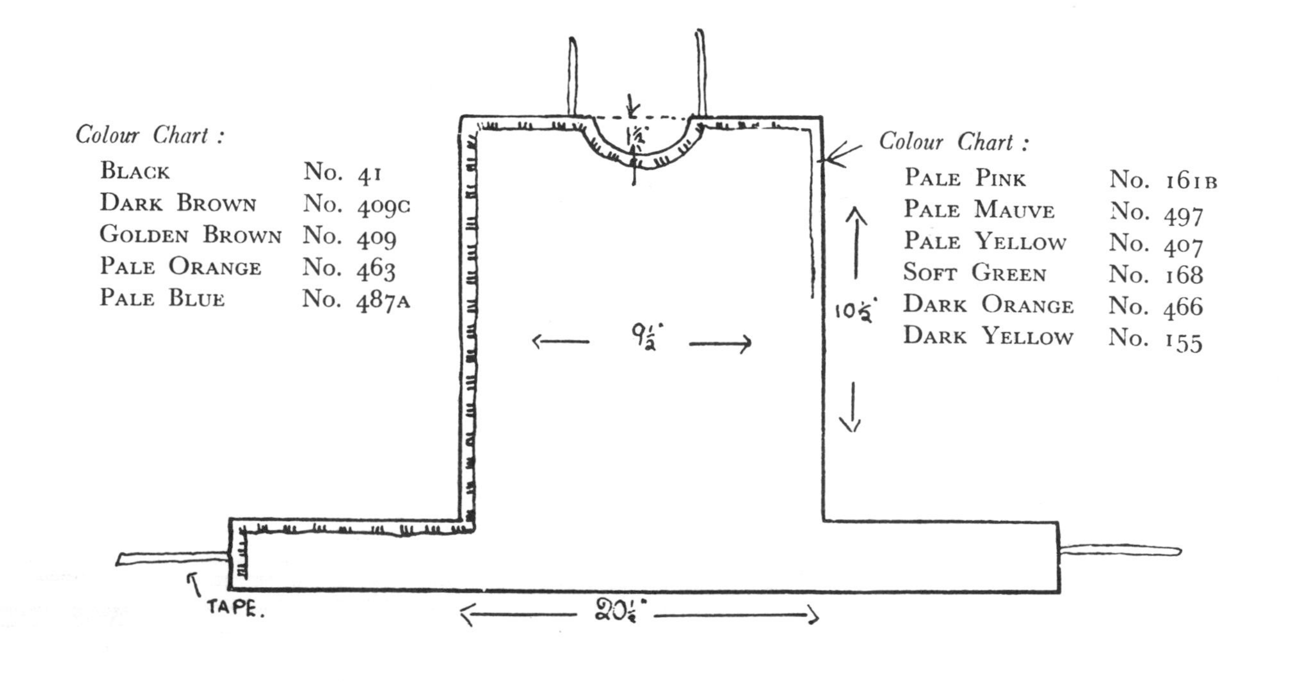

Colour Chart :

Black	No. 41
Dark Brown	No. 409c
Golden Brown	No. 409
Pale Orange	No. 463
Pale Blue	No. 487a

Colour Chart :

Pale Pink	No. 161b
Pale Mauve	No. 497
Pale Yellow	No. 407
Soft Green	No. 168
Dark Orange	No. 466
Dark Yellow	No. 155

SEVEN NEW STARS

Disney's Triumph —Laughton Again —General Releases

By OUR FILM CRITIC

Some of the dwarfs in "Snow White and the Seven Dwarfs," led by Grumpy

WHO is your favourite film star? How often do we argue hotly in favour of Garbo or Myrna Loy, Charles Laughton or Gary Cooper? Yet there are many who rank Donald Duck or Toby Tortoise higher than any of the human stars. And now Disney has given us seven new stars in one film.

"Snow White and the Seven Dwarfs" started as Disney's Folly and ended as Disney's triumph. The dwarfs are fascinating creatures, each one with a separate personality that is vivid and endearing. They and the animals are the best parts of the film. Snow White herself you may not like. She is just a conventionally pretty girl of uncertain age, with a childish treble voice. But the detail of her movements, though jerky, is marvellously complete.

Fascinating Dwarfs

Snow White, the Prince, and the Witch are Disney's concessions to the fairy story, but the animals and particularly the Dwarfs are his own creation, embodying everything that has made his short cartoons so popular and so fresh.

Now that he has given us the Dwarfs, I hope that he will not allow their adventures to begin and end with "Snow White." Everyone will want to see more of Dopey, the speechless simpleton (at times strangely reminiscent of Harpo Marx), of Sleepy, with his bothersome bluebottle, of Sneezy, whose sneezes blow them all off their feet, of Bashful, who is always blushing scarlet, of Happy, the fat and gay, of Grumpy, the old curmudgeon with a heart of gold, and of Doc, the leader with his spectacles and his spoonerisms (rather like Hugh Herbert). I hope Disney will make a series of shorts, featuring these lovable little men.

Children and the Film

A good deal of comment has been aroused by the Censor granting the film only an "A" certificate. Apart from the fact that the film is primarily for adult consumption, there are one or two scenes which might frighten children, especially as the introduction of human figures will make them take it more seriously than the adventures of Mickey or Donald.

The scene where the Wicked Queen becomes the hideous witch is very macabre, while the two leering vultures who accompany the witch on her visit to Snow White with the poisoned apple might upset a sensitive child. But I cannot see any nightmares being caused by these things, since the great part of the film is so charming and amusing.

Patience Rewarded

We have had to wait a long time to see Charles Laughton in "Vessel of Wrath." But the wait has been worth while, for his first independent picture is very good indeed and a great credit to British films.

Laughton plays the part of Ginger Ted, a drunken beachcomber in the Dutch East Indies. He is sleeping and drinking away his life when the missionary schoolmistress, Miss Jones, starts taking him in hand. The story is mostly about the conflict between these two opposites, and it takes an outbreak of typhoid and a danger of massacre to settle their differences. In the end we see them happily married, the proud (and teetotal) proprietors of a pub in Buckinghamshire.

The story is slight in dramatic incident, but rich in detail, atmosphere, and characterisation. For the last we have to thank Laughton and Elsa Lanchester, who give superb performances. The dialogue is full of wit and the production as a whole is first-class.

Garbo, Dietrich, and Temple

There is something for everybody in the April releases. If you are a Garbo fan, there's "Marie Walewksa," the spectacular production that tells the story of Napoleon's love for the Polish countess. Garbo is as good as ever, and she has in Charles Boyer a leading man who can act as well as she can. Then there's Marlene Dietrich in the Lubitsch picture "Angel." This is a highly sophisticated fable of a diplomat, his wife, and their mutual friend. Herbert Marshall and Melvyn Douglas are the men.

At the other end of the scale there is Shirley Temple dispensing light and sweetness in "Heidi." You may like to see Wallace Beery being tough and rascally in "Bad Man of Brimstone," or perhaps you would prefer Leslie Howard as the Innocent in Hollywood in "Stand-In." They are both on view this month.

British and Good

Four entertaining British releases can be recommended. The Scarlet Pimpernel returns, in the pleasant person of Barry K. Barnes, to give you some more adventures in the Paris of the French Revolution, while Jack Buchanan and Elsie Randolph track down jewel thieves —with lots of laughs en route—in "Smash and Grab." "Paradise for Two" has Jack Hulbert to recommend it, and that will be enough for most people, while the charming Annabella can be seen in "Dinner at the Ritz."

Here in a glittering glass coffin surrounded with flowers, the Prince found his Princess. He knelt sadly at her side and bent to kiss her lips

After the Queen had changed herself into an old witch, she started on the next step in her plan: a poison to get rid of Snow White

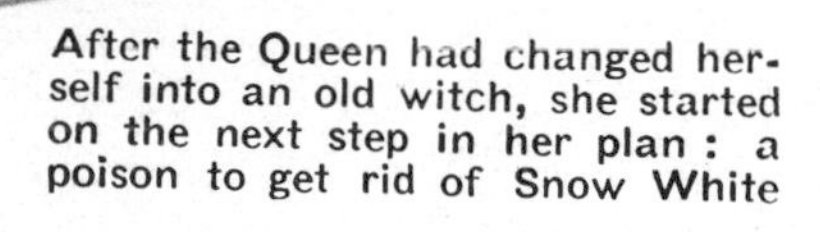

"This is a magic wishing apple," whispered the disguised Queen. "And you are so sweet I'll let you have a bite free! Then you'll get your wish"

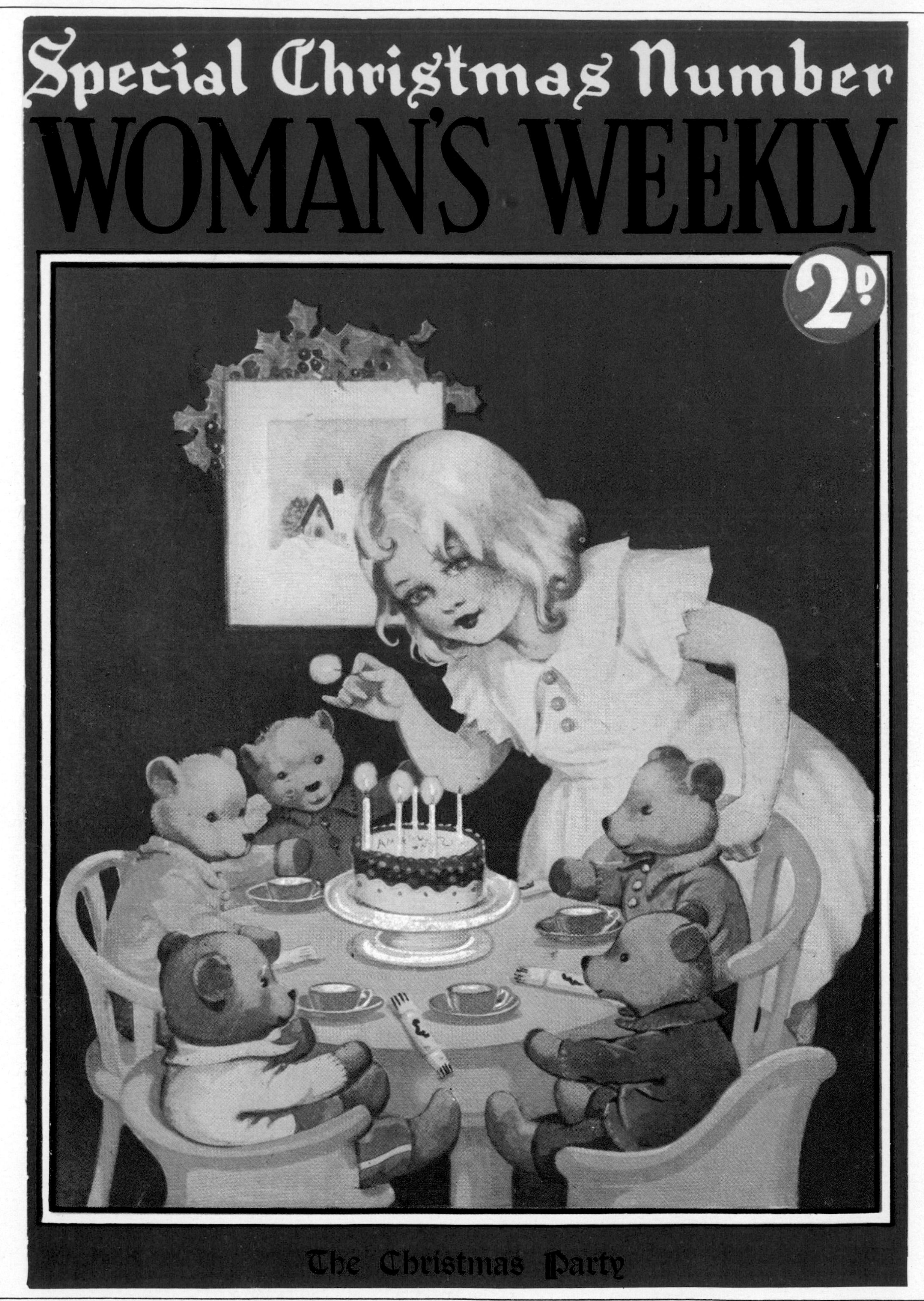
Special Christmas Number
WOMAN'S WEEKLY
2D
The Christmas Party

THE TEDDY TWINS!

The Teddies Measure 15 Inches High, And Can Be Obtained, Price 2s. 6d. Each, From Any Branch Of Marks And Spencer. The Outfits For The Two Teddies Cost Under 2s.

MATERIALS

THREE ozs. of Greenock 3-ply Super Fingering (obtainable only from any of the branches of SCOTCH WOOL & HOSIERY STORES) for the set, or 1 oz. for the frock and 2 ozs. for the jersey and knickers; a pair each of No. 11 and No. 12 Stratnoid knitting pins; 8 tiny buttons; ½ yard cord elastic.

TENSION AND MEASUREMENTS

WORKED at a tension of 8 sts. to the inch in width, on No. 11 pins, the following measurements are attained after light pressing:

THE FROCK.—Length from shoulder to hem, 9 inches; width all round body at underarms, 11 inches; side-seam, 6 inches.

THE JERSEY.—Length from shoulder to hem, 6 inches; all round body, 12 inches; side-seam, 3 inches; sleeve-seam, 3 inches.

THE KNICKERS.—Round waist, just below ribbing, 12 inches; side-seam, 3½ inches; centre-back seam, 4 inches.

ABBREVIATIONS

K., KNIT; p., purl; st., stitch; tog., together; inc., increase (by working into the front and back of the same st.); s.s. stocking-stitch (k. on the right side and p. back); rib is k. 2 and p. 2 alternately; m., make (by bringing the wool to the front of the pin and over it before working the next st.).

Master Teddy's Jersey

Master Teddy's Knickers

THE FROCK

TO WORK THE BACK.—With No. 11 pins cast on 104 sts. for lower edge, k. 2 rows plain, but do *not* work into the back of the sts. on the first row. Now work the scalloped border as follows:

1ST ROW: Inc. in each of the first 2 sts., * k. 1, k. 2 tog., k. 3 tog., k. 2 tog., k. 1, inc. in each of the next 4 sts., repeat from * ending the last repeat with inc. in last 2 sts.

2ND ROW: All k.

3RD ROW: Inc., * k. 2, k. 2 tog., k. 3 tog. k. 2 tog., k. 2, inc. twice; repeat from *, ending the last repeat with inc. once (88 sts.).

4TH ROW: K. 2, * p. 7, k. 4; repeat from *, ending the last repeat with k. 2.

5TH ROW: All k.

6TH ROW: K. 1, * p. 9, k. 2; repeat from *, ending the last repeat with k. 1.

Continued overleaf

THE TEDDY TWINS (Continued from previous page)

Now work 41 rows straight in s.s., beginning and ending with a k. row.

Change to No. 12 pins.

DECREASE ROW: P. 2 tog. across the row. (44 sts.) P. 1 row and k. 1 row.

Return to No. 11 pins and work 4 rows in s.s., beginning with a k. row.

TO SHAPE THE ARMHOLES:—Continue in s.s., decreasing at both ends of each of the next 6 rows. (32 sts.).

Work 10 rows straight in s.s

Change to No. 12 pins and work 12 rows in rib for yoke, beginning and ending with p. 1 on the 1st row. (Work only 10 rows here on front yoke.)

NECK ROW: Rib 8 and slip these sts. on a spare pin for first shoulder, cast off 16 sts. loosely (1 st. on pin), rib to end (8 sts. for second shoulder.)

On each set of shoulder sts. rib 3 rows and cast off.

THE FRONT.—Work as given on the Back until the neck row has been worked. Rib 7 rows on these 8 sts.

BUTTONHOLE ROW: (P. 1, k. 1, m. 1, k. 2 tog.) twice.

Rib 1 row. Cast off.

Join the wool to the neck end of the remaining 8 sts. and work exactly the same.

THE BUTTERFLY SLEEVES.—With No. 12 pins cast on 30 sts. for the arm edge. K. 4 rows.

NEXT ROW: Inc. in every st. (60 sts.)

Change to No. 11 pins and work 5 rows in s.s., beginning and ending with a p. row.

Continue in s.s., casting off 3 sts. at the beginning of each of the next 16 rows.

Cast off. Work a second sleeve in the same way.

TO MAKE UP THE FROCK

FIRST press all parts with a hot iron over a damp cloth on the wrong side of the work. Sew the front shoulders over the back shoulders at arm edge. Set sleeves into armholes. Sew the side and sleeve seams in one long line and press. Sew buttons to back shoulders, matching the buttonholes.

THE KNICKERS

WORK as for the boy's knickers, omitting the leg edging. In this case the border is worked with the No. 13 crochet-hook as follows: Join the wool to the leg edge, * 1 double crochet into a k. st. on the leg edge, miss 2 k. sts., 3 ch. and repeat from * to end, where join with a sl.st. to first d.c.

THE JERSEY

TO WORK THE BACK.—With No. 12 pins cast on 48 sts. for lower edge and k. 1 row into the back of the sts.

Now work in rib as follows:

1ST ROW (right side facing): P. 1, k. 2, * p. 2, k. 2; repeat from * until 1 st. remains, p. 1.

2ND ROW: K. 1, p. 2, * k. 2, p. 2; repeat from * until 1 st. remains, k. 1.

Repeat these 2 rows 4 times more.

Change to No. 11 pins and work 24 rows in s.s., beginning with a k. row.

TO SHAPE THE ARMHOLES.—Continue in s.s., decreasing at both ends of each of the next 8 rows, when 32 sts. will remain.

Work 8 rows in s.s.

Change to No. 12 pins and work 12 rows in rib as for lower edge. (Work 10 rows here on front.)

NEXT ROW: Rib 8 for first shoulder and slip these sts. on a spare pin, cast off 16 loosely (1 on pin), rib to end. (8 sts. for second shoulder.)

On each set of 8 shoulder sts. work 3 rows in rib and cast off.

THE FRONT.—This is worked exactly the same as the Back until the neck sts. have been cast off.

Work each set of 8 shoulder sts. as follows:

Work 7 rows in rib.

BUTTONHOLE ROW: (P. 1, k. 1, m. 1, k. 2 tog.) twice.

Rib 1 row more. Cast off.

THE SLEEVES.—With No. 11 pins cast on 12 sts. and p. 1 row for top of sleeve. Continue in s.s., increasing at both ends of every row until there are 44 sts. on the pins.

Work 4 rows straight in s.s.

Continue in s.s., decreasing at both ends of the next row and every following 6th row until 3 more decrease rows have been worked, and 36 sts. remain.

Change to No. 12 pins and work 10 rows in rib.

Cast off. Work a second sleeve in the same way.

TO MAKE UP THE JERSEY

FIRST press all parts with a hot iron over a damp cloth on the wrong side of the work. Wrap the front shoulder-edge over the back shoulder for about half an inch. Set sleeves into armholes, sewing through the double edges at the shoulders. Sew the sleeve and side seams in one long line. Press all seams, and sew two buttons on each shoulder.

THE KNICKERS

WITH No. 12 pins cast on 48 sts. for the waist edge.

Work 10 rows in rib.

Change to No. 11 pins and work as follows:

On the back work 4 rows in s.s. (Omit these rows on front.)

Continue in s.s., increasing into the 3rd st. at each end of the next row and every following 4th row until there are 60 sts. on the pins.

P. 1 row.

Cast off 8 sts. at the beginning of each of the next 2 rows, then cast off 6 sts. at the beginning of each of the next 6 rows.

Cast off the remaining sts.

The Front is worked as given on the Back.

TO MAKE UP THE KNICKERS

FIRST press both parts with a hot iron over a damp cloth on the wrong side of the work. Sew the side seams. To work the leg edging:—With No. 12 pins, pick up and k. 63 sts.

K. 2 rows and cast off. Press these edges and seams.

Sew the inside leg-seam, then thread elastic through waist-edge.

Miss Teddy's pretty little frock.

Simple in Silk

DRESS AND KNICKERS FOR A TWO-YEAR-OLD

MATERIALS

Three hanks of Briggs' Lightweight Crêpe in beige; 1 hank of the same silk in nigger; a pair of No. 12 Aero knitting pins; elastic for knickers; 1 press-stud.

HI! Look at me! Mummy has made me this lovely silky-slippery frock, and it's so cool and comfy. Yes—and the stripes go all round the back too—rather like my toy tiger, with some of his stripes rubbed off!

TENSION

Eight sts. and 10 rows to 1 in.

MEASUREMENTS

Length of dress—shoulder to hem, after pressing, 16 ins. Round hem, 38 ins. Length of knickers centre front and back, 10½ ins.

THE DRESS

THE *Back.*—Using the nigger silk, cast on 130 sts., and k. 4 rows. Then k. 4 rows in beige, 4 rows in nigger, and 4 rows in beige. Using the beige silk, work 8 rows in st.-st.

Next row: * K. 5, k. 2 tog., k. 6; repeat from * to end of row (120 sts.)

Work 5 rows in st.-st. Now k. 4 rows in nigger, 4 rows in beige, 4 rows in nigger, and 4 rows in beige. Work 8 rows in st.-st. in beige.

Next row: * K. 5, k. 2 tog., k. 5; repeat from * to end of row (110 sts.)

Work 5 rows in st.-st. Now k. 4 rows in nigger, 4 rows in beige, 4 rows in nigger and 4 rows in beige. Work 8 rows in st.-st.

Next row: * K. 4, k. 2 tog., k. 5; repeat from * to end of row (100 sts.)

Work 5 rows in st.-st.

On the next row make the back opening: Using the nigger silk k. first 50 sts. and place on a safety-pin.

From the centre of the work, using nigger silk, cast on 3 sts. for underlap. K. 4 rows nigger, 4 rows beige.

Now k. 4 rows in nigger, dec. for armhole at end of 1st and 3rd rows. Now k. 4 rows in beige, dec. at end of 1st and 3rd rows.

Using beige silk work 14 rows in st.-st., keeping 5 sts. at centre opening in garter-st., and continue to dec. on every k. row at armhole edge (42 sts. on pin). Put these sts. on to a safety-pin, and work other half-back to correspond, casting on 3 sts. at centre.

The Front.—Work exactly the same as the back, until 5 rows of st.-st. have been worked after the 3rd set of decreases (100 sts. on pin), then k. 4 rows in nigger and 4 rows in beige.

Now k. 4 rows in nigger, dec. at both ends of 1st and 3rd rows, and 4 rows in beige, dec. at both ends of the 1st and 3rd rows. Work 14 rows in st.-st., dec. at both ends of every k. row. Place remaining 78 sts. on safety-pin.

The Sleeves.—Using the nigger silk, cast on 52 sts., k. 4 rows, then k. 4 rows in beige. Now k. 4 rows in nigger, dec. at both ends of 1st and 3rd rows, and k. 4 rows in beige, dec. at both ends of 1st and 3rd rows.

Work 14 rows in st.-st., dec. at both ends of every k. row (30 sts. remain). Place these sts. on a safety-pin.

The Yoke.—With the wrong side of work towards you, place the 42 sts. of left half of back on to a knitting pin, next 30 sts. of first sleeve, then 78 sts. of front, then 30 sts. of other sleeve, and lastly 42 sts. of other half of back.

K. 4 rows in nigger, 4 rows in beige, 4 rows in nigger and 4 rows in beige. Using beige silk work 5 rows in st.-st., keeping border of 5 sts. in garter-st. at each end.

Next row: K. 5, * p. 3, p. 2 tog.; repeat from * to within 7 sts. of end, p. 2, k. 5 (180 sts.) Work 4 rows in st.-st.

Simple in Silk [CONTINUED FROM PREVIOUS PAGE]

Next row: K. 5, * k. 3, k. 2 tog.; repeat from * to last 5 sts. k. 5.

P. 1 row, then cast off 3 sts. at beginning of next 2 rows.

Now make hem for neck cord.

Using nigger silk work 5 rows in double knitting (k. 1, silk forward, slip 1, silk back). Cast off tightly.

To Make Up

Press well. Sew up side and sleeve seams. Thread a fine nigger silk cord at neck. Sew on press-stud, half-way up back opening.

The Knickers

Using nigger silk, cast on 50 sts., and k. 4 rows. Break off nigger silk, k. to within 12 sts. of end, turn; p. to within 12 sts. of end, turn.

and join beige. P. 1 row. On same pin, with beige silk cast on 30 sts. for gusset. Break off silk. On to same pin, cast on 50 more sts. in nigger. K. 4 rows on these 50 sts. only. Now break off nigger, join beige and k. 1 row across all sts. (130 sts.). P. 1 row, then commence the gusset and leg shaping.

Next row: K. 49, k. 2 tog., k. 28, k. 2 tog., k. to within 4 sts. of end, turn; p. to within 4 sts. of end, turn.

Next row: K. 45, k. 2 tog., k. 26, k. 2 tog., k. to within 8 sts. of end, turn; p. to within 8 sts. of end, turn.

Next row: K. 41, k. 2 tog., k. 24, k. 2 tog.

Continue in this way, working 4 sts. fewer at the end of every row and 2 sts. fewer between the gusset decs. on every k. row, until you k. to within 48 sts. of end, and p. to within 48 sts. of end.

Now continue across all sts, but dec. the gusset sts. on every k. row until 100 sts. remain on the pin.

Work 6 rows in st.-st., then k. 2 tog. at each end of the next and every 12th row until 90 sts. remain.

Work 11 rows in st.-st. Work 6 rows in double knitting. Cast off.

Work the other half to correspond.

To Make Up

Press well. Join side and gusset seams. Thread elastic at waist.

Carnival Time Again

Simple and Effective Suggestions For The Parade

A WICKED WITCH

An amusing idea for a small girl's carnival costume and bicycle decoration!

Fasten a birch broom, made with a bundle of twigs and a long handle, across the frame of the bicycle below the saddle and the handle-bars.

Cover the wheels with orange or white cardboard, on which are painted black triangles to form pumpkin faces.

The witch's costume consists of a divided skirt of emerald green, and a cape of scarlet cotton material. Make the tall hat of black buckram, and have an uneven fringe of grey wool hanging from beneath it to look like straggling wisps of grey hair!

A toy black cat could be tied to the centre of the handle-bars of the bicycle for an appropriate finishing touch.

A WICKED WITCH!

EASTER EGG

EASTER EGG

Any small child will enjoy representing a baby chick, and this idea is a novel way of decorating a pram. (It is also an excellent suggestion for a little girl's doll and doll's-pram.)

Cut lengths of crêpe paper, in two shades of green, in irregular points, and attach them round the body of the pram, one above the other, then arrange bare twigs and straw all round the top to resemble a large nest.

To represent the broken eggshell, cut jagged points along one edge of a wide band of buckram, which is shaped and fitted inside the pram, with the little chick sitting pertly inside.

Dress the chick in a yellow jumper, and a yellow cap, complete with a beak of American cloth and a round eye at each side.

A charming holiday study of the Duke and Duchess of Kent's children, Prince Edward and Princess Alexandra, in a Kentish cornfield.

A PRESENT FOR

MATERIALS REQUIRED: Baby doll, measuring 14 inches from top of head to soles of feet; 4 ounces of Bairns-wear Lambs Wool, or Baby Wool, 2-ply, and 3 ounces 3-ply; "Stratnoid" knitting needles, No. 10; $1\frac{3}{4}$ yards of baby ribbon. (NOTE: The 3-ply wool is used for cloak and bonnet only.)

MEASUREMENTS: CLOAK: Length, $13\frac{1}{2}$ inches; width at bottom, 20 inches. FROCK: Length from shoulder, $14\frac{1}{2}$ inches; width all round at bottom, 20 inches; sleeve seam, $2\frac{1}{2}$ inches. PETTICOAT: Length from shoulder, $13\frac{1}{2}$ inches; width all round at bottom, 16 inches. VEST: Length from shoulder, $5\frac{1}{2}$ inches; width at bottom, 14 inches.

TENSION: 7 sts. to 1 inch measured over st.-st.

ABBREVIATIONS: k. = knit; p. = purl; rep. = repeat; beg. = beginning; dec. = decrease; inc. = increase; sts. = stitches; st.-st. = stocking-stitch; g.-st. = garter-stitch; w.fd. = wool forward; tog. = together; s. = slip; w.t.n. = wool twice round needle; w.ft. = leave wool in front of work; pat. = pattern.

The Vest

Cast on 96 sts. and work in g.-st. for 4 rows. Change to st.-st., keeping 2 sts. at each end of needle in g.-st. until work measures 3 inches from cast-on edge.

Next row (right side of work).—k. 26, cast off 6 (loop on needle), k. 31, cast off 6 (loop on needle), k. 25.

Next row.—k. 2, p. 2 tog., purl to last 4, p. 2 tog., k. 2.

Next row.—k. 2, k. 2 tog., knit to last 4, k. 2 tog., k. 2.

Rep. last 2 rows twice, then still keeping 2 sts. in g.-st. at each end of needle, dec. at front edge only until sts. are reduced to 6. Continue without further shaping until work measures $5\frac{1}{2}$ inches from cast-on edge, then cast off. Re-join wool at 32 sts. of back, and work in st.-st. with g.-st. borders (dec. inside borders on first 4 rows = 24 sts.) until work measures $4\frac{1}{2}$ inches.

Next row (wrong side of work).—k. 2, p. 2, k. 16, p. 2, k. 2.

Next row.—Knit.

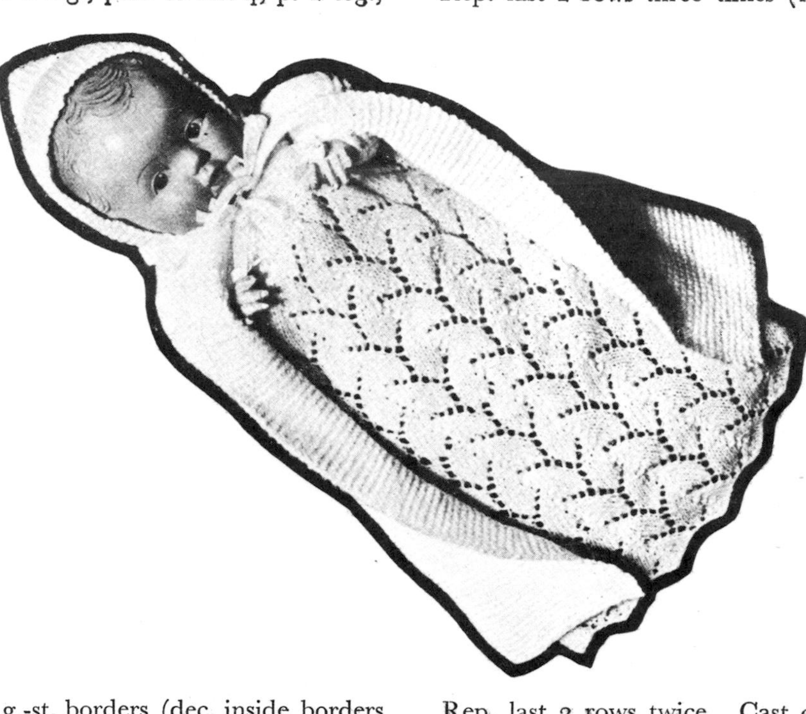

Rep. last 2 rows once.

Next row.—k. 2, p. 2, k. 2, cast off 12 (loop on needle), k. 1, p. 2, k. 2.

Next row.—k. 6.

Next row.—k. 2, p. 2, k. 2. Cast off.

Re-join wool at remaining sts., and work other side of shoulder to match. Re-join wool at remaining 26 sts. of left front, and work to match right front.

Making Up

Oversew shoulder seams. Stitch ribbons to front edges of right front in line with armhole and on left front to fasten.

The Petticoat

Back

Cast on 56 sts. and work in g.-st. for 6 rows. Change to all st.-st. until work measures $9\frac{1}{2}$ inches from cast-on edge, then divide sts. in half and continue in st.-st. (but keeping 2 sts. at opening edge in g.-st.) until work measures 11 inches from cast-on edge, then shape body thus:

Right side of work, k. 2 (k. 2 tog., k. 1) six times (k. 2 tog.) four times (18 sts).

Next row.—Purl to last 2, k. 2.

Next row.—k. 2, w.fd., k. 2 tog., knit to end.

Next row.—Purl to last 2, k. 2.

Next row.—Knit.

Next row.—k. 2, p. 2 tog., purl to last 2, k. 2.

Rep. last 2 rows three times (14 sts.).

Continue in st.-st. with g.-st. at each end of needle until work measures $12\frac{1}{2}$ inches from cast-on edge.

Next row (wrong side of work).—k. 2, p. 2, k. 10.

Next row.—k. 2, w.fd., k. 2 tog., knit to end.

Next row.—k. 2, p. 2, k. 10.

Next row.—Cast off 8 (loop on needle), k. 5.

Next row.—k. 2, p. 2, k. 2.

Next row.—Knit.

Rep. last 2 rows twice. Cast off.

Re-join wool at remaining sts., and work other side to match, but casting on 2 sts. at beg. of 1st row for an underflap, and casting off 10 sts. at neck instead of 8. Omit buttonholes.

A Long Clothes Baby Doll

A LITTLE GIRL

Front

Cast on 57 sts., and work in g.-st. for 6 rows.
Change to st.-st. until work measures 11 inches from cast-on edge, then shape body thus: (k. 1, k. 2 tog.) nineteen times (38 sts.).
Knit 5 rows without shaping, then keeping 2 sts. at each end of needle in g.-st., dec. inside these borders on next 7 rows (24 sts.).
Next row (wrong side of work).—k. 2, p. 2, k. 16, p. 2, k. 2.
Next row.—Knit.
Next row.—k. 2, p. 2, k. 16, p. 2, k. 2.
Next row.—k. 6, cast off 12 (loop on needle), k. 5.

Knit 8 rows st.-.st. with g.-st. borders, then cast off.
Re-join wool at remaining sts., and work other side to match.

Making Up

Oversew seams. Stitch two buttons on back to match buttonholes.

The Frock

Front

Cast on 71 sts., and work in pat. thus:
1st row.—s. 1, k. 1, p. 2 tog., * k. 2, w.fd., k. 1, w.fd., k. 5, p. 3 tog. Rep. from * ending p. 2 tog., k. 2, instead of p. 3 tog.
2nd row and every alternate row.—s. 1, k. 1, purl to last 2, k. 2.
3rd row.—s. 1, k. 1, p. 2 tog., * k. 1, w.fd., k. 3, w.fd., k. 4, p. 3 tog. Rep. from * ending p. 2 tog., k. 2, instead of p. 3 tog.
5th row.—s. 1, k. 1, p. 2 tog., * w.ft., k. 5, w.fd., k. 3, p. 3 tog. Rep. from * ending p. 2 tog., k. 2, instead of p. 3 tog.
7th row.—s. 1, k. 1, p. 2 tog., * k. 5, w.fd., k. 1, w.fd., k. 2, p. 3 tog. Rep. from * ending p. 2 tog., k. 2, instead of p. 3 tog.
9th row.—s. 1, k. 1, p. 2 tog., * k. 4, w.fd., k. 3, w.fd., k. 1, p. 3 tog. Rep. from * ending p. 2 tog., k. 2, instead of p. 3 tog.
11th row.—s. 1, k. 1, p. 2 tog., * k. 3, w.fd., k. 5, w.t.n., p. 3 tog. Rep. from * ending w.t.n., p. 2 tog., k. 2, instead of w.t.n., p. 3 tog.
12th row.—As 2nd.
These 12 rows form pat.
Continue in pat. until work measures 12 inches from cast-on edge, then shape body thus: k. 1 (k. 3 tog., k. 2) fourteen times (43 sts.). Continue in all g.-st. for 4 rows. Now shape armholes by casting off 3 sts. at beg. of next 2 rows, and dec. at each end of next 5 rows (27 sts.). Continue without further shaping until work measures 13½ inches from cast-on edge, then shape neck by casting off centre 7 sts., and dec. at neck edge on next 4 rows (6 sts.). Continue in g.-st. for 7 more rows, then cast off. Re-join wool at remaining sts., and work other side to match.

Back

Work as for front until body shaping is completed, then divide sts. in half, and dec. 1 st. at centre. Continue in all g.-st. for 4 rows, then shape armhole by casting off 3 sts. at beg. of next row, starting at seam edge, and dec. at same edge on next 5 rows (13 sts.). Continue without further shaping until work measures 13½ inches from cast-on edge, then shape neck by casting off 4 sts. at beg. of next row, starting at opening edge, and dec. at same edge on next 3 rows (6 sts.). Continue without further shaping for 8 rows, then cast off. Re-join wool at remaining sts., and work other side to match.

Sleeves

Cast on 27 sts., and work in g.-st. for 2 rows.
Next row.—k. 1 (k. 2 tog., w.fd., k. 1) to last 2, k. 2 (27 sts.).
Knit 2 rows of g.-st.
Next row.—k. 3 (knit twice into next and every alternate st.) eleven times, k. 2 (38 sts.).
Next row.—s. 1, k. 1, purl to last 2, k. 2.
Continue in pat. for two full pats., then dec. 1 st. at beg. of next 8 rows. Cast off.
Work another sleeve to match.

Making Up

Oversew seams. Fasten back of frock with tiny buttons, making loops to match. Pass ribbon through slots at end of sleeves.

The Cloak

Using 3-ply wool, cast on 130 sts., and work in g.-st. for 11 inches. Change to k. 1, p. 1, for 2 inches.
Next row.—k. 1 (w.fd., k. 2 tog.) to last st., k. 1.
Knit 4 rows g.-st., then cast off.

Making Up

Thread ribbon through slots and tie in bow.

The Bonnet

Using 3-ply wool, cast on 48 sts., and work in g.-st. for 5 inches; k. 24, then graft sts. tog. to form pixie bonnet.

Making Up

Stitch piece of ribbon at each side and tie in bow.

All FOUR GREW UP

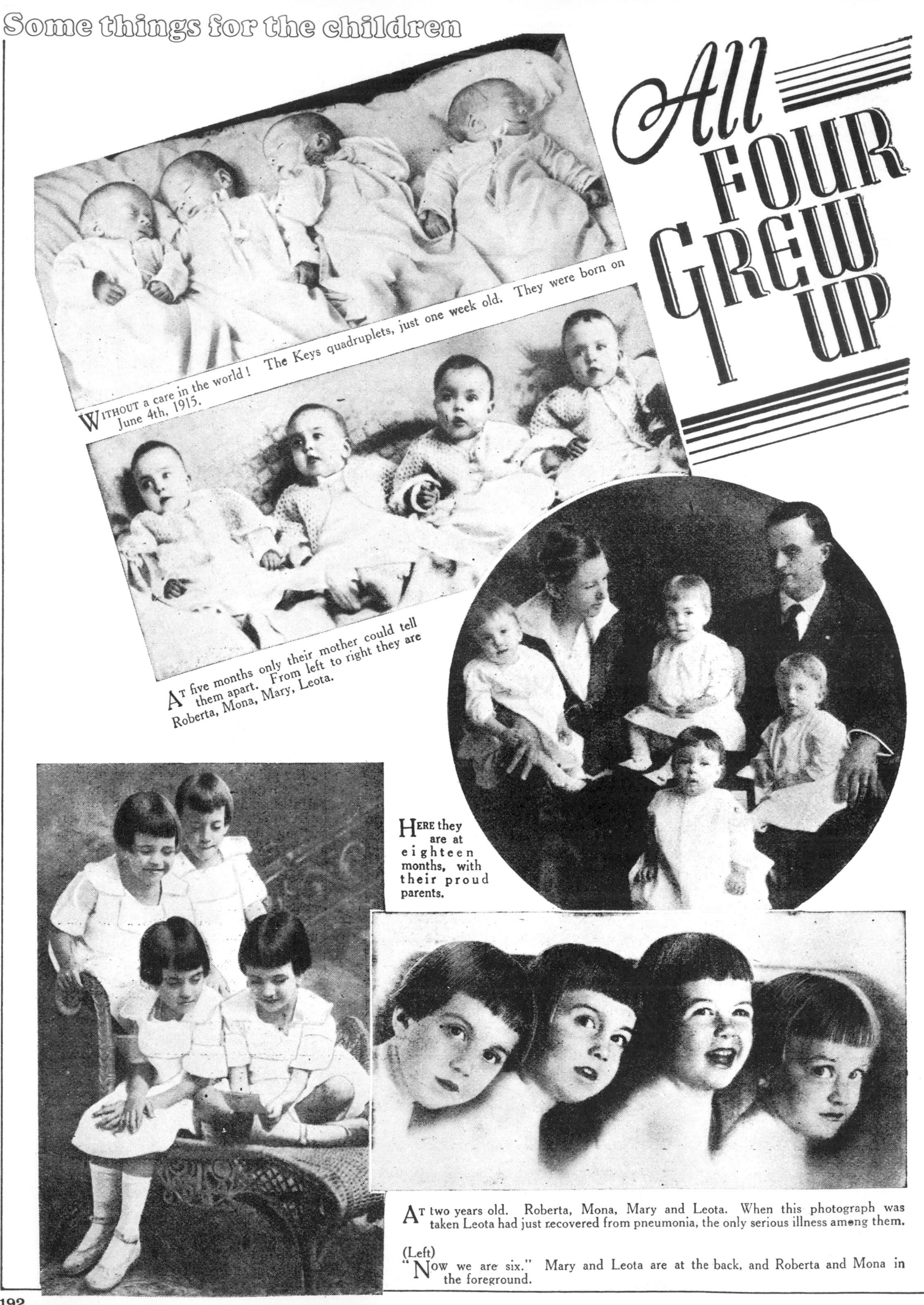

WITHOUT a care in the world! The Keys quadruplets, just one week old. They were born on June 4th, 1915.

AT five months only their mother could tell them apart. From left to right they are Roberta, Mona, Mary, Leota.

HERE they are at eighteen months, with their proud parents.

AT two years old. Roberta, Mona, Mary and Leota. When this photograph was taken Leota had just recovered from pneumonia, the only serious illness among them.

(Left)
"NOW we are six." Mary and Leota are at the back, and Roberta and Mona in the foreground.

PICTURE-STORY of the life of the famous Keys quadruplets, the only quads known to have lived to the age of twenty-three.

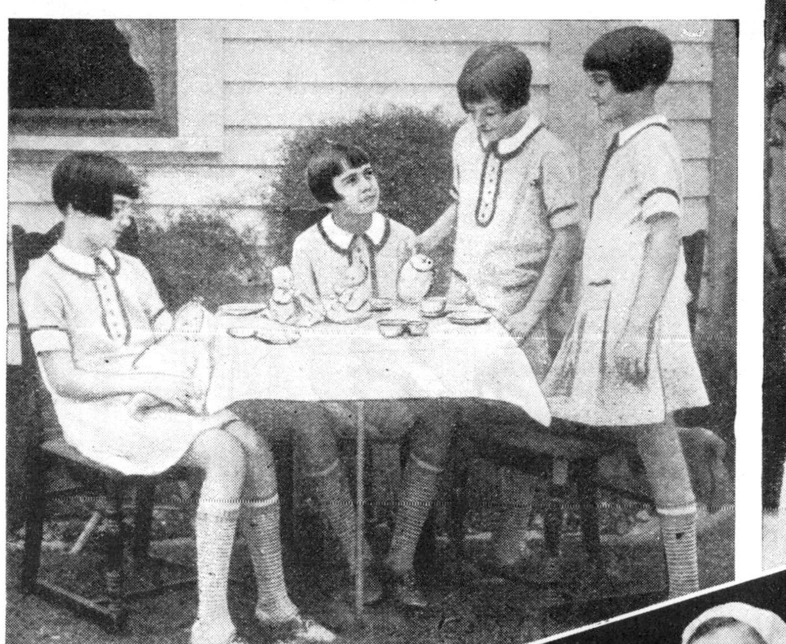

MONA, Roberta, Leota and Mary, aged eight, with their dolls.

WHEN they were twelve. By this time all four were already accomplished musicians. (From left to right, Leota, Mona, Roberta and Mary.)

(Above)
SIXTEEN years old and high school students. Quite a number of colleges were anxious to enrol the famous four.

HERE they are at 21 years old, practising archery. But so far Cupid's arrows have not found a target in the hearts of any of them. From left to right you see Mona, Roberta, Mary, Leota.

NO, they haven't really emptied father's pockets! To-day, at 23, these four attractive young women are making money on the stage and radio, but intend to devote their earnings to building an orphanage. Left to right, Mary, Mona, Roberta, Leota.

"When very

JACK OAKIE

JOAN CRAWFORD

FRED MacMURRAY

MARLENE DIETRICH

FREDRIC MARCH

HOW far back do your early recollections take you? If you cannot see a soft white woollen shawl without recalling your first party and the bits of woolly fluff that *would* get into your mouth, you have **Claudette Colbert's** sympathy. The memory of that first party, and the fluff in her mouth during the cab ride, is one of her early recollections. The rest of her childhood seemed to consist of sedate daily walks in the Bois de Bologne, near her home in Paris, with her nurse. Like most Parisian children in the decade before the War, she never went out without her nurse and did not play with other children unless the "bonne" was there, too, to prevent undue exuberance of spirits! Her childhood was very happy and carefree, in spite of the conventional restrictions. Claudette's parents moved to New York when she was just six. Business reverses made a move imperative, and M. Chauchoin—Claudette's real name is Claudette Chauchoin—thought he would try his luck in a new country. Though she was still guarded and chaperoned as in Paris, Claudette enjoyed the freedom of American school life.

At seven she had decided to become a second Pavlova. She begged her father to let her have ballet lessons. He, however, had other ideas. He looked into a future in which his beloved Lily—his pet name for her—was a famous grand opera star. She had a remarkable voice, and he started her on an intensive course of singing and voice training. Little over a year later a trivial "common cold" took a hand in her affairs. The cold turned into a series of severe colds which affected her voice, leaving it deep and husky, the very qualities that have made it so attractive on the screen! Singing lessons were discontinued. While still at school Claudette longed to be a dress designer, and later she obtained a post in a dress salon, but before she had attempted to design a single gown a chance meeting led her to the stage. At a tea party she was introduced to a producer who offered her a small part in a production. And her future was thus arranged by Fate!

DO you recall being made to recite "pieces" to admiring—apparently!—friends and relatives? Then your sympathy is with **Fredric March.** His very earliest recollections are of standing on a platform, in a dim gas-lit hall, reciting "Poor Little Mose" in a competition. Being the youngest competitor by some years, he won first prize, but he cannot see a lace collar on anyone, or in a picture, without recalling the horror of those awful moments when he was dressed up in a white suit with a big lace collar to compete for this prize. He would much rather have been left at home to play with his new boat. He always had, and still has, a passion for the water and for anything that will ride on it! He was an intensely serious little fellow, though, and put his whole heart and soul into whatever he had to do, and the concentrated energy and anxiety in his recitation endeared him to the whole audience. His elder brother tells a tale of how Freddie walked two miles to find him when he was staying with friends. The younger boy, then only six, had to buy a notebook for school, it transpired, and he wanted his big brother's

"I was Young"

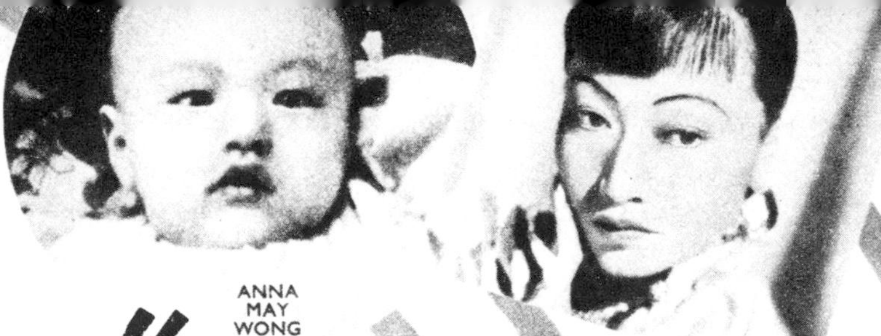

ANNA MAY WONG

GARY COOPER

Many favourite film stars cherish early photos of themselves, and—luckily for us—every little picture tells a story!

advice on the kind to get—whether it should open at the side like a book or at the top like a reporter's notebook!

WHEN Mrs. Elizabeth K. Peters, then living in Indiana, looked at the great blue eyes of her youngest baby, Jane, did she, I wonder, visualise a future in which her lovely chubby baby would be famous the world over? Whatever she knew, or did not know, she was convinced that little Jane would at least grow up carefree and gay, able to take "knocks," a thorough sport, and, perhaps, a bit of a tomboy. Her six-year-old sons, Freddie and Stuart, were going to take care of that! They were not going to allow their baby sister to grow up a "cissy!" She was not allowed to squeal or whimper, and she had to play football, climb trees, and ride a horse almost as soon as her plump little legs could hold her in an upright position. To-day, she is one of the most glamorous stars of filmland. She has a flair for gay light comedy, and is famous for her pranks and good friendship. Who is she? Why, **Carole Lombard,** of course.

A regular tomboy was **Fred MacMurray** in his boyhood days spent at Beaver Dam, Wisconsin. He was born in Illinois, but commenced a roving life at the age of three weeks, when his parents moved to the neighbouring state. He learned how to escape from his play-pen by climbing up the wire netting sides and toppling over in a heap of petticoats on the other side.

While still really only a baby, Fred would go anywhere to hear music, having inherited a love of music from his violinist father. He won all possible high honours at lessons, and was quickly the champion games player in Beaver Dam, though *how* he got through school so brilliantly no one ever knew, for he was never seen with a book! At nine years old he declared he could not sleep under a roof—and moved his bed into a huge packing-box in the garden! There was no more air in the box that in his large bedroom with several windows, but Fred slept with intense satisfaction.

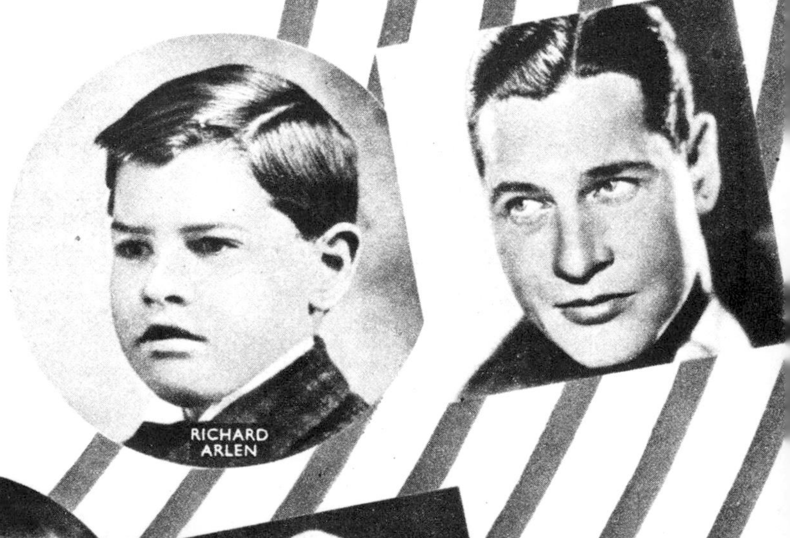

EVEN at four, **Marlene Dietrich** showed poise and glamour in her heavily starched white-embroidered muslin dress and hat, the latter with its under-brim massed with tiny starched frills of lace. There is serenity in her pose and in her now-provocative eyes; and her generous mouth seems ready to break into the lovely sensitive smile so famous on the screen. Born in Berlin, Marlene was the daughter of an officer in the Imperial army. Her mother was a member of a family of high social standing and old-world refinement with unusual musical talent.

CLAUDETTE COLBERT

RICHARD ARLEN

CAROLE LOMBARD

Let the Children

They can't begin sewing too soon! Simple things now pave the way to bigger things later, and they will always be very glad they started young.

138911 (*5 to 10*) and **138912** (*11 to 16*)
Simple as ABC and very smart! For 7 to 8 years; 54-inch material, 1⅜ yards; 36-inch, 2⅛ yards; trimming, ⅛ yard. Pattern 6d. For 13 to 14 years; 54-inch material 2 yards; 36-inch, 2⅞ yards; trimming, ¼ yard. Pattern 9d.

SMALL folk simply love to take a hand in doing useful, "grown-up" things, and if mothers, guardians and teachers of evacuated children are wise, they'll take full advantage of this fact, for it will solve quite a number of difficult problems for them.

The children in all parts of Britain who have been evacuated from their homes will, in the very near future, be needing new, warm clothes. Parents of the poorer ones will possibly be unable to provide them, and even the parents of the not-so-poor will be so busy with National Service and other things that they won't have the time to make the little garments they would like to.

Now you can be quite sure that any little girl will be as proud as Punch to be allowed to make her own clothes, or clothes for her little friends. Girls from the age of nine can make really charming little frocks and all kinds of underwear, and children much younger still can get a great deal of fun out of knitting simple squares which can be made, by what seems like magic, into the most attractive woollies.

Really pleasant afternoons can be spent in sewing and knitting; and if one girl reads an exciting story, the children will have something doubly attractive to look forward to. In the case of sewing classes at the schools, it is interesting to form small groups of five or six children and set them to work on one complete outfit. A special treat or a small prize for the group turning out the best sewn and knitted outfit would be an added incentive, and would create a spirit of happy competition.

Simple Instructions

With the help of the patterns sketched on these pages, which have been specially designed to take the least possible amount of material, and chosen for the extreme simplicity of the sewing, teachers and guardians will be able to do three very necessary things; provide the children with warm, attractive clothes at the smallest possible cost—keep them happily occupied—and leave themselves free to do the million and one small jobs needed for the care of young people.

Now for the garments themselves. The little frock above can be made in soft woollen material or velveteen, and is extremely simple to sew, as you'll see for yourself if you glance at the pieces of material

138921 (5 to 10 years)
FOUR simple pieces only. For 7 to 8 years; 35/36-inch material, 1⅞ yards. ½-inch lace, 2½ yards; 1-inch lace for hem of petticoat and knickers 4 yards. Pattern 6d.

Make These

used. First of all, lines of stitching are run at the waist level to form the sets of gathers. When this is done the seams of frock and sleeves should be stitched. "Run-and-fell" or French seams are strongest for these. Next the wrist edges of the sleeves should be gathered up and stitched between the edges of the wristbands. All that remains to be done after this is to neaten the neck and back opening, turn up the hem and stitch the sleeves into the armholes. The tiny tab collar pieces can be made by the youngest member of the group, and tacked on to the frock afterwards. Sufficient material for three sets of tabs is quoted, so that they can be changed easily for washing.

The petticoat and knicker set couldn't be easier to make, and will cost very little indeed in lawn or cambric. Feather-stitching can be used instead of lace for the trimming if further economy is advisable.

No. 138941 is a grand skirt to wear with a woolly jumper, and is made from just two pieces of material. Stitch the seams, turn up the hem, fix the top to a petersham band, make and fasten the placket and hey-presto! you've finished the smartest little skirt you could wish to find. The skirt No. 138931 for Miss Five-to-Ten is mounted on a simple two-piece lining bodice.

The attractive woolly is made from four straight strips of knitting. Two measuring 14 inches by 14 inches for the back and front, and two measuring 16 inches by 9 inches for the sleeves. These measurements are for a ten-year-old child, and you'll need 8 ounces of Sirdar Supreme wool, a pair of No. 10 needles and a pair of No. 7 needles.

138931 (5 to 10) and **138941** (11 to 16)
A SOFT tweed or woollen would make this smart skirt. For 7 to 8 years; 54-inch material ¾ yard. For 13 to 14 years 1¼ yards. Pattern 6d.

Front and Back (both alike)

With No. 10 needles, cast on 78 stitches and knit in ribbing of knit one, purl one for 2½ inches. Change to No. 7 needles and knit in stocking stitch till the work measures 14 inches from the lower edge and cast off.

Sleeves

With No. 10 needles, cast on 50 stitches, and knit in ribbing of knit one, purl one for 3 inches. Change to No. 7 needles, and knit in stocking stitch till sleeve measures 16 inches and cast off.

Press all the pieces with a warm iron over a damp cloth. Sew the front and back pieces together at the sides, leaving 6½ inches free at the top for the armholes. Lap the corners of the shoulder edges back over the front to about two inches and oversew them securely together as shown in the little diagram (on right). Sew the sleeve edges together, oversew the tops to the armhole edges, and there's your woolly! No fastenings are necessary, and a crisp white school collar can be worn with it if liked.

This particular woolly is made to fit a ten-year-old child, but it can, of course, be made to fit all ages, the measurements and quantities of wool being varied according to the child's size. Allow 11 stitches to 2 inches.

CAN YOU CROCHET?

For lovely laces, nothing can take the place of the age-old art of crochet, and nowadays hats, scarves and collars can all be made by this method. To refresh your memory, here is a pictorial lesson explaining clearly all the stitches used.

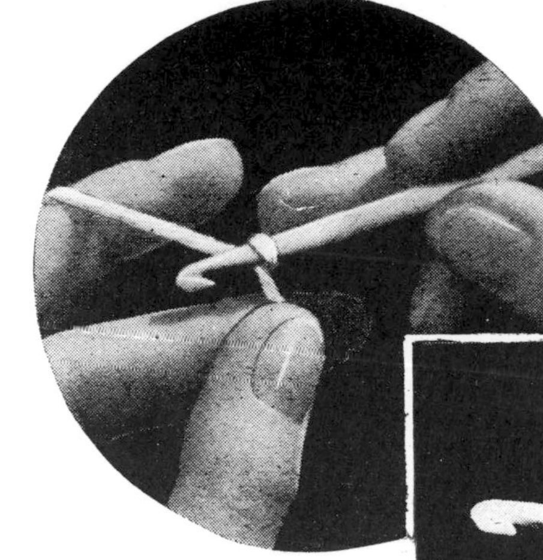

1.—To make first st., hold the end of the wool between the thumb and first finger of the left hand, and pass the wool from the ball over the first and second fingers, under the third and round the little finger. Holding the hook between thumb and first two fingers (as illustrated), insert it downwards under the thread in the left hand, from LEFT to RIGHT, and twist it round to normal position. Now pass the hook from front to back under the wool (held in the left hand), and draw the wool through the loop already on hook.

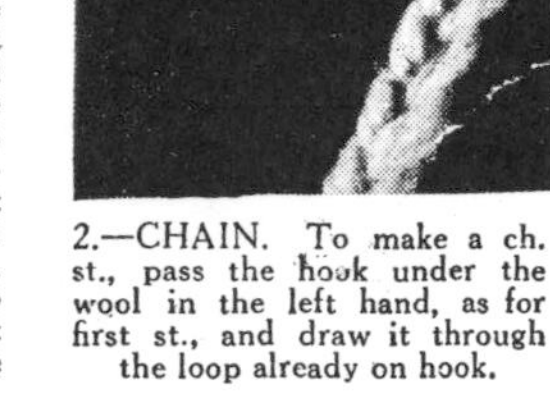

2.—CHAIN. To make a ch. st., pass the hook under the wool in the left hand, as for first st., and draw it through the loop already on hook.

3.—TURNING A ROW. When turning a row, always allow 2 ch. to turn a row of d.c., 3 ch. for a row of tr., 4 ch. for a row of long tr., and so on. Above shows a row of d.c. being commenced, when the hook is inserted under one or two threads of the third ch. from hook.

4.—DOUBLE CROCHET. Having inserted hook in st., pass hook under wool in left hand and draw loop through st. (2 loops on hook). Now pass hook under wool again and draw loop through both sts. on hook This forms 1 st.

5.—TREBLE. * First pass hook under wool, then insert hook in 4th ch. and draw wool through. There are now 3 loops on hook. Pass hook under wool (as illustrated), draw it through two loops, again pass under wool, and draw it through remaining 2 sts. Repeat from *

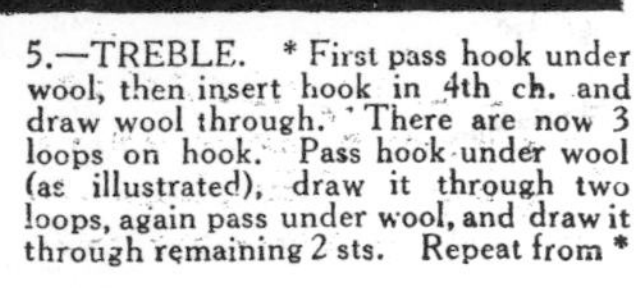

6.—SPACES. Make a length of ch., then work 1 tr. in 7th ch. from hook. This allows 2 ch. for bottom of sp., 3 ch. to turn and 2 ch. for top of sp. Now work * 2 ch. and 1 tr. in 3rd ch. from hook. Repeat from * along row. On all following rows, turn with 5 ch. (3 for turning and 2 for top of first sp.), and work each tr. into top of tr. of previous row.

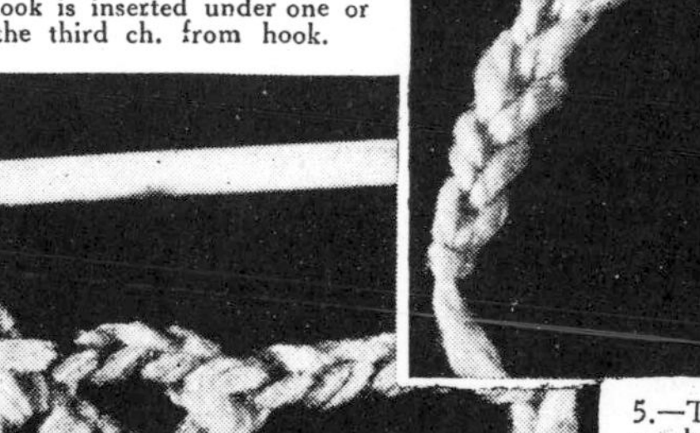

7.—LACETS AND BARS. These sts. are usually worked alternately. A BAR consists of 5 ch., miss 5 sts., 1 tr. in next st. When turning first row, work the first tr. in the 13th ch. from hook. Commence all other rows with 8 ch. and 1 tr. in first tr. (3 ch to turn and 5 ch. for bar.) LACETS. Turn with 3 ch. for first tr., then make * 3 ch., miss 2 sts., 1 d.c. in 3rd st., 3 ch., 1 tr. in following 3rd st. (or tr. of previous row). Repeat from *.

8.—WHEN WORKING IN ROUNDS, as for hats, etc., make 3 ch. to commence round, then work in tr., increasing as directed in instructions. To finish round, pass hook into third of 3 ch. that commenced the round (as illustrated), and draw loop of wool through this ch. AND the st. on the hook. Begin and end all rounds in this way

9.—PICOTS. These can be varied in size, according to requirements. To work as illustrated, make a length of ch., then work * 1 d.c. into first st., 8 ch., 1 d.c. into 4th ch. from hook, 4 ch., miss 3 ch. of foundation row and work 1 d.c. into next st. Repeat from * to end of row, working as many d.c. between each picot as required.

10.—BLOCKS AND SPACES. A BLOCK consists of 3 consecutive tr., which makes 4 consecutive tr., counting the tr. which ended the previous st. To work pattern illustrated, make 1 sp., 3 tr. in next 3 ch. (for block), then repeat all along. On second row, work spaces over blocks, and vice versa.

Credits and notes

Grateful thanks are due to all the magazines and their publishers which have so kindly granted permission to reproduce material, also to Richard Hughes for permission to reproduce *The Old Queen*, and to Ernest Shepard, Walt Disney and Meccano Ltd for permission to reproduce illustrations. I would also like to thank Mik Dunn, Zelide Cowan, Luise White, Helen Taylor and Tony and Leslie Birks-Hay for their help with the book. The sources of items are given below, and for the knitting patterns equivalent modern yarns and needle sizes are stated. If you want to use the very fine 2-ply and 3-ply yarns to keep the 'look' of the old garments, check your tension carefully first. Transfers and pattern pieces referred to in the text, which were supplied with the original magazines but are no longer available. are almost always illustrated and could quite easily be copied.

page

6 bottom left *The Home Companion* International Publishing Company (IPC)
top right *The Girl's Own Annual* The Lutterworth Press, The United Society for Christian Literature
7 *The Girl's Own Annual* The Lutterworth Press
8 top left *The Home Companion* IPC
top right *Modern Woman* IPC
bottom left *Woman's Weekly* IPC
10 *Wife and Home* IPC
11 *Wife and Home* IPC
13 *Modern Home* IPC
14 top Meccano Ltd
bottom *William the Detective* George Newnes Ltd
15 top right *Daily Express*
bottom left Walt Disney Productions Ltd
bottom right *Winnie the Pooh* Methuen
16 top left *Woman's Magazine* The Lutterworth Press
bottom right *Woman's Weekly* IPC
17 *Wife and Home* IPC
18 *Wife and Home* IPC
19 *Good Housekeeping* The National Magazine Co. and Walt Disney Productions Ltd
20 *Good Housekeeping* The National Magazine Co.
21 top *The Home Companion* IPC
bottom *Woman's Weekly* IPC
22–3 *The Home Magazine* IPC
24 *The Girl's Own Annual* The Lutterworth Press. Twilley's Stalite, No. 10 and 12 needles
25 top *The Home Companion* IPC
bottom *The Girl's Own Annual* The Lutterworth Press
26 *The Home Companion* IPC
27 *The Home Companion* IPC
28 *Woman's Magazine* The Lutterworth Press
29–31 *The Home Magazine* IPC
32–3 *Good Housekeeping* The National Magazine Co.

34–6 *The Girl's Own Annual* The Lutterworth Press. Jumper with striped border: Templeton's Shetland Fleece, No. 10 and 12 needles. Openwork design: Patons' Double Knitting, No. 7 and 11 needles
36 *The Girl's Own Annual* The Lutterworth Press. Any standard Double Knitting, No. 3.50 hook
37 *The Girl's Own Annual* The Lutterworth Press. Any standard Double Knitting, No. 9 and 10 needles, No. 3.00 hook
38–9 *Woman and Home* IPC. Any 4-ply Baby Wool, No. 10 needles, No. 2.00 hook
39 bottom *The Lady's Companion* IPC. Sirdar Double Knitting, No. 3.50 and 2.50 hooks
40 *The Lady's Companion* IPC
41 *Woman's Weekly* IPC
42 *Woman and Home* IPC
43 *Woman and Home* IPC
44–5 *Woman and Home* IPC
45 bottom *Good Housekeeping* The National Magazine Co.
46–7 *The Home Magazine* IPC
48–9 *Woman and Home* IPC. No. 0.60 hook
50–1 *Woman and Home* IPC. Any standard 4-ply, No. 9 needles
52–3 *Weldon's Series* IPC
54 top and right *Woman and Home* IPC
bottom left *Woman's Weekly* IPC
55 *Woman's Weekly* IPC
56 *My Home* IPC
57 *Woman and Home* IPC
58 *Woman's Weekly* IPC
59 *Woman's Weekly* IPC
60 *Bestway* IPC
61 *Weldon's Series* IPC
62 *Woman's Weekly* IPC
63–5 *Woman's Weekly* IPC
66–7 *Woman's Weekly* IPC
68, 71 *My Home* IPC. Tricel/nylon 4-ply (Sunbeam, Robin or Wendy) and Templeton's Shetland Lace, No. 2.50 and 3.00 hooks
69–71 *Woman and Home* IPC. Mother duck: any standard Double Knitting, No. 8 needles. Ducklings: any standard 4-ply, No. 12 needles, No. 3.00 hook
71 top *Woman's Weekly* IPC
72–3 *Good Housekeeping* The National Magazine Co.
74 bottom left *Woman's Weekly* IPC
right *Woman and Home* IPC
75 *Woman's Weekly* IPC
76 *Good Needlework and Knitting* IPC
77 *Woman's Weekly* IPC
78 bottom *Woman's Magazine* The Lutterworth Press
78–9 *Good Needlework and Knitting* IPC
80–1 *Woman and Home* IPC
82–3 *Woman and Home* IPC
84 *Wife and Home* IPC
85 *Wife and Home* IPC
86–8 *Wife and Home* IPC
89–90 *Woman's Magazine* The Lutterworth Press. Patons' 3-ply Baby wool, No. 11 needles, No. 1.50 or 2.00 hook
90 right *Wife and Home* IPC
bottom left *The Home Companion* IPC
91–2 *Wife and Home* IPC
93–4 *Woman's Magazine* The Lutterworth Press. Any 4-ply Baby wool, No. 9 needles, No. 2.00 hook
94 right *Wife and Home* IPC
95 *Woman's Magazine* The Lutterworth Press
96–7 *Woman's Magazine* The Lutterworth Press
98–9 *Woman's Magazine* The Lutterworth Press. Clark's Anchor Stranded cotton, any colours
99 right *Wife and Home* IPC
bottom left *Home Chat* IPC. Templeton's Shetland Lace, No. 2.50 and 4.50 hooks
100 *Woman and Home* IPC
101 *Woman and Home* IPC
102 *Good Needlework and Knitting* IPC
103 *Woman's Magazine* The Lutterworth Press
104–5 *Woman's Journal* IPC. Copley's Cobweb wool or Templeton's Shetland Lace, No. 3.00 hook
106 top *Wife and Home* IPC
bottom *Daily Mail*
107 *Woman's Magazine* The Lutterworth Press

108–9 *Wife and Home* IPC
110 *Woman's Magazine* IPC
111–12 *Wife and Home* IPC
113 *Woman and Home* IPC
114–15 *Woman's Magazine* The Lutterworth Press. Any standard 4-ply, No. 10 needles
115 top right *Woman's Magazine* The Lutterworth Press
bottom right *My Home* IPC
116–18 *Wife and Home* IPC
119 *Wife and Home* IPC
120–2 *Wife and Home* IPC
123–4 *Wife and Home* IPC
124 right *Woman's Magazine* The Lutterworth Press
125 *Wife and Home* IPC
126–30 *Woman and Home* IPC
131 *The Farmer's Home* (Supplement to *The Farmer and Stockbreeder*) IPC
132–3 *Woman's Magazine* The Lutterworth Press. Father and son: Sirdar Double Knitting, No. 8 and 11 needles. School frock: Patons' Camelot or Wendy Town'n'Country, No. 7, 9 and 12 needles, No. 3.00 hook
134 *My Home* IPC
135–7 *Modern Home* IPC
137 right *Woman and Home* IPC
138–40 *Good Housekeeping* The National Magazine Co.
141 *Woman and Home* IPC
142–3 *The Farmer's Home* IPC
144–7 *Good Housekeeping* The National Magazine Co.
147 bottom *Good Housekeeping* The National Magazine Co. Tricel/nylon 4-ply, No. 11 or 12 needles, No. 2.00 hook
148–9 *Wife and Home* IPC
149 right *Wife and Home* IPC
150 *Woman's Magazine* The Lutterworth Press
151–5 *Woman and Home* IPC. Camel and bear: any 4-ply wool, No. 3.00 hook. Penguin: Double Knitting, No. 9 needles. Elephant: Double Knitting, No. 11 needles, No. 3.00 hook
155 *Woman's Magazine* The Lutterworth Press
156 *Modern Home* IPC. 4-ply, No. 10 needles, No. 3.00 hook
157 *The Farmer's Home* IPC. Lister's Lavenda 4-ply, No. 8 and 10 needles
158 *Wife and Home* IPC
159–60 *Wife and Home* IPC
161–3 *Wife and Home* IPC
164 *Wife and Home* IPC
165 *Woman's Magazine* The Lutterworth Press
166–7 *Woman's Journal* IPC
168–9 *Woman and Home* IPC
169 *Wife and Home* IPC. Wendy 4-ply nylonised, No. 10 needles, No. 2.50 hook
170–3 *Wife and Home* IPC. Jumper: Jaeger Celtic Spun, No. 9 and 12 needles. Coat: Wendy Double Knitting nylonised, No. 9 needles, No. 3.00 hook. Dookie: Double Knitting, No. 12 needles
173 right *Mother* IPC
174–6 *Woman's Magazine* The Lutterworth Press. Sirdar Double Knitting, No. 12 needles
176 bottom *Good Housekeeping* The National Magazine Co.
177–8 *Woman's Magazine* The Lutterworth Press. Templeton's Shetland Fleece, No. 9 or 10 needles
178 right *Wife and Home* IPC
179–81 *Woman's Magazine* The Lutterworth Press. Clark's Anchor Stranded cotton
182 *North Bucks Home and Empire* IPC
183 *Good Housekeeping* The National Magazine Co. and Walt Disney Productions Ltd
184 *Woman's Weekly* IPC
185–6 *Woman's Weekly* IPC. No. 11 and 12 needles
187–8 *Wife and Home* IPC. Tricel/nylon 4-ply, No. 12 needles
188 bottom *Woman's Weekly* IPC
189 *The Farmer's Home* IPC
190–1 *Woman's Magazine* The Lutterworth Press. Lister or Ladyship 3-ply, No. 10 needles
192–3 *Wife and Home* IPC
194–5 *Mother and Home* IPC
196–7 *Mother and Home* IPC. Sirdar Double Knitting, No. 8 and 10 needles
198 Fox Photos
200 *Woman and Home* IPC